Unsung Heroes of the Market

Unsung Heroes of the Market

The 24 Underrated Economists You Need to Know

Edited by Robert M. Whaples with
Christopher J. Coyne, Gregory J. Robson,
and Diana W. Thomas

ISBN: 978-1-59813-428-5
eISBN: 978-1-59813-430-8
Library of Congress Control Number: 2026932276

Cataloging-in-Publication Data on file with the Library of Congress

Independent Institute
100 Swan Way, Oakland, CA 94621-1428
Telephone: 510-632-1366
Fax: 510-568-6040
Email: info@independent.org
Website: www.independent.org

Cover Design: John Caruso
Interior Design: Mike Mott

10 9 8 7 6 5 4 3 2 1

Contents

Introduction
Unsung Heroes

Robert M. Whaples

A RECENT ISSUE of *The Independent Review* marked the three hundredth anniversary of Adam Smith's birth with Nobel-laureate Vernon Smith's essay explaining how the earlier Smith's ideas are "foundational in understanding how the West grew rich because of its commitment to classical liberalism anchored in freedom."[1] As Kenneth Boulding so aptly put it, "Adam Smith . . . has strong claim to being both the Adam and the Smith of systematic economics."[2] Smith's contributions to economics have been keenly appreciated for over a quarter of a millennium. If you search through recent issues of *The Independent Review*, you won't be surprised to see that Smith is cited in every single issue—although many of his insights are woven so deeply into our understanding of economics and human nature that they go without mentioning. The same might be said of economists like James Buchanan, Milton Friedman, Friedrich Hayek, and Ludwig von Mises—who are routinely cited in *The Independent Review*. These economists, and others including Joseph Schumpeter and John Maynard Keynes, have been celebrated and, indeed, appreciated by economists, if not by the wider public.

This collection of essays, which grew out of a symposium published in *The Independent Review*, redirects our attention from these luminaries to economists who haven't been as widely appreciated. Who counts as an under-appreciated economist? As we put it in a call for contributions, "You tell us. Probably not, for example, Smith, Ricardo, Marshall, Mill, Marx, Keynes, Friedman, Samuelson, Hayek, Schumpeter, Becker, Arrow, Solow, Coase,

---

Robert M. Whaples is professor of economics at Wake Forest University and editor of *The Independent Review*.

and Stiglitz—all of whom were selected as 'favorite' economists in a poll of economists published in *Econ Journal Watch* about ten years ago."[3]

While the list of underappreciated economists could be extended at least a hundredfold, the contributions to this volume include a few economists that were new to me (Friedrich Lutz, Karl Mittermaier, and Earl Thompson) and some who are very well known, including Alexander Hamilton, Thomas Sowell, and Thorstein Veblen. The subjects are compelling, the writing sparkles, and the essays are packed with insights and interesting information, so read them in any order you wish.

I

Alexander Hamilton as Economist

A Proper Verdict

Richard M. Salsman

FEW SCHOLARS DOUBT that Alexander Hamilton (1757–1804) was a formidable American Founder—Revolutionary War aide to George Washington, prolific pamphleteer, main author of the *Federalist Papers,* champion of the US Constitution, first US Treasury secretary, architect of early US foreign policy. But do scholars consider him a great economist? No—but they *should.*

We have no polls, only impressions, but Hamilton is viewed as unoriginal in economics and, worse, a fan of "big government," public debt, fiat money, central banking, subsidies, and protectionism. Statists cite him as authoritative and helpful, whereas libertarians indict him as authoritarian and harmful.[1] Edward C. Lunt's review was mixed: "In one sense of the term—a political economist being the embodiment of politics, law, ethics, and economics—Hamilton has reached the foremost place" because he "brought out more clearly by his elucidation" "certain principles and laws," by a methodology that was both "deductive and inductive," and yet "our final judgment must be that however great Hamilton may be as a statesman, his rank as an economist is not high."[2]

In such hands, Hamilton isn't so much underappreciated as he is misused or abused. Defective analyses of "the Hamiltonian vision"[3] seem to stem from ideology (statism versus liberalism) or anachronism: out-of-context claims about Hamilton being responsible for whatever great good or evil has transpired in America since the 1790s. If America became the world's dominant

---

Richard M. Salsman is assistant research professor in the Philosophy, Politics, and Economics program at Duke University.

capitalist dynamo, *credit* Hamilton (unless you're an anti-capitalist) because he was (truly) the most pro-capitalist Founder; if instead America became illiberal, politically centralized, bureaucratically bloated, crony-ridden, and financially fragile, unjustified *blame* is heaped upon Hamilton because he established a strong, energetic federal government (true) compared with its predecessor. Let's not just split the difference between false extremes; instead, let's render an objective verdict as free as possible of ideological bias and anachronism.[4] Properly judged, Hamilton deserves greater appreciation as an economist than he's been given.

Political Economy Versus Economics

The term "economist" often denotes someone engaged in formal mathematical modeling detached from economic experience, one doing "positive" economics (purely scientific, logical) while eschewing "normative" (ethical, value-laden) economics. This dichotomy wasn't used in the 1790s. There was *political economy,* albeit an infant industry, which examined the *interplay* of politics and markets. Two Scotsmen led the way: James Steuart, a mercantilist (*Principles of Political Economy,* 1767), and Adam Smith, a liberal (*Wealth of Nations,* 1776). The more systematic Smith was the real founder of the field; he defended free markets (with exceptions) but also refuted mercantilism (the notion that the state should manipulate the economy to maximize its power and revenues) and physiocracy (the notion that agriculture alone creates economic value, which implies that other sectors are parasitic).

Hamilton used Steuart and Smith[5] plus David Hume's essays of the 1750s, Adam Anderson's *Origin of Commerce* (1764), Pelatiah Webster's *Political Essays on the Nature and Operation of Money, Public Finances and Other Objects* (1776–91), Wyndham Beawes's *Merchant Law Directory* (1761), William Blackstone's *Commentaries on the Laws of England* (1765–69), the *Memoirs* of Jacques Necker (France's finance minister, 1777–81), and Malachy Postlethwayt's *Universal Dictionary of Trade and Commerce* (1774).[6] Writing as "The Continentalist," Hamilton initially sympathized with mercantilism, believing it empowered Britain.[7] But his essays mainly bespeak liberalism; the fourth one counsels uniform tax and tariff rates: "the genius of liberty reprobates everything arbitrary or discretionary in taxation," for everyone, "by a definite and general rule," should know in advance "what proportion of his property the state demands." After reading Smith in the early 1780s, Hamilton embraced economic liberalism more consistently.

As Treasury secretary (1789–95), Hamilton delivered to Congress (by request) five carefully researched, influential reports on public credit, banking, money, taxes, trade, tariffs, and manufacturing. He proposed mostly liberal policies, reflecting his (and the Federalists') allegiance to security of private property and sanctity of contract.[8] A scholar recounted Hamilton's liberalism:

> The purpose of Hamilton's political economy was the preservation of private property and the liberty to pursue it. For him the chief functions of government were to protect property, to enforce a legal framework in which it was secured, and to provide a stable environment for economic activity and growth.[9]

Hamilton's political economy has a complex, little-recognized context. A nation builder and policymaker, he effectuated many difficult transitions. One was a shift from a wartime to a peacetime economy. Another was a removal of hyperinflated monies and defaulted debt, to foster monetary-fiscal rectitude and stability. Still another shift involved replacing an impotent and incompetent confederation of disunited states with a system of federally united states able to exercise sovereign power. A further shift was from an undiversified colonial economy to a freer, more independent, more heterogenous one. Another move was needed away from physiocracy to the recognition that all sectors can add value. A final, monumental shift might have been toward ending slavery, as Hamilton preferred.[10] In all of these cases, Hamilton was opposed by anti-Federalists.[11] Political independence was declared (1776), and the war was won (1783), but nothing guaranteed that next would come positive change, national unity, and the Constitution. That was Hamilton's dream but Thomas Jefferson's nightmare.

A precursor to the Constitutional Convention (1787) was a gathering the previous year at Annapolis of Hamilton, James Madison, and others seeking freer interstate trade. They also tried to quell debtor revolts and other assaults on property. Article 1, Section 8 of the Constitution empowered Congress to "lay and collect taxes, duties, imposts and excises, to pay the debts for the common defense and general welfare of the United States" and "to regulate commerce with foreign nations, and among the several states." The purpose was *not* to establish today's ultra-indebted welfare-regulatory-protectionist state but to create a durable, rights-respecting republic. "General welfare" meant no privileging of special interests, and to "regulate" meant not to *restrict* but to *regularize,* to keep economic activity flowing.

Hamilton adopted Smith's critiques of mercantilism and physiocracy, but he also rejected a few of Smith's fateful errors: his "labor theory of value" (that economic value reflects quantities of manual labor time); his belief that some labor (the service sector, military, courts) was nonproductive; and his assertion that public debt always diminished prosperity. Hamilton proved more astute than subsequent economists—David Ricardo, John Stuart Mill, Karl Marx—who perpetuated Smith's myths.

Money, Banking, and Debt

As Treasury secretary (1789–95), Hamilton almost single-handedly fixed America's shattered financial system; he set a high standard for policymaking and set America on a path to economic prowess. Hamilton implemented sound policy principles amid contentious political wrangling. Eight years prior, he wrote to Robert Morris about how to revive America's degraded finances.[12] A wealthy banker and finance chief under the Articles of Confederation, Morris couldn't raise enough taxes to pay for war; it was funded by cascades of successively depreciated money and debt. Hamilton didn't *cause* or *perpetuate* the debased money and defaulted debt; he *inherited* them, then *fixed* them.

Hamilton had seen degraded finances undermine America's war effort, and then, during the "critical period" (1781–89), he saw how they precluded prosperity. His plans for fiscal and monetary reform, once they were enacted by Congress, transformed a bankrupt nation issuing worthless paper money into an honorable debt-payer issuing gold- and silver-based dollars. Hamilton's reforms surely benefited bondholders and "monied interests," but all sectors benefited from more rational public governance. He wanted a system of sound and stable money (a gold-silver standard), a vigorous private banking system, public spending restraint, low and uniform tariff rates, minimal regulation, a diminishing public debt, and genuine credit (an adequate capacity to borrow).

That we lack many of these features today reflects a multi-decade *rejection* of Hamiltonian principles.

Foes of Hamilton's cures advised debt defaults, either explicitly or implicitly (by inflation), and even if debt was serviced, they wanted Treasury to discriminate against secondary bondholders (demonized as "speculators"). Hamilton, defending the sanctity of contract, refused. Foes also opposed his "assumption" plan to have the federal government assume all state debts. Independence had been won nationally, he argued; states should start fresh fiscally. Detractors claimed the plan would unduly empower federal governance, even though no government benefits by adding liabilities or having to raise taxes. Assumption was approved. Hamilton then helped reduce the national debt burden from 40 percent of gross domestic product (1790) to 20 percent (1795). Yet he worried that unrestrained democracy again would render America overindebted. He warned of "a general propensity in those who administer the affairs of government . . . to shift off the [spending] burden from the present to a future day—a propensity which may be expected to be strong in proportion as the form of the state is popular."[13] He advised further debt reduction through sequential budget surpluses generated by spending restraint.

For Hamilton, "a national debt if it is not excessive will be to us a national blessing; it will be powerful cement of our union."[14] Libertarians today love citing the "blessing" part, but Hamilton conceded that debts can be excessive.[15] Borrowing mustn't become a major funding source, nor should it ever be repudiated. In 1790, he told Congress that "so far from acceding to the position that 'public debts are public benefits,' a position inviting to prodigality, and liable to dangerous abuse," the body should codify "as a fundamental maxim, in the system of the public credit of the United States, that the creation of debt should always be accompanied with the means of extinguishment." Hamilton advised steady repayments such that "the whole of the debt shall be discharged" in a decade.[16] He endorsed what became the "golden rule of public finance,"[17] which says public borrowing is justified only if it promotes the creation (not redistribution) of wealth over the long term; because winning certain wars and building productive infrastructure can benefit future generations, they too should bear the cost. This golden rule has been abandoned, along with Hamiltonian principles.

Hamilton's reforms fostered nationwide banking and efficient tax collection through the Bank of the United States (BUS), chartered from 1791 to 1811. He made sure it was apolitical. "To attach full confidence to an institution of this nature," he wrote, "an essential ingredient in its structure" is that it "be under a private not a public direction, under the guidance of individual interest, not of public policy," never "liable to being too much influenced by public necessity," because "suspicion of this would most likely be a canker that would continually corrode the vitals of the credit of the Bank." If "the credit of the Bank be at the disposal of the government," it would be a "calamitous abuse of it."[18] The BUS succeeded because, unlike central banks today, its purpose wasn't to fund fiscal profligacy; privately owned and prudently operated, it issued gold- and silver-convertible money and lent very little to the federal government.[19] The states used corrupt chartering schemes to limit the freedom of banks to branch; state-level BUS foes denounced it as a nationwide "monopoly" but didn't repeal their own anti-banking policies. Thanks to the BUS, the number of private-sector banks grew rapidly after 1791. Central banks today issue fiat token money, monetize public debt, depress interest rates, cause inflation, and bail out bad banks. None of that is Hamiltonian.

Tariffs, Trade, and Foreign Affairs

Influenced most by Steuart (mercantilism) and Smith (liberalism), Hamilton was initially mixed on trade policy, but while contributing to the *Federalist Papers* (1787–88) he was unequivocal in advocating freer trade among the states. He also recognized that the main initial federal funding source would be tariffs; the Constitution excluded powers to tax income, property, or sales. It allowed for excise taxes, but when these were applied initially, in 1792–94 (on whiskey), taxpayers revolted.

Hamilton's policies were not mercantilist, for that system not only demonized trade deficits and saw money as wealth but also required officials to micromanage prices, wages, rents, and interest rates while maintaining constrictive labor guilds. None of that was Hamiltonian. Mercantilism was part of empire, imperialism, and colonialism—all precapitalist phenomena left unchallenged until the mid-1700s. Since 1620, the American colonies had been part of this system, partially helped but also unnaturally stunted by it. Colonial powers, wanting trade surpluses and net imports of cash (to enrich royals and build war chests), forced colonies to export commodities and import manufactured goods. Hamilton, wanting a durable independence from Britain, sought to *extract* America from the mercantile system, not perpetuate it. To become genuine *states,* colonies had to *unite* into a federalist whole. Hamilton wanted nation-state institutions so America could "grow up" quickly and safely. Foes misrepresented him as lusting after power and intent on perpetuating a new mercantilism, a Federalist American Empire.

Hamilton was no protectionist. He advised low and uniform tariff rates for the legitimate (and constitutionally sanctioned) purpose of raising revenues, not high and variable rates to discriminate against some nations (or goods) or privilege others.[20] Hamilton also didn't obsess about America's large trade deficit. If America's money and bonds were sound (and he ensured that they were), there'd be no dearth of incoming foreign investment. He knew that a capital surplus (net inflow), mirroring a merchandise deficit, was akin to an international vote of confidence in the United States. Funds *did* flow inward because of his reforms. Meanwhile, Jeffersonians sought to use tariffs as weapons to hurt Britain and help France and to artificially boost America's farmers at the expense of the nation's manufacturers. A trade scholar explained:

> Seeing imports as the critical tax base on which he planned to finance government expenditures and fund the public debt, Hamilton advocated modest, non-discriminatory import duties to ensure a steady stream of revenue into the Treasury coffers. He also wanted a stable commercial relationship with Britain to avoid any conflict that might disrupt imports and diminish customs revenue. By contrast, Jefferson and Madison saw trade policy as an instrument for achieving reciprocity, a weapon to be wielded against what they perceived to be Britain's grossly unfair discrimination against U.S. commerce.[21]

International trade involves foreign–military relations, and Hamilton, preferring prosperity, also wanted more (hence freer) trade. He never sought trade wars that might become militarized; he wanted nondiscriminatory, nonpunitive tariffs to minimize hostilities. He advised US neutrality toward Britain and France, which were warring in the 1790s. In contrast, Jeffersonians wanted policies that punished Britain, favored France, and jeopardized US security and prosperity.[22] At Hamilton's urging, Washington issued his Proclamation of Neutrality in 1793 to keep the US out of war. In 1796, he asked Hamilton to draft a farewell address; he made clear the links between peace, trade, and prosperity:

> The great rule of conduct for us, regarding foreign nations, is in extending our commercial relations to have with them as little political connection as possible. So far as we have already formed engagements let them be fulfilled with perfect good faith. Here let us stop. . . . Taking care always to keep ourselves by suitable establishments on a respectable defensive posture, we may safely trust temporary alliances for extraordinary emergencies. Harmony, liberal intercourse and commerce with all nations are recommended by justice, humanity, and interest. But even our commercial policy should hold an equal hand, neither seeking nor granting exclusive favors or preferences; consulting the natural course of things; diffusing and diversifying by gentle means the streams of commerce but forcing nothing.[23]

A Freer and More Diverse Economy

The mercantilist system under which American colonies labored lasted more than a century, until the revolts of the 1760s. It weakened as a result of war and liberal ideas. Hamilton knew that if an independent America was to flourish, it must shift from a subservient, agrarian economy to a freer, more diversified one. His foes, clinging to physiocracy, insisted that agriculture alone was noble and productive and thus that commerce, manufacturing, finance, and cities were inherently corrupt and parasitic.

Hamilton rejected physiocratic premises more consistently than did Smith; he rejected the latter's claim that some sectors used nonproductive labor. Hamilton was original in his embrace of the modern view that *all* sectors of an economy can be productive and mutually reinforcing, that a harmony of intersectoral interests is possible, preferable, and achievable. Belief in *intersectoral* antagonism (physiocracy) was as foolish as the later belief in *interclass* conflict (Marxism). Hamilton also had the radical view that *finance* is productive;[24] that view isn't widely accepted even today. Hamilton also believed (contra Smith) that *political actors* could be productive if engaged in legitimate state functions (law and order, justice, defense). In *Federalist* no. 12, Hamilton explained:

> The prosperity of commerce is now perceived and acknowledged, by all enlightened statesmen, to be the most useful as well as the most productive source of national wealth; and has accordingly become a primary object of their political cares. By multiplying the means of gratification, by promoting the introduction and circulation of the precious metals, those darling objects of human avarice and enterprise, it serves to vivify and invigorate the channels of industry, and to make them flow with greater activity and copiousness. The assiduous merchant, the laborious husbandman, the active mechanic, and the industrious manufacturer—all orders of men, look forward with eager expectation and growing alacrity to this pleasing reward of their toils. The often-agitated question, between agriculture and commerce, has from indubitable experience received a decision, which has silenced the rivalships, that once subsisted between them, and has proved, to the satisfaction of their friends, that their interests are intimately blended and interwoven. It has been found, in various countries, that in proportion as commerce has flourished, land has risen in value. And how could it have happened otherwise? Could that which procures a freer vent for the products of the earth—which furnishes new incitements to the cultivation of land—which is the most powerful instrument in increasing the quantity of money in a state—could that, in fine, which is the faithful handmaid of labor and industry in every shape, fail to

> augment that article, which is the prolific parent of far the greatest part of the objects upon which they are exerted? It is astonishing that so simple a truth should ever have had an adversary; and it is one among a multitude of proofs, how apt a spirit of ill-informed jealousy, or of too great abstraction and refinement is to lead men astray from the plainest truths of reason and conviction.[25]

Hamilton's distinctive political economy is best expressed in his Report on Manufactures, delivered in December 1791.[26] Congress had requested it in early 1790, but Hamilton uncharacteristically deferred delivery, seeing money, banking, and debt as policy priorities. Those fundamentals had to be fixed first, for they were akin to the body politic's central nervous system, vital organs that were a precondition for broader economic success. His reports on debt, banking, and money were delivered in a flurry, over the course of a year, through January 1791.[27]

One of Hamilton's great insights pertained to the power of specialization; it would enormously enhance human creativity, achievement, and enjoyment, he said, and contribute to a more diversified, sounder economy. Smith too had hailed the productivity gains possible from specialized labor, but he worried it would make workers stupid and torpid. Marx later used this notion (and Smith's labor theory of value) to condemn capitalism (especially finance) for its "alienation," "exploitation," and "expropriation." Hamilton committed no similar error; he appreciated the benefits of a fully free, diverse economy:

> As to the furnishing greater scope for the diversity of talents and dispositions, which discriminate men from each other, this is a much more powerful means of augmenting the fund of national industry than may at first sight appear. It is a just observation, that the minds of the strongest and most active powers for their proper objects fall below mediocrity and labor without effect, if confined to uncongenial pursuits. And it is thence to be inferred, that the results of human exertion may be immensely increased by diversifying its objects. When all the different kinds of industry

> obtain in a community, each individual can find his proper element, and can call into activity the whole vigor of his nature. . . . To cherish and stimulate the activity of the human mind, by multiplying the objects of enterprise, is not among the least considerable of the expedients by which the wealth of a nation may be promoted. Even things in themselves not positively advantageous, sometimes become so, by their tendency to provoke exertion. Every new scene, which is opened to the busy nature of man to rouse and exert itself, is the addition of a new energy to the general stock of effort. The spirit of enterprise, useful and prolific as it is, must necessarily be contracted or expanded in proportion to the simplicity or variety of the occupations and productions, which are to be found in a Society. It must be less in a nation of mere cultivators, than in a nation of cultivators and merchants, and less in a nation of cultivators and merchants than in a nation of cultivators, artificers, and merchants.[28]

Hamilton's report on manufactures also included some innocuous proposals for modest public subsidies ("bounties"), to foster "infant industries" that might be necessary for national defense. The report was no material departure from liberal principles; it sought to offset the artificial imbalances resulting from colonialism. Moreover, the proposals were temporary, like the twenty-year BUS charter.

For decades, statists have tried to use Hamilton to justify massive government subsidies, with politicians "picking winners and losers" through "industrial policy." They hope to enlist at least one Founding Father. But they fail, for Hamilton was no more a proto-Keynesian (on money and debt) than he was a proto-Stalinist (on manufacturing and military might). His desire to *encourage* American manufacturing didn't make him a central planner seeking a "comprehensive socialization of investment" (per Keynes); he sought to counteract prior policies that *discouraged* manufacturing. Nor did Hamilton believe the state could discern or should decree some "optimal" sectoral mix; that must reflect each nation's natural economic advantages, a prescription that mercantilism flatly rejected.

In his report on manufactures, Hamilton also welcomed immigrants, stating that many sought a more prosperous life, an "exemption from the chief part of the taxes, burthens and restraints which they endure in the old world." They sought "greater personal independence" under "a more equal government." It was in "the interest of the United States to open every possible avenue to emigration from abroad."[29] Unlike today's American nationalists, Hamilton was a pro-immigration individualist.

Hamilton also extolled the "system of perfect liberty to industry and commerce" in his manufacturing report; indeed, "the option ought, perhaps, always to be in favor of leaving industry to its own discretion." Yet he did *not* imply that government should (or could) keep its "hands off" the economy, as libertarians portray *laissez-faire* doctrine. Hamilton denied that a complete separation of state and economy was possible. A proper government, by protecting property rights and contracts, necessarily helps producers and harms robbers. For Hamilton, these were official, indispensable acts of justice, not privileges; moreover, legitimate functions (police, courts, military) require revenues, *unavoidably* from producers. Hamilton rejected *laissez-faire* not as liberalism's foe but as realism's fan.

Hamilton's Methods

Hamilton's methodology was scientific, deploying both induction and deduction. He also saw no necessary dichotomy between "positive" and "normative" economics: what *is* (facts) must inform what *should be* (policy). This is absent from contemporary economics. Hamilton remarked that "men give me credit for some genius," but "all the genius I have lies in this: when I have a subject in hand, I study it profoundly. Day and night it is before me. I explore it in all its bearings. My mind becomes pervaded by it. Then the effort which I have made is what people are pleased to call the fruit of genius. It is the fruit of labor and thought."[30] Harvard professor Frank Taussig described Hamilton's analytic prowess while assessing his report on manufactures:

> Considering the conditions under which he wrote, and the stage which economic theory had reached in his time, the report is a great intellectual feat. The marshaling of the op-

> posing arguments, the tireless examination of every aspect of the question, the careful investigation of the facts of industry and trade, the specific recommendations, and conclusions at the close, all bear the stamp of Hamilton's peculiar and powerful intellect.[31]

Hamilton's economic principles were derived from personal experience (business, law, policy positions) and from close study of primary sources and treatises. His specialty might be called *applied* economics, but his principles were also tested in the real world, in real time; they succeeded. Their validity could also be confirmed after his death (1804) as US prosperity tended to wax or wane as his principles were adopted or jettisoned. Hamilton's principles weren't merely *applied* but *verified.*

A Fair Verdict

Hamilton's political economy is misappreciated—either *overappreciated* by statists (hoping to recruit a formidable ally) or *depreciated* by libertarians (seeking a scapegoat to blame for today's statism). Because he helped *create* a great nation-state, its *current state* must be his doing. That's a non sequitur. In truth, his economics isn't mixed, statist, mercantilist, or corporatist. It is, simply, capitalist.[32] For critics, capitalism can't possibly be a morally legitimate social system entailing all social sciences; it's necessarily a corrupt system that favors a subgroup of "crony" capitalists. That was no more Hamilton's view than was that of Ayn Rand (1967), who in our time has expounded the broader view. Hamilton was no mere economist; he was a *political economist* and, rarer still, *pro-capitalist.* Although not an original economic theorist, nonetheless he was an astute *synthesizer* of principles and policies—and *correct* ones. His unique combination of talents marks him as an original practitioner of wise economic-financial policymaking. The ills felt so acutely in today's world are attributable not to a foolhardy embrace but instead to a tragic ignorance—and abandonment—of Hamiltonian principles.

2

Harriet Martineau

Economist as Storyteller and Traveler

David M. Levy and Sandra J. Peart

Martineau's Reputation in Her Own Day

ALTHOUGH HARRIET MARTINEAU is underappreciated today, her writings were widely read during her lifetime, and she was extremely influential in her own time. She successfully reached a wide popular audience with her monthly serials, published under the umbrella title *Illustrations of Political Economy.* She read widely in political economy and socialized and corresponded with many of the well-known political economists of her time, including James Mill and John Stuart Mill, Thomas Robert Malthus, William Godwin, and Francis Place.[1] She corresponded with a remarkable group of political and literary figures in both Britain (Prime Minister William Gladstone, John Bright) and America (Ralph Waldo Emerson, Harriet Beecher Stowe). Perhaps the most balanced appreciation of her *Illustrations* is found in a lecture by William Stanley Jevons, who rightly read her as a follower of Adam Smith.[2]

It is no exaggeration to suggest that her ideas were sometimes controversial and attracted negative attention. Indeed, both her ideas and her character were

---

David M. Levy is professor of economics at George Mason University and distinguished fellow of the History of Economics Society. His most recent book with Sandra J. Peart is *Towards an Economics of Natural Equals: A Documentary History of the Early Virginia School*, published by Cambridge University Press. Sandra J. Peart is E. Claiborne Robins Distinguished Professor in Leadership Studies and dean of the University of Richmond's Jepson School of Leadership Studies. She is a past president of the International Adam Smith Society and the History of Economics Society. With David Levy, she has written on the transition to postclassical economics.

flamboyantly attacked in *Fraser's Magazine*, where she was the first of three named economists to be vilified in the *Fraser's* "Gallery."[3] All three, Martineau, William Godwin, and Francis Place, were central to the controversy surrounding the implication of Malthus's *Essay on Population*. The central issue in the debate was at what age responsible people might marry. Martineau, like Malthus himself, advocated for couples to delay marriage until they could support their children. This seemingly innocuous recommendation was in direct contradiction to the orthodox Christian doctrine of that time that couples should marry as soon as possible to avoid the sin of fornication.[4]

Importantly, this controversy over marriage presupposed monogamy and a world without contraception.[5] Had polygamy been practiced, choice space would have widened beyond the question of earlier or later marriage. This simple point needs to be understood to appreciate what Martineau accomplished in her travels to America, to which we turn next.

Martineau's Travels to America

Martineau's *Illustrations of Political Economy* was a *de facto* textbook of political economy, formed from a monthly series of installments, a sequence of stories that began with the simplest of economic arrangements and gradually became more complex.[6] Queen Victoria was one of her students.[7] For our narrow purpose, Martineau's fourth installment of her *Illustrations of Political Economy,* titled *Demerara,* is the critical one. It was published a decade following the 1823 rebellion of thousands of enslaved persons in the British colony of Demerara.[8] It is important to separate what she wrote about slavery when in England and what she discovered on her American trip.

In *Demerara,* Martineau repeated the anti-slavery argument that property is a conventional right and "Man has no right to hold Man in property." In this story, she developed a theme that she greatly expanded later. She suggested that the system of slavery would lead to rebellions because enslavers would not punish rebellious slaves but instead would protect their (enslavers') assets. Thus, Martineau wrote, if the conventional punishment for murder were death by hanging, the slave owner might well prefer not to destroy his property but instead would attempt to disguise the crime and sell the enslaved person to a neighbor.[9] In her visit to the American South during the time of slavery, she was sensitive to political attempts to solve such collective action problems.

The economics lesson opens in a way unsurprising for anyone who has read Adam Smith's *Wealth of Nations* (1776). Because the product of their labor did not affect their wealth, enslaved persons had little incentive to work diligently. But Martineau added a complication absent in Smith. Her story features a character, Alfred, the son of a slave owner who has *also* read Smith and has become aware of the incentive problem associated with using enslaved labor. Alfred offers a solution to this problem—taskwork with wages:

> Mr. Bruce meanwhile was looking alternately at two gangs of slaves at work after a rather different manner. He was standing on the confines of two estates; and, in a field at a little distance, a company of slaves was occupied as usual; that is, bending over the ground, but to all appearance scarcely moving, silent, listless, and dull. At hand, the whole gang, from Cassius down to the youngest and weakest, were as busy as bees, and from them came as cheerful a hum, though the nature of their work rather resembled the occupation of beavers.
>
> "Task-work with wages," said Alfred, pointing to his own gang; "eternal labour, without wages," pointing to the other. "It is not often that we have an example of the two systems before our eyes at the same moment. I need not put it to you which plan works the best."[10]

Thus, in *Demerara* she laid out two interesting hypotheses about slavery: insufficient punishment because of the property interest and the idea of an incentive-compatible slavery. During her American travels, she found instances of both. Neither of these are our primary concern, so we will focus on what she discovered.

Power, Sex, and Racial Politics

When Adam Smith explained how slavery could exist even though it would not be materially profitable, he appealed to the masters' desire to dominate.[11]

Smith did not explain what he meant by domination. Martineau, who had been invited to visit the American South with the hope of changing the views she expressed in *Demerara,*[12] discovered something that filled the gap in Smith's argument. While traveling through the plantation South, Martineau was welcomed by the wives of plantation owners, who apparently spoke candidly about the sexual arrangements on plantations. On the basis of her conversations, she pointed to a terrible consequence of the lack of self-ownership. Plantation owners abused their female slaves sexually:

> Every man who resides on his plantation may have his harem, and has every inducement of custom, and of pecuniary gain,* to tempt him to the common practice. Those who, notwithstanding, keep their homes undefiled may be considered as of incorruptible purity.[13]

Martineau's footnote, marked by an asterisk, continues, "The law declares that the children of slaves are to follow the fortunes of the mother." Plantation owners were legally able to sell and bequeath their own enslaved children.

Martineau thus dropped the monogamy restriction of classical political economy and opened the door to the critical examination of racial politics:

> A gentleman of the highest character, a southern planter, observed, in conversation with a friend, that little was known, out of bounds, of the reasons of the new laws by which emancipation was made so difficult as it is. He said that the very general connexion of white gentlemen with their female slaves introduced a mulatto race whose numbers would become dangerous, if the affections of their white parents were permitted to render them free. The liberty of emancipating them was therefore abolished, while that of selling them remained.[14]

A father might well desire to emancipate his children, but the law closed off this possibility in order to prevent possible violent insurrection initiated by this mixed-race group.

Thus, as early as 1837, Martineau treated race as polychotomous, endogenous to the system of slavery. Recognizing that the white fathers of enslaved people might feel affection or obligation to their mixed-race children, she offered a straightforward explanation of why skin tone would matter in twenty-first-century estimates of income disparities.[15] If skin tone is a long consequence of miscegenation, children of a white father were likely wealthier than children of two enslaved persons.[16] In addition, when confronted by the "common boast," as Martineau put it, that slavery improved the morals of Southerners—there were fewer prostitutes in Southern than in Northern cities—Martineau countered that there would be no reason to resort to prostitutes for a fee when one could purchase women for life and sell the resulting children.[17]

Martineau's accounts rendered clear, as few before her had done, the terrible consequences of slavery: violence and sexual abuse. Both her position and her character were consequently attacked. Thomas Carlyle referred to her "fanatisms" and criticized her anti-slavery argument.[18] Attacks on her work on America were collected and republished after the publication of Harriet Beecher Stowe's 1852 *Uncle Tom's Cabin.*[19] Martineau's obscurity among twenty-first-century economists may be explained by her gender, coupled with the severe attacks by canonical authorities, which served to bury the significance of her work,[20] and by the fact that hypothesis discovery remains an uncommon procedure within economics.[21]

Yet with new genetic data sets and the ability to determine the geographic lineage of parents, Martineau's hypothesis may be tested in the data. If she is correct, women from Africa would contribute more to the American gene pool than men from Africa. That prediction is borne out by current genetic research. A recent study concludes: "An Americas-wide African female sex-bias can be attributed to known accounts of rape of enslaved African women by slave-owners and other sexual exploitation."[22]

Underappreciated by Whom?

Martineau's 1837 report about the sexual usage of American enslaved persons was noticed by the black historian and sociologist Carter Woodson in a 1918 article in his *Journal of Negro History.* Woodson was a careful reader of Martineau. However, there is little evidence that twentieth-century economists read her work; otherwise, they would not have been "startled" at what they

Period Ending	Cumulative Citations Economics	Cumulative Citations African American Studies
1944	1*	5
1960	1*	7
1970	1*	7
1980	1*	8

found in the slave economy.[23] Restricting ourselves to canonical economics, her insights were entirely neglected; rather, Martineau was subjected to intense criticism in her day and oblivion in ours. One instance will suffice: Under pressure from his funders, Gunnar Myrdal, who knew Martineau's work, if only from Woodson's report, moved the reference to sexual usage reported in her work from the body of *American Dilemma* to an appendix printed in a tiny font.[24]

To illustrate how the period of exclusion during which black scholars were absent from economics[25] has influenced our understanding of the early debates concerning race, we conducted a pair of JSTOR searches restricted (first) to the larger number of journals JSTOR considers as "economics" journals and (second) to the smaller number of journals it considers as "African American" journals. The first period is from the first issue of the journals in the respective fields through 1944, and then we pressed forward. The table reports cumulative citations. We searched for "Martineau" and "miscegenation."

The first citation in African American studies journals is Woodson (1918). We would have found many more articles had we searched for "Woodson" and "miscegenation" instead of "Martineau" and "miscegenation," with ten references in African American studies journals through 1944 and zero references through 1980 in economics journals. The only occurrence in economics (Newman 1944) cites Martineau as a supporter of the Union in the Civil War and miscegenation as an accusation that is not connected with Martineau's report. Because this has nothing to do with the issue, it is identified with an asterisk. Through 1980, there are no additional citations.

The difference in citations for "Martineau" and "miscegenation" across fields is truly remarkable. Economists have been writing about slavery for as long as there has been economics. Smith's appeal to domination was not made substantial until Martineau's account brought reports of sexual use of American slaves to the attention of the world. Her report was duly noted in African American studies journals and ignored in economics journals. Economists in the twentieth century were apparently hesitant to examine past evidence and debates concerning slavery, whereas those outside economics—who were perhaps excluded from the profession and tackled these issues as historians or sociologists—found the accounts of past commentators, accounts that came from within economics, illuminating.

Conclusion: The Consequence of Martineau's Visit to America

The importance of hypothesis discovery continues to divide economists. The controversy engendered by Rutledge Vining (1949) over how best to discover and test hypotheses shows no sign of ending.[26] The key issue is whether one first develops a theory that yields hypotheses or whether the data themselves yield the hypotheses in a discovery process. Whatever one's views on that methodological issue, Martineau's travel to America constituted a form of hypothesis discovery, one that had an impact on the economics of her time. Her novel about slavery offers no suggestion that slaves would be sexually used; she discovered this usage in America during her travels. Thomas Carlyle's (1849) characterization of the political economy of his contemporaries reveals that he was very much aware of Martineau's account.

As two of the most prominent essayists of their time, Carlyle and Martineau had initially enjoyed a cordial relationship, but that cordiality deteriorated into antipathy largely as a result of Martineau's sympathies for enslaved people in America. In the 1849 essay in which he referred to political economy as the "dismal science," Carlyle used the phrase "sweet blighted lilies, they are holding up their heads again" cruelly to characterize blacks in Jamaica. He continued, "Our beautiful black darlings are at last happy; with little labour except to the teeth."[27] His words echo Martineau's report of "[a]n epitaph on a negro baby at Savannah," which begins, "Sweet blighted lily," as Carlyle mocked her description of the hopes of the baby's heartbroken parents for the final resurrection.[28]

Indeed, as noted at the outset, Martineau was vilified in *Fraser's*; her originality, talent, and character were all questioned in her time. Even though her writings were extremely successful during her lifetime, today only specialists know of Martineau's work, and economists have downplayed her originality and sophistication. Both her subject matter and her method of collecting information via travel proved controversial from the beginning of her career. Perhaps for these reasons, Martineau disappeared from the scholarly landscape for close to a century after her death. As eugenic thought and racism emerged and flourished among social scientists, Martineau's important work was forgotten, and scholars lost the ability to appreciate her contributions. At least within economics, her work was neglected and eventually fell into near oblivion. It is now time to reevaluate and appreciate her important contributions.

3

Knut Wicksell

A Consistent Marginalist

Diana W. Thomas

> *As has been correctly observed, there can be justice only among equals. Justice from above to below always smacks of condescension or contempt. Justice from below to above has only too often been synonymous with revenge.*
>
> —Knut Wicksell[1]

JOHAN GUSTAF KNUT WICKSELL was born on December 20, 1851, in Stockholm, Sweden. Wicksell may seem like an unlikely candidate for a symposium on underappreciated economists because his legacy and impact on economics broadly and the areas of marginal productivity theory, monetary economics, and public economics are acknowledged in most history of thought textbooks.[2] Yet Wicksell's impact on economics was, in many ways, indirect, and his name is therefore known among only a select few. Beyond the fact that he is little known, his unanimity principle for public decision-making remains controversial and underappreciated. An essay reviewing his contribution to public finance in the context of his other work is therefore useful.

In his obituary following Wicksell's death, Bertil Ohlin (1926) highlighted three substantive areas of economic theory to which Wicksell importantly contributed: marginal productivity theory, public finance, and monetary theory. Ohlin argued that Wicksell was underappreciated, even among

---

Diana W. Thomas is coeditor of *The Independent Review* and associate professor of economics and director of the Institute for Economic Inquiry in the Heider College of Business at Creighton University.

economists of his time, for two reasons: (1) English-speaking economics was woefully unaware of many of his contributions, because they were published in German,[3] and (2) Wicksell was removed from practical life and had difficulty getting in touch with what Ohlin called "practical" economics. Ohlin blamed Wicksell's Austrian training for this lack of what we might today call "policy relevance" on Wicksell's part.

Most treatments of Wicksell's work more broadly begin with a description of his political activism, which preceded and inspired his formal training in political economy.[4] Uhr suggested that Wicksell was a social reformer before he became an economist and that his economic training was motivated by a desire to perpetuate social reforms. Wicksell's position on population control was to advocate for the development and wider distribution of contraceptives. This position was motivated by a desire to abate poverty and resulted in Wicksell being labeled a neo-Malthusian. He had a distaste for the empiricism of the German Historical School and focused, in his own work, on a deductive mathematical method. He opposed institutionalized Christian religion and was a proponent of an expansion of the public sector, of free public schooling, population control, and universal suffrage but also qualified majorities, benefit taxation for public goods that benefited only some, and ability taxation only for those public goods that clearly benefited most citizens. Although his varied positions may make him appear an enigma from today's perspective, Wicksell was a consistent proponent of marginal benefit calculus and its application to both economics and politics. In what follows, I review his career more broadly. Then I summarize his contributions to marginal productivity theory, capital and interest, and monetary economics and highlight similarities in approach across his different contributions, which suggest that Wicksell was a consistent marginalist who consistently applied the logic of economic science across the different areas to which he contributed. Finally, I describe his contribution to public economics, and in particular his articulation of the unanimity principle in greater detail, again highlighting how his contribution in this area was firmly rooted in a commitment to marginalism and a consistent application of the economic logic.

Wicksell's Academic Career and Social Reform Efforts

Wicksell joined the ranks of academic economists rather late in his life, at age forty-nine, after prolonged studies that were interrupted only by his social activism. He initially studied mathematics at Uppsala University, receiving his first degree at the age of twenty-one in 1872. As he continued in his studies, he became very engaged in student activities and the social reform movement. He developed a reputation as a gifted speaker and even served as president of the students' association from 1878 to 1879. As a result of his success as a speaker, he was invited to lecture on different topics relating to social reform. On one such occasion in 1880, addressing the temperance organization on the causes of and remedies for alcoholism, Wicksell pointed to abject poverty as the primary reason why males, in particular, turned to alcoholism. He blamed excessive procreation as the primary cause of poverty and advocated for the development and use of contraception to stop what he thought was a trend of overpopulation. The content of his talk was summarized in the local newspaper, which created a public outcry against Wicksell. He subsequently came to be considered a neo-Malthusian and a moral nihilist.[5]

As a by-product of the upheaval he had generated with his public activism and lectures, Wicksell studied the population question more carefully, reading Malthus's *Essay on the Principle of Population*. Inspired by the book, he turned to the study of classical economics more broadly. He finished his second degree in mathematics in 1885 and then turned his attention to economics more fully, spending the next five years in England, Germany, Austria, and France.[6] He obtained his doctoral degree in economics at the ripe age of forty-five, in 1895, and had to spend an additional four years after that studying law in order to be eligible for an academic appointment in political economy, which, in Sweden as in many other places at the time, belonged to the faculties of law. Starting in 1900, he served as assistant professor in political economy at Lund University, and he was promoted to full professor in 1904. His concerns regarding overpopulation and poverty remained, despite his training in economics, and he continued to publicly advocate for birth control and emigration. One talk he gave on the topic in 1908 even landed him in prison for two months for "violently offending the public against certain Christian beliefs."[7] During his time in prison, he published a special edition of his book on population, *Die Lehre von der Bevölkerung.* He retired from his position at Lund University in 1916.

Wicksell on Marginal Productivity Theory, Capital and Interest, and Monetary Economics

As outlined earlier, Wicksell made substantive contributions to several areas of economic theory, including marginal productivity theory, monetary economics, and public economics. Uhr described Wicksell as "a founder of the marginal productivity theory" and explained that Wicksell reconciled insights from William Stanley Jevons and Carl Menger regarding marginalist analysis with Eugen von Böhm-Bawerk's analysis of capital and the Walrasian general equilibrium theory in a way that revealed multiple causal connections between different variables in these models.[8] More concretely, Wicksell's insight into marginal productivity theory was that producers maximize profit by producing where the marginal rate of technical substitution between input factors equals the price ratio between said inputs, which is, to this day, one of the fundamental insights taught to students in intermediate microeconomics courses.[9] This insight is a direct application of the equimarginal principle to the production side of the economy, identifying the relevant choice variables (input price ratios and marginal rates of substitution) and their relationships in production equilibrium.

Beyond this important theoretical insight, Wicksell contributed to Austrian capital theory by extending Böhm-Bawerk's work on the topic. He articulated an explicit theory of interest as the marginal productivity of waiting and constructed a dynamic theory of the interplay between interest rates and capital accumulation, which was later extended into the Austrian theory of the business cycle by, among others, Friedrich A. Hayek.[10] With this, as with his contribution to marginal productivity theory, Wicksell again identified the relevant choice variables for economic actors in financial markets as well as the relationship between those variables in equilibrium.

Finally, Wicksell contributed to monetary theory by being the first to articulate aggregate demand and supply analysis and emphasizing the relationship between investment and savings.[11]

Across these different contributions to economics, a theme of consistent marginalist thinking emerges. Throughout all of his various contributions, Wicksell seems to have focused on the following logic of economic science. He:

a. identified the relevant choice variables for each economic problem (consumption, production, savings/investment),
b. articulated the particular equimarginal principle that characterizes equilibrium, and
c. gave an account of the dynamic effects of changes in the variables underlying the larger theoretical construct.

As a result, he was keenly aware of and able to articulate clearly

1. the information relevant for individual choice in each situation (consumer preferences, technological possibilities, relative scarcities expressed in the form of factor prices, time preferences), which is contained in the variables describing equilibrium conditions, and
2. potential disturbances to the theoretical apparatus he had described.

This pattern of clearly articulating the relevant choice variables, the equimarginal principle inherent in those choice variables, and potential disturbances to equilibrium is the blueprint for most of Wicksell's work. Mats Lundahl (2015), building on Johan Åkerman (1933), even made the case that it extends to his theory of population, which had otherwise been considered doctrinaire and lacking in originality. As I will argue later in this essay, the same blueprint of identifying relevant choice variables and their equilibrium conditions also applies to his theory of public finance articulated in *Finanztheoretische Untersuchungen.* His articulation of the unanimity principle as a tool for parliamentary decision-making that would ensure equality between value and countervalue—that is, the marginal benefits of public goods production to the individual would equal marginal tax prices for the same individual—may have been his most original insight. It also remains his most underappreciated and controversial idea.

The Unanimity Rule: Consistent Application of the Logic of Economic Science

Knut Wicksell began his essay titled "A New Principle of Just Taxation" in his book *Finanztheoretische Untersuchungen* (1896) with the declaration that although the title of his essay suggested a heterodox position, what he was actually doing was simply applying what has come to be known as the equimarginal principle to public service: "The principle as such is, in reality, nothing more than the benefit principle, the well-known principle of equality between Value and Countervalue." He continued that what was novel about his treatment of the principle of value and countervalue was simply the fact that he was applying it not only to public services and the individual's contributions for these services but also to parliamentary approval of taxes. His proposal was "to describe the conditions in which the Value and Countervalue principle could be used more or less automatically by parliamentary tax bodies."[12]

After a detailed discussion of the advantages of the benefits principle applied to public expenditures more generally, Wicksell turned his attention to the application of the principle to parliamentary decision-making. He began this discussion with the assertion that "It is not necessary either from the theoretical or from the practical point of view that tax distribution should be so rigid and pre-determined, nor indeed that it should be independent of the approval of expenditure itself."[13] Wicksell essentially questioned the now common practice of considering the benefits and the costs of public expenditure projects in isolation. Instead, he suggested that there are significant advantages to considering both the specific tax prices and the benefits of a public expenditure project simultaneously. This assertion implicitly suggests that by focusing on the levying of taxes for public revenue as distinct from the discussion of public expenditure projects, parliamentary bodies have intentionally separated considerations of benefits and costs of public goods projects in a way that has prevented application of the benefits principle to public goods production. He went on:

> Provided the expenditure in question holds out any prospect at all of creating utility exceeding costs, it will always

> be theoretically possible, and approximately so in practice, to find a distribution of costs such that all parties regard the expenditure as beneficial and may therefore approve it unanimously. Should this prove altogether impossible, I would consider such failure as an a posteriori, and the sole possible, proof that the state activity under consideration would not provide the community with utility corresponding to the necessary sacrifice and should hence be rejected on rational grounds.[14]

These few short sentences communicate the core of Wicksell's insight regarding a consistent application of the equimarginal principle, or the "principle of Value and Countervalue," as he called it, to the public sphere. His discussion suggests that most public expenditure projects cannot be justified unless they are able to command support from a majority of the constituents, because a failure to achieve unanimous support implies that the expected benefits from a public expenditure project do not exceed the costs in terms of additional taxation to the population. His discussion here is evidence that Wicksell was a consistent theoretical economist across all of his different contributions focusing on the equality of marginal benefits and marginal cost in equilibrium. As discussed earlier, this tendency of human systems to equilibrate and produce what he called economically just outcomes when the choice-relevant magnitudes are considered and allowed to equilibrate is consistent throughout all of Wicksell's work: population, marginal productivity of capital, monetary economics, and public finance.

Wicksell's proposal for unanimity in public decision-making stemmed from his desire to design a system that was economically just—in the sense that people should not have to pay for public goods and services in excess of the benefits they receive. Marianne Johnson (2010) quoted Wicksell as stating, "[M]y claim is now only that the degree of justice, which characterizes voluntary exchange, namely that nobody needs to pay more for a commodity than he believes it to be worth, should be adopted in public taxation."[15] A unanimity rule provided the requisite institutional structure that would ensure that everyone's preferences were politically represented and that no group, no matter how big or small, could be exploited by a majority as a result of limitations on the franchise or voting rules that allowed democratic preference domination.

Wicksell cared mostly about adopting a principle of public decision-making that would ensure voluntary consent. His proposal of adopting a unanimity principle was guided by the insight that economic justice was realized when individual marginal benefits equaled individual marginal costs. He believed that only the unanimity principle could ensure representation of the preferences of all social groups and that it would make public decision-making processes more like private decision-making process in markets. This preference for economically just taxation is also revealed in his admission that minority rights of veto or approximate unanimity were reasonable alternatives for unanimity.[16]

Unlike some of the most well-known later proponents of his unanimity principle, such as James Buchanan, Wicksell believed that a successful implementation of his principle (of voluntary consent) would result in an increase in the number of activities undertaken by government:

> If the distribution of taxes always rested on the principle of voluntary consent, it seems to me highly probable that many such activities which today can be undertaken only by private groups, would come to be incorporated into the operation of the state. The bitter opposition which now confronts the introduction of many very useful state institutions would largely disappear as soon as each individual could be certain that he would never be burdened with a larger share of their costs than he personally or his interest group had accepted through their representative in the legislature.[17]

Given that Wicksell seems to have had an Austrian process perspective on exchange as a type of human interaction, paired with the understanding that aggregate outcomes of individual choice would at least meet a standard of economic justice (albeit not necessarily a welfare maximum), it does not seem far-fetched to interpret his belief that the public sector would expand if it were modeled on the logic of equilibrating the relevant choice variables (i.e., individual marginal benefit and individual marginal cost) as a belief that rational agents would latch onto and use a process of public decision-making that reflected economic justice concerns more widely. Clearly, this had been the case with the market mechanism as a technology that expanded the scope for economic exchange.

Wicksell's theory was firmly rooted in Sweden's empirical historical reality wherein farmers, who were not otherwise represented in the Swedish parliament, nevertheless had the right to veto any imposition of new taxes.[18]

Despite this focus on economic justice, Wicksell also insisted on an inclusion of social justice concerns in public decision-making processes. He proposed mechanisms that would ensure a relatively more equal distribution of resources to allow for economically just outcomes. More specifically, Wicksell proposed confiscatory inheritance taxes, which would create a process of social leveling of opportunity, which he believed would yield greater overall utility for society than a free enterprise system.[19] Buchanan justified his arguments in favor of redistribution (and inheritance taxes specifically) along similar lines,[20] but also based on the fact that inheritances, as noncompensated transfers, represent rents, which come with all of the inefficiency costs of associated rent-seeking activities.[21]

Another way in which Wicksell's focus on economic justice and the equimarginal principle as a tool to achieve such justice is revealed is in his discussion of the enemies of political and economic justice.[22] Wicksell was particularly concerned with political injustice resulting from the following five sources: (1) the influence of a privately motivated executive; (2) the political power of the wealthy, who even with universal suffrage enjoyed undue influence by virtue of the fact that they were overrepresented in "the whole legislative and tax approval machinery";[23] (3) the potential for a tyranny of accidental parliamentary majorities; (4) the potential for an inefficient spending spiral; and (5) obstructionism by a minority with veto power. All of these sources of political injustice ultimately result in a movement away from a consistent execution of the equimarginal principle in the public sphere and therefore represent movement away from what Wicksell considered economic justice.[24]

Conclusion

Knut Wicksell's contributions to economics spanned productivity theory, monetary economics, and public economics. Beyond his scholarship in economics, he also published on and publicly discussed population theory. Across all of his contributions, Wicksell was a consistent marginalist and faithfully applied the logic of economic science consisting in the principle of value and countervalue (the equimarginal principle). His faithful application of what he called the principle of value and countervalue was inspired by his belief that a system based on this principle would produce economically just outcomes in the sense that "each man received his money's worth."[25]

4

Thorstein Veblen

The Drive for Status

Robert M. Whaples

AT FIRST GLANCE, it would appear that Thorstein Veblen is not underappreciated. He is probably the most well-known economist addressed in this volume. While he's no longer a household name—unlike Adam Smith, John Maynard Keynes, or Milton Friedman—many economists are familiar with his most important ideas. In fact, he ranked as the seventh most popular deceased twentieth-century economist in Davis, Figgins, Hedengren, and Klein's 2011 poll of economists, behind only Keynes, Friedman, Paul Samuelson, Friedrich Hayek, Joseph Schumpeter, and John Kenneth Galbraith—and slightly ahead of George Stigler, Joan Robinson, and James Tobin.[1] His life and ideas are discussed—sometimes in considerable detail—in most history of economic thought textbooks.[2] Robert Heilbroner's multimillion-selling *The Worldly Philosophers* (1953) accords him an entire chapter, "The Savage World of Thorstein Veblen"—an honor that he shares with only Adam Smith, Karl Marx, and Keynes. Moreover, the possibility of an upward-sloping demand curve for status symbols—known as a Veblen good—is named for him.

However, appreciation for Veblen is quite narrow.[3] Left-of-center economists laud him, but the mainstream virtually ignores him, and most classical liberals find him rather alarming. I will take each of these in turn.

Among the economists surveyed by Davis, Figgins, Hedengren, and Klein, Democrats outnumbered Republicans 2.33 to 1. However, among those who selected Veblen as being among their favorite three economists, Democrats outnumbered Republicans 4.6 to 1. The survey also asked economists'

Robert M. Whaples is professor of economics at Wake Forest University and editor of *The Independent Review.*

opinions on seventeen policy questions, creating from it a [classical] "liberalism" score.[4] The classical liberalism score for Veblen's supporters was one of the lowest among top-rated economists—similar to the score for supporters of Galbraith and Robinson (who once lauded Veblen as "the most original economist born and bred in the USA").[5]

While popularizers like Heilbroner love Veblen, and it may be true that in the early twentieth century "Veblen became the most visible and highly regarded social and economic critic of his time,"[6] Joseph Schumpeter was not impressed. His monumental *History of Economic Analysis* (1954) mentions Veblen only four times—a sentence or less in each case—in its 1,200 pages.[7] And it's pretty clear that mainstream economists have followed this lead. Veblen has rarely been cited in leading economics journals in recent decades. A JSTOR search for "Veblen" in all contents published in the *American Economic Review*, *Journal of Political Economy*, and *Quarterly Journal of Economy* indicates that he has been cited less than any of these other favorite twentieth-century economists since 2000. The *Journal of Political Economy*, which Veblen edited over a century ago, has mentioned his name just once since the turn of the millennium. Alfonso Giuliani's essay in the *Handbook on the History of Economic Analysis* tries to be sympathetic but notes "the negative judgment by the academic world"—the world of mainstream economists—that Veblen's theories have suffered.[8]

When I mentioned to a group of classical liberals that I would be writing on Veblen as an underappreciated economist, there was an immediate and striking reaction. "Veblen!?," they said, almost in unison. Then came a string of objections: "He was a statist. . . . He wasn't a friend of freedom. . . . He was a relativist. . . ." All these things may be true, but my contention in this article is that mainstream economists, especially those who are inclined in the classical liberal direction, should pay more attention to Veblen. They could improve their analysis by taking his central message about the importance of status more seriously and incorporating it into their work.[9]

Veblen's Life and Ideas

Thorstein Veblen (1857–1929) was raised among Norwegian-immigrant farmers in Wisconsin and Minnesota. His father's success as a "progressive" farmer allowed Thorstein to attend nearby Carleton College.[10] Then he studied philosophy and economics in graduate school at Johns Hopkins and Yale. Due to what may have been a bout of malaria or an "immunologic condition,"[11] he subsequently spent seven years unemployed but reading voraciously, as he lived with his family and his wife's family. He reentered academia, pursuing a second PhD at Cornell, and then moved with his mentor James Laurence Laughlin to the University of Chicago, where he lectured and published for several years before he gained public acclaim (and notoriety) for his most enduring work, *The Theory of the Leisure Class* (1899). He went on to publish a stream of other books including *The Theory of Business Enterprise* (1904), *The Instinct of Workmanship and the State of the Industrial Arts* (1914), *The Higher Learning in America* (1918), and *The Engineers and the Price System* (1921).

Veblen never secured a tenured faculty position and was eventually terminated at Chicago, later moving to Stanford, the University of Missouri, and the New School for Social Research. His career was marked by clashes with administrators due to his provocative ideas, his poor teaching reputation, his hostility to administrators and university donors, and his "flagrant and frequent violations of social mores,"[12] including his repeated marital infidelities.[13]

Unfortunately, grasping Veblen's ideas can be very difficult. Alvin Johnson, one of the cofounders of the New School for Social Research, recalled that as a graduate student he attended a seminar taught by Veblen. "Johnson was deputized by his colleagues to confront Veblen," who spoke in such a low voice that he could often not be understood, "and request politely that he speak up. Johnson did so. Veblen listened, looked up, and said quite clearly, 'Johnson, if you wish to create a cult, mumble.'"[14] The same can be said of Veblen's writing. It is cluttered with his hard-to-follow verbiage (mumbling) but also includes moments of sheer and clear insight. Lewis Haney echoes the sentiment that the obscurity was strategic: "Veblen . . . usually develops a peculiar terminology, and part of his prestige comes from a cult-like use of words."[15] In addition, he wrote as though every statement he made was authoritative. Many of Veblen's readers yearn to see a passage like this one from Eric Hoffer: "The reader is expected to quarrel with much that is said. . . . He is likely to feel that much has been exaggerated and much ignored. But this is not an authoritative textbook."[16] However, that was not Veblen's way. "Thorstein" means "son of Thor"—and a son of thunder like Veblen "made no intellectual compromises."[17]

Veblen's broad understanding of the economic world runs counter to many of the insights of classical, neoclassical, and classical liberal economists. His approach stressed studying the economy as a whole and focused largely on institutions—not merely formal institutions like corporations and laws, but much more the informal institutions that encompass our habits of thought and culture. He primarily took an evolutionary approach, focusing on change and the roots of change rather than equilibrium. Rather than the win-win view of buyers and sellers gaining from trade, he rejected a "harmony of interests" approach and saw clashes of interests everywhere, rejecting the *laissez-faire* approach and calling for massive reforms to the economic system. He attacked standard economic theory as a sterile, oversimplified "theology" used to justify private property and the propertied classes. Veblen dismissed the value of "captains of industry," arguing that they "sabotaged" the system, purposefully making it less efficient to garner more profits, and advocated a technocratic society in which managers and engineers directed economic affairs.[18] He generally argued that "predators" at the top were seizing almost all the wealth, so that the benefits of innovations did not accrue to workers.

In short, Veblen adopted the role of a pathologist performing an autopsy on society and the economy, who saw cancer everywhere—especially in healthy tissue. Somehow, he failed to appreciate the rapidly rising standards of living of the late nineteenth and early twentieth centuries. Real GDP per capita in the US (2017 dollars) rose from about $3100 at the time of his birth, to $5800 when he published *The Theory of the Leisure Class*, to $9800 in the year he died.[19] That's hard to miss—as are things like the spread of electricity and automobiles to the broader population by the time he died. In some sense he was preoccupied with people keeping up with the Joneses rather than figuring out why the Jones's standards of living kept rising.

Somehow, he also missed the vital role that entrepreneurs play in the economy (perhaps this is one reason Schumpeter pays him no heed) and viewed them merely as predators who wanted to exhibit their wealth. "The captain of industry is an astute man rather than an ingenious one," an unscrupulous man of "shrewd practise and chicanery."[20] Such sniping at capitalism and capitalists is standard fare for social critics. It's not unique (and often not very helpful). However, what sets Veblen apart from other social critics is his stress on—and creative, expansive examination of—*status*.

Veblen's Central Insight[21]

Stuart Chase summarizes Veblen's core argument in *The Theory of the Leisure Class* as follows:

> The thesis is simple. People above the line of bare subsistence . . . do not use the surplus . . . primarily for useful purposes. They do not seek to expand their own lives, to live more wisely, intelligently, understandingly, but to impress other people with the fact that they have a surplus. Ways and means for creating that impression . . . consist in spending money, time and effort quite uselessly in the pleasurable business of inflating the ego.[22]

Perhaps Chase could have boiled it down to saying, "People care about status and will bend every effort to gain more."[23]

Veblen's accomplishment is to convince readers that this is true, to explore its roots, and to explain its manifestations. He doesn't see the quest for status as genetic per se, as do modern evolutionary biologists. Rather, he sees the quest for status evolving through stages of human development—starting with a rather peaceable "savage" state, followed by a "barbaric" state in which the individual quest for status exploded, and then the modern stage of quasi-peaceable industry—although "human nature is *still* substantially savage."[24] During the barbaric stage, predation and warfare arose and a large enough surplus was accumulated that a leisure class came into existence, which exempted itself from labor—that is, from drudgery, which is "disreputable." The leisure class achieved its position through "exploit"—by violence, strain, self-assertion, and aggression in killing big game or seizing wealth from others. Seizure of wealth gave one status, which was originally visible to all in the form of trophies and booty—often captive women, who were the first true form of property. The "distinction between exploit and drudgery is an *invidious* distinction. . . . Those employments which are to be classed as exploit are worthy, honourable, noble; other employment . . . especially those which imply subservience or submission are unworthy, debasing, ignoble."[25] "Invidious" is the key word here. Veblen uses it 106 times in *The Theory of the Leisure Class.* "Invidious" can be defined as "likely to arouse or incur resentment or anger in others." The etymology of the term comes from the Latin *invidia*, meaning "envious."[26] Veblen's argument is about one of the seven deadly sins. While other moral critics of the economy focus on greed, his focus is on envy, which he sees as a far deeper wellspring of human action.[27] (As he also discusses arousing envy in others, he implicitly touches on the sin of pride too.)

The opening chapter of *The Theory of the Leisure Class* may strike some readers as odd. Veblen's historical sketch seems oversimplified and unhistorical.[28] But there's a degree of plausibility to it, and the logic of gaining status through prowess is compelling. A hot-blooded reader might wonder why he can't troop off, sack a city, and carry off some captives, but then Veblen brings the reader to the modern period, where things don't work this way anymore.

Veblen argues that the modern idea (implicitly held by most economists, as a glance at any intermediate microeconomics textbook will show) that the end of acquisition is the mere *consumption* of the goods accumulated is simply wrong. Yes, the incentive to achieve physical subsistence, the desire for comfort, and the goal of security are there, but "the motive that lies at the root of ownership" isn't the end use of the good—eating it, wearing it, driving it—it is "*emulation.*"[29] "Emulation" is commonly defined as the effort to match or surpass others in achievement. The Latin root comes from *aemula*, meaning a rival. Veblen sees this contest to possess more than other people—and to demonstrate it to everyone else—as especially fierce at the top but as permeating all of society. Initially prowess gave honor, and it was demonstrated in the booty obtained, but eventually it was the booty itself that gave the honor, and then *all* forms of wealth in settled societies.

However, this quest for status, which is a "consequence of the predatory habit of life,"[30] sets up an unhappy dynamic, a ratchet effect. "It is exceedingly gratifying to possess something more than others. But as fast as a person makes new acquisitions and becomes accustomed to the resulting new standard of wealth, the new standard forthwith ceases to afford appreciably greater satisfaction than the earlier standard did. The tendency . . . is constantly to make the present pecuniary standard the point of departure for a fresh increase of wealth; and this in turn gives rise to a new standard of sufficiency and a new pecuniary classification of one's self as compared with one's neighbors."[31] Because the goal of most people is to outclass others, "so long as the comparison is distinctly unfavourable to himself, the normal, average individual will live in chronic dissatisfaction with his present lot; and when he has reached what may be called the normal pecuniary standard of the community, or of his class in the community, this chronic dissatisfaction will give place to a restless straining to place a wide and ever-widening pecuniary interval between himself and this average standard."[32] The "desire for wealth can scarcely be satiated in any individual instance [with rare exceptions, people with 'aberrant temperaments,' especially those with 'strong religious convictions'] and evidently a satiation of the average or general desire for wealth is out of the question."[33] We're insatiable, always hungering and thirsting for more wealth and more status, because "*relative* success, tested by an invidious pecuniary comparison with other men, becomes the conventional end of action."[34] And wealth must be converted into consumption to be legitimate. "In the rare cases where it occurs, a failure to increase one's visible consumption when the means for an increase are at hand is felt in popular apprehension to call for explanation, and unworthy motives of miserliness are imputed."[35] "In order to gain and hold the esteem of men it is not sufficient merely to possess wealth or power. The wealth or power must be put in evidence, for esteem is awarded only on evidence."[36]

This is a hard pill to swallow. Although he heaps much odium on those at the top, Veblen sees such competition as ubiquitous—it is driven by the society-wide "instinct" for emulation—not merely keeping up with the Joneses but outclassing them. The law of diminishing returns holds for just about everything—with enough food, its marginal utility falls to zero—but not for status, as Veblen sees it. We are doomed to a zero-sum status game; we're virtually forced into it by public opinion. Moreover, the accumulation of wealth at the top "implies privation at the lower end of the scale,"[37] because it *compels* the lower ranked to spend more and waste more: "In modern civilized communities the lines of demarcation between social classes have grown vague and transient, and wherever this happens the norm of reputability imposed by the upper class extends its *coercive* influence with but slight hindrance down through the social structure to the lowest strata."[38]

Moreover, because we simply don't need all the things that the money buys, we consciously and unconsciously waste it. Those at the top begin to show their wealth by spending it on things that are of no use *except* for showing off their status. "The *need* for conspicuous waste . . . stands ready to absorb any increase in the community's industrial efficiency or output of goods, after the most elementary physical wants have been provided for."[39] This waste runs against another of our instincts—the instinct of workmanship—the proclivity for "the efficient use of means at hand and adequate management of resources available for the purposes of life,"[40] which presses us to do things efficiently—but the instinct for emulation often wins out.

In addition, labor—which people generally enjoy (at least up to a point)—becomes irksome because the wherewithal to enjoy leisure and its fruits is a better marker of status. However, leisure isn't idleness or quiescence. To merit one status, leisure time must be wasted productively—not by watching television, for example, but in quasi-artistic and quasi-scholarly pursuits and accomplishments, which allow one to flaunt status. For the "sake of his good name," one must "be able to give a convincing account" of his leisure.[41] People don't think you have class if you can quote *Seinfeld*, but they certainly do if you can spout some Latin, as Veblen does on the same page to demonstrate his status and drive home the point, quoting Juvenal: "Summum crede nefas animam paeferre pudori, Et propter vitam vivendi perdere causas."[42]

Veblen argues like an economist when he concludes that conspicuous leisure has declined relative to conspicuous consumption because as populations grow we encounter more people who don't know us and cannot witness our leisure but can witness our clothing, cars, and home. Moreover, he points out that the cost of living is effectively lower in rural areas, as there is less need to spend money showing off to the people who already know your status. Similarly, he argues that we discriminate in favor of visible consumption over invisible consumption—the outsides of our homes, which people can see, rather than in the insides. Domestic life is "relatively shabby"—privacy is "protective" of our resources.[43]

His take on common aesthetics is spot on. "True beauty must be expensive"[44]—for example, silver spoons are merely costliness masquerading as beauty. A beautiful flower that comes cheap is a weed. We disapprove of the "cheap" because it is inexpensive and therefore "intrinsically dishonourable"[45] —and believe that "a cheap coat makes a cheap man."[46] How much would someone appreciate a plot of land with a beautiful view of a lake or mountain unless they knew that other people knew he or she possessed it? Handmade "artisanal" goods are preferred to machine-made ones *because* of their flaws, which demonstrate that they are handmade and therefore costly, rather than "common."

He concludes that "with the exception of the instinct of self-preservation, the propensity for emulation is probably the strongest and most alert and persistent of the *economic* motives proper."[47] All of this sounds approximately true. So why don't economists pay more attention to it?[48] Imagine a world in which no one—not friends, neighbors, strangers, coworkers, or even God—is impressed or unimpressed by your consumption. How would you do things differently?

How does the desire to gain status play out now? As I see it, Veblen's central emphasis on status has endured the test of time. One might even argue that the quest for status is stronger than ever today[49] or at least that it has found new outlets that Veblen couldn't have imagined—such as competitions for more "likes" on social media, the ability to check out the latest net worth standings of the world's billionaires on Forbes,[50] or the ability to compare scholars' total citations or h-indexes as calculated by Google Scholar. Would he have foreseen young women adopting the style of baring their midriffs so they can show off the time and money they've spent at the tanning salon, or young men showing off how buff they are—evidence of time and money spent at the gym?

Veblen's Legacy Among Mainstream Economists

Veblen's most successful follower is certainly John Kenneth Galbraith. In *The Affluent Society* (1958), Galbraith identified the three primary benefits of wealth in "the satisfaction in the power with which it endows the individual . . . in the physical possession of the things which money can buy" and—bringing in Veblen's core idea—"in the distinction or esteem that accrues to the rich man."[51] However, he then argues that "all three of these returns to wealth have been greatly circumscribed in the last seventy-five years." Like Veblen, he contends that "wealth has never been a sufficient source of honor in itself. It must be advertised." But he suggests that—while the grandees of the late 1800s knew how to flaunt their wealth—"such display is now passé."[52] I doubt that Veblen, were he still alive, would have agreed that showing off one's wealth had gone out of style. Nonetheless, Galbraith took Veblen's argument that much of spending is wasteful quite seriously, effectively arguing that this meant the marginal utility of additional personal spending by most Americans had fallen to zero.[53] Why do Americans produce so much that our additional output is virtually worthless? Galbraith argues that "we have been deceived into thinking we need more production—tricked by history, by economists, and by Madison Avenue."[54] Veblen would approve of this sentiment. On the other hand, Galbraith argued that public goods (actually government-provided goods)—like good roads, clean parks, slum clearance, and education—were underfunded, concluding that a raft of reforms and programs along the lines of the Great Society should be adopted.[55]

Robert Frank is another important modern follower of Veblen. In *Choosing the Right Pond* (1987) Frank provides empirical evidence supporting Veblen's idea that status matters to individuals. Examining the incomes of automobile salespeople and real estate agents, he finds that incomes are much more equally distributed than the revenues the agents generate. After ruling out other explanations, he argues that high-wage workers are paid less than the dollar value of their marginal product because they have relatively high rank in their peer group, and low-wage workers are paid more because they are compensated for their low rank. In other words, workers' compensation has two components: a monetary payment and social ranking. Status matters, and real people will pay for it—receiving less money for the right to be a big fish in a pond with smaller fish. Status matters, and real people must be compensated for lack of it—receiving more money for the burden of being a small fish in a pond of bigger fish. Frank estimates these magnitudes and stresses that the equilibrium is driven by the ability of individuals to choose their own reference groups.

In *Luxury Fever* (1999), Frank argues that the spending of the wealthy is a virus that infects nearly everyone else in society. Very few people are immune to this disease because almost everyone has an intense, partially biological, desire for relative status. Harmful, wasteful rivalry infects much of human interaction from shouting at cocktail parties to use of anabolic steroids by athletes to SAT cram courses, arms races, advertising wars, and high heels—and especially to conspicuous consumption by buying nicer clothes, cars, and houses than our neighbors. What is "smart for one" (getting ahead) is "dumb for all" (wasting resources by jockeying for relative status). The marketplace is full of dealers peddling biased information and pushing conspicuous consumption. The "tendency to allocate too many resources to conspicuous consumption is in this sense no different in kind . . . from the addict's problem with cocaine."[56] Frank frames such spending as a negative externality: "Because each individual's consumption affects the frame of reference within which others must make important choices, the frame of reference is no less a legitimate object of public concern than the quality of our air and water."[57] He argues that just as we cannot ignore pollution, or indeed any vector which attacks us physically, we cannot ignore such psychological assaults as the high spending of others. Like other negative externalities, conspicuous consumption—ultimately all consumption—should be subject to a Pigouvian tax, as Frank sees it. Like Veblen, the analysis is verbal, not mathematical, although he attempts to make the argument more formal in later work.[58]

As discussed above, however, few mainstream economists pay heed to Veblen anymore. Jack Hirshleifer explores the "expanding domain" of economics, examines status, and concludes that "rank-oriented motivations are intrinsically malevolent, since one person's rise is another's fall"; notes how remarkable it is that economists have failed to incorporate this phenomenon into their models; notes that Veblen raised the issue in *The Theory of the Leisure Class*; but then concludes that Veblen's discussion is "more satirical than analytical," which appears to be the nub of the reason that economists usually ignore him.[59]

Despite the overall trend and Hirshleifer's verdict, there have been a few interesting attempts to incorporate status concerns and Veblen's ideas about things like conspicuous consumption in recent years. Some of these have been theoretical.[60] Some have been experimental.[61] Some have been historical.[62] Others have been empirical—such as Charles, Hurst, and Roussanov (2009), who document that Hispanics and blacks spend a greater than expected share of their incomes on visible goods (e.g., clothing, jewelry, and cars), arguing that this conspicuous consumption is an effective, though costly, form of status-signaling for these groups.

Economists should publish more studies like these, rather than ignoring the issue of status. They should bring it into their textbooks and classrooms too, but they seem overwhelmed by the idea of being dragged to the anti-market ideas that Veblen espoused. I don't see it this way, partly because I reject Hirshleifer's conclusion that "rank-oriented motivations are *intrinsically* malevolent."[63]

What Can We Do with Veblen's Insights?

Almost every American is part of the leisure class at this point. Robert Fogel estimates that around 1880, when Veblen was a young man, the average male household head experienced 1.8 leisure hours per day (time not allocated to sleep, meals, hygiene, chores, travel to and from work, work, and illness). This more than tripled to 5.8 leisure hours per day by the end of the twentieth century. He estimates that in 1880 about four-fifths of discretionary time was spent earning a living. By 1995 about 60 percent was spent "doing what we like" instead of working for money. Finally, he examines "expanded consumption"—the sum of conventional expenditure plus the imputed value of leisure time—finding that 49 percent of expanded consumption went to food in the late 1800s, with 12 percent for clothing, 13 percent for shelter, and only 18 percent for leisure. By 1995, these figures were 5 percent for food, 2 percent for clothing, 6 percent for shelter, and—the lion's share—68 percent for leisure.[64]

I see the evidence that we are a leisure class—that almost all of us have as much as we need (far more than we need?)—as liberating and a sign of the abundance that the market system has created. Americans in the bottom 5 percent of the income distribution have a consumption level that puts them at approximately the 95th percentile among all the people who have ever lived.[65]

Others see its chief implication—that the marginal utility from an additional dollar is essentially zero, except for the boost it gives to one's status—as frightening, as an admission that the market system *is* wasteful. They fear that if such waste is admitted then there is no good argument against progressives and socialists who would seize wealth from the rich (and middle classes and almost everyone else). This logic is mistaken. The seizure of this "excessive" wealth is illegitimate because it doesn't belong to those taking it—or those to whom it might be redistributed. (It is also likely that those seizing wealth will spend it much less wisely than those who earned it.) Anti-growth advocates take the admission that the marginal utility of additional consumption is near zero as a call to force people to consume less to save the planet's dwindling resources. But prices indicate that most natural resources have gotten less scarce in the long run, and if consumption generates actual negative externalities (such as smog), we need to measure the externalities correctly and make buyers and sellers bear their true costs, rather than derailing economic growth.

Many people *do* spend their wealth on conspicuous consumption. Veblen and his followers see this as a problem, but if the drive for status is so primal, then thwarting conspicuous consumption will only drive attempts to display status somewhere else—like a game of whack-a-mole—perhaps to something that is truly harmful. Veblen's idea that conspicuous consumption at the top has a "coercive"[66] effect is simply wrong, as this contention implies that we are spineless people who *must* follow the lead of others. Yes, other people influence us, but this is simply not coercion. We have free will and exercise it regularly—in making important, life-changing decisions, in deciding how to spend every minute of our time, and even in deciding how to spend our money. Equally important, the equation of "conspicuous consumption" with pollution falls flat. The polluter doesn't have the right to put smoke into the air others breathe because, among other things, he doesn't own the air. The conspicuous consumer owns his wrist, and few would deny him the right to put an overpriced watch there. People have a lot of trouble avoiding the polluter's smoke. Averting their eyes from the watch is *very* simple in comparison. Are you wearing a Rolex or a Timex? It turns out that I didn't notice.

Is conspicuous consumption a bad thing? Maybe some of it is. If it is driven by envy, then the fault is in the envious person, who should root it out. If it is driven by pride, again the fault is in the prideful person, who should root it out. But it seems like a fairly peaceful way to compete—and people can choose their own ponds and choose whether or not to be envious of proud people. Finally, people choose many ways to show off their status not just by consuming more and better—by their education levels, by the accomplishments of their children, by their looks, by success in their favorite hobbies—

from Sudoku to video games, by their ability to find mates, by how much alcohol they can drink, by their "luxury beliefs,"[67] and even by their outward holiness, as they "widen their phylacteries and lengthen their tassels."[68]

Read correctly, Veblen can be seen as warning us against being spineless and following the crowd, rather than taking charge of our own lives and leading them worthily.[69]

Acknowledgments: I thank John Dalton, Williamson Evers, Robert Hébert, Michael Munger, and William Shughart II for advice and comments.

5

Frank Fetter

The Fortunes of Subjectivism

Matthew McCaffrey

IN 1925, THE name Frank Albert Fetter (1863–1949) would have been familiar to any professional economist or reader of the major journals in the social sciences. In 2025, however, it is almost completely unknown, even among scholars who work in areas like the history of economic thought, in which there is greater emphasis on rediscovering underappreciated thinkers. The neglect of Fetter today is strange when viewed in the light of his achievements and of the professional recognition he received throughout his long career, which ran from the mid-1890s to his death in 1949 at the age of eighty-six.

Born in 1863 in the rural town of Peru, Indiana, Fetter distinguished himself in his early years as a student and a prize-winning orator, and later as a successful entrepreneur. He attended Indiana and Cornell Universities for his bachelor's and master's degrees before travelling to Germany, where he completed his doctoral studies in economics at the University of Halle. He then returned to the United States, where his scholarly energy and originality allowed him to quickly become an influential figure in the emerging economics profession. Although in his writings he could be a fierce debater, personally his colleagues and students found him "slow to criticize but quick to understand," a scholar who "helped others by wise counsel, seasoned with never-failing humor."[1] He was a loving husband and the father of three children, the eldest of whom, Frank Whitson Fetter, also became a notable economist.

Fetter's central contribution to economics was to develop a consistently subjectivist theoretical system based squarely on the work of the Austrian

Matthew McCaffrey is associate professor of entrepreneurship at the University of Manchester.

economists and their American sympathizers.[2] This involved a complete reconstruction of the theories of value, price, and distribution, with a particular focus on the themes of capital, interest, and rent.[3]

Professionally, he held his major academic positions at Indiana, Stanford, Cornell, and Princeton Universities, with visiting posts at Harvard, Columbia, Johns Hopkins, Northwestern, and Illinois, among others. In 1912, after many years of service as one of its officers, he served as president of the American Economic Association.[4]

Despite these and many other accolades, however, his reputation declined precipitously is his later years, and following his death, his ideas were carried forward by only a few writers, who in turn found themselves increasingly out of favor with the dominant trends in economics. These were mainly economists in the Austrian tradition, who for more than 125 years have been repeatedly rediscovering Fetter's insights and using them to expand our economic knowledge.[5] Yet even among modern Austrians—who place a high value on past wisdom—Fetter is not well known. Jeffrey Herbener is therefore entirely justified in calling him a "forgotten giant" of social science.[6] I would describe him somewhat less eloquently as the underappreciated economist's underappreciated economist.

Fortunately, little by little Fetter's works on a wide range of economic subjects are being rediscovered and integrated into modern research. This effort has been aided greatly by a variety of primary and secondary works, especially the republication of Fetter's writings on distribution theory edited by Murray Rothbard,[7] the extensive review of Fetter's economic system by Jeffrey Herbener,[8] and a roundtable discussion hosted by the Online Library of Liberty in 2019.[9] Scholars have also devoted individual studies to Fetter's theories of rent,[10] interest,[11] entrepreneurship,[12] business cycles,[13] and other topics crucial to Austrian economics. In addition, two volumes of Fetter's rare and unpublished writings are soon to appear in print, which will hopefully encourage renewed and sustained interest in his ideas.

In this chapter, I will explore an area of Fetter's thought that has yet to receive much attention: his work in the history of economic thought. Specifically, I will consider his account of the transformation of economics following the "marginalist revolution," and of the role of subjectivist Austrian economics in that transformation. This topic increasingly occupied Fetter's attention in the later decades of his career, as he witnessed the theoretical revolution falter and give way to what eventually became anti-subjectivist currents in economics. In Fetter's view, the promise of the revolution was never fulfilled, and was eventually undermined because subjectivism was never completely or consistently adopted in economics. This led to conflicts between classical and subjectivist theories, but also to internal disputes among economists who all nominally embraced the new value theory. These difficulties were often overlooked, leading to a false sense of agreement and unity among economists that masked substantial differences that would eventually undermine the accomplishments and prestige of the subjectivists like the Austrians. It became a widespread belief, even among their own ranks, that their insights had been completely integrated into economics, which had at last achieved the goal of becoming a unified, rigorous social science. Yet as Fetter showed, this view was inaccurate and failed to account for the uniquely valuable and revolutionary character of the work done by Menger and his followers. In a sense then, this chapter serves double duty in this volume, because it is an underappreciated economist's history of other underappreciated economists.

Below I trace Fetter's work on the history of subjectivism, focusing on a series of articles he published from 1912 to 1928 that surveyed trends in economic theory, particularly some key developments in the shift from classical to neoclassical periods. One hundred years on, Fetter's papers offer a fresh account of how and why economics failed to become more deeply and consistently subjectivist. They are especially notable for Austrians, who have a significant stake in understanding this history and, along with it, the rise, fall, and renaissance of the Mengerian tradition.

The Arrested Development of Subjectivist Economics

Fetter was a pioneer in advancing the subjective theory of value in the tradition that began with the "revolutionary" ideas of Carl Menger, William Stanley Jevons, and John Bates Clark. In fact, Fetter's project in economics could be summarized as an attempt to consistently apply the subjective approach to the entire body of value, price, and distribution theory. This in turn meant abandoning eclecticism and purging economics once and for all of any classical Ricardian baggage, paving the way for a consistent economic theory built on individual valuation and action.

Fetter carried out this project over several decades and through a variety of textbooks and journal articles.[14] His efforts earned him a reputation as a major theorist in the United States, and along with Herbert Davenport and Irving Fisher, he became known as a leader of the "American psychological school."[15] In this context, "psychological" meant roughly "subjective," that is, emphasizing the idea that valuation—and indeed, all of economics—has its roots in individual human minds, perceptions, and interpretations, rather than in the objective physical characteristics of the world. The aim was thus not "to merge economics with specialized psychology."[16] Rather,

> seen in the light of prevailing thought about 1870, [psychology] merely connotes [a] shift of the center of economic interest. The old ("classical") political economy began its explanations with the objective world, e.g., the scarcity of land, the limited power of an acre to produce food, the growth of population, and the increase of mechanical inventions, and thereupon formulated certain "laws" of rent, diminishing returns, wages, etc. The whole treatment was essentially materialistic and fatalistic. The new feature justifying the term "psychological economics" was not the mere mechanical or logical device of marginality but was the shift of the center of interest from the outer physical world to the feeling, mind, and needs of man. This was a truly revolutionary change.[17]

Unfortunately for Fetter and the other Americans who worked in the Mengerian tradition, their approach to economic theory failed to catch on. Instead, subjectivist marginal utility theory was introduced into economics in fits and starts, and never consistently, leading economists to embrace various eclectic theories combining classical cost-of-production and newer psychological elements. The most famous exemplar of this trend was Alfred Marshall in England. The famous "Marshallian scissors" acknowledge subjective value in the determination of demand but still assign to cost of production the key role in determining supply. Marshall in turn heavily influenced Frank

Taussig, the "American Marshall" and author of a leading textbook that had a major impact on teaching in the United States. The success of these and other writers meant that key components of classical economics persisted into the neoclassical era, while at the same time, more thoroughgoing subjectivist works were sidelined, and eventually lost out.

Fetter was at first slow to recognize the changing fortunes of subjectivism, and when he did he attempted unsuccessfully to fight them. As one of his critics pointedly observed,

> Fetter insisted that all the "old lumber" of Ricardian thought be "broken up for kindling." In [an article in] 1901 he declared it had happened; in [another article the same year] he predicted it was going to happen; in 1927 he lamented that it hadn't yet completely happened; but always he insisted it should happen.[18]

Over the years roughly from 1900 to 1926, Fetter charted different ways in which subjectivism succeeded and failed, and he noted the sometimes-subtle ways in which classical ideas survived, often by intermingling with aspects of emerging neoclassical theory. Notable examples included the general theory of price, as well as the theories of rent, interest, capital, overhead costs, monopoly, and monopolistic competition.[19] Crucially, however, these ideas came to be labelled by contemporaries as modern and "marginalist." Their eclectic elements were either ignored or treated as benign, and it became the conventional wisdom that all the insights of the pioneer subjectivists had been absorbed into economics, which was at last achieving doctrinal unity.[20]

At the same time, from the turn of the century onward, institutionalist economists like Thorstein Veblen launched new attacks on the subjective theory of value, especially its alleged assumptions and normative biases. These criticisms helped to tarnish the reputation of the new value theory and recast the "radicals" of the marginalist revolution as the "conservatives" of economics, as compared to the younger generation. This further dampened enthusiasm for what was fast becoming viewed as a doctrinal relic.

The promise of the revolution begun by Menger, Jevons, and Clark in the 1870s was thus never fully realized, and by the 1920s was losing ground. In Fetter's words,

> The mood of pessimism must often possess the economists of that generation that got its bent in the last quarter of the nineteenth century. Perhaps they planned to give their lives to perfecting the ideas [i.e., the ideas of subjectivism] that were then at the center of attention and that then promised fruitful developments in many directions.[21]

Thus, while Fetter began his career as an energetic and original thinker looking optimistically to the future triumph of subjectivism, he ended it in grim disappointment with the direction economics had taken by the end of the first half of the twentieth century. Well might he have recognized the sentiment of Ludwig von Mises, who wrote in his memoirs, "I set out to be a reformer, but only became the historian of decline."[22]

The Rise and Fall of Subjectivism

Over the course of his career, Fetter developed, in real time as it were, a subjectivist interpretation of the history of economic thought. This interpretation identified key differences between groups of economists that went unnoticed or unappreciated, or were only beginning to become visible in the early twentieth century. At a time when many writers were hopeful that economics was moving toward unity and consensus, Fetter showed that theoretical divisions ran deep even among thinkers who superficially agreed on essential issues. He did this by returning to the roots of economic theory, and by tracing the development of key economic concepts relating to value and price.

Fetter reflected on these trends in a series of articles published from 1912 to 1928. The first of these was an extensive survey of definitions of price that distinguished between several major traditions in price theory.[23] He followed this up in 1920 with a two-part article exploring how the scope and central topic of economics had changed over time, from a narrow focus on commercial behavior to the study of consumer value, and finally to a social science of human welfare.[24] In 1923 he added to this another pair of articles, this time describing the recent history of economics and suggesting some ways that future economics could make best use of subjectivist value theory while also pushing its boundaries.[25] Finally, in 1928, in a Festschrift for Friedrich von Wieser that he co-edited, Fetter contributed a paper summarizing the development of economics in the United States from the 1860s to the 1920s.[26] Together, these articles offer a detailed account of the rise of subjectivism in economics, particularly in America, how it failed to fully win over the economics profession, and eventually, how it declined. Within this larger history, the ideas of the Austrians play an especially important role, as in Fetter's view they had most consistently and effectively championed the new value theory.

Price Concepts and Price Theories

Fetter was keenly interested in terminology and argued that clear and consistent use of terms was indispensable for meaningful discussion and progress in economics. Subtle differences in definition are both cause and effect of wider divisions among economists, and can reveal or explain larger trends in the history of thought. A key example is the definition of price. In 1912, Fetter published an article with that name in the *American Economic Review*.[27] Its insight is simple, but powerful: there is great value in returning to the essential concepts of economics. In particular, price theory is the heart of economics, and the beginning of any price theory is inevitably a concept of price. From that one notion grow many of the ideas that come to define and distinguish different trends, traditions, and schools of thought.

Fetter surveyed 117 definitions of price drawn from across English, French, German, and Italian sources published from 1769 to 1911. From this extensive list he devised a six-part classification of types of price theory. He first grouped each definition as either an objective, subjective, or ratio-of-exchange concept. Objective views focus on the thing given in exchange, or "value in the sense of purchasing power."[28] Subjective views emphasize individual valuation, or "value in the sense of desirability, estimation, subjective value."[29] Ratio-of-exchange definitions describe "value in the sense of a mere ratio of exchange, or bare mathematical expression, or quantum."[30]

Each of these types in turn has monetary and non-monetary varieties. Monetary definitions express price in terms of a money unit, while non-monetary prices can be either money prices or barter prices.[31] Table 1 summarizes this classification and provides some exemplars of each type. Fetter him-

Table 1. Fetter's Typology of Price Concepts, with Exemplars

	Monetary	Non-Monetary
Subjective	*J. B. Clark* *Ely* *Kemmerer*	*Menger* *Böhm-Bawerk* *Fetter* *Schumpeter*
Objective	*Ricardo* *J. S. Mill* *Marshall* *Taussig*	*Smith* *Malthus* *J. Mill*
Ratio-of-exchange	*Jevons* *Rambaud* *Davenport*	*Ippoliti* *Gunton* *Fisher*

Source: Adapted from Fetter (1912).

self and the Austrians used a subjective, non-monetary price concept.[32] In fact, Fetter concludes his article by stating, "We can hardly improve upon Menger's wording: 'Prices are the quantities of goods appearing in exchange.'"[33]

Fetter's survey reveals several notable trends. Prior to Adam Smith, definitions of price had been mainly subjective. From Smith until the years of John Stuart Mill's prime influence, objective definitions were dominant. In particular, from Ricardo through Mill, definitions of price are almost entirely given in monetary terms. After Menger, however, subjective definitions became increasingly common. Yet they remained just barely in the minority even through 1911, and even then were often intermingled with ideas from classical economics or incipient mathematical economics that clashed with the spirit of economic theory stemming from Menger. Two examples are worth mentioning.

First, the persistence of classical doctrines is seen in the group of subjective monetary definitions. These emerged in the mid-nineteenth century through "hybridizing" the subjectivist views of German economists with the monetary approach of the English Ricardians.[34] They are noteworthy because they were adopted by leading American economists like J. B. Clark, Richard T. Ely, and Edwin Kemmerer, who in turn transmitted them through their own research and teaching. This group thus offers a useful case study of the way in which more consistently subjectivist Austrian views were sidestepped, leading some Americans to adopt an eclectic account of price.

Second, the importance of mathematical economics is evident when examining the ratio-of-exchange group. By conceiving price as a ratio, this third group of concepts moves sharply away from taking individual valuations as the basis of economics:

> The hope [of the ratio concept] is not only to dematerialize purchasing power by making it mean no longer the other thing [offered in exchange], but to despiritualize it also, so that it remains nothing but a cold mathematical expression. All qualities cease to be, except in the mathematical aspect. The concept of the quality value becomes merely a mathematical expression.[35]

An unintended consequence of adopting the ratio definition was the creation of conceptual confusions around words like value and price, as well as the needless multiplication of terms. A more pressing problem was the way that the ratio view abstracted away from the concrete reality of human action, the way it "despiritualized" it. As Joseph Salerno explains, a price is "a brute fact of history, an *event* occurring at a specific moment in time as the outcome of interaction among specific persons."[36] It cannot be appreciated fully without understanding this interaction and the subjective valuations that make it possible.

For his part, Fetter argues that even otherwise subjectivist theorists like Herbert Davenport and Irving Fisher had inconsistently fallen into ratio definitions, effectively abandoning a subjective account of value in this aspect of their theorizing.[37] This presaged later confusions and concessions that undermined the gains won by the Austrians in the previous decades.

Economics: A Science of Price, or Welfare?

Having laid some groundwork in his 1912 article, Fetter took up a similar topic in 1920 in two articles on "Price Economics Versus Welfare Economics."[38] He built on his discussion of prices by examining the role they play as a definitional concept in economics. He begins his inquiry with a question: "What is the central theme of economics?", hurrying to add, "Or perhaps it would be better to ask, 'What should it be?'" According to Fetter, "Every serious economic student should face this question and seek to make a decision upon it."[39]

To answer his questions, he again surveys economic literature from the late seventeenth through the early twentieth centuries. He explains that

> From the beginnings of political economy as a separate branch of study, two more or less conflicting conceptions of the subject have been present in the minds of men. According to one conception the aim of economics is to study prices, profits, and trade; according to the other, it is to study the relations between wealth and human welfare.[40]

The first of these conceptions Fetter calls "price economics," the second "welfare economics":

> In price economics as a goal, it is prices, exchanges, commercial statistics, and financial operations. In welfare economics it is the relation of men to their environment, social and physical, consisting of the objects of their choice, as affecting their sustenance, their happiness, and their welfare. The best in price economics, modestly interpreted, is but a small part of the means to the end found in welfare economics.[41]

Thus, in Fetter's opinion, price economics has its proper place, but it should be a secondary place: human welfare should be at the center of economic inquiry.

Fetter identifies Smith as a thinker of broad sympathies and an early welfare economist whose views were unfortunately misappropriated by the very mercantile privilege-seekers he criticized so effectively. After Smith, the welfare approach was distorted, and it declined until it was decisively replaced by the price economics of Ricardo, which dominated most economic opinion from roughly 1817 to 1860. Price economics is essentially classical Ricardian political economy. It had three major characteristics:

1. A rigid belief in *laissez-faire*, together with the assumption that existing institutional arrangements (e.g., the distribution of property) reflected a "natural state" that therefore could not or should not be altered or reformed.
2. An insistence on studying economic questions from the perspective of employers and production rather than consumers and valuation.
3. An insistence on expressing and measuring economic phenomena in terms of prices and profits.

The scope of price economics is thus limited to the commercial world of an employer's business behavior, which is motivated only by monetary profits. Money and money profits are taken as the measure of human motivation and well-being.[42] Price economics is therefore almost synonymous with the concept of the "economic man."

In contrast to this view, economists like the Austrians viewed economics as fundamentally concerning human choice and its causal implications. Menger, for example, began his analysis with human wants and the scarce goods used to satisfy them,[43] and praised the humanitarian impulses of Smith and other early political economists.[44] For Menger, Böhm-Bawerk, and Wieser, the entire productive process existed to satisfy consumers, not consumers to satisfy producers. The market economy is a vast, complex process geared toward improving the well-being of all individuals and thereby of society generally.[45] By thus focusing on individual action and the complex motives that influence it, the Austrians were from the outset oriented more toward welfare economics than price economics.

In 1920, Fetter was highly optimistic that price economics was on the wane, and that the trend of opinion, especially in the United States, was strongly toward varieties of welfare economics. He further recognized that the Austrians had played a role in this shift, both as critics of classical economics and as original theorists.[46] Nevertheless, he noted that influential economists in several countries still adhered to price economics to one degree or another.

These writers included Alfred Marshall, Frank Taussig, Wesley C. Mitchell, and even Herbert Davenport.[47] Fetter further implied that the assumptions of classical theory continued to threaten the progress made since the beginning of the marginalist revolution:

> If, indeed, the change of opinion [from price to welfare economics] had been as complete as it seemed, it would put a terminus to our inquiry. . . . But the conception of price economics had very tenacious roots, and sprang up vigorous again in the writings of authors where it had been blasted in leaf and branch. We even hear it seriously contended now that price economics is the ideal for the future, not the outgrown error of the past.[48]

Fetter's warning went largely unheeded at the time, but the resurgence of price economics became all too evident with the rise of mathematical formalism, general equilibrium theory, and other developments of mid-twentieth century economics.[49] Austrian-style contributions to value and price theory were mostly lost or ignored during this period, and with them, a subjectivist approach to welfare economics.

Whither Subjectivism?

In 1923, Fetter published a two-part sequel article to his work on price and welfare titled, "Value and the Larger Economics," which featured updated discussions and some hopeful predictions for the future of the science.[50] He remained optimistic about the prospects of subjective-value welfare economics as opposed to a classical price economics, but was obliged to recognize new challenges as well. It was unquestionable, for example, that subjectivism had made serious gains in economics. Even its critics had no choice but to acknowledge, first, that the subjective theory of value was vastly superior to the Ricardo–Mill theory; second, that the subjective approach adequately explained the real world of market prices and distribution; and third, that a return to a pre-marginalist era was unthinkable.[51]

The problem was rather that critics and even some advocates of subjectivism poorly understood or poorly communicated its central claims. This was leading by the 1920s to a confused and eclectic economic theory. As Joseph Salerno explains, "It was not so much that the approach had been rejected but that—due partly to its own deficiencies—it had been uncomprehendingly conflated with competing approaches."[52]

As an example, Fetter points to the criticism of "marginal utility" economics by Thorstein Veblen. Veblen and his students attacked marginalism on the grounds that it was based on hedonistic calculus. Yet while this was partly true of the systems of Jevons and Marshall, it was untrue of many non-English theorists, whose ideas were not colored by Benthamite utilitarianism. Subjectivism as advanced by Fetter and the Austrians, for instance, begins with individual perception and interpretation rather than strong assumptions about utility calculus.[53] I return to this point below.

More broadly, Fetter argued that criticisms like Veblen's gained acceptance because economists were confused about their own recent history. In particular, the "marginalist revolution" had been misinterpreted in a way that eventually led to the downfall of much subjectivist economics, especially in the Mengerian tradition. In fact, for Fetter, the terms "marginalist revolution" and "marginal utility" were misnomers and sources of multiple confusions. First, the conceptual revolution in economics was not the discovery of marginal decision-making. This had existed, for example, in classical economics since at least Ricardo's theory of rent, and survived in Marshall's adapted version of it as well. Instead, the revolution was in subjectivism and in the recognition that individual values of consumers are the ultimate source of the economic process. Second, "utility" was a poor word to describe the new understanding of choice because it carried with it the philosophical baggage of hedonist utilitarianism. In addition, it implied an objective capacity to satisfy—an emphasis on a good itself rather than "the individual's feeling, estimation of, or desire for" it.[54] Emphasizing marginality and utility thus ultimately reflected a failure to more fully and consistently extend the ideas of subjectivism and to cleanly break from both classicism and from those versions of neoclassical economics inconsistent with Mengerian value theory.

Wither, Subjectivism

The last of Fetter's writings discussed in this paper was a survey of the history and then-present state of economics in the United States. It was written in 1926 and eventually appeared in 1928 in a Festschrift for Wieser. As with the other papers discussed so far, it is long and rich in detail and cannot be fully summarized here. Instead, I focus on its relevance to the history of subjectivism and of the Austrian tradition.

Fetter's survey pays special attention to Austrian influence on economic thought in the United States, and it was hailed by Austrians at the time as a brilliant treatment.[55] Fetter goes so far as to claim that "it still may be truthfully said that in large part the output of economic theory in the thirty years beginning 1888 is connected with and inspired by the Austrian theory, directly or indirectly."[56] Due to the efforts of Menger, Böhm-Bawerk, Wieser, and their English-language translators and interpreters, "the newer doctrine" enjoyed "an early and widespread acceptance" among economists.[57] To take one example:

> It may be said (with some qualification in details and variations of emphasis) that all the important general American textbook writers since 1895 have gone at least as far as had Marshall in adopting the marginality conception, and most of them have gone further.[58]

Despite this notable progress, however, the "incorporation [of subjectivism] in the general body of doctrine . . . was far from complete."[59] The reason is that while Austrian influence was generally positive, it was also hampered by poor translations of terms from German into English. Fetter notes especially the confusion around the word "utility" mentioned above. This issue alone resulted in decades' worth of criticism of Austrians and other proponents of the newer value theory on the grounds that it relied on Benthamite hedonism:

> The mischief and misunderstanding became greater in America after 1900 when, utilitarianism having become discredited in psychological circles, critics of the marginal

> doctrine thought by this fact to discredit the marginal "utility" theory in economic circles.[60]

Of course, Austrians could easily reply that "the views reflected both in the criticism and in the proposed changes [to theory] evidence the failure to see fully the implication of their doctrine."[61] Yet it was difficult to convince critics who lumped Austrians together with other traditions to accept that their common terminology meant anything other than that they were in fundamental agreement. In this way it became easier for critics to dismiss the ideas of the Austrians, while more sympathetic writers found it easier to accept those ideas as merely slight variations of their own. This is the view that began to dominate in American economics and around the world.

In an unpublished manuscript on the theory of overhead costs, Fetter noted that many ideas from classical cost theory still survived, usually because economists had been unwilling to embrace the logical conclusions of complete subjectivism. "Marginalism" had become an umbrella term containing mutually inconsistent theories that were nevertheless taken to be essentially the same. Fetter complained that

> To make the hallmark of the psychological school the marginal utility method, or to group that school with nearly all recent theory . . . under the title of "the marginal utility school" as is not infrequently done . . . reveals a gross misunderstanding or no understanding at all of the major issues in value theory since 1870.[62]

Fetter points to Frank Knight as one source of this mistaken view,[63] which was also advanced by Jacob Viner and other influential economists.[64] Even Mises and F. A. Hayek suggested versions of it.[65] In consequence of these and other problems, "By the mid-1930s there was no longer an Austrian School to speak of in the sense of a self-conscious, institutionally embedded community of scholars engaged in active research and dialogue within the Mengerian tradition."[66] This was a direct result of the historical developments and confusions Fetter had noted since at least 1912. They played a significant role in explaining why subjectivism, especially the Austrian variety, ultimately lost out to Marshallian and Walrasian equilibrium theories in the interwar period.

Conclusion

Frank Fetter continues to be underappreciated even among economists who work in the same intellectual traditions he did. His original contributions to economic theory and policy are becoming better known, but they still have much to offer contemporary scholars, most of whom remain unaware of them. The same is true of Fetter's work on the history of economics. As part of his larger project to chart the development of fundamental doctrines—from specific concepts to high-level discussions of the scope of economics—Fetter created an original history of subjectivist economics, one particularly associated with the Austrian tradition of Carl Menger.

Fetter shows how the early Austrians' subjectivism was never fully adopted or even understood by their contemporaries, and that they themselves sometimes failed to advance their own theory consistently. This led to the mistaken belief that by the 1920s or so all the essential insights of the Austrians had been incorporated into economics, and there was no need to identify any uniquely Austrian tradition. Yet the lack of a strong, clearly defined subjectivism made it easy to dismiss Austrian ideas along with any others, new or old, that did not fit a new orthodoxy. Fetter correctly diagnosed this problem, although he could not have predicted the extent of its consequences.

Fetter's history is not without faults, of course. To take only one example, he is too harsh on advocates of *laissez-faire*, and too quick to assume that they were untrained polemicists motivated by partisan politics, class interests, and the intent for special pleading on behalf of industry. Fetter also could not have foreseen that some of his criticisms would be resolved by later writers. For instance, his call for a "larger economics" would be realized in the work of Ludwig von Mises, whose "praxeology" takes action as the starting point of theory, and thereby incorporates all of the "psychic" welfare considerations Fetter believed were fundamental to the science. Moreover, Mises's theory of economic calculation provided the missing link between the economic analysis of price and value on the one hand, and social welfare on the other, that Fetter believed was missing. Mises's explanation of the economic process in terms of entrepreneurial planning and forecasting using the price system offered an account of social order and progress that had been only hinted at by the early Austrians.

6

Clark Warburton on the Great Depression and Federal Reserve

Thomas F. Cargill

CLARK WARBURTON IS an underappreciated economist by any reasonable meaning of the term. Warburton anticipated many of the important aspects of the Monetarist Revolution that dominated the profession in the 1960s, 1970s and 1980s—and remains important today—and confronted the Keynesian views based on *The General Theory*.[1] The monetarist literature convinced many economists that Keynesian policies and their reliance on discretionary government stabilization policies were based on a faulty theoretical framework, lacked empirical foundation, and, most important, were far too influenced by the then widely accepted view of the Great Depression. During the Great Depression and for over a decade after World War II, it was widely but erroneously held that the Great Depression was nonmonetary in origin, the Federal Reserve, despite easy monetary policy, was impotent, and a market-based economy was incapable of achieving economic stability and growth. It is difficult to overstate the impact the Great Depression had on political economy institutions in the United States and elsewhere, and on world history.[2]

Warburton stood alone against the professional and political trends of his time, and while not the only critic of the Keynesian perspective of the Great Depression, Warburton was the most significant in terms of the number of aspects of the Monetarist Revolution he anticipated, the number of detailed empirical results he presented, and the number of times he clashed with the

---

Thomas F. Cargill is professor of economics emeritus at the University of Nevada, Reno, and research fellow at Independent Institute.

Keynesian perspective in leading economic journals. This record justifies the claim that Warburton "stood alone against the profession."

Warburton's views were formulated during almost a decade of close study of the banking collapse in the 1930s and Federal Reserve policy. Based on this inductive research, Warburton came to the conclusion that the Great Depression was largely the result of mistakes made by the Federal Reserve. Warburton illustrated how government policy not constrained by rules was prone to policy errors that turned what would have been an unremarkable and probably serious economic decline into the major economic catastrophe that it became. This was his most important contribution; however, he anticipated the Monetarist Revolution on many issues, many of which are now widely accepted.

There is a caveat to any evaluation of Warburton's work that one should keep in mind, however. It is easy to overstate Warburton's contributions with regard to many topics because they are now seen in the context of the Monetarist Revolution, which occurred in an inflationary environment not nearly as severe as the collapse of real economic activity in the 1930s, had the benefit of theoretical, econometric, and historical rigor unavailable to Warburton, and happened at a time when the initial enthusiasm for Keynes had waned and some in the profession were willing to reconsider the Keynesian perspective on its inherent logic. It is one thing, for example, to empirically show that changes in money had a long and variable lag impact on the economy and that there was a close relationship between money and economic activity using simple statistical methods, as Warburton did, but another to estimate the lag with modern econometrics, develop the long and variable lag results into an indictment against activist monetary policy, and develop detailed models of how money and economic activity were interrelated. The emergence of public choice theory in the 1950s and 1960s also strengthened the monetarists' claims about discretionary policy.

This caveat does not apply with regard to Warburton's most important contribution. By the early 1980s, monetarists had convinced the profession on many of the points Warburton had anticipated—money and economic activity are closely related, money impacts the economy with a long and variable lag, monetary policy is more powerful than fiscal policy in the absence of monetary accommodation, and Federal Reserve policies in the Great Depression intensified and prolonged the financial and economic distress. However, the fundamental difference between Keynesians and monetarists regarding the inherent stability of a market system and the role of activist government policy continues. In this regard, the Keynesian-monetarist terminology is far too limiting and might better be replaced with the activist–nonactivist terminology.

Franco Modigliani, in his presidential address to the American Economic Association in 1976, most succinctly expressed this point. He acknowledged the monetarists had been successful in many technical areas, but a fundamental difference persisted:

> In reality the distinguishing feature of the monetarist school and the real issues of disagreement with nonmonetarism, is not monetarism, but rather the role that should probably be assigned to stabilization policy. Nonmonetarists accept what I regard as the fundamental practical message of *The General Theory*: that a private enterprise economy using an intangible money *needs* to stabilized, *can* be stabilized, and therefore *should* be stabilized by appropriate monetary and fiscal policy. Monetarists by contrast take the view that there is no serious need to stabilize the economy: that even if there were a need, it could not be done, for stabilization policies would be more likely to increase than to decrease instability; and, at least some monetarists would, I believe, go so far as to hold that, even in the unlikely event that stabilization policies could on balance prove beneficial, the government should not be trusted with the necessary power.[3]

Warburton's most important contribution was to show that discretionary policy—with its inherent tendency to make errors in the presence of long lags and incomplete understanding of how the economy reacts to monetary policy—turned what would have been a normal decline in economic activity into a major crisis that lasted almost a decade. This perspective stands in sharp contrast to Modigliani's view expressed almost three decades after Warburton ceased publishing his views. Perhaps Warburton didn't make the case in the detail made in Milton Friedman and Anna Schwartz's *A Monetary History*

(1963), but this is a distinction without a difference. In my opinion, Warburton's view on the Great Depression remains the most important contribution for understanding the fundamental debate so well articulated by Modigliani.

Warburton, Research Economist

Warburton received his undergraduate and master's degrees in economics from Cornell University in 1921 and 1928, respectively, and PhD degree in economics from Columbia University in 1932. He held a few short-term teaching positions but soon discovered research was his comparative advantage. Warburton worked for a short time at the Brookings Institution on the national income account project but joined the newly formed Federal Deposit Insurance Corporation in 1934, where he continued until his retirement in 1965. Warburton then joined the Department of Economics at the University of California, Davis, as a visiting lecturer for a short period, where I, as a second-year graduate student, attended a seminar he gave. This was not a pleasant time for Warburton because of some health issues, adjusting to retirement knowing that his research had been largely ignored, and inexperience in the classroom. Warburton returned to McLean, Virginia, around 1967, where he resided until his death on September 18, 1979.

During his career as a research economist, Warburton published a large number of papers and made many presentations. His most important research citations can be found in Bordo and Schwartz,[4] Cargill,[5] and Warburton.[6] To my knowledge, these papers did not represent his official duties for the Federal Deposit Insurance Corporation (FDIC). The majority of research was conducted at his home office in McLean, and as far as I can determine, Warburton had no meaningful research assistance. The volume of work is remarkable given Warburton's limited resources. In sum, Warburton was a one-man operation, and though he had access to the monetary and financial database at the FDIC and was permitted to use publicly available data, he maintained a professional separation between his views and his responsibilities at the FDIC.[7] It would be an error to view his research as part of his FDIC responsibilities, though the two are not completely unrelated.

Warburton's Contributions

Warburton did not start out to stand alone against the Keynesian Revolution, to become a critic of government fiscal and monetary policy based on Keynes, and, most important, to hold the Federal Reserve largely responsible for the Great Depression. He came to these positions over a period of years at the FDIC through his official responsibilities at the FDIC. Warburton's first assignment at the FDIC was to determine the size of the deposit insurance premium to fund the FDIC based on a study of the banking crisis from 1929 to 1933 and how future business fluctuations might influence the FDIC fund. It was in studying the day-to-day unfolding of the banking crisis and the role of Federal Reserve policy that he came to realize the banking crisis and the Great Depression were due to monetary factors, primarily caused by the Federal Reserve's failure to understand its lender of last resort role and how banks responded to changes in monetary policy, allowing a 25 percent decline in the M2 money supply from 1929 to 1933, and focusing on interest rates as an indicator of monetary policy. Warburton came to view the Federal Reserve as the primary cause of the most intense period of financial and economic distress ever experienced in the United States, and one that provided the foundation for the administrative state.

This interpretation of the Great Depression and its implication for the political economy of government stabilization policy are his most important and enduring contributions, but the following selected list of other contributions is significant: changes in the money supply were necessary and sufficient to cause changes in real and nominal economic activity in the short and long run, respectively; changes in the money supply had a long and variable lagged effect on economic activity; changes in deficit spending required a change in the money supply to have an impact on economic activity, or otherwise deficit spending without monetary accommodation was subject to crowding out; activist policy was not required to stabilize the economy—what is required for a growing economy is a stable monetary growth rate to stabilize the value of money and allow market forces to allocate resources; banks did not passively respond to central banking policy; inflation was inherently a monetary phenomenon; and interest rates were a poor indicator for conducting and understanding central bank policy.

Over a decade from 1943 to 1953, Warburton's views were expressed in a series of papers, often with detailed empirical evidence, many of which appeared in leading journals including the *American Economic Review, Journal of Political Economy,* and *Review of Economics and Statistics.* Warburton's "The Misplaced Emphasis in Contemporary Business Fluctuation Theory" (1946) is included in *Readings in Monetary Theory.*[8] This and other *Readings* volumes included the economic research of the most prominent economists of the day selected by a committee of the American Economic Association.

Yet Warburton had very little impact, was largely ignored,[9] and sometimes was regarded as a nut.[10] Why, then, was Warburton so widely published? Editors and reviewers concluded Warburton's work met professional standards to merit publication and offered a lone opposing view to the Keynesian perspective.

Warburton Was Ignored and Then Cancelled by the Administrative State

The General Theory was enthusiastically embraced by the majority of economists in academia and government because it offered a new foundation for building macroeconomic models to guide stabilization policy. But most important, it offered not only an explanation of what happened in the Great Depression but offered a solution to preventing further economic instability. The progressive movement that had started at the turn of the century also saw the Great Depression and the widely accepted view of why it happened as an opportunity to fundamentally change US institutions to accommodate a more activist government and commenced a political movement that continues to the present. Warburton was ignored not only because his views appeared to be contradicted by the Great Depression, but just as importantly, his approach to economics, rooted in classical economic thought, was considered in the trash bin of history as the progressive movement found its moment of opportunity in the 1930s. Today, it is difficult to appreciate how fast and completely *The General Theory* dominated the economics profession and how many accepted the Federal Reserve's claim that it did everything possible to prevent and then reverse the economic and financial decline. This fit so well in the progressive view of the administrative state.

Other aspects of Warburton's work also contributed to his failure to influence the profession, however. Warburton had no graduate students nor held an academic position that might have expanded his audience, and the FDIC was not notable as a government entity focused on academic research—especially research that raised questions about government's role in the Great Depression. Warburton's writing style (which some have characterized as obtuse), reliance on the Equation of Exchange framework, tendency to argue intensely over minor technical issues, and too often turning his typewriter into a flame thrower on those who disagreed with his perspective contributed to his inability to influence the profession. These factors, however, pale in comparison to the fact Warburton's views were rejected primarily by a profession that overnight enthusiastically accepted Keynesian economics and the political trends of his time. It would have made no difference who criticized this perspective in the environment of the Great Depression.

Not only did Warburton fail to convince the profession, but he increasingly found his views unacceptable to the new and rapidly growing administrative state that emerged from the Great Depression. No government agency likes to be criticized, especially if one attributes the most significant decline in economic activity experienced in the United States to their policies. It was only a matter of time for Warburton to become a target and subject to cancellation. In 1953, he came under pressure from the US Treasury to cease publishing and presenting his views. I became aware of these events from various sources. In preparing an overview of Warburton's work that started in 1973, I interviewed a well-known economist at the time who had knowledge of these events and was informed, off the record, that yes, Warburton was close to being terminated at the FDIC, but because of the intervention of several economists who had influence in Washington, DC, the termination threat ended when Warburton agreed to cease publishing and presenting his views at conferences. There, of course, is no known documentation of these events, but in light of how the administrative state functions, few would now find it difficult to reject this reason for the sudden end of Warburton's publishing in 1953. In 1958, Warburton began to express his views again in congressional testimony,[11] but by then, times had passed the one-man operation of Warburton and attention turned to Milton Friedman, Anna Schwartz, and others who formed the Monetarist Revolution.

Warburton Comes in from the Cold

Starting in the late 1950s and accelerating in the 1960s, a new generation of economists was armed with stronger economic theory and econometrics and a more extensive historical review of the relationship between money and economic activity. Much of this effort was led by Friedman and the so-called Chicago School of economists. As admitted by Modigliani in 1977, many of the major technical issues of the Monetarist Revolution were decided in their favor. By the 1980s, the profession no longer argued money does not matter, but instead claimed that it was too important to be left to any rules-based framework and government had the right and responsibility to use monetary policy and other policies to promote the general welfare.

Accepting Warburton's conclusion that the Federal Reserve's policy errors contributed to the intensity and length of the Great Depression came much more slowly because of the political economy implications of that view, but even that view is now generally accepted after many years of debate since the publication of *A Monetary History* in 1963. The most telling admission was made by Ben Bernanke in honor of Friedman's ninetieth birthday:

> Let me end my talk by abusing slightly my status as an official representative of the Federal Reserve. I would like to say to Milton and Anna: Regarding the Great Depression. You're right, we did it. We're very sorry. But thanks to you, we won't do it again.[12]

This was a remarkable and admirable admission from an official of the Federal Reserve but, unfortunately, Warburton's contribution to this admission has now been relegated to the history of economic thought.[13] Warburton is now recognized by those who consider the history of economic thought important for understanding today's debates, and fortunately, at the end of his life, Warburton witnessed the long overdue attention.

A significant recognition of Warburton's work came from Friedman and Schwartz in their introduction to *A Monetary History*:

> We [Freidman and Schwartz] owe an especially heavy debt to Clark Warburton. His detailed and valuable comments

> on several drafts have importantly affected the final version. In addition, time and again, as we came to some conclusion that seemed to us novel and original we found that he had been there before.[14]

This passage initiated a research journey for me. As one of three students in Warburton's seminar in 1967, I expressed to Warburton after a class that he must be pleased that Friedman and Schwartz were generating so much controversy and widespread discussion about money, the Federal Reserve, and the Great Depression. He responded that yes, he was, but he had made many of the same points a decade earlier. As a second-year graduate student, I did not fully comprehend Warburton's response and conferred with Thomas Mayer, my dissertation chair. Yes, Warburton was correct, and I would be advised to review *A Monetary History* again, especially the introduction.

That event began a journey that resulted in bringing detailed attention to Warburton's work and relationship to the Monetarist Revolution,[15] along with Bordo and Schwartz;[16] Humphrey;[17] Seldon;[18] Tavlas;[19] and Trescott.[20] That journey eventually included the writing of a tribute to Clark Warburton on the occasion of his death.[21]

Warburton Remains Underappreciated in the Most Important Sense

Warburton's contributions are rather remarkable considering the environment in which he worked. While ignored for many years, his contributions are now recognized by those interested in the history of economic thought, but not by many of the current generation of economists. In broad perspective, however, Warburton's most important insights about the Great Depression—expanded by Friedman and Schwartz and others who contributed to the monetarist perspective in the 1960s, 1970s, and 1980s—have not been appreciated by the profession or central banks to the degree they deserve.

Despite the overwhelming evidence that the Federal Reserve contributed to the depth and length of the Great Depression, and Bernanke's admission to Friedman and Schwartz in 2002, much of the profession and all of the government agencies assigned with stabilization policy responsibilities reject the implications of that finding. In contrast, they accept Modigliani's perspective that the economy needs to be stabilized by government discretionary policy, can be so stabilized, and therefore government has the right and responsibility to carry out the fundamental message of *The General Theory*. Perhaps the administrative state and the Federal Reserve have come to play such a major role in the new century that they control the narrative, and the views of Warburton, Friedman, Schwartz, and others are easy to push off as not relevant in today's environment.

Nonetheless, the record of discretionary monetary policy is not impressive by any standard. The Federal Reserve shares much of the responsibility for the severity and length of the Great Depression, as well as the Great Inflation from 1965 to 1985, yet *The General Theory* continues to influence the economic profession and government policy. These two major policy failures have had no impact on confidence in discretionary monetary policy. Despite Bernanke's admission in 2002, the Federal Reserve commenced an expansionary monetary policy in the shadow of Japan's deflationary process in the 1990s and into the first decade of the new century that contributed to the bubble in house prices (2002 to early 2006), the burst of the bubble (early 2006), and the Great Recession, which began with the financial meltdown in 2008 and continued for several years. In response to the fallout from the burst of the house-price bubble, the Federal Reserve shifted to even greater excessive ease and adopted Bank of Japan's zero interest rate and quantitative ease policy to stimulate the economy. As in Japan, these nontraditional monetary policies did not prevent a rather sharp decline, which ended in 2009 and saw the economy grow at a slow rate until 2015.

It is remarkable that of the four major periods of economic and financial distress in the last century, the Federal Reserve's discretionary policy and outright errors contributed importantly in every case. Yet faith in discretionary monetary policy remains firm and, if anything, has strengthened, as the Federal Reserve continues to claim it can "float like a butterfly, sting like a bee" and continues to emphasize its independence from political forces. Despite the many contributions of the monetarist school that are now widely accepted, the fundamental message of *The General Theory* is widely accepted by government and much of the economics profession.

Warburton is now recognized as the most prominent and persistent critic of the Keynesian view and anticipated many of the important elements of the monetarist perspective. In this sense Warburton is no longer underappreciated; but there are two caveats: first, this recognition had only come from those interested in the history of economic thought who wanted to set the record straight, and second, Warburton's most important contribution remains underappreciated, as the fundamental message of *The General Theory* continues to guide monetary policy as well as virtually every government stabilization and regulatory institution.

7

Ursula K. Hicks

Reviewer, Editor, and Gatekeeper

Marianne Johnson

URSULA KATHLEEN WEBB HICKS (1896–1985) was the University of Oxford's Lecturer in Public Finance for nearly twenty years. She published a dozen books on public finance and economic development. She cofounded the *Review of Economic Studies* and served as its managing editor for twenty-eight years, which made her the first woman editor of a leading economics journal. In addition to her appointment at Oxford, Ursula Hicks held visiting professorships at the University of Chicago, Harvard University, Northwestern University, and the Australian National University and at universities in Brazil, India, and Japan. She was an economic adviser for the United Nations on India and consulted for governments throughout the developing world on tax finance. A. C. Pigou considered Hicks's economics "excellently done."[1] Simeon Leland declared her history of finance "skillful," "brilliant and thoroughgoing," and full of "good judgement."[2] Essays in her Festschrift by leading public finance scholars of the subsequent generation—Martin Feldstein, John G. Head, and Alan R. Prest—further illustrated "the high regard in which her work has been held by theoretical and applied economists."[3]

Yet contemporary references to Hicks are sparse; for example, she did not receive a single mention in Robert Cord's nearly thousand-page history of the London School of Economics and Political Science (LSE).[4] Surveys of midcentury public economics similarly relegate Hicks to the sidelines.[5] Joyce Jacobson suggested this may be because "the principles she espoused

---

Marianne Johnson is distinguished professor of economics at the University of Wisconsin Oshkosh.

are so basic as to the way public finance is nowadays taught that it is not considered necessary to cite references for them."[6] Others might speculate her gender played a role. Indeed, the systematic undervaluing of work produced by women economists has received significant attention in recent years.[7] However, it is not only the work of women that often goes unappreciated in the discipline—so too does the work of journal editors, referees, and book reviewers. Indeed, historiographic examinations of the influence of such roles on the evolution of the discipline are few. In this essay, I argue for the importance of this type of work—work that defines the boundaries of a field and grades the quality of what is produced. In doing so, I also make a case for Ursula Hicks as an underappreciated economist.

Background and Education

There was little in Ursula Hicks's background to suggest she would become a leading British authority on public finance.[8] Born in Dublin to Quaker parents, she was educated at the Alexandra School and Roedean School before studying history at Somerville College, Oxford. She graduated in 1918 with an undistinguished BA in modern history. After brief employment with the Agricultural Wages Board, Ursula returned home to spend the next decade caring for her elderly parents. Volunteer work for the Workers' Educational Association during this time led her to develop an interest in economics. Following her parents' deaths, she enrolled at LSE. She earned her BSc in Economics in 1932 with first-class honors and immediately began graduate study. Her MA thesis—a history of British government finance[9]—was completed under the supervision of Lionel Robbins.[10]

In 1935, Ursula married fellow LSE student John R. Hicks. John was knighted in 1964 and awarded the Nobel Prize in Economics in 1972 for his contributions to welfare economics. John spent their first two married years in Cambridge, where he had a fellowship at Gonville & Caius College; Ursula remained affiliated with LSE.[11] In 1938, she was asked to become the head of the economics department at the University of Liverpool. The same year, John was named Stanley Jevons Chair of Political Economy at the University of Manchester. After the war, they spent a year in the United States before taking positions at Oxford University. There, Ursula was associated first with Nuffield

College and later with the Linacre House/College. Beginning in the 1950s, she developed an interest in the public finance problems of developing nations, inspired by a visiting professorship at the Delhi School of Economics. Work for the United Nations, the World Bank, the Colonial Office, and the governments of Ceylon, Jamaica, Uganda, Nigeria, and Malaysia ensued. Ursula Hicks took Fellow Emeritus status in 1966; though she retired from teaching, she remained active in Oxford economic circles until her death in 1985.

Contributions to Economic Thought

Public finance during the 1930s had not yet shaken off its parochial roots and distinct national traditions. At LSE, however, the conditionality of public finance theory on historical and political circumstance likely seemed increasingly anachronistic, given the consolidation of microeconomics and welfare theory. Hicks provided a bridge, recognizing the usefulness of a coherent theoretical foundation for the field while still acknowledging the importance of social and historical context.[12] Accepting that "each writer naturally has in mind the background of his own country," she argued that public finance theory nonetheless should have general relevance;[13] see also Hicks.[14] The insight first emerged in her thesis.[15] Hicks's *Public Finance* offered a more comprehensive exploration of the same theme, perhaps best evinced by her discussion of tax incidence, consumer surplus, and welfare theory and their relation to policy.[16] Whereas theory was deterministic, the application of theoretical insights required a thorough understanding of contemporary and historical perspective;[17] see also Hicks.[18]

Another recurrent theme in Hicks's work was the inability of traditional public finance to competently address the growing size and scope of government—to properly adjust to "a complete alteration in the social outlook" that initially included wartime price controls and rationing and later the rise of the welfare state.[19]

> As the economic functions of government expand, the technical aspects of finance . . . assume a new importance[, and as] professional economists come more and more to take a direct part in the shaping and administration of public

> policy, a general knowledge of the functioning of those parts of the administrative machine . . . becomes . . . a necessary part of their equipment.[20]

To understand and manage the vast expansion of the public sphere required "a clear idea of the principal components of the public sector and their relative importance at different stages" in history.[21] Hicks argued that there were two fundamental tensions in the application of public finance theory to actual governance. The first was that public officials rather than consumers determined the provision of social or public goods—those "wants of such a nature that the means of satisfying them cannot be split up into units and sold through the market mechanism . . . [and] have therefore to be satisfied by collective provision."[22] Provision was divorced not only from preferences but also from costs. "Since services of this nature cannot be paid for directly by the users," compulsory taxes are necessary.[23] However, these taxes often had no correspondence to the desire for or the use of public services. In this, Hicks anticipated the central problem of midcentury public economics, as distinct from more traditional public finance.

Despite her interest in the public sector, Hicks held few illusions about the effectiveness of many government interventions. Her work on wartime policies and forays into macroeconomic stabilization and economic development illustrated the practical limitations faced by policymakers who sought to manage market outcomes.[24] In this, Hicks shared with other LSE economists "the common viewpoint or common faith . . . a belief in the free market."[25] This classically liberal orientation may help explain her enthusiasm for the public-choice research program that emerged in the 1960s.

Reviewer, Editor, and Gatekeeper

Histories of economics tend to emphasize original contributions to economics in the form of books and journal articles. Often, what happens behind the scenes—for example, the work of editors and reviewers—goes unnoticed despite the importance of such roles in shaping the trajectory of the field.

Book Reviewer

Although Hicks's contributions to public finance theory and practice were staples for a generation of British students, it was in her roles as reviewer and editor that she was able to shape the larger landscape. Hicks served as a global clearinghouse of information at a time when international mail and book dispersion were slow and frequently disrupted.[26] Facilitating an internationalized perspective of the field, Hicks produced more than fifty reviews for British, American, German, and Scandinavian journals of books by Hugh Dalton, Harold Groves, William Vickrey, Mabel Newcomer, Henry Simons, Luigi Einaudi, Fritz Neumark, Richard Musgrave, Alan Prest, and James M. Buchanan. Read together, the reviews are an argument to expand the boundaries of public finance concomitantly with deepening its theoretical foundation.

An early voice for public economics over public finance, Hicks argued that the field needed to break "from the narrow Victorian outlook on the subject which emphasized the tax side almost to the exclusion of everything else."[27] An analysis of the "distribution and expenditure of tax revenue" was needed.[28] Although her own textbook offered little by way of a theory of expenditures, she did not hesitate to prod others. For example, setting Prest's (1960) carefully conscribed vision of public finance against Musgrave's (1959) expansionary conceptualization, she asked readers to consider "where were the limits to be drawn," particularly regarding "stability or growth . . . closely related questions of welfare, of income distribution, of the balance of payments, and above all, to the field of its fellow, monetary and credit policy?"[29]

Tax incidence provided Hicks with a convenient vehicle by which to compare tax treatises and advance her argument for a globalized theory of public finance. She defined incidence as

> the search . . . for the "locale of the final burden of a tax." It sets out from the point where the revenue authorities pitch on a particular group of producers and extract a tax from them. These then proceed to throw the tax, as it might be a tennis ball, at the consumers. If the latter hang onto the ball, our search is at an end; the tax has "come to rest" . . . but the consumers may throw it back again, or alternatively in the

> first instance the producers may have thrown it not to the consumers (a forward shift) but to another group of producers (a backward shift); and so the rally goes on.[30]

However, despite its origin in classical price theory, the emergence of various national incidence traditions in the nineteenth century complicated comparison and evaluation—a problem exacerbated by imprecise terminology and analysis. Study of incidence required the application of rigorous logic and "a systematic chain of reasoning" that considered demand, cost, and market conditions.[31] Neither the "crude view" endorsed by Americans, in which incidence was expected to have a direct effect on prices, nor the "almost equally misleading view, frequently fathered on Ricardo," that many taxes could not be shifted, met Hicks's bar for technical precision.[32]

Hicks's reviews were frequently bent on clarifying and standardizing terminology; as such, they can be seen as extensions of her own work.[33] And although her reviews invariably slanted positive, Hicks did not hesitate to take to task authors whose theoretical analysis was not up to standards. She declared that Neumark's views on incidence were old-fashioned[34] and Otto von Mering's were "quite unnecessarily complicated."[35] Groves's analysis was "something less than adequate";[36] Buchanan's consideration of incidence was "rather worse than other parts of the book."[37] It was not until Musgrave's *Theory of Public Finance* (1959) that she felt incidence was treated with appropriate "clarity"—and that, Hicks declared, was a significant improvement over Musgrave's earlier articles.[38]

Simultaneously with enforcing a rigorous and internationalized standard in public finance theory, Hicks's reviews provided keen cross-country comparisons, particularly between the United Kingdom and the United States,[39] but also between the United Kingdom and Sweden[40] and between the United Kingdom and Germany.[41] Her comparative analyses and reviews were later extended to myriad developing countries. Such work was especially useful for practitioners who sought to foster comparability and create shared international standards across postwar tax systems.

Editor and Gatekeeper

With LSE colleagues Paul Sweezy and Nicholas Kaldor, Hicks founded the *Review of Economic Studies* in 1933; she served as managing editor through October 1961. Established independently of an academic institution or school of thought, the journal sought to "supplement the facilities for the publication of new work in theoretical and applied economics, particularly by young writers."[42] Early board members included Abba Lerner, John R. Hicks, A. Neumann, Joan Robinson, Harry Johnson, and Paul Samuelson. Although the journal was not lacking for managerial talent, its success has been widely attributed to Hicks's "skillful management of its affairs and her careful selection of the various papers."[43]

Editors play an important role in the evolution of disciplinary communities; they establish the boundaries of a field and shape views on what constitutes relevant and important work.[44] As Hicks explained, the job of an editor was "to advise and assist in editing articles in your particular field, & assist with finding good articles—either by supplying them yourself or making other people write them."[45] Additionally, "[a] prudent editor always expects the flow of good articles to dry up without notice."[46]

As gatekeepers, editors decide what should be sent for review and to whom. They set the standard for what constitutes good communication in the field. Their ability to solicit comments and rebuttals to articles can shape debates. As editor, Hicks demonstrated a keen sensitivity to such responsibilities. Writing to Samuelson, she explained:

> I have read the Klein-Rubin note to the best of my ability [Klein and Rubin 1947]. . . . It seems an ingenious bit of mathematics, and I guess we have a big enough public for that sort of thing to make it worth including. It is a pity it is written in such a very condensed form, but if you could, as suggested, append a short note discussing its empirical significance (which isn't very clear to me, I must admit), and the linearity business (which seems a rather serious limitation) that would greatly add to its usefulness.[47]

An extensive correspondence, along with regular seminar attendance in Oxford and London, kept Hicks on top of the field. Her active solicitation from and promotion of promising graduate students and young visiting scholars at Oxford and LSE—"encouraging the young"[48]—launched careers while simultaneously establishing the *Review* as a locus for cutting-edge research. For example, when Samuelson's paper with Wolfgang Stolper on the relationship between the relative prices of output and factor rewards was rejected by the *American Economic Review* in 1941, Hicks secured it for the *Review,* believing it contributed an important "new point in the theory of international trade."[49]

Editorship of the *Review* also allowed Hicks to prosecute arguments in public finance. In collusion with Samuelson, Hicks engineered to publish Nancy Ruggles's doctoral thesis as the definitive welfare theoretic answer to the ongoing "marginal-cost controversy."[50] The debate had begun during the previous decade, when Harold Hotelling (1938) resurrected Jules Dupuit's argument in favor of marginal-cost pricing for railways. For a decreasing-cost industry, Hotelling claimed that "the optimum of the general welfare corresponds to the sale of everything at marginal cost," with fixed costs covered by general government revenue.[51] However, because excise taxes would generate deadweight loss, maximization of social welfare along Paretian lines required the use of lump-sum taxes. The problems associated with implicit redistribution via lump-sum taxation, compensation payments, and actual versus potential Pareto improvements generated a transatlantic controversy that elicited contributions from Samuelson, Buchanan, Lerner, Coase, and James Meade, among others.[52] Nancy Ruggles provided an incisive analysis favoring the position of Samuelson and John Hicks on the use of potential Pareto improvements to identify possible welfare-improving choices.[53] Any specific choice from among those possible would, however, require some sort of subsequent interpersonal welfare comparison: "As Samuelson has said, the economist cannot say that the change *should* be made and the compensation paid; he can only say that the change *could* be made and the compensation could be paid with an increase in welfare."[54]

As editor, Hicks was a savvy protector of the *Review*'s reputation, her extensive personal and professional connections often providing insight into how to manage situations and egos—whether it be Kaldor's proclivity to lose papers, Sandy Henderson's loss of employment and editorship due to his "inveterate Don Juanism,"[55] or Robbins's peculiar grudges.[56] Writing to Samuelson, Hicks explained:

> I am sorry, but I don't think we should publish the Fels note in the Review, I am therefore returning it by sea mail—I hope that's all right. It really is not a very diplomatic note, and I don't see why [we] should get ourselves into Arthur Burns' black book gratuitously [sic]. However, we shouldn't mind that so much if we thought it was a really good note.[57]

Robinson provided a regular source of exasperation. Commenting on what she perceived as a late and not particularly novel contribution to capital theory, Hicks wrote to Harry Johnson (who had by then replaced Samuelson as the *Review*'s American editor): "Now for the big problem. I had not thought Joan would land this on us. . . . If you and Nicky [Kaldor] can make Joan withdraw some of the quite ridiculously rude and patronizing phrases that she uses I suppose that she will do herself more harm than us if we publish it."[58] Hicks's ability to navigate such situations contributed both to the *Review*'s status as a preeminent journal and to the fondness authors and later editors had for her management.[59]

Conclusion

In this essay, I make a case for Ursula K. Hicks as an underappreciated economist. Even though her contributions are now generally considered so standard as not to merit citation,[60] Hicks played an important role in the transition from the normative and descriptive work that characterized public finance into the 1930s to the modern theoretical public economics of the postwar period. What makes Hicks's contributions difficult to assess is that they came less from her books and journal articles than from her work as an editor and reviewer. In more than fifty book reviews of works produced across a half dozen countries, Hicks synthesized midcentury public finance, pushing for a consistent theoretical basis in welfare economics and shared, precise terminology. During the twenty-eight years she served as editorial adviser for the *Review of Economic Studies,* Hicks played a similar role, shaping the field of economics, evaluating the quality of work produced, resolving controversies, and defining boundaries—her influence particularly evident at the intersection of welfare theory and public finance.

Jim Thomas speculated that the unusual organization of the *Review*—established as an outlet primarily for graduate students run by graduate students—may have facilitated Hicks's success in the role of editor at a time when women economists were few and frequently marginalized.[61] Indeed, that Hicks's contributions to economics may be undervalued because they operated through the less obvious channels of editing and reviewing is difficult to disentangle from the institutional and societal constraints that limited the ability of women to make contributions to the field during the postwar period. Nevertheless, despite such limitations, Hicks had a profound impact on British and postcolonial public finance as an "economist, teacher, scholar

---

Acknowledgments: I would like to thank Maria Cristina Marcuzzo and Jim Thomas for their helpful comments and suggestions.

8

W. H. Hutt

An Economist for the Twenty-First Century

Art Carden and Ilia Murtazashvili

It is a good rule, after reading a new book, never to allow yourself another new one till you have read an old one in between.
—C. S. Lewis[1]

THE STOCK OF knowledge need not always grow. Infrastructure in Britain crumbled after the Romans withdrew because no one left had the knowledge and skill necessary to repair and rebuild the Roman roads and walls. After Tasmania was cut off from the Australian mainland, it started to regress technologically. We run the risk of doing something similar intellectually when we cut ourselves off from our intellectual forerunners or even expel them. Many economists don't merit serious study today, but there remains a lot of gold in the history of economic ideas. There are particularly rich veins in the work of the twentieth-century British-turned-South-African economist W. H. Hutt (1899–1988). His are old books to which we can turn for new insights. These do not just help us understand society better in our role as social scientists. They will, if taken seriously, advance the cause of a just and humane society.[2]

As Thomas Hazlett wrote in a 1983 article for the *Wall Street Journal*, W. H. Hutt "may be the most important economist of this century."[3] Hutt's University of Dallas colleague Samuel Bostaph prophesied that Hutt might

---

Art Carden is Margaret Gage Bush Distinguished Professor of Business at Samford University, senior fellow at the American Institute for Economic Research, and research fellow at Independent Institute. Ilia Murtazashvili is associate professor in the Graduate School of Public and International Affairs at the University of Pittsburgh.

be one of the most important economists of the twenty-first.[4] Economists who know W. H. Hutt likely only know him because he popularized the phrase "consumers' sovereignty." This is unfortunate because he made many more substantial contributions that deserve revisiting in the twenty-first century. They still have much to teach us about how free societies function and flourish. Hutt was a thoroughgoing individualist from an early age, the son of a typesetter who took a dim view of organized labor, and eventually an unexpected academic who answered an advertisement in the *Times of London* for a lecturer at South Africa's University of Cape Town. He told his mentor, Edwin Cannan, that he thought he had a "small contribution" to make to economics. His contributions, ultimately, were many, and they were more than modest.[5] He is perhaps less well known than he should be because his post in South Africa meant he was far from the intellectual epicenters of the economics profession.

Hutt despised coercion in all its forms, and he distinguished between *private* coercion on the part of strikers and boycotters and *public* coercion on the part of the government. The role of coercion of various kinds in inhibiting coordination played an important role in his work from his first book, *The Theory of Collective Bargaining*, through the end of his long and colorful life. He was an outspoken dissenter from the popular progressive religion of the labor movement, arguing that labor unions reduce aggregate incomes and especially harm the politically impotent they push out of competition.[6] His analysis of labor markets, institutional change, price flexibility, and discrimination demonstrate his foresight and continued relevance. In *The Economics of the Colour Bar*, for example, he explained that racist policies in South Africa—the color bar (restrictions on opportunities for black laborers) before 1948, apartheid after—were not merely a result of racial prejudice but were deeply rooted in rent-seeking by interest groups that had coalesced around race.[7] In 1908, miners struck because of "the fear of the White unionists that non-Whites were becoming too effective competitors."[8] Similar shenanigans would motivate Hutt's analysis of labor market conditions in *The Theory of Collective Bargaining* (1930), *The Economics of the Colour Bar* (1964), and *The Strike-Threat System* (1973).[9]

Hutt, born in 1899, did a stint in the Royal Flying Corps during World War I before attending the London School of Economics, where he studied under luminaries like Edwin Cannan, Lilian Knowles, and Arnold Plant. Knowles's influence is particularly noteworthy because her course inspired one of his most influential articles, "The Factory System of the Early 19th Century," which was published in *Economica* and which would be republished in *Capitalism and the Historians*, edited by F. A. Hayek and T. S. Ashton.[10] Unfortunately, she passed away before Hutt could show her the article.[11]

After he graduated, he worked at London's Individualist Bookshop but remained restless, thinking that perhaps he could do more for the individualist cause in academia or elsewhere.[12] He landed at the University of Cape Town, where he would become the dean of the Faculty of Commerce and eventually the founder of the Graduate School of Business. All of this he did while teaching his courses and producing a steady stream of important contributions. In 1964, he retired from the University of Cape Town, published his devastating *The Economics of the Colour Bar*, and decamped for the United States, where he would be something of an academic nomad before settling down at the University of Dallas in the 1970s, where he remained for the rest of his career.

While he is most famous for coining the phrase "consumers' sovereignty" and his criticisms of J. M. Keynes, his analysis of and proposals for peaceful institutional change also deserve renewed attention, particularly in light of ever-evolving conflict in the Middle East. People working to stay abreast of new contributions to economics and other social sciences would do well to intersperse the new books they are reading with one or more of Hutt's contributions. There are a lot of excellent options; perhaps the three best would be his *Economists and the Public* (1936), *The Theory of Idle Resources* (1939), and *The Economics of the Colour Bar* (1964).

Hutt emphasized the role of race as an organizing principle informing interest groups' actions. Race is a useful focal point for social organizing as people can blame their problems easily on disfavored minorities. There were, he argued, strong antisemitic elements to the anti-sweating movement during the early British Industrial Revolution.[13] The themes he explored would be echoed and elaborated on later in work by the economist Jennifer Roback.[14] Hutt's opposition to apartheid and his defense of economic freedom led to the South African government withdrawing his passport, a testament to his uncompromising stance on individual liberty and justice.[15]

Oppression and Hutt's Heretical Labor Economics

> *The only such forces for which I myself, after a lifetime of study in the field, can discern are in the nature of restraints which prevent under-privileged workers from bettering their condition and prospects by offering their labor in competition with the privileged.*
>
> —W. H. Hutt on what consigns people to poverty[16]

Hutt is an economist for the twenty-first century whose work should be more widely read and studied, even three and a half decades after his death. Hutt's political economy was *humanomic* in that it treated acting man as a whole person rather than a mere consumption maximizer or constrained optimizer. His work and his outlook had three pillars: free markets are better than socialism, individual autonomy is crucial, and people and progress are basically good.[17]

An economist to the core, he welcomed competition and competitive institutions on the grounds that they served people in all the roles they inhabited in a commercial society—as producers, workers, consumers, shareholders, and so on. Where others saw antagonism between labor and capital, Hutt joined the economists in seeing opportunities for mutual gain. His criticisms of strike-threats were grounded in his conviction that it was impossible to transfer wealth and income from capitalists *as a class* to workers *as a class* for several reasons. First, workers who saved and invested were themselves capitalists. Second, any gains workers enjoyed from the strike-threat system came at the expense of other workers who were shut out of the market and consumers who were paying higher prices. Throughout *The Strike-Threat System*, he argued that the system's apologists failed to answer the important ethical question about why one class (investors) should be expropriated for the benefit of another class (workers), noting further that "the easy assumption that investors are rich and workers poor is rather dubious today."[18] With so many Americans owning the means of production through pension funds and retirement accounts, it is even less clear in the twenty-first century.

Hutt's analysis of rate-for-the-job rules mirrors many economists' analysis of inflation: the consequences are insidious but opaque. Many seem to believe that when the minimum wage changes, the only things that change are workers' and investors' incomes with workers getting more and investors getting less. However, as Hutt argues, "rate for the job" rules—effectively minimum wages—are mandatory discrimination against the unproductive. What's more, if low productivity is highly correlated with race and gender due, for example, to low investment in education for women and indigenous Africans, a minimum wage is *de facto* mandatory discrimination against these groups. We did them and the rest of the world no favors, Hutt argued, by shutting them out of the jobs for which they were most competitive:

> I am pleading here, among other things, firstly for the rights of the low-grade worker who has to be classified as such by reason of his inborn qualities, even in the occupation in which his productivity is highest; and secondly, for the rights of the worker who must be classified as low-grade solely by reason of lack of opportunity. The incentive to invest in human capital through "on the job training" can often be destroyed if persons who are in a position to benefit from the training cannot be employed *at what they are initially worth*, while the value of their efforts is being built up.[19]

Here, he argues that someone might be "low grade" for two reasons. First, they might simply lack skills because of cognitive and physical handicaps. This, he thought, is inevitable in a large, complex, and diverse world. Second, Hutt was very clear about non-innate sources of difference. Many people had fewer skills because they had been systematically denied the opportunities others enjoyed. Hutt recognized that, for the most part, these workers were unskilled through no fault of their own, but he also recognized that trying to undo the past was like trying to unscramble an egg. The circumstance was to be lamented, but it was not clear it could be remedied in a way that would ultimately benefit the oppressed and their descendants. In this respect, he recognized that on-the-job training was an important source of human capital. Workers' compensation is not just wages and benefits, or even wages, benefits, and working conditions. It also includes the ability to learn on the job. Rate-for-the-job minimum wage rules took away people's opportunity to be paid with learning opportunities.

Hutt held rate-for-the-job and "standard rate" minimum wage laws in special contempt because they "came to be tacitly recognized as a highly effective stratagem for protecting the status quo while nominally conceding equality of civil rights."[20]

Strike-threats exercise private coercion in the service of raising rivals' costs. By threatening "scabs," unionists reduce the supply of people willing to step in and the wages strikers refuse. The strike-threat has the additional consequence of creating destructive social capital: "One of the most effective forms of exercising privately contrived coercive power in the United States is 'the honoring of picket lines' by all unions."[21] The strike-threat, he argued, could only be successful if governments stood by and did not protect the integrity of persons or property threatened by the strikers:

> Such is the cupidity of man that, when managements have stood on principle to resist strike pressures, they have at times been in danger of their lives (as have nonstrikers). Even the police have often been compelled to defend themselves against violence when they have tried to protect managers and nonstrikers from physical assault; and when the police have, in self-defense, answered physical force with physical resistance, allegations of "police brutality" have become routinely common.[22]

By contrast, the market process is "social" and "democratic"; it relies on people's willingness to "vote" for patterns and operations with the fruit of their own labor.[23] He wrote, "The most important freedom denied through union power is the right of every individual to accept any employment which he believes will improve his earnings and prospects."[24] He argued throughout his work that union power meant mandatory discrimination against "non-preferred" groups with fewer developed capabilities.[25]

Hutt's most overlooked contributions come from his constitutional political economy. He did not think it was sufficient to merely condemn South African racial discrimination. Seeing the system as grossly immoral did not require a great deal of moral courage, nor was it an outstanding philosophical achievement. His interest was in the kinds of institutional reforms that might make it possible to move from an obviously unjust and inefficient system of privilege and oppression to one that has *both* equal opportunities and freely operating labor markets. In other words, taking out the racist institutions is insufficient; all manner of restrictions must be removed for all.

But Hutt was not content to point out the problems with restrictionism. He devoted substantial attention to the complex interrelationship between politics and economics. The major problem he saw was the distribution of veto players who somehow had to be convinced to go along with the transition peacefully. To this end, he proposed income guarantees that would provide incumbents who stood to lose economic rents from labor market liberalization to provide them with the incomes to which they had grown accustomed. Paying for it, he thought, would not be a serious problem because the additional output from a more efficient South African economy would prove more than sufficient to provide the taxes and transfers that would be required.

He explained this in an article for the South African Institute of Race Relations titled "Distributive Justice and Colour Antagonism," and in this article, he said he would elaborate on the plan in a later book along with draft legislation aimed at preserving incomes for those who stood to be harmed by sudden liberalization. It was published in 1943 as *Plan for Reconstruction*, and while James M. Buchanan did not think it deserved careful study as late as 1989, he nonetheless pointed out that Hutt's work prefigured a lot of contributions that would come later from scholars like Mancur Olson, Douglass North, and Barry R. Weingast, among others studying institutional and social change. Furthermore, it complements Sheilagh Ogilvie's analysis of the competition-thwarting work of the medieval guilds. Successful rent-seeking coalitions like labor unions and guilds obstructed price flexibility, with consequences for long-run economic growth and short-run economic stability.

Flexible Prices and Free Markets

Price flexibility was central to Hutt's analysis. He argued, therefore, that resource idleness was due to specific rules that kept prices from adjusting to new underlying economic realities. This was especially true in labor markets, where labor union contracts kept wages artificially high and prevented labor from moving to where it was most urgently needed. He was especially critical of "rate for the job" rules in South Africa and minimum wages elsewhere—as well as provisions like the US Davis–Bacon Act—because they interfered with price flexibility and macroeconomic adjustment.

When economists write and teach about "consumers' sovereignty," they are channeling Hutt's most enduring rhetorical contribution. As Hutt defined it, the consumer is *sovereign* when he has not delegated to political authority the decision-making power he can exercise by buying, selling, and refraining from buying and selling. Specifically, "The consumer is sovereign when, in his role of citizen, he has not delegated to political institutions for authoritarian use the power which he can exercise socially through his power to demand (or to refrain from demanding)."[26]

The free market, Hutt argues, is a social space where, in the price-mediated conversations happening between people in their roles as buyers and sellers of goods and services, people decide what is to be produced when, where, how, and for whom. He thought the alleged antagonism between labor and capital was an illusion because, ultimately, people acting in their roles as consumers were the ultimate employers.[27] He saw South African apartheid as an affront to free markets and economic coordination precisely because it interfered with the sovereign consumers, usurped their authority, and vetoed their consensus, all for the benefit of the politically privileged. The market is an ongoing referendum where every penny is a vote. Contrary to the notion that the very rich exert disproportionate power, the elite criticism of the free market is that people tend to vote with their pennies for the wrong things (dollar stores and Walmart) rather than the right things (boutique grocers selling organic foods).

One implication of this is that worker-owned cooperatives are not generally viable. Nothing, Hutt explained, stops people from experimenting with them.[28] The experiments should be especially easy in a competitive capital market: if owners and bosses are an implicit tax on workers who add no value, it should be especially easy for a group of workers to organize a leveraged buyout, fire all the executives, managers, and bosses, and then run a successful worker-owned and worker-managed enterprise. The enterprise's efficiencies would manifest themselves in higher profits (which would accrue to worker-owners), making them a very attractive credit risk. Furthermore, by removing superfluous and parasitic layers of management, they should be able to attract capital and high-quality labor. As Hutt explained,

> If the workers really wanted to undertake entrepreneurship, they could do so by sharing it—which I recommend in my 1982 *Policy Review* article—or by taking it outright. They would have to borrow the funds from their union or somewhere else, and buy out the whole company, all of its assets, and appoint their own managers, or appoint the same ones, then run it under their direction so as to maximize the aggregate yield so that the workers would get more than their rate of interest on what they put in.[29]

However, since they occupy no more than a small share of the market, they must have disadvantages relative to more conventionally organized firms. But for-profit firms' real comparative advantage seems to be in managing risk. Hutt explains this in the *Policy Review* article to which he referred: "That they never actually do this in practice is because the arrangement of risk-taking under the present system of entrepreneurial direction is so much better. That is, the workers benefit enormously from contracts under which they agree to accept the commands of others in return for no risk."[30]

It is fashionable to declare that corporations need to be held "democratically accountable." Some commentators object that corporations can act independently of any democratic oversight, but in Hutt's analysis, this would be a mistake. As he explained in his unpublished autobiography,

> But I had subsequently come to perceive that this notion has most far-reaching implications for political theory. Consumers' sovereignty is a system of voting which, in a free society, people in their entrepreneurial capacity must recognize. Through such voting, not only is the composition of the community's assets stock determined, but equally the composition of the stock of valuable skills acquired—at least to the extent to which the workers perceive their prospectively most productive employment outlets.[31]

Hutt's political economy was ultimately humane. In an interview with Morgan Reynolds, he explained that "the present system is impoverishing, not only in material terms but even worse, in human terms."[32] His criticism of the color bar and other restrictions created in an oppressive, racially stratified society was not merely that it meant less food, clothing, shelter, and material provision but that it impoverished our souls.

Constitutional Political Economy

How, according to Hutt, could societies escape from sclerotic institutions that ossified the structure of production and made it less responsive to changing underlying conditions? His analysis complements the work done by Gary W. Cox, Douglass C. North, John Joseph Wallis, and Barry R. Weingast on the violence trap.[33] Political stability is precarious, but the rent-seeking society makes it possible lest society devolve into a war of all against all or into the resolution of disputes by actual violence rather than merely threatened violence. In other words, transitions that expropriated those who held existing positions of privilege or substantially subverted their expectations about their future income paths ran the risk of springing the violence trap.[34] He suggested this might be a feature rather than a bug for the Soviet Union and its satellites, writing, "It almost seems as if it has been their aim to prevent at all costs a bloodless abandonment of colour injustices. They have sought to provoke sheer envy and the desire for vengeance."[35]

Hutt concentrated his attention on Great Britain during and after World War II and on post-colonial Southern Africa, but there are clear lessons for efforts to plant liberal, democratic, free-market institutions in places where they have yet to take root. Efforts to plant these institutions in soil not prepared to receive them have been largely unsuccessful.[36] Hutt was largely concerned not with what the ideal society looked like but with how to eliminate political privileges while also avoiding a bloodbath. When he proposed a weighted franchise, it was not because he did not think indigenous Africans *deserved* less political influence than whites but because he did not think white Africans would be willing to let go of political control without "ironclad" constitutional protections of their private property rights.[37] Hutt the idealist mixed with Hutt the realist; while he did not shy away from recommending policies that might at first seem "politically impossible," he was nonetheless with Adam Smith: "When he cannot establish the right, he will not disdain to ameliorate the wrong; but like Solon, when he cannot establish the best system of laws, he will endeavour to establish the best that the people can bear."[38]

In his 1989 contribution to the *Managerial and Decision Economics* symposium on Hutt's work, Buchanan called him a "gains from trade" economist as opposed to an "allocation" economist. As he explains, "The allocation economist, having identified failure by specific distortions in resource use, calls explicitly for a shift in allocation, independently of direct reference to the institutional setting."[39] Meanwhile, "The gains-from-trade economist, if he remains consistent, does not place arguments from efficiency, as such, in the front rank of his rhetorical presentation. His reform emphasis is directed toward the removal of restrictions, with the enhanced value in exchange relegated to a position of necessary consequence."[40] Hutt was firmly in the latter camp, seeing markets not as mere tools for achieving particular equilibria but as processes whereby people discovered new ways to cooperate advantageously and to use assets productively.

Hutt was a lifelong opponent of privilege in all its forms, emphasizing early that labor union privileges and the strike-threat system created economic rents for the politically powerful at the expense of the politically powerless. He emphasized the racial dimension of the color bar in articles for the South African Institute of Race Relations and later in his 1964 book. His work was sufficiently influential that it led to symposia in *Managerial and Decision Economics* in 1989, the *Journal of Labor Research* in 1997, and the *Review of Austrian Economics* (forthcoming).

Hutt continually emphasized the consequences of minimum wages and other labor market regulations for the people they were ostensibly there to help, and it was no small source of frustration for him that those who were hurt the most rarely protested and even embraced the policies that oppressed them.[41] The "standard rate," for example, gives people the impression they are being helped while actually shutting them out of the market.[42] As he explained in 1965,

> By preventing the non-Whites from discounting the prejudice against employing them, from discounting their initial inferiority of background and education, and from discounting the additional costs of employing them (due to the hostility of White labour, segregation provisions in the

> Factories Act and other legislation), minimum wage rates excluded Coloureds, Indians and Africans from the more productive and better-paid opportunities of employment.[43]

He was dismayed that the oppressed not only went along with it but embraced it, noting, "The races harmed have acquiesced. They have been indoctrinated into believing that their real enemy has been that fictitious abstraction, 'the capitalist exploiter.'"[44] He nonetheless remained hopeful, citing the example of the South African Indian minority: "The free market and scope for profit-seeking have allowed them to progress in spite of powerful race prejudice."[45]

Conclusion

In its obituary, the *Times of London* wrote, "Hutt's defence of capitalism centered on his belief that the competitive market was the institutional arrangement that best assured members of the working class of opportunity to improve their welfare."[46]

W. H. Hutt is not a household name, not even among professional economists, even though we have likely used his phrase "consumers' sovereignty" in the classroom at one point or another. He is, however, anything but the kind of "defunct economist" to whom "madmen in authority" frequently find themselves enslaved.[47] He offered many original insights that advance economic science and help us understand and explain how social institutions emerge and evolve. He also offered many original insights that, if taken seriously, would mean a better world for us and our descendants. And since populist politicians seem to be dueling over the kind of restrictions, and because political violence is an ongoing problem in much of the world, Hutt remains an economist for the twenty-first century whose advice and insight any policymaker—and any economist—would do well to take seriously.

Acknowledgments: This article is adapted from several projects in progress. We thank the special collections libraries at Stanford University's Hoover Institution and the London School of Economics for assistance locating documents. We thank ChatGPT, Perplexity, Grammarly, and Google Gemini for their research and editing assistance.

9 Friedrich A. Lutz

A Forgotten Monetary Economist and Social Philosopher

Lachezar Grudev

THE TWELFTH CHAIRMAN of the Federal Reserve, Paul Volcker, who is credited with ending the long period of inflation that challenged the US economy in the 1970s, recalled that as a student at Princeton University, he acquired his economic knowledge from two German-born economists: Oskar Morgenstern, who taught introductory courses in economics as well as game theory, and Friedrich Lutz, who taught monetary theory and banking.[1] Volcker continued: "But it was only money and banking and monetary policy that really caught my attention,"[2] and "[Lutz] taught us that too much money created inflation."[3] Without any doubt, the student understood the lessons of his master. However, compared with the extensive literature on Oskar Morgenstern, whose contributions have been held in the highest esteem, Lutz's intellectual legacy has fallen into neglect, among both economists and historians of economics.

There are three reasons to revitalize Lutz's research program. First, his publications in the areas of monetary economics, monetary policy, and international monetary theory established him as an expert in the field of money and banking.[4] Second, Lutz was very well connected to top-tier American economists, and this was why the Austrian economist and social philosopher Friedrich A. Hayek (1899–1992) thought of Lutz when envisaging the appropriate person to write a US version of *The Road to Serfdom*.[5] Further evidence of his being well-connected was Lutz's membership in the Bellagio Group, in which leading monetary economists discussed topical theoretical and practi-

---

Lachezar Grudev is interim professor of political economy at the Faculty of Business and Economics at the University of Applied Sciences Zwickau, Germany.

cal problems of international monetary policy.[6] Third, he has been remembered as an inspiring teacher who was able to explain complex phenomena in a clear and straightforward manner, something that many students described as influential in their decision to study monetary economics.[7]

The Early German Years

Lutz was born in 1901 as the third child of the brewery owner Friedrich Lutz and his wife, Amélie Lutz, née Metzger, in Saarburg, Lorraine, which was then part of the German Empire. Lutz's father died three months before the birth of his youngest child. World War I brought many tragedies to Lutz's family. Lutz lost his older brother on the battlefield, and his native Lorraine became part of France. The latter forced the family to leave their newly occupied hometown and move to Stuttgart, in Southwest Germany. After graduating from high school in 1920, Lutz studied at the universities of Heidelberg and Berlin. During his Berlin years (1921–25), an acquaintance with the young assistant professor Walter Eucken (1891–1950) would turn out to be fateful for Lutz. Eucken would later become one of the founders of the Freiburg School of Economics, whose ideas would influence German economic policy after World War II, thereby initiating the German economic miracle.[8]

Eucken's early research program, and his debate with the German Historical School, which still dominated German economic thinking after World War I, shaped Lutz's ideas as a young scholar. Eucken and Lutz belonged to a generation of economists who accused the representatives of the Historical School of failing to explain the causes of hyperinflation between 1920 and 1923 and thus failing to provide recommendations for how to fight this disastrous phenomenon, which shattered the basis of the German economy.[9] The descriptive methods of members of the Historical School were oriented toward collecting and analyzing facts about historical epochs, countries, and even single industries with the aim of inductively deriving theory from their research. However, this approach made them helpless regarding the explanation of urgent problems. At the same time, members of the Historical School did not hide their abhorrence of the abstract-deductive theoretical approach, which isolated German economic thinking more and more from the theoretical achievements of their Austrian and Anglo-Saxon colleagues.[10]

Lutz himself became a victim of the Historical School's dominance, which made his path to an international reputation anything but easy. With Eucken's mediation, Lutz submitted his doctoral thesis to Hermann Schumacher, one of the leading representatives of the Historical School. Schumacher rejected Lutz's thesis with the explanation that "it was too abstract." This was a calamity for the young scholar because German students were required to submit a doctoral thesis in order to graduate from their study of economics. Hyperinflation had already destroyed his mother's savings, which meant that Lutz could not finance his study until he found another supervisor.[11] This firsthand experience of the social effects following hyperinflation was highly influential on Lutz's later decision to research monetary economics and monetary policy. Luckily for Lutz, Eucken was appointed professor of economics at the University of Tübingen, not far from Stuttgart, in 1925. Eucken accepted the young scholar as his first doctoral student. Lutz defended the thesis *A Controversy on Capital Theory* (1927), which provides a short glimpse of Lutz's ability to present a history of economics. He classified the research programs of leading economists such as Eugen von Böhm-Bawerk, Gustav Cassel, and John Bates Clark according to how they explained the formation of capital. On the basis of this classification, Lutz analyzed how the theory of capital had evolved since the writings of Adam Smith. This book was later included by the Austrian economist Friedrich A. Hayek in the mandatory reading list for his economics classes at the London School of Economics and Political Science (LSE).[12]

In 1929, Lutz became Eucken's assistant at the University of Freiburg in Southwest Germany, where Eucken had moved in 1927. There, Lutz finished his habilitation thesis, "The Business Cycle Problem in Economics" (1932). This type of thesis was then an indispensable prerequisite to starting an academic career in the German-language area. Lutz's thesis provided a historical account of how the explanation of causes and persistence of economic crises evolved from the theories of David Ricardo, Jean-Baptiste Say, and Thomas Malthus to the contemporary business cycle research of the 1930s. Lutz criticized the still dominant nineteenth-century approach initiated by the French medical doctor Clément Juglar, which was oriented toward proving that crises were an inevitable phenomenon of capitalism. This approach neglected the institutional factors that affected the recovery process from economic crises.

Lutz claimed that business cycle theorists either described or just replicated the idea of the wavelike movements of capitalism by constructing mathematical models without explaining the reason for the occurrence and persistence of economic crises. Lutz became Eucken's first student to be granted the right to lecture at the university. As a lecturer at Freiburg, Lutz taught Current Disputes in Monetary Policy, Currency and Money, and Problems of Business Cycle Theory, as well as statistics tutorials.[13]

A crucial moment in Lutz's career was Hayek's decision to send his doctoral student Vera Smith to Freiburg, where she was able to study the German monetary history in the context of her doctoral thesis, "The Rationale of Central Banking and the Free Banking Alternative" (1936).[14] The thesis had been favorably reviewed by Austrian economists because it analyzed the foundation of central banks as institutions intended to support the treasury and thus state policy in general. This supported the Austrian view that central banks always tended to destabilize the value of money.[15] Hayek's advice to Smith to spend several weeks in Freiburg was hardly a coincidence, because Eucken already had a reputation as an economist who had explained German hyperinflation between 1920 and 1923 as being the result of expansive monetary policy conducted by the German Central Bank. In this sense, Eucken debunked the common view that hyperinflation was a result of the balance of payments—a view promoted by the infamous Historical School.[16] When Vera arrived in Freiburg, Lutz had already been teaching monetary theory and policy, lectures that he inherited from his teacher. According to Hayek, Smith convinced Lutz to apply for a Rockefeller Fellowship in order to study the English banking and monetary system. As Hayek recalled, "She came back bringing Lutz to London, and after a while they married."[17]

Lutz and the Years of High Theory

In October 1934, Lutz embarked on a ship to London for his one-year fellowship in England, where he intended to spend nine months at LSE and three months after that at Cambridge. Lutz's British sojourn took place during a period that Hayek described as the decade of high theory, when economic theory was transformed and formalized.[18] The surviving correspondence between Eucken and Lutz documents how Lutz himself experienced these years. He learned new instruments of analysis, such as consumer and producer surplus, supply and demand elasticity, and indifference curves that were developed by Alfred Marshall and Francis Y. Edgeworth and refined by young LSE scholars such as R. G. D. Allen and John R. Hicks. As an economist trained in the Historical School's tradition, Lutz not only was surprised by this completely new theoretical approach but also recognized the increasing division between German and Anglo-Saxon economics in the 1930s.[19]

During his London stay, Lutz studied the British monetary and banking system and participated in the famous Grand Seminars at LSE organized by Hayek and Lionel Robbins.[20] Lutz established lifelong connections with the two professors, who later played an instrumental role in his academic career. In Cambridge, Lutz participated in a discussion with John Maynard Keynes. In one of his letters, Lutz related that Keynes was completing "a new book on monetary theory that [was] supposed to be published in the end of October 1935. But the message of this book [had] changed once again" (Lutz to Eucken, May 20, 1935).

Upon his return to Germany in 1935, Lutz recognized that his teacher had been involved in opposition to the former rector Martin Heidegger. The Nazis had considered the famous philosopher to be a fitting person to establish Nazi ideology in the traditionally independent University of Freiburg and condemned any opposition against him.[21] The intellectual nexus to Eucken would be one of the reasons why the Nazi Party vetoed Lutz's appointment at several universities in Germany.[22] Furthermore, Lutz's research of institutionally based economics was met with strong criticism by Nazi-oriented economists who started dominating German economics. An example of such criticism is provided by a review of his book *The Fundamental Problem of the Monetary Constitution.* In this book, Lutz analyzed the performance of the German, American, and English banking systems during the Great Depression. Lutz concluded that the Peel Banking Act of 1844, which assigned exclusive note-issuing power to the Bank of England, contributed to the higher resilience of the English banking system during the Depression. The lack of such legislation in Germany made the German banking system more vulnerable to shock, which plunged the whole German economy into deep crisis.[23] A Nazi-oriented economist rejected Lutz's conclusion that a monetary institutional framework, such as the British one, would have saved the

German banking system from collapse. The disastrous state of the German economy was actually a result of an infernal plan created by England and the United States, according to this critic. Such a parochial explanation of economic events was unimaginable for Lutz, but this review probably made him aware of the newest trends of economic thinking that he would have to tolerate if he was to continue researching in Germany.[24]

The Forced Emigration

This hostile academic environment was the reason why he applied for another Rockefeller Fellowship in 1936, but this time to visit American universities. On March 31, 1937, before he sailed to America, he married Hayek's doctoral student Vera Smith, who would play an instrumental role in Lutz's acclimation to US academia. After several stays at leading American universities, the German scholar joined Princeton University in September 1938 as an instructor. Five months later, he became an assistant professor. In 1943, he was affiliated with the Institute for Advanced Study, and he became a full professor in 1947, teaching a variety of courses such as Money and Banking, International Monetary Economics, Public Finance, and Advanced Microeconomics.[25] When Lutz joined Princeton, he had already made a grand entrance into the US economics scene with his essay "The Outcome of the Saving-Investment Discussion" (1938), published in the *Quarterly Journal of Economics.* Lutz analyzed how the Cambridge economists D. H. Robertson and Keynes, as well as the representatives of the Stockholm School, formulated the relationship between saving and investment when they explained the business cycle phenomenon. Lutz concluded that the relationship between saving and investment was no longer useful in the analysis of the business cycle phenomenon because even if there was equality between saving and investment, this would not guarantee that there would be economic equilibrium. The paper provoked discussion in the 1939 issue of the *Quarterly Journal of Economics,* where leading economists such as Oskar Lange (1939) and Abba Lerner (1939) responded to Lutz's critical statement.[26]

As an assistant professor at Princeton, Lutz focused on interest rate and monetary theory. His paper "The Structure of Interest Rates" (1940), which also gave rise to extensive discussions in the pages of the *Quarterly Journal of*

Economics, formulated a theory of interest rate structure by postulating the assumption of rational expectations developed by John R. Hicks in his book *Value and Capital* (1939). Several papers in the *American Economic Review*[27] and the *Quarterly Journal of Economics*[28] focused on how interest rates affected the investment decisions of firms. These ideas provided the basis for Lutz's highly technical book *The Theory of Investment of the Firm* (1951), written jointly with his wife. Besides writing about interest rate theory, Lutz published seminal works on international monetary economics and discussed the associated topical problems. With his essay on Keynes and Harry D. White's proposal regarding the creation of the Bretton Woods system, Lutz launched a new series of essays on international finance at Princeton.[29] Further essays and lectures established him as a leading expert in international monetary economics and finance.[30]

Lutz as a Transatlantic Interlocutor and Classical Liberal

During his Princeton years, Lutz did not forget his Freiburg alma mater. Immediately after the end of World War II, Lutz became a guest professor at Freiburg, where he introduced the economics taught at American universities. Thus, he contributed to overcoming the increased academic isolation that German economics students suffered during the war.[31] One cannot imagine a more suitable person for this integrative role than Lutz. As a young German scholar, he had initially faced the difficulties of adopting the modern Anglo-Saxon economic approach, but he went on not only to actively contribute to the newest developments in modern economics but also to become an outstanding teacher at Princeton. Lutz's students praised him for his didactic skills. He was able to explain the most complex and intricate theories in a simple way, so that even graduate students attended his introductory lectures.[32] Volcker himself remembered Lutz as "very good and logical" and recalled that his lectures made Volcker believe that money and banking economics was "more precise than other economics."[33] These skills can be recognized in his writings, in which he was able to clearly explain the most complex economic issues without using mathematics.

In 1947, Eucken invited Lutz to be a cofounder and editor of the Freiburg-based journal *ORDO—Jahrbuch für die Ordnung von Wirtschaft und Gesell-*

schaft, which aimed to popularize the Freiburg School's research program on institutionally based economics. After Eucken's sudden death in 1950 during a lecture tour at LSE organized by Hayek and Robbins, Lutz was considered to be the natural successor to Eucken's chair. However, because of bureaucratic issues, he was deprived of this opportunity. In 1953, Lutz accepted a financially superior position at the University of Zurich, where he taught Theory and History of Social Economics until the end of his life. During the Zurich years, Lutz remained loyal to Freiburg. He was the cofounder and a lifelong board member of the Walter Eucken Institute in Freiburg, the aim of which was to preserve Eucken's intellectual legacy. He remained the coeditor of *ORDO,* in which he published papers in the tradition of his teacher's research program.[34]

Lutz considered it his duty to seek conversation with scholars and students outside the narrow scope of economics. In several public lectures held at Zurich, Lutz accentuated the relevance of institutionally based economics and the role of the history of economics for the development of economic theory. All of these lectures were summarized in his book *Political Beliefs and National Economic Theories* (1971), which aimed to make a broader readership familiar with the contemporary problems of economics. During this period, Lutz published his influential book *The Theory of Interest* (1956), which traces the development of interest rate theory from the Austrian economist Eugen von Böhm-Bawerk to the modern concepts developed by Don Patinkin. The book is considered to be the standard reference work on the history of capital and interest rate theory.[35]

In Switzerland and Germany, Lutz played an active role in several organizations dedicated to economic research. He was a director of the Swiss Office of International Studies, the aim of which is to organize seminars and lectures in order to discuss topical social and economic problems. Lutz took over supervision of the research department of the Bank for International Settlements in 1956, and at the same time he was a member of the Board of Academic Advisors at the German Ministry of Economics until 1974. Lutz also advised the Swiss and German Central Banks as well as the Bank for International Settlements. At these three banks, Lutz adopted a strong anti-Keynesian stance, in opposition to the dominant Keynesian views that engulfed monetary policymaking during the 1960s and 1970s.[36] Such a confident position did not come out of nowhere. Lutz was able to draw on his experience as an adviser at the Federal Reserve in the 1940s, where, following Morgenstern's mediation, Lutz consulted with the Board of Governors on the proper monetary and interest rate policy.

Further evidence for the high esteem of Lutz's reputation was his appointment as a publisher of several books that are still considered standard reference works in economics. The American Economic Association appointed Lutz and the Chicago monetary economist Lloyd W. Mints as chairmen of a committee to select articles for republication in the authoritative volume *Readings in Monetary Theory*, a compilation of the most important essays on monetary economics.[37] In 1958, Lutz became chairman of the Programme Committee of the Corfu Conference on the Theory of Capital, which later gave rise to the Cambridge capital controversy. Among the active participants were eminent economists such as Paul Samuelson, Robert Solow, Evsey Domar, John R. Hicks, Nicholas Kaldor, and Piero Sraffa. Lutz was coeditor of the conference volume, *The Theory of Capital: Proceedings of a Conference Held by the International Economic Association*.[38] In chapter 1, "The Essentials of Capital Theory," Lutz provided a lucid summary of the Cambridge capital controversy, which dominated economic thinking from the early 1950s until the end of the 1960s.[39]

Lutz was a founding member of several societies that were intended to preserve the intellectual foundations of liberalism and the functioning of free-market economies, as well as social order, during the postwar era. Lutz was among the founding members of the Bellagio Group, the purpose of which was to discuss issues of international finance and monetary economics. This group was founded by his Austrian colleague Fritz Machlup, who invited economists with an international reputation to join, such as Robert Triffin, Peter B. Kenen, Robert Mundell, William Fellner, and Gottfried Haberler. During the first meetings (in 1961–63), they examined alternative monetary plans that might solve the balance of payments difficulties.[40] Lutz supported the idea of flexible exchange rates as the best solution to the balance of payments difficulties. He argued that if exchange rates were allowed to fluctuate within well-defined limits, then speculation would be thwarted, the confidence in currencies would be preserved, and any exacerbation of balance of payments difficulties would be avoided.[41]

Lutz was also invited by Hayek to the founding meeting of the Mont Pèlerin Society in 1947. Because of his teaching engagements at Princeton, he declined, but he was able to attend the society's next business meeting in Basel in 1948. Hayek envisaged the society as an opportunity to gather scholars from all over the world to discuss the intellectual program of a new liberalism, thus providing an alternative to the dominant planning tendencies after World War II.[42] Lutz not only played an instrumental role in the formation of the society's position on topical economic and political problems but also was the only member who served twice as its president.[43]

Friedrich Lutz died in Zurich on October 4, 1975, and Vera passed away on August 20, 1976. Despite the passage of time since then, Lutz's intellectual legacy can still inspire regarding how to conduct research on monetary and banking issues. Several events show that Lutz's monetary economics embedded in institutional analysis is more than necessary today. The 2007 financial crisis demonstrated that without taking into account the institutional framework within which banks interact, we cannot understand the fragility of the banking sector and its contagious effect on the real economy. The 2019 LIBOR (London Interbank Offered Rate) scandal proved that the banks could form a cartel that can manipulate the interbank interest rate, the benchmark for pricing loans and derivatives. The subject of forming a cartel has been neglected by many monetary economists and policymakers. The recent banking crisis following the failure of Silicon Valley Bank provides further evidence of the fragility of the banking system, which once again proves the necessity of an institutional analysis of the monetary and banking sector in the tradition of Friedrich A. Lutz.

10

Eric Hoffer, Mass Individualism, and Economic Freedom

Alberto Mingardi

THE LOCUTION "MASS SOCIETY" is typically used with a broadly derogatory meaning. It casts a dubious shadow on what others have called "the Great or Open Society where millions of men interact and where civilization as we know it has developed."[1] Mass society is thus purported to mean one in which communal links have broken down and alienated individuals, who hence fall prey to the worst passions and ideas. Eric Hoffer often thought otherwise. His insights into both the "supply" and the "demand" for mass movements and into what motivates human actions like work, trade, and proving one's worth make him an underappreciated economist, though he was not an academic economist at all.[2]

Karl Mannheim saw mass society as being "rationally" organized at the level of industrial production but fostering all sorts of irrational impulses at the individual level, producing "an accumulation of unsublimated psychic energies which, at every moment, threatens to smash the whole subtle machinery of social life."[3] Hannah Arendt contrasted "mass" and "class" and held that "masses grew out of the fragments of a highly atomized society whose competitive structure and concomitant loneliness of the individual had been held in check only through membership in a class."[4] Such masses were the constituency of totalitarian movements.[5] As Judith Shklar observed, "in post-Marxist speculative sociology, the failure of the proletariat to appear and the success of fascism meant that class society was dead and had

Alberto Mingardi is associate professor of history of political thought at IULM University in Milan and a presidential fellow in political theory at Chapman University.

been replaced by an undifferentiated 'mass,' which was easily held together by ideologies, propaganda, and terror."[6] Indeed, "the content of the idea of mass society is an inversion of the myth of progress, reason, freedom, and civilization."[7]

This is but a short summary of an ample tradition. Whatever the influence of a particular author may be, "mass society" keeps echoing what is alienating and rotten in our world. It is often also associated with a sense of cultural decay.[8] A few take a different view, among them Edward Shils, who recognized that "this new order of society, despite all its internal conflicts, discloses in the individual a greater sense of attachment to the society as a whole, and of affinity with his fellows,"[9] and maintained that the problems of high culture in mass society were not necessarily new nor specific to industrialized ones. "Mass society" can be seen, in a more descriptive fashion, as the result of modern economic growth, which means industrialization and population growth:[10] it is a society where a *mass* of humans is eventually able to provide for itself.

Eric Hoffer (1902–83) had profound insights on the nature of "mass society," which he associated with the United States he lived in. He is best remembered as a critic of "mass movements," but did not think that the masses were destined to become violent mobs. The same experience of change which drove disappointment and rage could actually make the masses creative and productive.

His work can illuminate our view of what modern economic growth accomplished. Some would argue that Hoffer was no economist. But they might also argue that he wasn't a bona fide philosopher. Either way, his philosophical and economic insights are undeniable. A self-educated essayist, he has been dubbed "the longshoreman philosopher." Hoffer did not deny that dramatic change after the Industrial Revolution brought uneasiness to the societies it changed: "[T]he independent individual constitutes a chronically unbalanced entity. . . . The soul of the autonomous individual has the aspect of a volcanic landscape."[11] Yet he saw that this volcanic landscape could be the most fertile of soils, and not only for the educated few. Hoffer saw twentieth-century America as a society that enjoyed "mass flourishing." If it did not sound all too paradoxical, we could label his political thought *mass individualism*.

Today's reader is unlikely to have heard of his insights. Hoffer achieved substantial success in life as a public intellectual but was soon relegated to the zoo of historical curiosities after his death.

This is because he did not have an academic background. He had discovered, almost by surprise, that he could write persuasively and had something to say about the mid-twentieth-century United States. And that something is as much "outside" the academic consensus of his and our times as he himself was the ultimate outsider.

An Unlikely Success

In his biography of Eric Hoffer, Tom Bethell writes about "the enigma Eric Hoffer." Hoffer, born in 1902 (but even that is hardly sure), was not part of the republic of letters before 1951, when he abruptly came out with *The True Believer.* That book was a sensation and catapulted him onto the reading lists of US presidents and put him before national television audiences.

Bethell speculates that Hoffer "quite possibly . . . was born in Germany and never became a legal resident of the United States."[12] That may explain his German accent, which Hoffer himself traced back to his "Alsatian immigrant parents." In interviews, Hoffer claimed that "my life is not important. . . . It is not even very interesting. Ideas are all that's important."[13] This show of false modesty raised some suspicion in later biographers like Bethell. Certainly Hoffer had peculiar ways of framing himself. "For all of his idolizing of America," he did not "really consider himself an American," as he thought he lacked such "American traits as forbearance and the readiness to help others" and recognized that he still "spoke with an accent."[14]

Little is known of his childhood. Hoffer remembered learning to read in English and German by the age of five, that his mother died when he was a kid, and that he had a rather solitary childhood.[15] He "repeatedly said that he went blind at the age of seven or eight and then recovered his sight at sixteen." His blindness "has functioned in all accounts as an alibi, explaining why he didn't go to school, didn't have friends, spoke with a German accent, had 'shadowy" recollections and so on."[16] Bethell questions the story and points to Hoffer's inconsistency, including a lexical one: It is one thing to be "blind" and quite another to be "practically blind." Plus, recovering eyesight is something that requires one to bathe in the Pool of Siloam or some similarly miraculous occurrence.

Such inconsistencies can perhaps be best explained by looking at the whole of Hoffer's life. Of his later years, we know more. The Eric Hoffer who was quizzed by journalists, and may have embellished his life, was a man with no formal education, who lived in Los Angeles's Skid Row for quite a while, then worked as a migrant worker in California's Central Valley picking oranges, peas, and peaches. He achieved a certain stability (consisting of renting a room in San Francisco) only after Pearl Harbor. In 1941, Hoffer wanted to enlist but "was turned down by the U.S. Army because of a hernia."[17] Thus he joined the longshoremen's union in San Francisco and built a life for himself at the docks. He was "a natural loner"[18] who self-described as "rather lusty" but limited his love life to commercial intercourse. His only known romantic engagement was with Lili Fable, the wife of his colleague Selden Osborne, though they later divorced.[19]

During his itinerant life, Hoffer found consolation and entertainment in reading. He "knew whorehouses the length and breadth of California" but "as he knew all the whorehouses, Hoffer knew all the libraries in the state."[20] It is no exaggeration to claim that "Hoffer had no mentor or formal education during his youth or in his adult years, but he had books to read from the public libraries of California."[21] In particular, Hoffer recounted that he was on his way to be a gold digger in Sierra Nevada in 1936 when he stopped in a bookstore in San Francisco. He wanted to buy the thickest volume they had, so that he could entertain himself as long as possible. Luckily he stumbled upon Michel de Montaigne's *Essays*, which became the model for his own writing. Montaigne gave him "a taste for the good sentence."[22] Montaigne inspired not only Hoffer's terse and brilliant prose, but also his method of reasoning by introspection. Other major influences on Hoffer's works include Jacob Burckhardt,[23] Henri Bergson, Blaise Pascal, Alexis de Tocqueville, and Ernest Renan.

Writing became a career years later. Hoffer ran into a journal called *Common Ground*, a publication addressed to the foreign-born, which he most likely found "during one of his frequent visits to one of the Carnegie libraries," as the magazine was sponsored by the Carnegie Corporation.[24] Hoffer mailed them an article and received a response from editor Margaret Anderson, who did not run his submission, but encouraged him to continue writing. "Her continuing interest and support sustained Hoffer through his solitary years struggling to write *The True Believer*."[25] It was Anderson who in 1949 received the manuscript of the book—she passed it to Harper & Brothers and came up with the title.[26]

The book was a success. In such success, the author's oddity played a part. Before sending the text to the printing presses, the publishers wanted to make sure Hoffer actually existed and was not a literary invention himself.[27] "A 1956 profile in *Look* magazine identified Hoffer as 'Ike's Favorite Author,' elevating this blue-collar working man to the level of President Eisenhower's bedside table."[28] Hoffer would keep writing while working as a longshoreman. He retired from the docks at the mandatory age in 1967, but beginning in 1964 he had started to teach at Berkeley, as the university offered him a job in spite of his having no academic background whatsoever. His appointment at Berkeley made Hoffer meet the world of counter-culture, which he did not sympathize with.

In his lifetime, Hoffer was not made famous by scholars commenting on his work or by the support of a "school" of disciples, but by the market for ideas. In 1967, Eric Severeid interviewed him for CBS News. "Critics were unanimous in their praise. . . . Jack Gould in the *New York Times* called the interview 'fascinating [and] pragmatic.' . . . Amid the predictable humbug of so many authorities, [Hoffer's] down-to-earth philosophy was a provocative breeze that challenged the thinking mind. . . . Hoffer's books soon sold out from every bookstore,"[29] and he was invited to the White House for a private chat with President Johnson. Later Johnson appointed him to the Commission on the Causes and Prevention of Violence, convened after the assassinations of Martin Luther King Jr. and Robert F. Kennedy. Later, in 1983, the year he died, he was awarded the Presidential Medal of Freedom by President Reagan.

In the late 1960s, Hoffer held intellectual positions that made him unpopular with the new consensus. He had little patience for student radicalism, revealing a "law and order" attitude, and he maintained that Johnson's effort would lead to a rapid end of the Vietnam War. Yet, on the matter of American interventionism abroad, Hoffer suggested that the United States as a rule should avoid interventions in the first place: "The better part of statesmanship might be to know clearly and precisely what not to do, and leave action to the improvisation of chance."[30] In fact, Hoffer indicates that "it might be wise to wait for enemies to defeat themselves," as they might fall upon each other with the United States out of the picture. He feared that the coming of the best and brightest into power might infantilize foreign policy: "[T]o an intellectual in power liberalism, the readiness to compromise, and moral considerations are the marks of a paper tiger, and the sight of a paper target incites him to a most reckless ferocity."[31] A strong feeling for human imperfection runs through his work. He thought man was "perpetually unfinished . . . it is this incurable unfinishedness which sets man apart from other living things. For in attempting to finish himself, man becomes a creator."[32]

What made Hoffer so popular during his lifetime may explain his lapsing into obscurity in recent years.[33] Academic scholarship is hardly welcoming to outsiders. *The True Believer* remains a text of historical significance, and its enduring popularity is aided by such a keen title. But Hoffer's production is seldom considered as a consistent *oeuvre*, in spite of the fact he himself identified the subject he always struggled with: change. His major work is perhaps his second substantial essay, *The Ordeal of Change* (1963). Hoffer's penchant for brilliant words also led him to write aphorisms, beginning with his second published book, *The Passionate State of Mind* (1955). Either when writing aphorisms or longer essays, Hoffer's style reminds the reader more of an eighteenth-century essayist than a modern professor. That would have pleased him, but it limited scholarly interest in his work.

True Believers: The Supply and Demand for Mass Movements

In Tom Stoppard's *The Real Thing*, playwright Henry observes that "public postures have the configuration of private derangement."[34] This could have been an aphorism by Eric Hoffer. In fact, he had a similar one: "We all have private ails. The troublemakers are they who need public cures for their private ails."[35] The "thoughts on the nature of mass movements," which Hoffer published in 1951 as *The True Believer*, explore precisely how private derangements produce public postures. As George Will noted a while ago, "Hoffer thinks extremism is a personal problem rooted in human nature."[36]

The main topic of the book was "mass movements," being understood as "popular political movements with an implied element of spontaneity" aiming at overthrowing the status quo.[37]

It may well be, as a commentator maintained, that the book succeeded because it "argued for equating America's prior, Nazi enemy with its current, Communist enemy on ethical, moral, and psychological ground."[38] The idea that communism and national socialism were both totalitarian ideologies threatening Western "liberal" societies is a common feature of what historian Alan Kahan has called "third wave liberalism," emerging in the 1920s and reacting to the threat of totalitarianism.[39] A number of liberals pointed to the existence of common philosophical roots in German idealism; others emphasized that national socialists' economic policies showed a socialist inspiration. Ludwig von Mises observed that both communists and Nazis relied on "polylogism" (the notion that different groups have different versions of logic, hence the bourgeois is intellectually enslaved by her circumstances), as they lacked logical arguments against their adversaries.[40]

Hoffer's analysis was broader, and extended to *all* forms of mass movements, of which fascism and socialism were only the most egregious examples. He did not consider them to be a consequence of fractures in society caused by industrial progress but searched for their causes in the psychology of individuals. Hoffer was fond of an apocryphal Hitler quotation: "The petit bourgeois Social-Democrat and the trade-union boss will never make a National Socialist, but the Communist always will,"[41] the point being that mass movements' leaders well understood their followers to be interchangeable.

Hoffer hence searched for common traits of mass movements in general. All of them revolved around a "holy cause," whose mere advocacy was far more important than its possible contents. "However different the holy causes people die for; they perhaps die basically for the same thing."[42] The willingness of people to buy into such holy causes was motivated by their lack of self-confidence, and the need to find substitutes for what they felt lacking in their own individual life. "Faith in a holy cause is to a considerable extent a substitute for the lost faith in ourselves."[43]

The True Believer focuses both on the demand and on the supply side of mass movements. The account of the first involves "the ferment of frustration."[44] This is not associated exclusively with poverty, let alone extreme poverty or, to use a more contemporary lexicon, widening inequalities. Having been a cash-poor worker himself, Hoffer did not buy into the idea that poverty was enough to breed revolutions:

> Where people toil from sunrise to sunset for a bare living, they nurse no grievances and dream no dreams. Discontent is likely to be highest when misery is bearable; when conditions have so improved that an ideal state seems almost within reach. A grievance is most poignant when almost redressed. De Tocqueville in his researches into the state of society in France before the revolution was struck by the discovery that "in no one of the periods which have followed the Revolution of 1789 has the national prosperity of France augmented more rapidly than it did in the twenty years preceding that event." He is forced to conclude that "the French found their position the more intolerable the better it became."[45]

People react to "change," in the customary sense that they need to deal with tumultuous evolution in technology and society. "The True Believer" was indeed "a plastic human type thrown up by a century of ceaseless change."[46] Rapid change forges its discontents. Yet they "locate the shaping forces of our existence outside ourselves. Success and failure are unavoidably related in our minds with the state of things around us."[47]

Hoffer is careful to distinguish the kind of attitude which brings people to join a mass movement from their willingness to enter a party or a trade union as a means to improve their lot by gaining greater bargaining power through group action. Mass movements win hearts, offering the hope of nirvana, not the satisfaction of petty needs:

> There is a fundamental difference between the appeal of a mass movement and the appeal of a practical organization. The practical organization offers opportunities for self-

> advancement, and its appeal is mainly to self-interest. On the other hand, a mass movement, particularly in its active, revivalist phase, appeals not to those intent on bolstering and advancing a cherished self, but to those who crave to be rid of an unwanted self. A mass movement attracts and holds a following not because it can satisfy the desire for self-advancement, but because it can satisfy the passion for self-renunciation.[48]

Here the supply side of mass movements comes in. Discontent (or poverty) per se would not fuel political engagement. It takes leadership—and a general understanding that the future of society can be reshaped with the proper tools. Hoffer sees mass movements to be the product of an intellectual leadership, reinforced by a belief that social reality can be twisted and improved at will: "The fanatic deals with men the way the scientist deals with matter."[49]

Mass movements thus command loyalty not because they provide people with direct benefits (this happens only in a later, more "institutionalized" phase[50]) but because the chief passion of the frustrated is "to belong." Mass movements can be demanding and still worshipped, as they are in the business of providing "substitutes" for self-respect. Paradoxically, "self-sacrifice" turns out to be easier than "self-realization."[51] The orchestra conductors are "faultfinding intellectuals," men of words who invariably pioneer future mass movements.[52]

The idea that society can be molded at will into a particular shape may surprisingly go together with a sort of worship of nature. In his later writings, Hoffer showed little sympathy for the fledging environmentalist movement. He then located a change of attitude among the intellectuals in the Romantic age. If "the intellectuals entered the nineteenth century flushed with their conviction that they were the new makers of history," industrialization shocked them: "One morning they woke up to discover that power had fallen into the hands of their middle-class relatives. . . . The revulsion from a middle-class society that came to dominate the nineteenth century alienated the intellectuals from the machine age."[53]

These are only a handful of Hoffer's often forgotten insights. Some may sound prescient: The autodidact Hoffer lacked the modern tools that are now used for a perusal of the political mind,[54] but he pointed in a direction unlikely to be taken by modern cognitive psychology. He proposed to look into private derangement as part of the process of understanding public postures.

Markets, Liberty for the Masses, and Mass Flourishing

If *The True Believer* is Hoffer's most celebrated work, his *magnum opus* is perhaps another slender pamphlet, published a few years later, *The Ordeal of Change.* Ruminating on his own reflections, he deduced his own subject was actually "change," understood in his different dimensions "from backwardness to modernity, but also . . . from boyhood to manhood, from poverty to affluence, from subjection to equality."[55]

Hoffer understood the psychological challenge that change poses to people. It may ultimately turn them into raw material for a political mass movement. "Even in slight things, the experience of the new is rarely without some stirring of foreboding." In 1936, writes Hoffer, he was picking peas. But in summer he had to pick string beans. "I still remember how hesitant I was the first morning as I was about to address myself to the string bean vines. Would I be able to pick string beans? Even the change from peas to string beans had in it elements of fear."[56]

This sense of being tested and having to adjust to the unknown is all the more stressful when we are to cope with drastic change. But such stress was not *wrong* per se. Drastic change produces a "population of misfits" who discover their own skills to be outdated and feel themselves out of place. This would indeed make them "unbalanced, explosive, and hungry for action."[57] Such hunger for action could be channeled in a productive direction or end up in politics: "When a population undergoing drastic change is without abundant opportunities for individual action and self-advancement, it develops a hunger for faith, pride, and unity . . . drastic change, under certain conditions, creates a proclivity for fanatical attitudes."[58]

But that is not necessarily the case. It was not the case in the United States that Hoffer knew firsthand, which was very different than fascist Italy or Nazi Germany or Soviet Russia, which he never visited. America proved that change can be a source of good social developments too.

> The millions of immigrants dumped on our shores after the Civil War underwent a tremendous change, and it was a highly irritating and painful experience. Not only were they transferred almost overnight, to a wholly foreign world, but they were, for the most part, torn from the warm communal existence of a small town or village somewhere in Europe and exposed to the cold and dismal isolation of an individual existence. They were misfits in every sense of the word, and ideal material for a revolutionary explosion. But they had a vast continent at their disposal, and fabulous opportunities for self-advancement, and an environment which held self-reliance and individual enterprise in high esteem.[59]

These immigrants could "plunge into a mad pursuit of action," as the context allowed their self-reliance and industrious spirit to flourish. Hoffer largely identifies this context with the industrial West and particularly with the United States of his own times: a "mass society," in which everyone could give it a go as *an individual.*

Political mass movements are a collective response to the pressure of change. The alternative is "mass flourishing," as economist Edmund Phelps later called it. Phelps wrote that

> The modern economy, seen as a vast, unceasing project to conceive, develop, and test ideas about what would work and what people would like, has had profound consequences for work and society. Its predecessor, the mercantile economy, offered little work. . . . In modern economies, work is nearly universal . . . work is central to people's experience, particularly their mental life, and shapes their development.[60]

Western societies, and particularly America as Hoffer knew it, unleashed individual energy through work. Observing contemporary socialism, Hoffer noticed that "the uppermost problem which confronts leadership in a Communist regime" was "to make people work—how to induce them to plow, sow, harvest, build, manufacture, work in the mines, and so forth."[61] Which, on the other hand, came rather easily in the West.

Not that the Soviets could not be at the forefront of technology. They indeed knew how "to foster the exceptional skills requisite for the manufacture of complex machinery . . . even the harnessing of the atom and the launching of Sputniks. But it seems helpless in anything which requires an automatic readiness on the part of the masses to work day in, day out."[62] Famously, the Soviet Union was not producing tampons for women, who needed to rely on substitutes, and had problems in delivering basic consumer goods. Hoffer's insight complements the points raised by Austrian economists in the "economic calculation debate": The features of economic inefficiency due to over-centralization revealed a cultural bug.

This cultural bug can be traced to what Hoffer saw as the antagonism between men of words and men of action. Communism was simply the social order in which "the intellectual so completely comes into his own. . . . No other regime has treated the masses so callously as raw material."[63] "An economy run by intellectuals" was "colossal: big plans, big statistics, gigantic steel plants, factories, dams, powerhouses. The biggest ever! The intellectual cannot be bothered with the prosaic business of producing food, clothing, and shelter for the people."[64] Capitalism, instead, was "ideally equipped for mastering things but awkward in mastering men. It hugs the assumption that people will perform tolerably well when left to themselves."[65] It was this reluctance to "manage men" that made capitalism "modern." He saw "the cleavage between management and labor" as "a source of strain and strife," but thought struggle in society was needed to foster a "constant effort to improve and advance. . . . In human affairs, the best stimulus for running ahead is to have something we must run from."[66] The immigrants coming to America had the opportunities offered by a vast continent at their feet but were also *free* to pursue them.

Hoffer contrasted "the scribe," who was "from the beginning an adjunct of management rather than a member of the labour force," with "the trader." For him, "trading is a form of self-assertion congenial to common people—a sort of subversive activity; endocrine, unheroic, and uncoordinated, yet ceaselessly undermining and frustrating totalitarian domination."[67]

Mass flourishing happens when this latter activity becomes pervasive: in a society in which everyone becomes in some measure a merchant. Socialism saw the hegemony of intellectuals bossing the masses around. The capitalist

"Occident" (a word that Hoffer preferred to "the West") instead left the greater mass of individuals ever relatively free (certainly, freer).

For Hoffer, the West became rich because it saw the mass emergence of the autonomous individual.[68] He explicitly contrasts such a change with "the psychological effect of some religious ideas or doctrine,"[69] i.e., to the impact of the Reformation. Like Deirdre McCloskey later,[70] Hoffer considers the turning point to be a cultural one, due to "a fortuitous combination of circumstances."[71] Perhaps reminiscent of Burckhardt, he places it in the Renaissance, which "was born in the market-place, in the workshops of artisans. Pure science emerged from the pursuits of architects, navigators, and craftsmen."[72]

From the Renaissance on,

> Whether he willed it or not, the Western individual . . . found himself more or less on his own. . . . The separation of the individual from a collective body, even when it is ardently striven for, is a painful experience. The newly emerging individual is an unstable and explosive entity.[73]

Such an individual existence is "beset with fears," but happily the Western individual's "most vital need is to prove his worth, and this usually means an insatiable hunger for action. . . . The majority prove their worth by keeping busy. A busy life is the nearest thing to a purposeful life."[74]

For the first time in Western capitalist societies, work was not viewed as "a curse, a mark of bondage, or, at best, a necessary evil."[75] The "practical sense" became a vital part of everybody's quest for meaning, vis-à-vis the traditional aristocratic mentality. "The intellectual sees man's handiwork as a defacement. . . . With common people it is the other way around: they see man's work as an enhancement of nature."[76]

Hoffer did not sing the praises of the autonomous individual as the eccentric genius or the man who makes a cause out of his liberty. His autonomous individual was the average Joe in America, a "business civilization" which was deprecated for its "worship of success, the cult of the practical, the identity of quality with quantity, the addiction to sheer action, the fascination of the trivial." But it also showed "a superb dynamism, and unprecedented diffusion of skills, a genius for organization and teamwork, a flexibility which makes possible an easy adjustment to the most drastic change, an ability to get things done with a minimum of tutelage and supervision, an unbounded capacity for fraternization."[77]

This is possible because of liberty: "When the mass of people are free to work they usually act as if they are driven to work. Freedom releases the energies of the masses not by exhilarating but by unbalancing, irritating, and goading."[78]

Conclusion

A mass society for Hoffer is one where Mandarins and scribes exercised a limited influence. He thought the masses made America in the sense that the individual freedom offered to so many made possible unprecedented advancements for all. The view that liberty is at the root of our prosperity is often contrasted with an understanding of it as unsettling and psychologically threatening. Hoffer held both views but did not see the latter as necessitating a drift towards populism or autocracy, as many do. Change creates misfits, but such misfits could propel economic growth and progress under the proper conditions. These conditions are a free society that is not ruled by people of allegedly superior culture telling their fellow men what to do.

All through the Western countries, these days, we see something different: bureaucratic micromanagement, on one side, and on the other widespread cultural hostility toward "rugged individualism." Hoffer feared, in his times, "the diversion of talent and ambition from business," which may imply "a diminution of economic venturesomeness and drive."[79] He feared the twentieth century was "the age of the intellectual," implying such a diversion of energies from productive work into the sort of sterile *otium* intellectuals traditionally idolized.[80] He maintained that capitalism was not doomed by its inner contradictions, but challenged by a class of highbrows who despised its dynamics and values. His views came from a life at the waterfront, in which he was a laborer. This detail made him all the more detestable to, and hence artfully forgotten by, intellectual champions of the working classes.

11

Kenneth Boulding

Knowledge, Conflict, and Power

Yahya Alshamy and Christopher J. Coyne

KENNETH BOULDING WAS born in Liverpool, England, on January 18, 1910.[1] He earned a scholarship to Oxford University at New College in 1929, where he studied chemistry. Several life-altering events occurred during his time at Oxford. First, he joined the Religious Society of Friends (Quakers). His commitment to religion and pacificism would influence him for the rest of his life, both personally and professionally. Second, under the influence of Lionel Robbins, then a tutor at Oxford, Boulding shifted his focus of study to economics.[2] This led to the publication of his first academic paper in the *Economic Journal*, which was then edited by John Maynard Keynes.[3]

In 1932, Boulding traveled to America on a fellowship to spend time at the University of Chicago, where he studied with Frank Knight, Henry Schultz, and Jacob Viner. He returned to Britain in 1934, without completing his PhD, as an assistant lecturer at the University of Edinburgh. He remained there until 1937, when he returned to America, taking a position at Colgate University. During his time at Colgate, he married Elise Bjorn-Hansen, a sociologist who would later teach at Dartmouth College and also work on issues of peace and conflict. After four years at Colgate, Boulding made several short-term moves—to the League of Nations Economics and Financial Sec-

Yahya Alshamy is assistant professor of public policy and economics at Alfaisal University and associate research fellow at the King Faisal Center for Research and Islamic Studies (KFCRIS). Christopher J. Coyne is professor of economics at George Mason University and associate director of the F. A. Hayek Program for Advanced Study in Philosophy, Politics, and Economics at the Mercatus Center at George Mason University.

tion at Princeton University (1941–42), Fisk University (1942–43), Iowa State College (1943–46, returning in 1947–49), and McGill University (1946–47). In 1947, he moved to the University of Michigan, where he would remain until 1967. During his time at the University of Michigan, he cofounded the *Journal of Conflict Resolution* in 1957 and founded the Center for Research on Conflict Resolution in 1959. His final professional move was to the University of Colorado in 1967, where he remained until his retirement in 1980.

Is Kenneth Boulding an underappreciated economist? One could argue that he is not. He produced an enormous body of work, including three dozen books and at least eight hundred articles. The breadth of his work is staggering, including work in economics, political science, sociology, philosophy, social psychology, peace research, and the humanities. One clear indication of his diverse intellect is the multiple volumes of sonnets he published during his lifetime.

Boulding was also well decorated with professional accolades. He was the winner of the John Bates Clark Medal in 1949. The Clark Medal is awarded every other year by the American Economic Association (the top professional association in economics) to an economist under the age of forty who has made significant contributions to the discipline. Boulding held the presidency in numerous professional associations: the Society for General Systems Research (1955–59), the American Economic Association (1968), the International Peace Research Society (1969–70), the Association for the Study of the Grants Economy (1970–89), the International Studies Association (1974–75), the American Association for the Advancement of Science (1979), and the section on economics of the British Association for the Advancement of Science (1982–83). He received honorary doctorates from more than thirty universities and was a member of the National Academy of Sciences, the Institute of Medicine, and the American Academy of Arts and Sciences. He was also nominated for both the Nobel Prize in Economics and the Nobel Peace Prize. When he passed away in 1993, the *New York Times* ran an obituary—"Kenneth Boulding, an Economist, Philosopher and Poet, Dies at 83."[4]

Despite this success, we argue that Boulding is underappreciated. For one, Boulding himself feared that he had failed to make a lasting impact. In the introduction to the first volume of his collected papers, Boulding wrote, "In many ways I see myself as a voice crying in the wilderness, to which nobody has paid much attention."[5] In a review essay of Boulding's collected works, Robert Heilbroner (1975) speculated as to why a school of thought failed to develop around Boulding as it had with Milton Friedman, Paul Samuelson, and Joan Robinson. According to Heilbroner, Boulding's work tended to be insightful but abstract, such that "[w]e do not know what to do with these insights."[6] The abstract nature of his work, according to Heilbroner, led to ahistorical work that was "'above' the real world" and failed to attract a large number of dedicated followers.[7]

Yet another reason, not mentioned by Heilbroner, might be the breadth of Boulding's work. Simply put, it may be difficult for scholars in any one field to know what to make of Boulding. Although he was an economist by training, his work was highly interdisciplinary in nature. As Mancur Olson stated upon Boulding's death, "His talks, his writing were so full of brilliant asides that no summary does them justice." He described Boulding in the following way: "Imagine someone who was half Milton Friedman, half Mahatma [Gandhi]."[8] What made Boulding unique as an intellectual—the scope, diversity, and eclecticism of his scholarship—also makes it difficult to neatly categorize him and his ideas in a single school of thought in a single discipline.

In what follows, we provide an overview of some of the key, and neglected, themes in Boulding's scholarship. Given the breadth of his body of scholarship, we can't hope to cover all of his contributions. Instead, we discuss three of Boulding's books, *The Image* (1956), *Stable Peace* (1978), and *Three Faces of Power* (1989). These books reflect Boulding's emphasis on individual agency, subjectivism, the nature of knowledge, open-ended processes, and the role of institutions.

The Image

One of Boulding's critical insights into the study of social systems is his concept of image. In *The Image,* Boulding (1956) offered a novel way to understand the role of knowledge in governing human behavior. The book was written as an argument against behaviorism, which he believed overemphasized the role of external stimuli in governing human behavior.[9] Instead, Boulding argued that human behavior is influenced by one's *image* of the world. "Image" refers to a person's subjective knowledge stock, ranging from the individual's worldview, web of relationships, roles in organizations, and emotions.

Unlike behaviorists, Boulding sharply distinguished between a person's image and "new messages," defined as stimuli of information based on experiences to which the person is exposed. The sharp distinction is based on individuals' capacity to subjectively interpret messages and position them as they see fit in their image of the world. Subsequently, he offered two propositions: (1) a person's behavior is governed by the person's image of the world, and (2) the meaning of novel messages is the change it produces in the person's image. Like Friedrich Hayek (1943), Boulding postulated that the facts of the social sciences are not mere stimuli but the subjective meanings that people attach to physical items and events in the world.

Boulding's conception of the image was not committed only to methodological individualism in the sense that only individuals act. It also identified the individual as a precursor to action; only individuals form images and interpret stimuli that govern their actions. He emphasized that the image is always the possession of individual persons, never of organizations.[10]

Yet Boulding's methodological individualism does not postulate an atomistic interpretation of human behavior and recognizes how social embeddedness helps form *public images*. Public images refer to the role individuals play in their environment or organization. Shared public images of one another's roles can be analogized as images of organizations themselves and are essential for coordination in complex societies characterized by specialization. However, Boulding maintained that one must not take the analogy of public images too far, maintaining that only individuals form images of their roles.[11] For all practical purposes, the only way to study the public image and dynamics of images in society is to first study the images and changes in images of the individuals constituting society and the organizations within society.[12]

One's image is not static; it is dynamic and malleable. Boulding explained that "[t]he image not only makes society, society continually remakes the image."[13] A great amount of effort in each society is dedicated to transmitting and protecting its public image as a form of inertia. Yet unusually charismatic and creative individuals, who do not follow the transmitted public image, can bring great changes to the public image of societies. They restructure the different roles of individuals and innovate new ways to coordinate society.[14]

Under the influence of these innovators, the old images of society continuously change, and new ones arise.[15]

Why does the concept of the image matter for the social sciences? There are at least three reasons. First, many social scientists still cling to behaviorism, which treats human decision-making as a direct response to external stimuli. This removes individual agency in the process of interpreting and responding to these stimuli. Beyond methodology, this matters for practical policy. For instance, assumptions of behaviorism will often make its proponents overly confident about the ability of government interventions to achieve their desired ends because people are assumed to be passive responders who act in a predictable manner.

Second, Boulding's conception of image permits economists to move beyond the mere mechanics of narrow self-interest and utility maximization. Though these abstractions may be useful in static decision-making scenarios, they fail to explain institutional change through time. To explain institutional change, we must appreciate the process of image formation by individuals and how that leads to image changes in society.

Third, recognizing the subjective, methodologically individualistic understanding of knowledge allows us to resolve what Israel Kirzner called the "Shackle-Boulding paradox."[16] Kirzner identified G. L. S. Shackle and Kenneth Boulding as an entry point to differentiate the Austrian perspective on the unknown unknowns and discovery from the mainstream treatment of known unknowns and search theory. Boulding said: "We have the paradox . . . implicit in the very concept of knowledge, that we have to know what we want to know before we can start looking for it. There are things we ought to know, and which we do not know that we ought to know, that remain largely unknown and unsought for."[17]

Search theory is not capable of explaining the gradual removal of ignorance of things we do not know that we do not know, because it assumes we know information is available if one wishes to incur the cost of search. Search is certainly important, but so too is the process of discovery, which tends to be neglected by economists. In this regard, there are clear affinities between Boulding and those working in the Austrian tradition.[18]

Stable Peace

Boulding was a founding father of conflict and defense economics with his book *Conflict and Defense: A General Theory* (1962), considered a foundational text in the field. He built on this earlier work with *Stable Peace* (1978), which offered a process-based approach to understanding conflict and peace. Boulding differentiated between nonconflict and conflict situations.

"Nonconflict" refers to situations in which one party's gain does not occur at another's expense. These situations are peaceful in that there is no violence. Conflict, in contrast, refers to actions that benefit one party at the expense of another. A key issue is how people navigate conflict situations. Conflict situations can be resolved peacefully, as in economic competition, or violently, as in war. Peaceful conflict situations involve formal and informal rules that govern competition by nonviolent means.

Boulding's interest was in understanding the factors that cause transitions from peace to war, and from war to peace, through time. He offered a framework defined by four phases of war and peace: stable peace, unstable peace, unstable war, and stable war. "Stable peace" refers to a situation in which parties have no plan to engage in war against each other, and each party is aware of the other's intent. "Unstable peace" refers to a situation in which parties are not engaged in war, but the possibility of war is practically considered in each party's plans. "Unstable war" refers to a situation in which parties are involved in war, but the possibility of peace is practically considered in each party's plans. Finally, "stable war" refers to a situation in which parties are engaged in war and have no plans to transition into peace.

Boulding offered a process view of the war-and-peace system grounded in human agency. Societies can move between phases through time. And the choices made by people can influence the speed and direction of the transition for better or worse.

To describe the transitions from one phase to another, Boulding introduced the concepts of "strain" and "strength." Strains are elements of the system that are conducive to phase change, whereas strengths are elements that make the system resist the sort of breakage that occurs under strain. Boulding cited several important factors that strain war phases and strengthen peace phases.

The first is the "habit of peace," which refers to having a history of peaceful relations. Boulding noted the paradoxical fact that the longer peace between two parties lasts, the better chance it has of persisting. Second, he discussed the role of professional specializations dedicated to discovering peace. Professional specialists include mediators, conciliators, and diplomats who use their creativity to find context-specific solutions to conflicts and make a living doing so. Third, he discussed the role of increasing travel and communication between parties. An increase in communication facilitates the formation of integrative relationships and lowers the cost of bargaining to avoid violent conflict.

The fourth factor is the formation of a web of economic interdependence. Boulding described what is today termed the capitalist peace hypothesis, stating that market transactions can lead to economic interdependence that shifts the budget constraint for war, raising the cost of violence. Fifth, Boulding explained the importance of the formation of mutually compatible self-images, referring to the formation of a positive, integrative relationship that does not include the use of force against one another. The formation of these images entails considering each party's conception of justice and equity and finding opportunities for mutual benefit. Finally, he explained the importance of a taboo line against the use of violence in general. He explained that there is a taboo line that divides everything a person can do into two parts—what a person does, and does not, refrain from doing. After all, international peace cannot be maintained without a shared taboo against using armed forces to resolve conflicts.

A key theme in Boulding's work is that people consistently overrate the role of threat systems in achieving their desired ends, including peace. For example, he noted that the reduction of banditry may be the result of technological advancements that give rise to alternative occupations more so than the successful threats of legal enforcement or conversion by saints.[19] Similarly, he believed that the reduction of wars of conquest was the result of the discovery that imperialism is not nearly as profitable as domestic economic development as a result of military defeats.[20]

Boulding's discussion of these issues was not confined to historical analysis. He expanded to discuss the future of peace and the folly of the overuse of threat systems in a regularly practiced political theory—deterrence theory.

Schelling defined deterrence as the prevention of action by fear of consequences.[21] Deterrence theory suggests that with an increase in the cost of war, where an act of aggression would result in a counter-aggression, both parties will be less likely to attack. Boulding emphasized the inherent instability of deterrence, despite its ability to potentially maintain short periods of unstable peace.[22]

Consider the case of nuclear deterrence. For deterrence to work, the likelihood of the use of a nuclear weapon must be greater than zero, for it were zero, it would not deter. Deterrence must always have a positive probability of breaking down, which means that it will break down over a sufficiently long period of time. As Boulding put it, "[n]uclear deterrence may be more like a one-hundred-year flood, with a probability of 1 percent per annum (this is just a guess), but even this would have a 63 percent probability of occurring in a hundred years and a 98 percent probability in four hundred years. It is an illusion, therefore, to think that deterrence can be ultimately stable."[23]

Another pathology of deterrence is that it exposes nations to the security dilemma. In deterrence theory, relative power matters more than absolute power; hence, an increase in military acquisitions and spending of an adversary may pressure increases in defense spending that do not increase the overall security of the nation as a whole, had the adversary not increased its defense spending. The paradoxical result is that investing in security against war can increase the likelihood of war. Boulding argued that studies of the "incidence of war in a historical sample of societies all over the world cast grave doubt on the old adage that, if you want peace, you should prepare for war, for most societies prepared for war seem to get it, which is not wholly surprising."[24] In making these arguments, Boulding called into question the "peace through military strength" view that dominated during the Cold War period and still exists today.

Three Faces of Power

Throughout his career, Boulding was interested in issues of power and the interplay between the economic, social, and political arenas. His most well-developed treatment of these issues is his book *Three Faces of Power* (1989), which built on his earlier work on the topic.[25] Boulding started by offering a simple definition of power—"the ability to get what we want."[26] On the basis of the different means of getting what we want and their consequences, he divided power into three categories.

First, there is the destructive power of threat systems. A threat system is based on a relationship in which A tells B, "You do something I want, or I will do something you do not want."[27] It is particularly associated with political power. Second, there is the productive power of exchange systems, based on a relationship in which A says to B, "You do something I want, and I will do something you want."[28] An exchange takes place if B has a choice to accept or reject the offer and accepts it. Exchange systems are particularly associated with economic power. Third, there is the integrative power of love. Integrative systems are based on a relationship in which A tells B, "You do something for me because you love me."[29] Love in the relationship can also be substituted for other feelings that motivate action, such as respect, pride, guilt, and shame. The ability to evoke these feelings to inspire action is associated with social power.

Boulding observed that elements of the three faces of power are found in all organizations, though one element is often likely to prevail. Consider the role of integrative systems in supporting threat systems. Unless a ruler is loved or respected, the power to organize threats increases and may even become prohibitively costly, as the history of revolutions illustrates. The need for legitimacy by threat systems, such as national military organizations, is exemplified in their rebranding from war departments to departments of defense to signal to the citizenry and international community their claims to defense as opposed to conquest.

As another illustration, consider that property relations, based on exchange systems, are characterized by elements of a threat system, such as legal enforcement, to protect and maintain. Legal enforcement operates as a threat to those who would seek to violate property rights. Integrative systems also contain elements of exchange, given that friends may start to become distant if they are not offered mutual love and respect.

Boulding's taxonomy is valuable because it underlines the choice over what kind of power we choose as a means to our ends. He offers the example of cutting down a tree.[30] Because we cannot bribe a tree or persuade it to cut itself down, we have to use destructive power. We also cannot threaten or persuade clay to turn into a pot, so productive power is all we have.[31] In building genuine friendships, threatening people is useless; we cannot beat people into becoming our friends. We also cannot bribe people into friendship, though mutual gift-giving when signaling care helps. Instead, we have to charm them with subtle communication and persuasion.

One can see how the themes in *Three Faces of Power* connect to common themes that run throughout Boulding's body of work. Choices about the type of power exercised will depend on people's image of themselves and of society. Where threat systems dominate, they are likely to contribute to an unstable peace. The future of peace for societies stuck in a precarious unstable peace requires people to choose better means of power to achieve their end, expanding their options to integrative and exchange systems. This, in turn, requires changing the images held by warring parties to expand the viability set to include alternative, peaceful solutions to conflict.

Conclusion

Kenneth Boulding is an underappreciated economist and social theorist. But why? As we discussed, Robert Heilbroner speculated that it had to do with the abstract and ahistorical nature of Boulding's work.[32] But perhaps there is another explanation.

Boettke argued that there was a shift in the economics profession over the course of the twentieth century toward formal, equilibrium theorizing.[33] This shift drained economics of institutional context and the purposes and plans of human beings *qua* human beings. This was at odds with the "mainline tradition" going back to Adam Smith.[34] This tradition is delineated by the following three propositions: "(1) there are limits to the benevolence that individuals can rely on and therefore they face cognitive and epistemic limits as they negotiate the social world, but (2) formal and informal institutions guide and direct human activity, and, so (3) social cooperation is possible without central direction."[35]

Kenneth Boulding was part of the mainline tradition, which meant that his work, although recognized by the profession while he was alive, was still often at the fringes of the discipline. This helps explain why his work was, and is, underappreciated. At the same time, the resurgence of the mainline tradition offers a unique opportunity to reengage Boulding's work to better understand the realities of the social world and to offer insight into a variety of issues related to individual flourishing and well-being.

12

Bruno Leoni

Underappreciated Economist

Michael C. Munger

Unless I am wrong, there is more than an analogy between the market economy and a judiciary or lawyers' law, just as there is much more than an analogy between a planned economy and legislation. If one considers that the market economy was most successful both in Rome and in the Anglo-Saxon countries within the framework of, respectively, a lawyers' and a judiciary law, the conclusion seems to be reasonable that this was not a mere coincidence.[1]

—Bruno Leoni

BRUNO LEONI IS "underappreciated" for three reasons. First, the depth and breadth of his contributions are remarkable, and his influence on "Austrian Economics" (through F. A. Hayek), on "Public Choice" (through James Buchanan), and "Law and Economics" (through George Priest) have not received anything close to the recognition they deserve.[2] Second, Leoni's tragic early death, the details of which I believe have not been shared before in English, prevented him from writing any kind of syncretic book that made clear how his various works fit together.[3] Third, Leoni's work that was published—other than *Liberty and the Law*, which the Volker Fund sponsored for simultaneous publication in English—was for the most part available only in Italian. It was not widely read or considered in Italy, because at the time he

---

Michael C. Munger is senior fellow and former coeditor of *The Independent Review* at Independent Institute and professor of political science, economics, and public policy and director of the Philosophy, Politics, and Economics Program at Duke University.

was writing the political climate was simply too hostile to his radical ideas, and it was not translated for reasons that in retrospect are hard to understand.

It is misleading to try to boil down the thought of a thinker as complex and nuanced as Leoni, but it is also still useful to try. So, with the usual caveat that "you should read and decide for yourself," this is what I see as Leoni's approach and contribution.

- The key explanandum, or in modern social science parlance the "dependent variable," for Leoni is "*the certainty of the law.*"
- The key independent or causal variable was "*institutions,*" the broad set of rules and conventions for governing society.[4]
- Importantly, Leoni was also concerned about the *certainty about* certainty of law, in the sense that it is not enough to be able to read exactly what the law is today; what is required is the assurance that the law can be understood clearly today, and that it will have the same content and meaning indefinitely into the future.
- As the quote presented above suggests, Leoni made an analogy between the relationship between "common law" and "legislation" compared to "market processes" and "central planning." His view of the common law, however, was different from the received conception of the English common law, where the specific language of "precedent" cases takes on the force of law. He thought that "lawyers' law" was at most conceptual, and provided a baseline for interpreting agreements only if there was no explicit contractual language that applied.
- Perhaps most fundamentally, the "task" of law was to settle disputes, *if the law is invited to do so by parties* to the disagreement. Otherwise, the only constraints on behavior are private agreements: most citizens can go about their business, and never encounter the law at all.

It is useful to give an overview of Leoni's life, after which I will turn to describe his contributions in greater detail.

A Frenetic Life and a Shocking End

Bruno Leoni was born in 1913, in Ancona, Italy (the "calf of the boot," on a map). By the time he was murdered, in 1967, he had already had what Alberto Mingardi described as "a frenetic life."[5] He completed his studies in Turin and was awarded an academic chair at the University of Pavia. He participated in World War II, first on the Italian side, but after Italy was defeated he was part of the "A Force," which according to Bradsher rescued Allied POWs who had been captured by Italy but had not been released under pressure from Germany.[6] He reassumed his position at the university in 1945 and was made head of Political Sciences at Pavia from 1948 to 1960. His field was what we would call political philosophy, but what was in post-Fascist Italy still jarringly called "the Doctrine of the State."[7]

After founding *Il Politico*, a highly respected journal still published today, Leoni worked on many things at once and built a significant international reputation.[8] In 1958, at Claremont McKenna College, Leoni presented the work that became *Freedom and the Law*, published in 1961. He shared that stage with F. A. Hayek, who was presenting the outline of what became *The Constitution of Liberty* (1960), and with Milton Friedman, who was working on *Capitalism and Freedom* (1962). This conference, directed by Arthur Kemp, and funded by the Volker Fund, showed that Leoni was thought of as one of the leading events of the growing international libertarian movement. Leoni also wrote book reviews and articles on a range of subjects, and was admired enough by Hayek—who called Leoni a "Renaissance Man"—to be made secretary of the Mont Pelerin Society after its founding in 1947.[9] Nearly two decades later, at the French meetings of MPS, with the strong support of Hayek behind the scenes, Leoni was elected president of MPS and began service in that office in September 1967.[10]

But he was only president for two months before the tragic events of early November. As far as I know, the account of his untimely death has not been told before in English,[11] and I ask the reader's indulgence to give a more extended account than might be customary for an article such as this.

Leoni's Death

Leoni managed some economic assets of the Olivetti family, working for Countess Magda Olivetti,[12] and there was a close relationship between the Olivettis and the movement Leoni helped found in Italy. But the relationship was also Leoni's undoing.

A printer named Osvaldo Quero[13] lived in one of the houses owned by the Olivettis, and Leoni contracted with Quero to collect rent from other tenants in the area. The subaccounts that Quero managed were about 80,000 lire (less than $150 US in 1967; around $1,400 today) in arrears; he had been collecting them but not turning them over to Leoni. Opinions about Quero vary; at the print shop where he worked, his superiors said he was their "best worker." Others who worked in the rent collection and processing operation for Leoni said he was quarrelsome and constantly pursuing women instead of working. Leoni had decided to fire him and demanded that Quero settle up the entire amount owed.

Quero replied that he would send the contracts and money by "registered mail." Days passed, but nothing arrived. Angry and impatient, on the afternoon of Tuesday, November 21, 1967, Leoni went to the post office to inquire, but was told by the clerk that he could not even check for the letter without a numbered receipt. Waiting at Porta Nuova, Turin's main train station, Leoni called the printer.

"Look, Quero," the professor angrily asked, "are you sure you sent me those documents?"[14]

Of course, he had not sent the documents or the check, but he insisted on the lie: "Very sure, by registered letter."

"Then bring me the receipt."

They set the appointment for 9:30 p.m. on the arrivals side of Porta Nuova. The professor arrived in his Mercedes, and Quero in his Fiat. Having in fact no receipt, Quero tried to buy time, saying he had left the receipt at home.

Leoni was an authoritative and decisive man. He ordered, "Then let's go and get it at your home!"[15] The Mercedes remained at the parking lot; they took the printer's small car, sitting in close, uncomfortable (I assume) silence.

After they got to Quero's house in Apignano (about fifteen kilometers from the train station), they began arguing more violently. Quero apparently killed Leoni by repeatedly bashing his head against a wall. Some tenants in nearby apartments heard Leoni shouting and calling for help, but no one did anything; it was a rough neighborhood. Quero dragged the disfigured body—the face was smashed beyond recognition—back into the garage. In a rage, he continued to bash the corpse, and then tied up the body so it would fit into a box, which he then left in the garage, tied tightly in rope.

Around midnight, Mrs. Leoni called the Queros to look for her husband. Rosina Quero told her that she hadn't seen him.

"My husband also hasn't returned: they will still be out together."

The printer finally came into the house just before three. He appeared stunned and quiet, his raincoat, suit, and shirt quite bloody.

"Don't be scared," his wife claimed he told her. "I helped a man hit by a car."

The phone rang, and it was Mrs. Leoni again. Quero replied that "I left your husband after 1:00 a.m. in Porta Nuova."

Quero was agitated and distracted, and his wife was afraid to press him. She said that he washed himself for a long time, and then she watched him make two bundles of his bloody clothes and put them under the armchairs in the bedroom.

"It was a bad evening, I'm exhausted," she said he told her. He fell asleep within minutes.

Meanwhile, and throughout the night, Mrs. Leoni searched for her husband in the hospitals and repeatedly telephoned the police: "I'm begging you, look for a Mercedes with Pavia license plate (number)."

Quero woke up and saw his wife next to him, staring at him with red eyes from being awake and crying. "Rosina," he told her, "I had an argument with the professor last night and I killed him. He's down in the garage." He hurriedly got dressed, took some money, and then drove away quickly, back towards Turin.

Then, in a scene that would be cut from a movie because it is too implausible, Quero resolved to create a diversion. He contacted the widow anonymously and claimed to have kidnapped Leoni. Signing the kidnapping note, "The Sardinians,"[16] he threatened to kill Leoni (who was, remember, already dead, and in a box in Quero's garage) unless Leoni's wife paid a substantial ransom. The police believed that the message was slipped into the mailbox by the murderer in the morning, just before the discovery of the body. Apparently, by faking a kidnapping, Quero hoped to gain time and divert the search. It appears he planned to return to the garage, load the boxed body into his car, and then dump it somewhere where it would not be found and traced to him.

But the plan was hopeless from the beginning. In the early afternoon Quero saw a newspaper headline that the body had been discovered. He drove to Rome; there, believing he was about to be captured, he tried to kill himself by drinking bleach. Surviving the suicide attempt, he was arrested, tried, and sentenced to twenty-four years in prison.[17] He died August 29, 1997, having lived quietly the last few years of his life.

The reason these details are important is that Leoni's murder changed the course of Italian politics, the development of Austrian economics in Europe, and the history of the Mont Pelerin Society. As Hartwell points out, the attempt to appoint a successor as president of MPS centered on Milton Friedman (who begged off, as too busy, and was opposed to the idea of an American president), and then settled on Daniel Villey, a French economist then at the University of Paris (Sorbonne).[18] But Villey, who seemed to be recovering from heart surgery, died of a heart attack on April 25, 1968. Günter Schmölders, an economist at Cologne, took over the presidency, and then was followed by Milton Friedman as president of MPS in 1970.

The details in this section are provided because I was unable to find much of this account anywhere in English, and it is important that the story be known. But it is time to turn to Leoni's contributions as a thinker and writer.

Leoni's Contributions

As noted at the outset, Leoni's central interest (though he had others) was the "certainty of the law." In some ways, this focus developed independently, but Leoni had an important disagreement with Hayek. As Hayek said, "I doubt whether the significance which the *certainty of the law* has for the smooth and efficient working of economic life can be exaggerated."[19]

Hayek's formulation of law sought to promote generality, equality, and certainty as components of "rule of law." But the fact that there are "definitely written formulae," and that "rules be general, clearly stated, and published in advance," while *useful* for Hayek, were *problems* for Leoni. For Leoni:

> The usual process of law-making . . . is by way of legislation. But the legislative process is not something that happens once and for all. It takes place every day and is continually going on. This is particularly true in our own time. In [Italy] the legislative process now means about two thousand statutes every year, and each of them may consist of several articles. Sometimes we find dozens or even hundreds of articles in the same statute. . . .

Leoni introduces a distinction between what he called "long-run uncertainty" and "short-run uncertainty" in the law. Written, legislated, or statutory laws and rules can be seen and understood, and their meaning interpreted, but there is little certainty that such laws are stable. An economic actor, an entrepreneur, or even just a citizen cannot make a reliable prediction that the law will be the same in the future. Leoni contrasted statutes with what the English call "common law" and what he called "lawyers' and judges' law." This law can be fuzzy and unclear in some of its particulars, but it is certain in the long run because certain principles are established and are thereafter difficult to change quickly.

Unfortunately, after Leoni was killed in 1967, his ideas were almost forgotten. He was seen as "too radical" for Italy. In the rest of the world his reputation was hampered by the fact that very little of his work was available in English, and what was available was "not put in a systematic framework."[20] He became, in the words of Masala, the "man of one book," though Masala notes that this was only because the other work had not been translated.[21] There were important ideas in *Freedom and the Law*, but both in his earlier and later work Leoni buttressed and expanded those arguments in many important ways.

Interestingly, the fact that one book—*Freedom and the Law*—was available in English, along with F. A. Hayek's generous crediting of Leoni for changing his thinking on common law, distorts Leoni's contribution, since that contribution was much larger than the "one book." Still, it is true that Leoni was important, and perhaps essential, in influencing some of the changes in Hayek's approach between *Constitution of Liberty* (1960) and his later, larger work *Law, Legislation and Liberty* (1973).

The central organon of Leoni's thought was the investigation of how the workings of the market, and market-like processes, could produce social order, extending even into the space of politics and the state.[22] According to Masala, it is important to see "two pillars" of Leoni's mature thought.[23] The first is the argument in *Freedom and the Law*: Leoni saw economic planning and legislation as both suffering from the same limitation, because they were both constrained by what we would now call "the knowledge problem." Just as economic planners lack the local information about resources and their uses that would be necessary to "plan," members of assemblies lack the local information about norms and agreements that will solve social problems.

Thus, the "production" of law by an isolated and poorly informed parliament will result in distortions, and often the "overproduction" of law in settings where formal rules are not necessary and may be actively harmful. Leoni argued that the errors of "centrally planned law" in Italy were quite recent, and that the interpretive tradition of law in Italy had been in place for centuries with very little centralized control. Interestingly, Leoni used the term "discovery" ("*processo di scoperta*") to describe how the law should be "made." Where a parliament debates and votes to "discover" the law, and where markets use exchange to generate prices to "discover" scarcity values, Leoni thought that the law could be "discovered" by judges and lawyers who were actively looking for the best solution. The goal was not to find what the law should be, but to find the solution to problems of disputes in agreements and contracts, and to identify the principles or concepts, assign liability, and resolve problems that blocked cooperation.

Roman and English law worked from broad principles to generate general rules that allowed citizens to coordinate their expectations with certainty, in a way that also produced relatively efficient outcomes, in Leoni's view. Consequently, he argued that parliaments and legislatures should be sharply restricted in the scope of their mandate to create written statutes. Most of the time, in most settings, there is simply no need for formal law, if common law principles can be used instead.

Another advantage of this "discovery" process, as noted above, is precisely that it is slow and deliberate. Citizens cannot be certain of parliamentary law, even if it can be read in very precise language *today*, because it may be

Table 1. Analogy Between Common Law and Markets, and Legislation and Central Planning

	Civil	Commercial
Discovery Process	Common Law	Market Processes
Imposed Top Down	Legislation	Centrally Planned Economy

changed or replaced tomorrow. Leoni tried to advance an analogy, claiming that common law and market processes both share a "discovery process," in which people actively search for improvements, while legislation and centrally planned economies share the feature that they are imposed, from the top down, and that neither legislators in law nor planners in commerce possess the information they would need to carry out their tasks. These differences are depicted in Table 1, above.

The second "pillar" of Leoni's work was a comprehensive political philosophy of law and rights. He wanted to know two things: First, how could we know if the laws are right and fair? Second, given a set of laws, which should be kept and which should be changed?

Because of his early and unexpected death, Leoni was unable to complete much work on this "second pillar," but some outlines of his answer can be glimpsed. To succeed, he would have to work out an important tension, between two sources of "discovery": reason and trial-and-error. To begin with, Leoni would dismiss political popularity as a source for "right," because voting had no capacity for "processo di scoperta." What was necessary was to *look at human behavior*, human action in the Misesian sense, or how things actually work in the Coasean sense, and determine which laws are consistent with individual liberty and prosperity.

Rights, for Leoni, are based on the claim of an individual, the assertion of a right ("this is mine, this is not yours," etc.) that others are *anticipated* to respect. Theft is then the assertion of a right, or the exercise of a right, that others do not recognize, and cannot be expected to respect. I take when no one else recognizes my right to take.

For Leoni, these kinds of claims or rights have three elements:

1. A personal interest—some connection or basis for the claim, or association

2. A forecast, a prediction about behavior—anticipating others will accept the claim
3. The opportunity to determine the claim's legitimacy through resolution of the dispute, in a way that others will also accept as legitimate

There are many kinds of such claims, in Leoni's view, far more than simply property claims. In Roman law, the guiding principle was *Ex Eo Quod Plerumque Fit*, or "From That Which Usually Happens" in the society.[24]

This observation seems quotidian, almost tautological, but for Leoni it was fundamental. There are three aspects behind "what usually happens":

1. The fact that expectations are formed out of experience with what works
2. An element of statistical probability, in the sense that actions satisfy expectations
3. The process of selection of principles of law, or patterns of dispute resolution, that fit particular circumstances

Taken together, this means that "what usually happens" is not the result of a random process of generating norms, but rather a process of selection of norms or principles that work, with "work" being defined as an outcome that produces mutual benefits and does not produce constant appeals and further litigation. Further, this principle is widely enough recognized and internalized that most people in the society coordinate their expectations on outcomes arising from this principle. Finally, the principle is a reliable and "certain" guide to future action, because it is constant and stable over time.

As was emphasized in Table 1, there is for Leoni a kind of unity between common/lawyers' law and market processes. Both are based on the fundamental ignorance of participants, with information emerging from a discovery process. Prices are a *social*, almost deliberative, phenomenon, and so are laws. Of course, this suggests the problem presented by natural law: there is no reason to expect that an evolutionary process will change toward better outcomes, because evolution simply emphasizes survival. There need to be no *telos*.

Leoni had wrestled with this problem in his own mind, but the contradiction was cast in stark relief by the review of *Freedom and the Law* published by Murray Rothbard soon after the book came out. Rothbard admired the valid critique Leoni had leveled at Hayek on "rule of law," but then pointed out a problem that Leoni had not dealt with adequately, or at all.

> A great defect in Leoni's thesis is the absence of any criterion for the content of the judge-made law. It is a happy accident of history that a great deal of private law and common law is libertarian, that they elaborate the means of preserving one's person and property against "invasion." But a good deal of the old law was antilibertarian, and certainly custom can not always be relied on to be consistent with liberty. . . . Suppose ancient custom decrees that virgins be sacrificed to the gods by the light of the full moon, or that red-heads be slaughtered as demons? What then? May not custom be subject to a higher test—reason?[25]

Leoni's response was to begin to write about what he called the "empirical recovery" of natural law. That is, the laws that result from the evolving process of finding what works, the process of judges and lawyers looking to uncover the principles or laws of correct dispute resolution, will tend also to illuminate laws of virtue and justice.

After all, evolved law is what is; natural law is what should be. The principles of natural law await discovery, in Leoni's view, as they are nothing more than the elaborated implications of reason. And the essence of "judge-made" or "lawyers' law" is the application of reason to disputes. Yet Leoni was unable to proceed very far, because he recognized that reason needed premises, and the path of reason that emerged from an emphasis on efficiency in dispute resolutions could be quite different from the path of reason that emerged from a foundation of virtue.

At the time of his death, Leoni was groping towards "empirical recovery" as way of reconciling the paradox. He argued that reason needs a historical experience or context. It is fair to say, as Rothbard argued, that only reason can say whether historical experience has led to good outcomes. But only historical experience can say whether reason leads to workable rules, and it is likely that reason alone will fail to suggest rules that "work" without considerable groping and trial-and-error. Thus, the common law process of evolving cases will generate principles, and then the task of reason is correcting the principles that emerge, rather than the impossible task of generating workable new rules de novo, as was suggested by more abstract political philosophers. The common law is evolved law, and so is consistent with actions and expectations. Natural law must be derived from the systematic application of reason but can at best be used to correct common law.

Conclusion

As was discussed in the previous section, Murray Rothbard admired Leoni's achievement, but he was frustrated with Leoni's description of how the process of law generation would work:

> While Leoni is vague and wavering on the structure that his courts would take, he at least indicates the possibility of privately competing judges and courts. To the question: who would appoint the judges. Leoni answers with the question: who now "appoints" the leading doctors or scientists in society? They are not appointed, but gain general and voluntary acceptance on their merits.[26]

Rothbard was right; it is by no means clear how this would all work. To be fair, Leoni had not even worked out for himself how it might work, and he certainly hadn't written it down before his untimely death. But there are certain core principles of the systematic treatment that Leoni was groping towards.[27]

- First, the law should leave you alone unless you ask the judge or presiding official to settle a dispute. You can go about your business, and the law never affects you.
- Second, the law, in meaning and application, is literally limited only to the facts in *that* dispute. The litigants are bound by the decision, because they contracted to have the dispute resolved. Other disputants may use the concepts of the decision to guide their own resolutions, but the specific linguistic choices of the judges are not binding and certainly have no force as precedent.

- Third, citizens are welcome to "contract around" the common law rules, which exist only to resolve disputes where contracts have been breached, or where parties disagree about breach.
- Fourth, the job of the judicial system is to "discover" the law; literally no one is authorized to "make" the law. Laws emerge from the search for principles that satisfy efficiency and reason, but those laws exist only as general principles, rather than having specific enforceable words and phrases. At most, the concepts in previous decisions are "the law," meaning that the language of a decision is simply an explanation of the principles. Most of what today is seen—in Supreme Court decisions, for example—as enforceable law would be no more than *obiter dicta* for Leoni. Fetishizing specific language was entirely foreign to his intuition about the law. To put it a little differently, Leoni rejected legal positivism and a focus on specific language to a degree that many (present author included) would likely find disconcerting.
- Fifth, and finally, the "law" is embodied in the conceptual solutions that are the result of repeated choices by individuals in similar fact sets being unable to resolve their dispute with the existing legal tools. A judge then offers a conceptual solution; if other judges find this useful also, then that conceptual approach ("last clear chance," "first appropriation") becomes "the law" because it has been "discovered." The precedent is not one authoritative resolution from a superior court, but an *emergent* pattern of similar decisions in similar constellations of fact. The most important takeaway: the common law is more certain, and more stable, than statutory law.

Ultimately, the most important takeaway from Leoni's tragically uncompleted work is the clarification of what "certainty" means in the law, and why it is important. Statutory law seems "certain" at any moment in time, because you can look up the precise language and be sure it is the law. But that certainty is misleading, even chimerical. The statute you memorize today may not be the law tomorrow, and it may not even be the law tomorrow morning:

> The Roman jurist was a sort of scientist: the objects of his research were the solutions to cases that citizens submitted

> to him for study, just as industrialists might today submit to a physicist or to an engineer a technical problem concerning their plants or their production. Hence, private Roman law was something to be described or discovered, not something to be enacted—a world of things that were there, forming part of the common heritage of all Roman citizens. Nobody enacted that law; nobody could change it by any exercise of this personal will. This did not mean absence of change, but it certainly meant that nobody went to bed at night making his plans on the basis of a present rule only to get up the next morning and find that the rule had been overturned by a legislative innovation.[28]

Because common law is conceptual rather than specific, and because it evolves into a consensus rather than being produced by a single entity or group, it is both easier to understand and much more reliably stable. The analogy Leoni drew between judge/lawyerly law and market processes is interesting and important in its own right. But it is also clear that much of the work that Leoni started can be seen to have borne fruit in the later work on efficiency of the common law,[29] and in the "evolutionary" theory of F. A. Hayek in *Law, Legislation, and Liberty* (1973). While one might wish for more, these are significant—and underappreciated—achievements.

13

Edith Penrose

Seeing into the "Insides" of the Firm

Richard N. Langlois

IT MAY SEEM inappropriate to include Edith Penrose in a volume focused on underappreciated economists. In the early twenty-first century, one scholarly article described her as "one of the more influential economists of the twentieth century."[1] According to Google, her seminal book *The Theory of the Growth of the Firm* (1959) has been cited more than forty-six thousand times. In fact, however, the authors making this pronouncement were not economists but management scholars writing in a management journal. And the vast majority of the citations to Penrose's book (henceforth *TGF*) have been in management and strategy. It is telling that, as others have noticed, the blurbs for the 1995 reprint of *TGF* came from two noted management scholars and an economist noted for being heterodox. As an economist, and among economists, Edith Penrose is indeed underappreciated, unread, and perhaps even unknown in the more fashionable precincts of the profession. As John Kay has pointed out, Penrose's name never appeared in the indexes of the most influential Nobelist-authored industrial organization textbooks of the late twentieth century (Milgrom and Roberts, *Economics, Organization and Management*, 1992, and Tirole, *Theory of Industrial Organization*, 1988).[2]

Penrose's life was largely coextensive with the twentieth century, and she was present for, and sometimes involved in, many of the signal events of her era. Hers was a life of adventure and sometimes tragedy, and her academic path was a complex and unusual one. This may speak in part to the originality

Richard N. Langlois is professor of economics at the University of Connecticut.

of her work—though, as is often the case, there may be a certain amount of endogeneity in such a judgment. The theory she developed in *TGF*, both its enduring value and some of its limits, must be understood in the context of the postwar era during which she wrote, a period dominated by large, vertically integrated corporations under the control of salaried managers rather than individual entrepreneurs.[3]

Edith Elura Tilton was born in 1914 in Los Angeles and grew up in San Luis Obispo.[4] Her father was a surveyor and road engineer who was involved in designing not only some of the most scenic stretches of California's storied Route 1 but also the entry road to William Randolph Hearst's San Simeon estate. As a result, the young Edith often found herself in road camps, where on one occasion her mother was forced to defend her by shooting a rattlesnake. A stellar student, Edith matriculated at the University of California Berkeley at the height of the Great Depression, and by accident fell into the study of economics. She was active in debate and campus politics at Berkeley, apparently taking a progressive but liberal-centrist stance during this highly polarized time. While still an undergraduate, she married law student David Denhardt. In 1938, while running for district attorney in the rural Central Valley of California, Denhardt was shot and killed in what may or may not have been a hunting accident.[5]

Entrusting her newborn son to her parents in Sacramento, Edith returned to Berkeley to work as assistant to the British economist Ernest F. Penrose, known to her as Pen, for whom she had worked briefly as an undergraduate. In 1939, Pen moved to the International Labor Office in Geneva. Edith came with him, taking a position as a researcher. It was during this period that she began honing a craft that would later serve her well. After the war broke out, she and Pen were active in helping Jews—including the economist Ludwig von Mises and his wife[6]—escape to the United States. Before long, ILO staff, including Pen and Edith, were themselves forced to flee across France and Spain to Portugal before returning to North America.

In 1941, John Winant, the head of the ILO (and formerly the first head of the Social Security System), became US ambassador to Britain, bringing Pen along to London as his economic advisor. Once again, Edith came too. Still in her mid-twenties, she would meet and interact with some of the most significant economists of the century, including F. A. Hayek, James Meade,

Lionel Robbins, and Austin Robinson. It was in this environment that she would be exposed to the inner negotiations between John Maynard Keynes and his American counterpart Harry Dexter White that would shape the postwar Bretton Woods monetary structure. After the war, she began working for the newly formed United Nations, where she assisted Eleanor Roosevelt in the writing and passage of the Universal Declaration of Human Rights.

In 1947, Pen accepted a professorship in geography and international relations at Johns Hopkins. Edith, now his wife, enrolled in the graduate program, working with the émigré Austrian economist Fritz Machlup, who had been a student of Mises in Vienna. She received her PhD in 1951, with a dissertation on the international patent system that would be published by Johns Hopkins University Press.[7] (Her central argument was that international arrangements should require compulsory licensing of patents, especially in less-developed countries, and that those countries ought not to be forced to sign international enforcement treaties.) She stayed on at Johns Hopkins to work on another Machlup project—on the growth of firms. But this was the era of the second Red Scare, and Owen Lattimore, a distinguished sinologist at Johns Hopkins, was accused of having been one of the American "China hands" who had "lost" China to communism. The Penroses rose to Lattimore's defense, and Edith became secretary of his defense fund.[8] Although charges against Lattimore were eventually dropped, the Penroses became disillusioned with life in the US, and they began to take gigs outside the country as Pen neared retirement, first in Australia and then in Baghdad.

In 1959, Edith took up a position (soon to become a chair) at the School of Oriental and African Studies of the University of London, moving to INSEAD in Fontainebleau, France, in 1978. Much of her later work focused on the multinational enterprise, especially in the oil industry, with which she had come into contact in Baghdad. She also traveled extensively, especially in the Middle East and Africa. When Pen died in 1984, she retired to Waterbeach in Cambridgeshire, remaining active until her own death in 1996. Indeed, it would not be until after her retirement that Edith Penrose would rise to prominence in the academic world—even if not perhaps in economics.

The Theory of the Growth of the Firm

Along with G. H. Evans, then the head of the economics department at Johns Hopkins, Fritz Machlup had secured a grant from the Merrill Foundation to study the growth of business firms.[9] This was mostly an empirical exercise, but Penrose's role in the project would be to provide the theory. Supported by a grant from the Foundation for Economic Education, she spent the summer of 1954 embedded at the Hercules Powder Company.[10] One of the powder companies spun off in the court-ordered breakup up of DuPont in 1911, Hercules had become a large, successful maker of chemicals and related products. Penrose's understanding of the nature and growth of the firm would spring from this inside view of corporate decision-making.

Having absorbed her mentor's attitude toward economic semantics, she argued that "the firm" has no fixed and unambiguous meaning: the term's definition should depend on the questions being asked.[11] For Penrose, the firm is distinguished from the market in that it is an administrative organization, one whose coherence as an entity emerges from the *collection of productive resources* it employs. The "primary economic function of an industrial firm is to make use of productive resources for the purpose of supplying goods and services to the economy in accordance with plans developed and put into effect within the firm. The essential difference between economic activity inside the firm and economic activity in the 'market' is that the former is carried on within an administrative organization, while the latter is not."[12]

The productive resources within a firm can be tangible or intangible, so long as they are durable resources that continue to generate services over time.[13] Resources thus include not only plant and equipment but even the human capital of the workers themselves, who can be considered durable assets in the sense that the firm suffers a capital loss when knowledgeable workers leave the firm. Workers, including managers, acquire human capital over time in contexts that are specific to each firm, which implies that firms assemble unique bundles of resources: firms inevitably differ from one another in what they know how to do well.[14]

The firm grows to the extent that entrepreneurs—very much including managers within an administrative organization—perceive and seize opportunities to profit from applying the services of the resources the firm has at its disposal. Because resources are lumpy, a firm always has "excess" resources, overheads that it could apply cheaply to new activities. "For the most part, resources are only obtainable in discrete amounts, that is to say, a 'bundle' of services must be acquired even if only a 'single' service should be wanted."[15] This means that the growth of the firm is what we would nowadays call path-dependent: which resources are available at any time for new uses will depend on resources inherited from the past and thus on decisions made in the past. Growth in this model is thus opportunistic. The firm seeks out new profitable activities that can take advantage of existing excess resources. Of course, existing resources may not be adequate or a perfect fit for the new entrepreneurial activity, which means that the firm will have to create new resources in the process of utilizing old resources. These new resources will also be lumpy, and the firm will then look for more opportunities to use these new resources—and the process will proceed indefinitely, rather like assembling a large jigsaw puzzle.

As Penrose realizes, what she has created is in the end a theory of growth through related diversification. Significantly, she sees "relatedness" not in terms of the products or services the firm generates but rather the relatedness of the resources it uses to produce. "Each type of productive activity that uses machines, processes, skills, and raw materials that are complementary and closely associated in the process of production we shall call a 'production base' or 'technological base' of the firm, regardless of the number of types of products produced."[16] A firm can have more than one production base, and each production base can generate many different, seemingly unrelated products in multiple markets. Here is where industrial research comes into the picture. Research is often closely related to existing technological bases, but it generates new resources, which can then be applied to new opportunities.

Sometimes firms develop resources without any clear idea what opportunities might arise to use them. For example, during World War II, Hercules developed a new cellulose gum in an effort to replace a lubricant that had become unavailable.[17] But the firm was sure there would be many other uses. They simply didn't know what those uses would be. So they placed an ad in the trade press challenging potential customers to come up with uses for the product.[18] Soon a wide variety of companies were buying the substance for a wide variety of seemingly unrelated products:

> Thus whether research be originally undertaken merely because the firm is convinced that profitable new opportunities will come out of it, or because it is considered necessary for survival in a competitive world, it enables at least the large firms to turn aside the process of "creative destruction" and to thrive on the novelty which might otherwise have destroyed them.[19]

Penrose and Strategic Management

To the extent that *TGF* had an early influence on the academic literature, it was in the context of the so-called managerial theory of the firm,[20] one of whose main proponents, Robin Marris, was a Penrose acquaintance.[21] In the days when salaried managers rather than stockholders seemed to be in control of the large corporation, this literature attempted to model the discretionary behavior of managers rather than to assume that those managers maximized shareholder value. The work of Penrose entered solely as part of an argument that, because resources could not be instantaneously acquired, management would necessarily become a constraint on the rate of growth of firms—an idea that came to be called the "Penrose effect."[22]

This was also the era in which policy-oriented industrial organization had coalesced around the structure-conduct-performance (SCP) paradigm of antitrust analysis. This approach was sometimes called the Harvard School, in that it emanated from the students of Edward S. Mason, notably Joe Bain[23] and his student and colleague Richard Caves.[24] The SCP paradigm envisaged market competition as a process in which firms constantly position themselves to earn rents in product markets by various strategies that effectively throw up barriers to entry. In one of the most significant moves in the history of management theory, Michael Porter, a student of Caves, flipped the script of the SCP paradigm: if economists could analyze strategic positioning and barriers to entry for purposes of antitrust, why couldn't management scholars—and consultants—use the same ideas to instruct managers in how to use to their advantage these very same forms of strategic positioning and barriers to entry?[25] Porter's "five forces" quickly became a dominant approach to strategic management.

Yet the 1980s were a period in which American firms were being pummeled by foreign competition and technological innovation. Mere strategic positioning in product markets seemed to be of little avail. Indeed, one of the lessons of Japanese competition seemed to be not that the Japanese were better strategists but that they were simply better at making high-quality, low-cost products. Thus, when in 1984—the year of Penrose's retirement—Birger Wernerfelt proposed an alternative to Porter that came to be called the Resource-Based View (RBV) of the firm, it instantly struck a responsive chord.[26] Drawing explicitly on Penrose, Wernerfelt argued that managers and management theorists should worry less about positioning in product markets and pay attention instead to their underlying resources—Penrose's production bases—as a source of competitive advantage. The RBV came to dominate thinking in strategic management, as managers were told in no uncertain terms to turn inward to the supply side—to stick to their knitting and build their "core competences." And Edith Penrose became the guiding light of strategic management theory.

As a number of authors have pointed out, however, despite the footnotes and references lavished upon Penrose by the RBV, in the end that approach actually incorporates surprisingly little of what was novel in Penrose and strays far less than advertised from mainstream economics or even from the Harvard School.[27] The principal objective of the RBV strategist is to profit from differential rents accruing to superior factors of production whose services are not easily imitated by others.[28] Although RBV theorists do see a heterogeneity among resources and differences in the costs of acquiring and protecting them, they "forget that it is the actual application in production, and not the mere possession, of resources that creates revenue."[29] The RBV became a theory of how to manipulate existing knowledge bases to advantage and not—like that of Penrose—an account of the nature and creation of knowledge bases.

Penrose, Chandler, and Richardson

The ideas of Penrose also made their way into business schools along a quite different path. Not long after Penrose had spent time at Hercules, Alfred Chandler, then an associate professor of history at MIT, was asked to work with Alfred P. Sloan, the recently retired head of General Motors, on what would be Sloan's second autobiography, *My Years with General Motors*. Chandler had already begun to theorize about the nature and structure of the American corporation,[30] an inclination that set him apart from the antiquarian style of contemporary business historiography and set him on the path to create the modern field of business history. Working with Sloan, Chandler had access to the GM archives.[31] The result was his first major work, *Strategy and Structure* (1962), which both chronicled and theorized about the multidivisional (or M-form) structure at firms like GM and DuPont. Only when the book was near publication did Chandler become aware of Penrose and *TGF*:

> While using somewhat different data and asking somewhat different questions, Dr. Penrose's findings have many similarities with mine. Her superlative study focuses on the economics of growth and not on structure and on its relation to strategy. My empirical data, however, certainly do help to support her theoretical concepts about the growth of the firm which are defined more rigorously than the more impressionistic generalizations developed here.[32]

The Penrosean theory of the growth of the firm would be at the heart of Chandler's *magnum opus*, *The Visible Hand* (1977), which narrates the growth of the large multiunit enterprise in the nineteenth and twentieth centuries and interprets that growth as deeply connected to the rise of the professional manager. Although Chandler thinks that the large firms sometimes took on new activities for "defensive" reasons—reasons not unlike those envisaged by the later RBV—he focuses principally on "productive" diversification, which involves precisely the process Penrose described: "Because the large integrated industrial had more and different types of operating units than other kinds of business enterprises, the likelihood that units might be underutilized was greater. It was rare for all units in such an enterprise to be operating at the same speed and capacity. Such disequilibrium provided constant pressure for the growth of the firm."[33] Here Chandler footnotes Penrose and *TGF*.

Another important figure deeply influenced by Penrose was George Richardson—himself an unjustly neglected economist who might well have merited his own place in this volume.[34] In "The Organisation of Industry," Richardson argued that "production has to be undertaken (as Mrs. Penrose has so very well explained) by human organisations embodying specifically appropriate experience and skill." In his view, "we cannot hope to construct an adequate theory of industrial organization and in particular to answer our question about the division of labour between firm and market, unless the elements of organisation, knowledge, experience and skills are brought back to the foreground of our vision."[35] What Penrose had called *resources*, Richardson calls *capabilities*, the "knowledge, experience, and skills" of the firm.

Unlike Penrose, Richardson explicitly considers ways of creating and coordinating capabilities *outside* of the structure of the firm. Years earlier Ronald Coase had considered markets and firms as alternative ways of coordinating economic activity,[36] even if in 1972 his ideas remained "much cited and little used."[37] A central thrust of Richardson's argument is that market actors have at their disposal a wide array of coordinating mechanisms—what we would now think of as relational contracts and hybrid organizational forms—that lie between the ideal types of the anonymous market on the one hand and the managerial enterprise on the other.

In Richardson's capabilities account of economic organization, capabilities can be either *similar* or *complementary*. (They can also be completely unrelated, of course.) Capabilities are similar when the knowledge, experience, and skills useful in activity A could be cheaply adapted to activity B. This is the fundamental idea in the Penrose-Chandler account of related diversification. But along a chain of production, capabilities are necessarily complementary to each other—even if they are quite dissimilar. (A simple example: the woodworking skills needed to make rifle stocks are dissimilar from the metalworking skills necessary to turn the barrels; but they are complementary in that both sets of skills are necessary to making rifles.) "Where activities were both similar and complementary," Richardson wrote, "they could be co-ordinated by direction within an individual business. Generally, however, this would not be the case and the activities to be co-ordinated, being dissimilar, would be the responsibility of different firms. Co-ordination would then have to be brought about either through co-operation, firms agreeing to match their plans ex ante, or through the processes of adjustment set in train by the market mechanism."[38] As Brian Loasby put it, we need both a theory of growth and a theory of coordination, and the use and accumulation of idiosyncratic knowledge must be the raw materials of both.[39]

The idea of capabilities—and eventually of "dynamic" capabilities—would also find its way into management and strategy as a development of the resource-based approach.[40] Yet, despite adopting Richardson's terminology, this approach would be influenced to some extent by Penrose but essentially not at all by Richardson. A conception of capabilities fundamentally similar to that of Richardson would be reinvented through another channel.

Penrose and Economics

In the middle of the twentieth century, economist Richard Lester sent questionnaires to American firms asking them if they behaved the way the basic neoclassical model predicted, that is, whether they set price equal to marginal cost. Almost all the respondents said no; many had no idea what marginal cost meant. We set price by simply adding a markup to what we pay for our inputs, Lester was told. Not surprisingly, this ignited a heated response from mainstream economists, in what came to be called the marginalist controversy.[41] In the forefront of the response was Fritz Machlup, who would later summarize his defense of marginal analysis in a presidential address to the American Economic Association.[42]

Another economist who had entered the fray was Armen Alchian.[43] Suppose, said Alchian, that thousands of motorists set out from Chicago on a variety of different routes. Suppose also that there are gas stations on only one of the routes. We can safely predict that only motorists who happened to pick the route with gas stations will get very far. But we can be assured in our prediction not because we assumed any of the motorists consciously selected the best route; rather, the lucky motorists were themselves selected by the impersonal forces of the environment. What looks like fully informed rational choice is really Darwinian selection.

There were two responses to Alchian's idea (and to related defenses of marginalism). The dominant response was to breathe a sigh of relief: because there is a Darwinian mechanism operating in the background, we can stop worrying and go on with our optimizing models as usual. Milton Friedman held that "given natural selection, acceptance of the [maximizing] hypothesis can be based largely on the judgment that it summarizes appropriately the conditions for survival."[44] But there was another response, rarer and more interesting. If what really lies behind economic activity is some kind of selection mechanism, then perhaps we should pay much more attention to analyzing how that mechanism works.

In a comment on Alchian's selection argument, Penrose pointed out that in biological evolution, selection operates on traits that can reproduce themselves.[45] But in the story about drivers dispersing from Chicago, there is no reproduction. If another thousand drivers leave again the next day, they have retained no information from the previous day and are on average no better at finding gas stations than the drivers the day before. In an important sense, rational economic agents are also much like Alchian's drivers. They too have no persistence of memory; they take each day afresh as they search for a new optimal solution. But for selection to operate, there has to be at least some stickiness, some repetitiveness of behavior. As Sidney Winter put it, "to make a 'natural selection' argument plausible in economics, some mechanism playing the role of genetic inheritance must be discovered."[46]

An obvious candidate model, already long aired within social science, would be to suppose that economic agents follow rules. Rules are sticky almost by definition; and rules, or something very like them, might be a good candidate for the genetic element in an evolutionary story. In the 1950s and 1960s, the arrival of the digital computer made the rule-following model all the more salient. Influenced by the computer—and indeed interwoven with the field of computer science—the Carnegie School of Richard Cyert, James March, Herbert Simon, and others proposed accounts of rule-like human behavior.[47] Simon famously argued that humans are subject to severe cognitive limitations that make it impossible for them constantly to optimize in any strong sense. Humans are "boundedly rational," Simon suggested, and as a result they must often "satisfice" rather than optimize.[48] And satisficing typically means the following of rules in a world too complex for nonstop optimization.

Influenced by the Carnegie School, Richard Nelson and Sidney Winter painted a sophisticated portrait of an evolutionary approach to economics. In their account, both individual agents and organizations follow *routines*, which are rule-like forms of behavior. The forces of selection then operate on the routines, which serve as the analogue of genetic material: routines are genes.[49] Organizations thus appear as a collection of routines—of ways of doing things—that exist independently of the individual personnel who follow the routines. An automobile assembly plant, for example, continues to operate—and learn—even as workers come and go.[50] For Nelson and Winter, routines are organizational memory, "the organizational analogue of individual skill."[51] Like Richardson, they called these organizational skills *capabilities*.[52]

As Nelson and Winter were developing their version of capabilities theory in the 1970s, economists were also beginning to use Coase's little-used 1937 paper. At the forefront of this revival was Oliver Williamson.[53] Williamson too was influenced by the Carnegie School. He had been a doctoral student at Carnegie during the first years of the 1960s, a time of great interdisciplinary intellectual ferment.[54] This experience had initially led him to become one of the early practitioners of the managerial theory of the firm.[55] But his interests soon turned in a Coasean direction. Just as Coase had seen the firm as arising because of limitations to the market—"a cost of using the price mechanism"[56]—Williamson saw the firm as arising because of the limits and complexities of market transactions.

David Teece, a student and colleague of Williamson, was among the first to attempt to bring these two lines of research together—to connect the Nelson-and-Winter account of the capabilities of firm, with a dash of Penrose, to the Coase-Williamson account of the boundaries of the firm.[57] As had happened with Penrose, however, this new instantiation of the theory of capabilities found its home in business schools far more readily than in economics departments.

Clearly, the work of Penrose made little inroads in economics because it challenged conventional models of the firm. In her foreword to the third edition of *TGF* in 1995, a time by which she had attained prominence in related realms of the academy, Penrose seemed willing to cast herself as something of a critic of the economists' model of the firm. "Few economists thought it necessary to enquire what happened inside the firm—and indeed their 'firm' had no 'insides' so to speak."[58] Yet she believed that it was not useful to "integrate" the two approaches. Famously, she held, theorists should tend their own gardens.[59]

Many have found it ironic that Fritz Machlup, who championed the marginalist firm against its detractors, was Penrose's close friend and mentor. It is a "fascinating paradox."[60] Of course, tending one's own garden was part of

Machlup's worldview as well. More fundamentally, however, Machlup was not defending the hardcore Walrasian model of the firm that was becoming increasingly central as the twentieth century wore on. He was defending the kind of common-sensical price theory we teach to freshmen.[61] Brought up in the Austrian tradition, Machlup had as his marginalist lodestar Carl Menger, not Léon Walras.

Indeed, we might see both Machlup and Penrose as Marshallians in a loose sense. Brian Loasby has made this argument compellingly for Penrose and Richardson:

> The central notion is a combination of Smith and Marshall: the division of labour, both within and between firms, leads to the development of skills and the perception of possibilities, while firms within a similar line of business will develop somewhat different skills and perceptions. Enterprise grows out of management, as Say and Marshall had argued; and it is driven by human purpose, seeking to discover and exploit causal relationships by producing new goods for new markets, in accordance with Menger's theory.[62]

14

Warren Nutter

Dissident Statistician of the Soviet Economy

Phillip W. Magness

FOR MUCH OF the twentieth century, leading figures of the American academy looked upon the Soviet Union's economic performance with what may be legitimately described as a sense of credulous envy. According to David Levy and Sandra Peart, the sudden collapse of the Soviet Union in 1991 "surprised many western students of economics in part because its economy had long been portrayed in textbooks as a viable alternative to democratic capitalism."[1]

Although it was a smaller economy than the United States, the Soviets' official numbers consistently projected a growth rate that would soon overtake their Cold War rival and, in doing so, validate the claimed inevitability of the socialist economic system on which it was built. Even as American economists rejected the Marxist philosophy behind Soviet planning, they settled into a curious postwar habit of disseminating economic projections that depicted the Soviet economy overtaking the United States in the near future.

Beginning with the 1961 edition of his bestselling economics textbook, Paul Samuelson included a graphic displaying the comparative growth rates of the American and Soviet economies. Per this forecast, the Soviet gross national product would overtake the United States at some point between twenty-three and thirty-six years in the future. Curiously, by the 1980 edition of the textbook this same graph had shifted forward by two decades so that the point of projected intersection would still take place between twenty-two and thirty-two years in the future. Similar claims appeared in competitor

Phillip W. Magness is senior fellow and David J. Theroux Chair in Political Economy at Independent Institute.

textbooks from the time and generally transferred over into the specialist literature on the Soviet economy as well.[2]

For many decades prior, economist G. Warren Nutter (1923–79) provided one of the lone dissenting voices to challenge what had become a matter of conventional wisdom among Sovietologists. Whereas others perceived vibrancy and vitality in the socialist society's industrial growth, Nutter recognized its long-term economic decline concealed behind a politically crafted veneer of propaganda about socialist industrial prowess. From 1956 onward, Nutter labored on providing a statistical corrective to the official Soviet numbers that painted a picture of a society gradually succumbing to the weight of its own central planning and the wasteful accretions of a graft-riddled and politically repressive bureaucracy.[3]

Nutter's conclusions sent a shockwave through the academic establishment. Appearing almost concurrently with Soviet leader Nikita Khrushchev's declaration to Western ambassadors that "we will bury you," they defied not only the optimistic economic assessments of the Soviet Union on the sympathetic Left, but also the military rationales for ramping up the American defense industry to meet the coming Soviet challenge. Henry Hazlitt was among the first to recognize the implications of Nutter's empirical work, writing in *Newsweek* in 1957 that "far from there being any 'miracle' of Communist production, the lands behind the Iron Curtain are going through an economic crisis," as per Nutter's statistics.[4] Hazlitt, and by implication Nutter's data, came under fire from economist Rendigs Fels in his 1961 book *The Challenge to the American Economy*. Per Fels, the Nutter "results are in striking contradiction to the figures cited" in his own book, which "proved that Communist output grows twice as fast as American." Fels attributed the difference to ideological bias, because, in his words, "Hazlitt is a stronger believer in capitalism and a vigorous critic of any other economic system."[5] Similar assessments from the period ranged from polite dismissiveness to outright attacks on his work. As his student Steven H. Hanke later recalled, "Nutter's findings flew in the face of virtually all the works by Sovietologists and economists, including Paul Samuelson and John Kenneth Galbraith," but "Nutter was cool, tough, and loved to swim against the tide."[6] In fact, Nutter had scooped the field and accurately identified an economy with deep structural problems—most of them directly traceable to its destruction of a functional price mechanism through the tools of state management.

Nutter's assessment was no abstraction, but rather the result of years of close study of the relationship between state policy and industrial concentration in the United States—the subject of his dissertation at the University of Chicago. But he also possessed an uncommonly keen eye for extracting observations from his surroundings. He deployed the latter during a twenty-eight-day visit to the Soviet Union in 1956 as a self-described "tourist" researcher, which he juxtaposed against other American experts whose longer visits occurred under the heavy scrutiny and management of handlers from the Soviet government.[7] Whereas others largely picked up on what the Soviets wanted them to see and incorporated curated factory tours and contrived statistical claims into their assessments, Nutter apparently had a knack for discerning beneath the surface from everyday observations of his surroundings—simply by keeping an eye on the types of goods in the shop window, the patterns of workers entering the factory in the background, and the way that the people he encountered described even the most mundane economic transactions of their daily lives.[8]

From Chicago to Virginia

Gilbert Warren Nutter came from a humble background. Born in Topeka, Kansas, in 1923 to a Jewish mother who was widowed around the time of his birth, Nutter grew up in tight economic circumstances. His small family migrated around the Depression-era rural Midwest in search of stable income, eventually settling in Iowa. A promising student, he received a break to attend the University of Chicago, where he came under the mentorship of the economist Henry Simons as an undergraduate.

Nutter's path to completing his studies encountered an unexpected diversion with the United States' entry into World War II. He served in an infantry unit in the European theater, earning a Bronze Star in combat during the invasion of Europe. The fierce combat of the war's final months put him in the direct line of fire more than once. He directly witnessed the horrifying revelations that came with the liberation of the Nazi concentration camps as his unit advanced into Germany. The horrors of Hitler's death camps haunted him for the remainder of his life. He seldom detailed what he witnessed, but he referenced the event as an ever-present reminder of the evils that a tyrannical government was capable of committing.

During his wartime service, Nutter exhibited an autodidactic skill at learning foreign languages—reportedly with a near-perfect ability to replicate accents as if a native speaker. This skill would serve him well over his career, initially by bringing him to the attention of Army intelligence, where he completed a brief stint after the surrender of Germany.

He returned to Chicago after the war with an intention of completing an economics degree and continuing to his graduate studies under Simons, then working on monetary theory. Simons's untimely death in 1946 nearly derailed Nutter's continuation on this trajectory until law professor Aaron Director, a mentor of sorts from his studies, brought him under the guidance of a newly hired economics professor by the name of Milton Friedman. Graduating in 1949, Nutter became Friedman's first doctoral student to enter into academic life. After a brief stint on the economics faculty at Yale, he soon settled at the University of Virginia in 1956. The move to UVA apparently came about through connections to Rutledge Vining, a fellow Chicago graduate who studied under Nutter's former teacher Frank Knight.[9] The somewhat irascible Vining facilitated the dual-recruitment of Nutter and his Chicago classmate James M. Buchanan, then at Florida State University, to invigorate a Chicago-style economic research program following the retirement of longtime department chair Tipton Snavely. Buchanan and Nutter would alternate as chair over the next decade. Of equal significance, they cofounded the Thomas Jefferson Center for the Study of Political Economy—a research unit affiliated with the department that recruited an all-star lineup of faculty, including Ronald Coase, Gordon Tullock, and Leland Yeager.

Shortly after their arrival, Nutter and Buchanan found themselves pulled into Virginia's tumultuous debates over education policy in the civil rights era. In 1956, the state's segregationist political establishment, under the machine of US Senator Harry Flood Byrd Sr., vowed "massive resistance" to the 1954 *Brown v. Board of Education* ruling by the Supreme Court. Byrd's strategy involved non-compliance with Court-ordered school desegregation by shuttering the affected public schools and transferring their students and funding to private "segregation academies" that, in his mind, stood a better chance at resisting the courts and maintaining segregation. One of the first major tests of Byrd's strategy came in 1958, when Charlottesville's school system responded to an integration order by shuttering Venable Elementary School.

Along with many UVA faculty families, Nutter's children attended Venable. Unwilling to send them to the private "segregation academy" favored by the Byrd machine, Nutter and a group of other professors set up the Parents Committee for Emergency Schooling and began operating a makeshift classroom for the affected students in the basement of his home. While the Nutter classroom was just one of several operated by UVA faculty for their children, it became the showcase in a national media story about the fallout from the school closures. Reporters from Washington descended on their street in a quiet suburban neighborhood, and CBS news showcased the basement classroom on its national broadcast. To his academic friends, Nutter quipped that he had accidentally stumbled into running a school system upon moving to Virginia.[10]

After the courts struck down the "Massive Resistance" laws in early 1959, Byrd and other segregationist hardliners vowed to press on by defying the courts. Nutter recognized an alternative path to attack the segregationists' flank by enlisting a proposal associated with his mentor Milton Friedman: school vouchers. Collaborating with Buchanan as his coauthor, they drafted a short paper on how a voucher or tuition grant system would operate in Virginia.[11] Friedman's earlier writings on this subject made the case that vouchers could become a potent economic weapon against segregated schooling by allowing parents the option of transferring their children to different schools for almost any reason of their choosing.[12] Friedman predicted that, in time, competition and moral suasion would cause integrated schools to grow at the expense of segregated schools. He reasoned that integrated schools had a competitive incentive to make classroom offerings more appealing to a larger base of students. By contrast, segregated schools would dwindle away with the loss of students from competition, eventually becoming uneconomical to operate.

Between the court rulings against "Massive Resistance" and the unpopularity of school closures, Byrd overplayed his hand and created an opening for a political realignment in Richmond. A group of moderate "cushioners," who wished to constrain the implementation of *Brown* to a gradual pace, found new common ground with desegregationists from the Washington, DC, suburbs in the form of a tuition grant measure. In early 1959 this coalition outflanked the Byrd machine and jettisoned the previous school closure policies.

Nutter and Buchanan recognized the unfolding events as a chance to test Friedman's theory in action and published a statistical report in 1965 examining the operation of the program. The report, as well as the immediate context of Nutter's experience during the school closure period, provides further evidence of their objectives. The two economists had little patience for the segregationist maneuvers of the "Massive Resistance" movement, contrary to certain recent claims.[13] Their 1965 report on the tuition grant program calls attention to a peculiar anti-voucher alliance that emerged between segregationist hardliners and Virginia's largest teacher's union, the Virginia Education Association (VEA).[14] Nutter knew the architect of this alliance, Charlottesville attorney John S. Battle Jr., as the segregationists' legal counsel during the school closure episode of 1958. By targeting the VEA for this specific criticism, the economists signaled their own expectation that the voucher system would erode segregation through economic competition.

Echoing Friedman's arguments from the other side, Battle predicted that tuition grants would undermine "informal" segregationist efforts to prevent integration by capping student enrollments. According to Battle, the swapping of schools by grant recipients for any reason would open up seats in classrooms, leading to the "negro engulfment" of previously all-white schools. In no small irony, Battle's objections to the program vindicated Friedman's prediction that vouchers would lead to greater integration.

As the tuition grant study revealed, Nutter had an interest in the policy applications of economic principles. He differed somewhat from his coauthor Buchanan on this margin. Whereas Buchanan would occasionally comment on current events, most of his energy went into dense theoretical works on the economics of the public sector. Nutter remained adjacent to the nascent Public Choice subfield that was developing around him at Virginia, and he clearly shared overlapping interests. At the same time, his own research had more conventional policy applications, including operating directly within the American political system. Nutter's first national political foray came in 1964 when Republican presidential candidate Barry Goldwater tapped him as an economic policy adviser and writer for the campaign. He was more conventionally conservative than Buchanan and joined Friedman as an early member of the Philadelphia Society, a debating organization at the heart of the 1960s Fusionist political movement uniting traditional conservatism, anti-communism, and free-market economics.

While Goldwater lost the election, temporarily thwarting a likely appointment of Nutter to an economic advisory position in the White House, he had another chance before the decade's end. In 1969, President Richard Nixon appointed Nutter as Assistant Secretary of Defense for international security affairs, where he applied his knowledge of the Soviet Union to Cold War–era efforts to contain the spread of communism. He resigned this position in 1973 to return to teaching at Virginia, although with a very different department. Coase, Tullock, and Buchanan each departed amid a long-running spat with UVA president Edgar Shannon and Robert Harris, the dean of Arts and Sciences. Although the department produced an impressive record of research in top scholarly outlets and developed a nationally respected PhD program, the university's administrators—and particularly Harris—took issue with its philosophical persuasion. Under Nutter and Buchanan's alternative chairmanships, the economics department often bucked the orthodoxies of mid-century Keynesian theory. The central office retaliated by restricting their budget, denying promotions, and disparaging individual faculty behind their backs. By the end of the decade, only Nutter and Yeager remained from the core group that founded the Virginia Political Economy tradition.

Measuring Marxism

Despite his foray into politics, Nutter's most enduring contribution remains his efforts to measure the Soviet economy. Later revelations vindicated his specific conclusions about the Soviets' exaggerated growth claims, but the most enduring contributions came from Nutter's innovative techniques for gathering and evaluating data in the presence of intentional Soviet obfuscation. He accordingly produced what is arguably the most comprehensive and well-rounded assessment of the Soviet economy to emerge from the Cold War.

Nutter had no formal training in Russian and does not appear to have claimed fluency, describing his 1956 tour as having taken place "under the severe handicap of not knowing the language."[15] Yet Nutter's language skills, as cultivated in the US Army during the liberation of Europe a little over a decade prior, again came into play. In reading his travelogue, one gathers that he may have gleaned more from observing the surrounding conversations than he let on—or that, importantly, his Soviet guides realized at the time. His colleagues and family members would later recount seeing Russian-language periodicals on his bookshelves, and his knowledge of the Soviet Union's economy, culture, and daily life are readily apparent in his scholarly works.

Following his visit, Nutter embarked on a multiyear project of compiling a more reliable measurement of the Soviet economy than the communist government's sources permitted. His work culminated in a statistical compendium drawn from data sampling at the industry level, unofficial indicators, and observation. "It has been said that the Soviet Union is more than a mystery," Nutter observed in framing his study, "it is a secret." The country lacked "a coherent body of relevant and reliable statistics" owing to gaps in the historical record, inconsistent measurements, and above all, the political incentives that distorted Soviet statistical reporting. As he further notes, "No government or other statistical agency can be relied upon to resist the temptation to stretch figures to its own account if it feels it can get away with it."[16] Locked in a geopolitical contest with the West, the Soviet Union faced every temptation to do just that. Per Nutter's evaluation, "Centralized authoritarian direction of the economy thus generates forces with opposing effects on the reliability of statistics."[17]

To overcome these challenges, Nutter and his colleagues gathered official Soviet statistics at the industry level, deducing that economic sectors with greater importance to political objectives, such as Stalin's industrialization plans, would also have finer-grained data. They further reasoned that aggregated measures of Soviet output, which arguably carried the greatest political implications, also suffered from greater ambiguity and opportunity for political distortion. Aggregate claims about Soviet output therefore tended to exaggerate growth more than narrow data for a specific and closely reported product. Even these data suffered from overreporting at intermediate stages of production, as incentivized by a statistical collection system that rewarded exaggerated claims to meet or exceed the government's production quotas. Year-over-year output totals almost invariably trended upward across most reported industries. By contrast, "poor performance is habitually masked by silence or evasion."[18]

To grapple with these issues, Nutter and his team divided the Soviet economy into specific sectors and products where data existed. They paid particular attention to reported patterns in final goods and their inputs from intermediate stages of production. Using industry-specific data from the United States, where more reliable and comprehensive numbers existed, they could then perform comparative analysis to approximate plausible ranges of finished production. To approximate growth over time, they constructed sector-specific weighted indexes from reported output statistics and used price averages to calculate approximate values. This incomplete sampling of sectors and industries nonetheless gave them a basis to impute other missing and unreported industries. This gave them a means to approximate the size of larger sectors of the Soviet economy over time, leading to their own aggregation. As anticipated, official Soviet aggregations dramatically outpaced Nutter's estimates based on their components.

Working with Israel Borenstein and Adam Kaufman, Nutter published this work with the National Bureau of Economic Research in 1962. Despite drawing multiple detractors from Sovietologists at the time, the book offers a model for making empirical inferences in the absence of reliable economic data. Similar approaches continue to have applications today, not only in other closed economies but also in historical work that predates modern national accounting practices and data availability.

Nutter's interest in the Soviet Union would continue for most of his academic career. In 1969 he turned his attention to the more practical matter of daily life under a socialist system of government. The result was *The Strange World of Ivan Ivanov*, a short yet hard-hitting indictment of the economic and political repression that so often follows from attempts to structure a society around Marxist ideology and centralized economic planning. Nutter began his work on *Ivan Ivanov* in 1967 as part of a debate with the Marxist historian Herbert Aptheker at the University of Western Ontario. As was a common theme at the time, Aptheker enlisted the history of racial segregation in the

United States to build a sweeping indictment of "capitalism" as an economic system, including assigning it blame for inculcating racial and other forms of discrimination. Nutter's rejoinder, "I choose capitalism," contains the starting point of his larger qualitative project on life under a Marxist regime.

The retort to Aptheker did not shy from confronting the problem of racism in the United States. Yet as Nutter explained, discrimination appeared to be a persistent curse of the human condition. Far from solving this problem, the socialist approach of the Soviets had actually systematized it into the instruments of the state. Noting that state action carries with it a far greater degree of coercive power, Nutter reframed the question of discrimination by asking his audience to judge a society on whether it availed the individual of a means to escape the very same instruments. In the Soviet Union, state policy had become a means of carrying out anti-Semitic and other ethnic persecutions under the guise of economic redistribution, property appropriation, and even genocidal persecutions and famines. Though Nutter avoided implicating his opponent by name, Aptheker himself had weathered the Stalin years as an apologist for the Soviet state's most notorious atrocities.

The cheerful depictions of life under socialism from the Marxist intellectual amounted to a political deception. They entailed a false comparison between an idealized form of egalitarian socioeconomic organization, as proposed on the far Left but never realized, and the observed faults of Western capitalism as it existed. Aptheker was comparing a constructed fantasy to a disliked reality—and declaring that fantasy the victor on account of its unrealized promises. Yet as Nutter stressed, the reality of life under socialism often reduced those under it to abject impoverishment and immiseration.

Far from being "solved" by socialism's promises, discrimination on ethnic and religious lines, along with deeply inegalitarian political distributions of resources and power, were endemic features of the Soviet system. Even as these features also manifested in the West through private and state-sanctioned discrimination, capitalism itself was an escape mechanism to the very same problems that the Soviet state, through its absolute and uncontested control of social life, denied. A socialist economy is inescapably dependent upon political mechanisms to allocate scarce resources, whereas a capitalist society offers an escape from politics through voluntary market exchange.

Shortly after the debate, Nutter shared a written transcript of his comments with William F. Buckley, indicating he would likely "toss them in the wastebasket" if the conservative editor of *National Review* could find no use for them.[19] Nutter's papers contain few clues as to why he changed his heart, but within a year's time he had expanded the transcript into a series of lectures on how the Soviet government treated its ordinary citizens. He delivered one version the following year at a conference for the American Bar Association.[20] At some point shortly thereafter, David Appel, a features editor at the *Philadelphia Inquirer*, approached the economist about developing the theme into a multipart series on daily life in the Soviet Union. Nutter composed ten articles for the paper, drawing on the previous two decades of his research and developing its implications for Ivan Ivanov, a generic Soviet counterpart to the American John Doe. After the series ran in March of 1968, he compiled its contents and edited them into a standalone manuscript.

Nutter's assessments of the Soviet economy offered not only empirical and qualitative analysis, but a warning to the world. The poverty, fear, and coerced subordination of Ivan Ivanov's life were not aberrations of a socialist revolution gone astray—they were the entirely predictable results of that same socialist system. And as socialism's human toll stretches from the Eastern Bloc to China to Cuba to Venezuela, its results continue to repeat with alarming certainty whenever and wherever it is attempted.

Reviving an Interrupted Legacy

The dissolution of the Soviet Union, membership in a star-studded faculty that included two future Nobel prize winners, and an untimely death from cancer in 1979 have somewhat overshadowed Nutter's own substantial résumé as a scholar. Curiously, as we mark three decades since the fall of the Berlin Wall, the primary subject of his scholarship is attaining renewed significance.

Political calls for socialism have regained a sense of fashionability on the far Left. Rehabilitated by academics and activists who present themselves as "democratic" expositors of centralized planning, practitioners of the modern, euphemized versions of Marxism are all too eager to dissociate their brand from its notorious and deadly twentieth-century iterations. Thus the recent two hundredth anniversary of Karl Marx's birth was met with an outpouring of editorials and academic commentaries celebrating the claimed relevance of the discredited philosopher's theories for "solving" income inequality, climate change, and a slew of similar progressive political tropes in the present day. Echoes of the Soviet Union's self-aggrandizing statistical claims continue to reverberate in the practices of the Chinese Communist Party's self-reported economic successes, and even more acutely in China's outlandish official claims of having reduced COVID-19 cases to zero through the dystopian lockdown regimes of 2020. Nicolas Maduro, the Marxist dictator of Venezuela from 2013 to 2026, has similarly enlisted data manipulation as a primary propaganda technique, ranging from implausible claims of extravagant growth in his country's faltering economy to the manufacturing of alternative election results to sustain his own tenure in office. We have entered into a new era of economic data manipulation, linked to the same brand of unfree regimes. Warren Nutter gave us the techniques and tools to meet this challenge in the international arena.

Acknowledgments: This essay is adapted and expanded from the introduction to the fiftieth-anniversary edition of Warren Nutter, *The Strange World of Ivan Ivanov* (American Institute for Economic Research, 2019). The author thanks Coleman Nutter for sharing several reminiscences about his father that informed this essay and opened new avenues of research.

15 Israel M. Kirzner and the Entrepreneurial Market Process

An Appreciation

Rosolino Candela

ISRAEL M. KIRZNER, more than any other economist in the post–World War II era, has revived our understanding of the systemic role of the entrepreneur as the driving force of open and competitive markets, understood as a process of discovery, error correction, and learning. During his prolific career, his contributions to the theory of capital and interest, economic methodology, history of economic thought, and, especially, the economics and ethics of entrepreneurship, have been integral to reviving the Austrian school of economics in the tradition of Carl Menger, Eugen von Böhm-Bawerk, Friedrich Wieser, Ludwig von Mises, and F. A. Hayek. The implications of his work have also been crucial in reframing our understanding of the roles of antitrust,[1] advertising,[2] and distributive justice[3] in the market process.

Indeed, Kirzner's work has been recognized and applied not only in economic theory but also in the study of entrepreneurship, business economics, and economic management, for which he was awarded the International Award for Entrepreneurship and Small Business Research in 2006.[4] True to his own understanding of his work, Kirzner was puzzled at being so honored, given that his scholarship explains that the source of economic development can be found in the entrepreneurial market process but that this research *cannot* explain the secrets of successful entrepreneurship itself.[5] Upon being

---

Rosolino Candela is senior fellow in the F. A. Hayek Program for Advanced Study in Philosophy, Politics, and Economics and program director of academic and student programs at the Mercatus Center at George Mason University. He is also research fellow at Independent Institute.

awarded the International Award, Kirzner made a point of acknowledging the influence of Mises on his scholarship: "I have always emphasized that my own contribution is simply an expansion and deepening of insights articulated by my teacher, Ludwig von Mises."[6] However, Kirzner has done more than just expand and deepen the insights of Mises. The hallmark of Kirzner's scholarship has been to take his inspiration from Mises and develop his own unique appreciation of the entrepreneurial market process, not for the purpose of illustrating where mainstream economic theory of his time had gone wrong per se, but to explain why its focus on equilibrium states painted an *incomplete* picture of the market process.

In spite of a growing awareness of the importance of the role of the entrepreneur in economic theory, the importance of Kirznerian entrepreneurship to understanding the market process remains relatively neglected. To the extent that entrepreneurial explanations enter into the dynamics of the market process, the predominant account is one that was first expounded by Joseph Schumpeter.[7] Before providing an overview of the importance of Kirzner's scholarship, I will first outline the intellectual context within which Kirzner entered the academic profession and explain how Kirzner's contributions remain underappreciated. In doing so, I hope to establish the significance of Kirzner's analysis to understanding the entrepreneurial market process as well as its continued relevance.

According to Kirzner, the year 1954 marked a professional turning point in his life. Upon completing his undergraduate studies at Brooklyn College, Kirzner enrolled in the MBA program at New York University (NYU), initially aiming to pursue a career in accounting. However, while searching for courses to take in fulfilling the requirements for his MBA, which he completed in 1955, he enrolled in a course with Ludwig von Mises. It was taking Mises's course that led Kirzner to decide to pursue a PhD in economics, completed in 1957 under the supervision of Mises. Upon earning his PhD, Kirzner joined the faculty of NYU, where he spent the entirety of his academic career.

It was also during this time that, in spite of the work of classical economists and, later, early neoclassicals, such as Frank Knight and Joseph Schumpeter, who had explicated the dynamic function of the entrepreneur in the marketplace, the role of the entrepreneur had been all but rendered into obscurity by the mid–twentieth century. This was a result of the preoccupation with analyzing markets as an equilibrium state of affairs rather than processes of equilibration. One way in which to situate the importance of Kirzner's seminal contributions is in terms stated by his student Don Lavoie: "Mainstream economics, according to Kirzner, is not so much wrong as simply incomplete."[8] Building on this point, the work of Kirzner is a critical juncture in the history of economic thought, first by rendering explicit what had been implicit in classical economics, and then by reinserting what had been left behind as a consequence of the marginal revolution: the entrepreneurial element of human action as the basis for equilibrating market processes in an open-ended world of uncertainty.

From Kirzner's standpoint, the market process, as understood by classical political economists, was not so much flawed as it was simply incomplete in its explication of entrepreneurship and the role that pure entrepreneurial profits play in driving the market as a competitive process of discovery. Kirzner elaborated as follows:

> The volume of *pure* profit won by entrepreneurs surely refers to only a small fraction of capitalist "profits" in the broad sense of the word used by the classical economists (and especially by Marx). It is no accident, it could be conjectured, that pure profit did not loom more importantly in the classic discussions of capitalist justice; the phenomenon was simply not important enough.[9]

This early neoclassical period, pioneered by William Stanley Jevons, Carl Menger, and Léon Walras, was distinct from the preceding period of classical political economy because of a gradual receding of institutional analysis into the background of economic theory. What would emerge in the foreground of economic analysis during this period was *the study of price formation and adjustment* based on subjective marginal utility. However, the preoccupation with proving the existence, stability, and uniqueness of competitive equilibrium in markets, as had been pursued by Nobel laureate Kenneth Arrow[10] (as well as Gerard Debreu and Frank Hahn), would lead him to conclude that economic theory has *no theory of price adjustment.* In a paper ironically titled "Toward a Theory of Price Adjustment," Arrow argued the following:

> Under conditions of disequilibrium, there is no reason that there should be a single market price, and we may very well expect that each firm will charge a different price. . . . The law that there is only one price on a competitive market (Jevons' Law of Indifference) is derived on the basis of profit- or utility-maximizing behavior on the part of both sides of the market; but there is no reason for such behavior to lead to unique price except in equilibrium, or possibly under conditions of perfect knowledge.[11]

With this intellectual background in mind, the evolution of Kirzner's scholarship can be understood as a consistent explication of the entrepreneurial role in the market process, as well as its normative implications. Kirzner's own understanding of entrepreneurship began with his doctoral dissertation, a topic recommended to him by Mises. Completed in 1957, it was later published in 1960 as Kirzner's first book, *The Economic Point of View.* Kirzner's argument was that the transformation of economic theory can be understood as evolving from a science defined as studying the accumulation of *material wealth* to a science broadened to encompass the study of *human action.* By tracing out that evolution from Adam Smith onward, Kirzner sowed the seeds for his refinement and articulation of the entrepreneurial element of human action: "The 'propensity to truck' must be understood as the faculty that men possess of recognizing situations in which the device of exchange, understood in this sense, would prove profitable."[12]

Despite Kirzner's own understanding of the intellectual trajectory toward which economic science had evolved—as he had learned from Mises—by the 1960s, mainstream economic theory had been immersed in a preoccupation with analyzing the conditions of a perfectly competitive market. Such an analytical focus came at the expense of understanding the process that creates tendencies toward a perfectly competitive outcome, and a process that entails the mutual coordination and adjustment of buyers' and sellers' plans. Kirzner's second book (and his only textbook), *Market Theory and the Price System* (1963), was written to fill the gap that had opened not only in mainstream economic theory but also in its pedagogy. By reducing the attention paid to perfect competition, Kirzner redirected economic analysis away from assessing the inefficiency of real-world markets versus the textbook ideal of perfect competition. Instead, the efficiency of market processes, according to Kirzner, should be assessed in terms of communicating errors to entrepreneurs in the form of current losses, which create future profit opportunities that are realized by correcting inefficiencies in the misallocation of resources toward their most valued consumer uses.

Throughout the 1960s and early 1970s, Kirzner continued to deepen and refine his account of the entrepreneurial market process through a series of papers,[13] culminating in his most well-known book, *Competition and Entrepreneurship* (1973). The impact of that book, along with *The Economic Point of View* ([1960] 2009) and *An Essay on Capital* (1966), have been recognized by the History of Economics Society (HES), which named Kirzner a distinguished fellow in 2018.[14] According to Kirzner, entrepreneurship refers not to a particular talent that is unique to a subset of individuals in society; rather, it is the central element of *all* human decision-making. The entrepreneur acts as an agent of change, discovery, and error correction through his or her "alertness" to pure profit opportunities. As Kirzner states:

> It is this entrepreneurial element that is responsible for our understanding of human action as active, creative, and human rather than as passive, automatic, and mechanical. Once the entrepreneurial element in human action is perceived, one can no longer interpret the decision as merely calculative—capable in principle of being yielded by mechanical manipulation of the "data" or already *completely implied* in these data.[15]

The best way to articulate Kirzner's unique contribution to the theory of entrepreneurship in the market process is by juxtaposing Kirzner's theory of the entrepreneur with that developed earlier by Joseph Schumpeter in the pre–World War II era.[16] According to the Schumpeterian account of entrepreneurship, the analytical point of departure for understanding the role of the entrepreneur is to begin in a state of equilibrium, in which all profit opportunities have been exhausted. Economic development, according to Schumpeter, "is a distinct phenomenon, entirely foreign to what may be observed in . . . the tendency towards equilibrium."[17] Therefore, the Schumpeterian entrepreneur is an innovator who has a *disequilibrating* effect on the market process, namely, by *creating* profit opportunities through technological innovation and therefore disrupting a preexisting state of equilibrium. Thus, entrepreneurship results in what Schumpeter referred to as "creative destruction."[18] The Kirznerian account of entrepreneurship, however, begins in a world of disequilibrium as its starting point, implying that a particular state of affairs at any moment of time and place is "nothing but a seething mass of unexploited maladjustments crying out for correction."[19] When he or she perceives such inefficiency from unrealized gains from trade, the Kirznerian entrepreneur captures pure profit and exhausts the available gains from trade by redirecting resources from less valued consumer uses to more valued consumer uses. In effect, the Kirznerian entrepreneur is an arbitrageur who *discovers* previously unnoticed profit opportunities by purchasing resources allocated toward a less valued consumer use at a lower price and reselling them in a higher-valued consumer use at a higher price. Thus, the Kirznerian entrepreneur has an *equilibrating* effect on the market process by creating a tendency toward one price across all markets for a particular productive resource, consumer good, or service.

One particular avenue of research in which Kirzner's account remains relatively underappreciated has been in the study of economic development. Much of the resurgence in attributing economic development to the relative allocation of entrepreneurship toward productive or unproductive activities can be traced back to William Baumol's seminal paper "Entrepreneurship: Productive, Unproductive, and Destructive" (1990).[20] Baumol's central claim is that the relative allocation of entrepreneurship between productive, unproductive, and destructive activities "depends heavily on the rules of the game—the reward structure in the economy—that happen to prevail."[21] Thus, entrepreneurship is ubiquitous, but its manifestation is institutionally contingent.[22] Indeed, an entire literature on entrepreneurship has taken inspiration from, and built upon, Baumol's Schumpeterian framework.[23] By his own admission, however, Baumol concluded that the Schumpeterian entrepreneur provides an incomplete basis for explaining, in the words of Eric Jones, "the European Miracle."[24] Given that, for most of its history, Europe was both a cultural and technological backwater compared with China,[25] this empirical fact presents a puzzle that cannot be explained solely by a

Schumpeterian account of entrepreneurship. This was admitted by Baumol, who provided a *Kirznerian* answer as to why this is the case:

> To derive more substantive results from an analysis of the allocation of entrepreneurial resources, it is necessary to expand Schumpeter's list, whose main deficiency seems to be that it does not go far enough. For example, it does not explicitly encompass innovative acts of technology transfer that take advantage of opportunities to introduce already-available technology (usually with some modification to adapt it to local conditions) to geographic locales whose suitability for the purpose had previously gone unrecognized or at least unused.[26]

The unintended, and unexpected, economic transition of the West from subsistence to exchange was fundamentally predicated on *creative arbitrage*,[27] namely (as Baumol put it), innovative acts of technology transfer by arbitraging it from one geographic location (with a less valued use) to another geographic location (with a more valued use). These creative acts of arbitrage were facilitated by Kirznerian productive entrepreneurship, which had been uniquely adapted to the commercial demands of European commerce and facilitated by political fragmentation and interjurisdictional competition.

Moreover, the importance *and* relative underappreciation of Kirzner's contributions to economic theory can also be understood in terms of their public policy implications. For example, Harold Demsetz's work, like that of Kirzner, provided a fundamental challenge to the prevailing orthodoxy of textbook perfect competition and the apparent prevalence of "market failures" associated with deviations from this ideal model to which the market ought to conform. Those perceived imperfections include the allegation that the markets are prone to create monopoly power, externalities, macroeconomic instability, under-provision of public goods, and inequality in the distribution of income. Nevertheless, Demsetz argued, while not denying the renewed importance of the entrepreneur to economic theory, that Kirzner had not accounted for anything substantially different from what had already been accounted for in the standard neoclassical market model. Because "alertness itself is a form of investment under conditions of uncertainty," it "is in principle indistinguishable from the analysis of such investment problems."[28]

Whether Demsetz was indeed correct in claiming such redundancy in Kirzner's analysis can best be illustrated by its public policy implications. For example, the failure to distinguish entrepreneurship from the ownership of capital only reinforces the particular argument that regulation is justified for the purpose of correcting a "market failure" associated with monopoly power based on economies of scale, which are regarded as a barrier to entry. Such an argument has been the basis for recent calls to regulate digital platform economies. However, the role of limited liability, which may be regarded as the source of corporate power, is, according to Demsetz, the very basis for its *discipline and erosion.* This is because "limited liability considerably reduces the cost of exchanging shares by making it unnecessary for a purchaser of shares to examine in great detail the liabilities of the corporation and the assets of other shareholders."[29] Although he acknowledged this disciplinary role of limited liability,[30] what Demsetz's assertion overlooks is that the *institutional* importance of limited liability in disciplining monopoly power is *fundamentally* predicated on there being an analytical distinction between entrepreneurship and capital ownership. Entrepreneurial profits, according to Kirzner, are not discovered by virtue of the fact that firm owners are owners of capital. Indeed, capital is required to later realize an entrepreneurial opportunity, but the ownership of capital is a *consequence* of having first discovered that a profit opportunity exists.[31]

This being said, Kirzner never asserted that markets are perfect, nor that the presence of market imperfections require government regulation. For Kirzner, market "imperfections" that deviate from the textbook ideal of perfectly competitive equilibrium do not necessarily prevent the price system from coordinating economic activity but in fact *depend on it*, because such deviations from the ideal represent entrepreneurial profit opportunities that fuel tendencies toward equilibrium. The relevant inquiry, then, is not whether government regulation is necessary to correct for market imperfections but *how* different sets of policies incentivize the discovery of particular types of profit opportunities by entrepreneurs.

The key to understanding why the correction of market imperfections hinges on the entrepreneurial market process, rather than government regulation, is the context-specific nature of profits *and* losses, as explained in Kirzner's "The Perils of Regulation" (1985). Within an institutional environment of private property and freedom of contract under the rule of law, entrepreneurs are residual claimants of the consequences of their decision-making, meaning that they bear both the costs *and* benefits of their choices. What is more important, however, is that the very process of rivalrous competition generates knowledge of profit opportunities, which is not available to any single person independently of such rivalrous market competition. Therefore, such economic knowledge is *context-specific* to entrepreneurs competing and therefore is not accessible to individuals operating in nonmarket settings, such as government regulators. However well-motivated and well-intentioned the public sector's regulators may be, they simply cannot correct alleged market imperfections, precisely because they are operating outside a private property context and do not face the discipline of competitive market forces. The implication is that government regulators are precluded from acquiring the knowledge that is necessary for correcting any perceived market failure because it *simply does not exist* for them in the form of entrepreneurial profits *and* losses.[32]

From a Kirznerian perspective, the very notion of "perfect competition" is an oxymoron because a situation in which all relevant information concerning consumer preferences, technology, and resource availability is given would no longer require a market (or government regulation, for that matter) for reallocating resources toward their most valued consumer uses. The "perils of regulation," as Kirzner referred to them, therefore, do not rest on any behavioral asymmetry between entrepreneurs and regulators. Both seek to further their own interests in an open-ended world of uncertainty, and neither entrepreneurs nor regulators can foresee future market conditions. Rather, they rest on the fact that when entrepreneurs bear losses for incorrect decision-making, such costs are concentrated upon them *and* communicated as future profit opportunities to themselves and other alert entrepreneurs to guide them toward an efficient allocation of resources. The imposition of regulatory constraints by government actors, however, creates what Kirzner referred to as "wholly superfluous discovery processes," which introduce profit opportunities regarded as undesirable in terms of the regulation's intent.[33]

The differences in outcomes in market processes and political processes, therefore, are based on the differences in planning horizons across *time* and the different feedback loops available to entrepreneurs and regulators. Whereas entrepreneurs respond to price signals that emerge through the exchange of anonymous individuals, and to the benefit of individuals they may not know, regulators, precluded from such price signals, can only respond to the knowledge available to them. That is, if regulation introduces undesirable consequences, they can respond in the short run only by introducing new regulation to correct for new profit opportunities that would not have existed if such regulation had not been imposed in the first place. Kirzner argued that "government regulations drastically alter and disturb opportunities for entrepreneurial gain, but they do not eliminate them."[34] Airline regulation under the Civil Aeronautics Board (CAB) from 1938 to 1978 is illustrative of Kirzner's point.[35] In an attempt to regulate price competition among US airlines, the CAB did not reduce nonprice competition among airlines. Rather, CAB regulation unintentionally changed the *manifestation* of entrepreneurial competition between airlines by creating profit opportunities for competition on other margins, such as food service and convenient flight schedules. Because the airlines could not compete by offering lower passenger fares, they began offering more sumptuous meals. From the standpoint of the CAB, the airlines' responses had an unanticipated and undesirable effect of creating the famed "sandwich wars" between airlines, after which the CAB began regulating the sizes of sandwiches! Frequent flights between major city pairs meant that just half of the seats were occupied, on average, adding considerably to operating costs and undermining the profitability of the CAB's regulatory regime. Therefore, the question of public policy is not whether a *deus ex machina* of government intervention must save imperfect markets from failing to live up to the ideal of perfect competition. Rather, if such market imperfections exist, as they always do, the relevant question becomes whether specific public policy measures, such as in the forms of taxes and regulation, will erect barriers to entry that either stifle or redirect entrepreneurship toward counterproductive activities, thus setting the market process up for failure.

Kirzner's understanding of entrepreneurship and how alternative institutional arrangements guide entrepreneurial activities toward productive or unproductive outcomes has important moral implications for the distributive justice of the market process. To the extent that mainstream economic theory frames the market in terms of equilibrium states of affairs, in which the entrepreneur, by definition, has no role, it also fails to account for the economic and moral relevance of discovering pure entrepreneurial profit. Economists have been able to demonstrate, in the best-case scenario, only that the distribution of income through the market mechanism is *not unjust,* meaning it will be unable to justify the discovery of entrepreneurial profits and the pattern of income distribution that emerges from such discovery.[36] At worst, profits earned by capitalists are categorized as "unearned rents," as claimed by Piketty.[37] Thus, any account of the morality of the market process must first begin with the notion that the distribution of income is the outcome of realizing pure entrepreneurial profits. It is not only the final product that is *created* through entrepreneurial discovery, but in the process of such discovery, the economic value of those inputs that are part of the production process are discovered and communicated through the price mechanism. For Kirzner, production is an *ex nihilo creation resulting from entrepreneurial discovery.* "There is nothing automatic or predetermined about the productive efforts put forth in the market economy."[38] Rather, each and every transaction in the market process expresses an entrepreneurial element of discovery, implying that all income earned in the market process is *discovered income.*

The profound importance of this insight complements and reinforces other theories of distributive justice based on private property, whether that be a Lockean labor-mixing theory of distributive justice[39] or a Nozickian entitlement theory of distributive justice.[40] From Kirzner's standpoint, any account of distributive justice based on a labor-mixing theory with unowned resources, as in the case of Locke, or an entitlement theory of income based on exchange between consenting adults with just holdings of property rights, as in the case of Nozick, must be preceded by how such resources are *discovered* in the first place. Perhaps most important, it also clarifies that Marxist accusations of capitalist injustice have been entirely misdirected because the "'profits' of capitalists which Marxist criticism, for example, saw as exploited away from labor, were not pure profits at all, of course, but a conglomerate of analytically disparate income categories,"[41] the value of which must be discovered through rivalrous competition between entrepreneurs actively bidding for land, labor, and capital in the first place.

Israel Kirzner is the living embodiment of Hayek's claim that "nobody can be a great economist who is only an economist—and I am even tempted to add that the economist who is only an economist is likely to become a nuisance if not a positive danger."[42] The power and continued relevance of Kirzner's scholarship is not only evidenced by its theoretical implications for microeconomic theory but also illustrated by its policy relevance. More important, perhaps, centering the case for individual liberty on the entrepreneurial element of human action has normative implications that transcend the distinction between economics and philosophy. To conclude in Kirzner's own words, individual liberty secures the "individual's freedom *to identify for himself what the opportunities are* which he may endeavour to grasp" and hence secures the possibility for productive entrepreneurship and human flourishing.[43]

Acknowledgments: I thank Peter Boettke and Christopher Coyne for their feedback and comments on this paper. Special thanks are particularly due to Caleb Fuller, whose comments and conversations were crucial to sharpening many critical points in this paper. I am also very grateful to the editorial comments and feedback provided by William Shughart II on an earlier draft of this article. Any remaining errors are entirely my own.

16 Thomas Sowell

Uncommon Perspectives on Culture, Society, and Economics

Art Carden and Brian C. Albrecht

WHO COULD SAY that Thomas Sowell is underappreciated? Sowell is one of the most famous economists of the past few decades. On April 28, 2023, he had four of the one hundred bestselling books in "Economics" on Amazon, a wide-ranging category that includes many books that are not economics by any economist's definition.[1] In 2011, when economics professors were surveyed about their favorite economists, Sowell ranked number 15 in the category "Economists over 60" who were alive at the time. He was the highest-ranked person on the list not to have won a Nobel Prize, falling right behind John Nash and Daniel McFadden.[2] Yet within academic circles, he is too often seen as merely a popularizer of economics or, worse, just a political pundit. According to Google Scholar, his most cited work is *Ethnic America: A History* (1981), with more than 1,562 citations. This is an impressive number for mortals but far behind the most-cited works of John Nash (13,865) or Daniel McFadden (24,014).[3] Sowell has made seminal contributions to cultural economics, information economics, and the history of social thought. The imbalance between Sowell's academic citations and the quality of his insights is why we argue that he is underappreciated.

Thomas Sowell was born in North Carolina to parents he never knew and was raised in New York by his extended family. In various places, he has written that his academic preparation lagged far behind that of his classmates.

Art Carden is Margaret Gage Bush Distinguished Professor of Business at Samford University, senior fellow at the American Institute for Economic Research, and research fellow at Independent Institute. Brian C. Albrecht is chief economist at the International Center for Law & Economics.

Sowell's intellectual life did not begin to blossom for him until he learned, at age eight, that he could *borrow* books from the public library across the street. Sowell would go on to drop out of high school, teach pistol-shooting while learning photography in the United States Marine Corps during the late 1940s and early 1950s, attend and graduate from Harvard University, and at the age of thirty-eight (but with a distinguished publication record already), earn a PhD in economics from the University of Chicago under the direction of the famously abrasive George Stigler, who would win the Nobel Prize in Economic Sciences in 1982. Sowell's main areas of research were in the history of economic thought, and he produced a pathbreaking analysis of Say's Law, published in 1972 by Princeton University Press. Sowell held a series of faculty positions and appointments at major research institutes before he landed for good at Stanford University's Hoover Institution in the 1980s, where he would spend the rest of his long and productive career producing serious scholarly volumes for his colleagues, popularizations for the thoughtful layperson, and columns of commentary on current events that were syndicated in newspapers around the country and the world.

During the past few decades, Sowell has been best known as a leading conservative commentator, which was especially surprising for a black economist. He and his colleague and friend Walter Williams used to joke that they were not allowed to fly on the same plane because if the plane crashed, there would be no black conservatives left. This framing is unfortunate because it limits Sowell's reach by emphasizing *black* and *conservative* rather than *economist.*

He writes with a sometimes abrasive style and, like his adviser Stigler, does not suffer fools gladly or easily. He holds himself, other scholars, and the entire academic enterprise to high standards. He resigned from Cornell University in response to pressure to lower the standards in a special program he was running for minority students. Throughout his career, he has argued that affirmative action programs are objectionable mainly because they hurt precisely the people they purport to help.

A World View

Sowell takes a *world view* of policies such as affirmative action, phenomena such as poverty, and sins such as slavery. As a result, he has developed a series of broad insights, noting that many phenomena look as if they have special causes but are instances of more general patterns. Throughout a long and distinguished career, Sowell has followed theory and evidence wherever it has led him, regardless of whether he liked the conclusions. Across his prodigious body of work, Sowell sets standards of intellectual integrity and rigor that we should all hope to achieve.

Sowell counters stories about the legacy of slavery, the desirability of affirmative action, and other claims by looking worldwide to see just how much explanatory power these have. Particularly in his later career, Sowell has worked to understand general causes rather than specific causes. Something that has been a part of virtually every society, such as slavery, cannot be the explanation for differences between those societies. European slave traders, colonizers, and imperialists did horrible things wherever they went, but this has been true of virtually every conquering group throughout history. If exploitation per se could explain how the West grew rich, it presumably would have happened somewhere else long ago.[4]

We have to look elsewhere. He repeatedly emphasizes that *prosperity,* not poverty, needs to be explained. Repeatedly, Sowell has explained how patterns intellectuals attribute to unique society-specific causes have reappeared throughout history and worldwide. For example, persecution of unfavored minorities and set-asides for the allegedly exploited are common across societies. Furthermore, many group differences, Sowell explains, are due to demographic differences (including differences in average age) and some historically accidental head starts. Lighter-skinned mulattoes, for example, had more privileges than darker-skinned slaves in the antebellum era; as Sowell points out, they therefore learned to read, write, and move in urban society before slaves on plantations.

In books such as *Wealth, Poverty, and Politics* (2015), Sowell pointed out the effects of random factors, such as geography, which might keep people isolated from one another and therefore cut off from the social conversation. He instances Aboriginal peoples in Australia and the Canary Islands, noting that they had no concept of iron and its use even though, in the case of the Australian Aborigines, they were amid one of the world's largest deposits of iron ore. However, he notes that "geographic determinism" is refuted by the experience of the Soviet Union, which, as he points out, was more richly endowed with "natural resources" than just about any country in history. And yet, the Soviet Union had trouble feeding itself—though it somehow found resources for a war machine. Africa, Sowell points out, has less coastline than Europe, fewer deep natural harbors, and rivers that "are only intermittently navigable."[5]

The Role of Culture

Sowell emphasizes *cultural prerequisites*, arguing that objects' physical characteristics are irrelevant unless people have the human capital needed to harness those characteristics. Sowell's emphasis on culture has exposed him to the criticism that he is "blaming the victims" or arguing that, in the case of persistent economic gaps between blacks and whites, he is functioning as a venal mouthpiece for people who want to hear what is "wrong" with black people.

Sowell offers example after example of groups who have started in conditions of abject poverty (such as Jews) and ascended quickly, going from the bottom of the income distribution toward the top in a generation or two. Throughout his work, he tells similar stories about the overseas Chinese or Indians in the societies they inhabited. In case after case, a persecuted ethnic minority creates jobs. It performs services no other group would do but is blamed by local demagogues for being responsible for the poverty of the majority.

Throughout his work, Sowell has little patience for received narratives such as the notion that Europe and its overseas extensions (the "neo-Europes" of Canada, the United States, Australia, and New Zealand) owe their prosperity to slavery, imperialism, and colonialism—in other words, to exploitation. This is more vision than fact, however. As Sowell pointed out, "Europe's economic impact on Africa was far greater than Africa's economic effect on Europe."[6] Trade between colonized Africans and colonizing Europeans was an enormous fraction of African international trade but a small part of European international trade.[7]

Attempts to explain existing patterns of injustice in the West as the product of uniquely and particularly Western sins are bound to miss a lot. What is unique about the relationship between slavery and Western civilization is that the West was the first civilization to turn against slavery. This institution was not "peculiar" but had existed worldwide for pretty much all of history. Sowell put it this way:

> [S]lavery was in fact one of the oldest and most widespread institutions on Earth. Slavery existed in the Western Hemisphere before Columbus's ships appeared on the horizon, and it existed in Europe, Asia, Africa, and the Middle East for thousands of years. Slavery was older than Islam, Buddhism, or Christianity, and both the secular and religious moralists of societies around the world accepted human bondage, not only as a fact of life but as something requiring no special moral justification. Slavery was "peculiar" in the United States only because human bondage was inconsistent with the principles on which this nation was founded. Historically, however, it was those principles which were peculiar, not slavery.[8]

Historians and economists can point to histories of exploitation in every economy that has been Greatly Enriched. This does not mean that the exploitation led to the Great Enrichment, because there are similar patterns of exploitation in societies that remain poor today. Breathable air also existed in societies that are rich today. That doesn't mean breathable air was sufficient—though it was necessary!—for a Great Enrichment.

One way that societies differed in their approach to slavery, according to Sowell, is that in some societies, slavery required extensive ideological justification if it was to persist because the practice was so obviously at odds with liberal principles, such as those of the American founding. He wrote:

> Slavery in a free society raised heated issues that kept political controversy alive throughout the history of the institution in the United States. It forced ideological justifications that other slave societies had not found necessary. Essential to these justifications was the assertion that the enslaved peoples were so different that the principles and ideals of the country did not apply to them—that they were inferior in intellect and lacked the feelings that would cause them

> suffering from degradation, hard work, or the destruction of family ties.[9]

The phrase "in a free society" is important here. In unfree societies where slavery is taken for granted, no ideological justification is necessary because it is simply the way of the world.

One of Sowell's largest and most notable projects was his 1990s "cultures" trilogy: *Race and Culture* (1994), *Migrations and Cultures* (1997), and *Conquests and Cultures* (1999). Throughout his career, he has been animated by the need to think clearly about group differences. Why, for example, are there "gaps and disparities" between black and white Americans in income, education, and so on? Are the "gaps and disparities" the result of "root causes" like poverty? Or are they lags to be overcome?[10] He noted, in *Race and Culture* and elsewhere, that many of the pathologies we associate with American black culture are the inherited pathologies of Southern white culture, which are in turn the inherited pathologies of regions of Scotland and England from which Appalachian settlers came.[11]

Whereas cultural explanations were relatively uncommon within economics when Sowell started writing on culture, the intellectual landscape is different today. After rediscovering the importance of institutions in explaining economic growth, economists rediscovered the role of culture in growth.[12] Although the recent work follows many of the trends in modern economics that are absent in Sowell's work, such as a heavy emphasis on formal modeling and causal inference, it shares with Sowell's work an emphasis on the causal role of culture in explaining growth or income and the recognition that cultural explanations cannot be based on simply comparing two groups but require a world perspective of culture. Sowell's work prefigured more recent work, even if Sowell was largely uncited.

Knowledge and Decisions

Sowell's 1980 book *Knowledge and Decisions* is his crowning achievement. It is a book-length analysis and application of the principles F. A. Hayek explained in his 1945 article "The Use of Knowledge in Society." The title for Hayek's review of the book—a title Hayek chose—was "The Best Book on General

Economics in Many a Year."[13] *Knowledge and Decisions* is also where Sowell developed as a social theorist, expanding his analysis to include political, social, and legal trade-offs. Sowell wrote that "various decision-making processes differ . . . in the extent to which they are institutionally capable of making incremental trade-offs, rather than attempting categorical 'solutions.'"[14] Therefore, the social theorist's task is to identify and explain how institutions affect people's ability to identify and make trade-offs within the institutions.

This raises an important theme in Sowell's work. He emphasizes the importance of incentives, costs, and benefits throughout social systems and structures. Third-party observers, he argued, could not be trusted to arrange society. The incentive problem is apparent. Intellectuals have relatively weak incentives to get things right or identify the right social validation processes because they enjoy no meaningful benefit from being right and bear no significant cost for being wrong. Moral, political, and economic surrogates, as Sowell would call them in his 1987 book *A Conflict of Visions*, cannot be trusted not because they are necessarily bad people but because they are not subject to social validation processes that provide reliable feedback. Sowell has no special place in his heart for "the totalitarian thrust of the intellectual vision."[15]

Intellectuals

Sowell has little patience with the "rampaging presumptions" of intellectuals who think themselves fit to rule. He explained his argument in detail in his 2009 book *Intellectuals and Society*. Adam Smith's discussion of the "man of system" is appropriate here:

> He seems to imagine that he can arrange the different members of a great society with as much ease as the hand arranges the different pieces upon a chess-board. He does not consider that the pieces upon the chess-board have no other principle of motion besides that which the hand impresses upon them; but that, in the great chess-board of human society, every single piece has a principle of motion of its own, altogether different from that which the legislature might

> choose to impress upon it. If those two principles coincide and act in the same direction, the game of human society will go on easily and harmoniously, and is very likely to be happy and successful. If they are opposite or different, the game will go on miserably, and the society must be at all times in the highest degree of disorder.[16]

The progressive presumptions of the men (and women) of system have by no means been benign. Eugenics was the "settled science" of the Progressive Era, and august intellectual bodies such as the American Economic Association and the American Sociological Association were founded by racists to promote racist ends. For example, Francis A. Walker and Edward A. Ross traveled in the highest ranks of intellectual life and were committed to racist visions and the pursuit of racial purity. Gunnar Myrdal, who shared the Nobel Prize with Friedrich Hayek in 1974, oversaw eugenic sterilization programs along with his wife, Alva.[17]

Sowell argues that group resentments begin with intellectuals. The leaders of the Bolshevik Revolution were intellectuals. Mao Zedong has been euphemized as an anti-colonial intellectual.[18] In taking a world view of intellectuals and race, Sowell points out that in society after society, the intellectual leaders among the elites move disproportionately toward the humanities and social sciences rather than the hard sciences and more technical subjects such as economics. In Malaysia, students of Malay descent (for whom affirmative action policies had been developed) tended to study the liberal arts, and "[i]n much of Latin America, technical and scientific careers were long regarded with condescension."[19] As Sowell put it,

> Not only Hispanic and Portuguese cultures, but also the cultures of much of the Third World make business and commerce far less attractive to the educated classes than government employment or work in the professions.[20]

Jobs in business have been left to despised "middleman" minorities such as Jews and overseas Chinese, whom indigenous demagogues could then blame for "exploiting" the badly off.

Visions

One of Sowell's most popular books is his 1987 classic *A Conflict of Visions*, which Art Carden used to assign in his introductory economics courses at Rhodes College (following the practice of his colleague Mark McMahon). Sowell's subtitle is *Ideological Origins of Political Struggles,* and he worked to explain why, in his words, "the same familiar faces can be found glaring at each other from opposite sides of the political fence, again and again."[21] He continued:

> It happens too often to be coincidence and it is too uncontrolled to be a plot. A closer look at the arguments on both sides often shows that they are reasoning from fundamentally different premises. These different premises—often implicit—are what provide the consistency behind the repeated opposition of individuals and groups on numerous, unrelated issues. They have different visions of how the world works.[22]

At first glance, it seems odd that once we know someone's views about gun control, we can very likely predict the person's views about abortion and school choice with surprising confidence. Sowell, however, noted that these are not empirical disagreements based on different readings of the evidence but fundamental disagreements about fundamental principles. One of Sowell's exemplars of the unconstrained vision, William Godwin, did not fit neatly into either the "pro-liberty" or "anti-liberty" camp. He was a libertarian, like F. A. Hayek and Adam Smith, but a libertarian of a different kind who argued that people are perfectible but corrupted by social institutions. Godwin's was a high liberalism, unlike the low liberalism of Smith, Hayek, and Sowell. Like others who share his unconstrained vision, he sought to throw off any social constraint and condemn it as oppressive.

The constrained and unconstrained visions differ in important respects. First, individual intentions are largely irrelevant in the constrained vision, whereas they are essential to the unconstrained vision. Good and bad things happen in the constrained vision as the unintended consequences of systemic forces such as market exchange and democratic choice. Good and bad things happen in the unconstrained vision largely because people make them happen deliberately for articulated reasons. Human nature—particularly human cognitive and moral limitations—is essential to the constrained vision. In the unconstrained vision, enlightened moral and political surrogates can perfect and condition people. In the constrained vision, these pervasive moral and cognitive limitations mean that systemic social characteristics (such as prices) are essential, and no one can run another's life. In the unconstrained vision, moral and intellectual inequality burden the Anointed—a term Sowell used in his book *The Vision of the Anointed* (1995) to describe this group very generally—with the Glorious Purpose of making everyone else equal. Economic and social equality demand political inequality, at least in the short run.

The two visions differ fundamentally in the way they understand knowledge:

> Knowledge as conceived in the constrained vision is predominantly experience—transmitted socially in largely inarticulate forms, from prices which indicate costs, scarcities, and preferences, to traditions which evolve from the day-to-day experiences of millions in each generation, winnowing out in Darwinian competition what works from what does not work.[23]

What we consider *scientific* knowledge represents a tiny fraction of socially useful knowledge. Later, Sowell wrote, "Knowledge is thus the social experience of the many, as embodied in behavior, sentiments, and habits, rather than the specially articulated *reason* of the few, however talented or gifted those few might be. . . . The specially articulated *reason* of the few," those with "cultivated" minds, is in the unconstrained vision the total of socially meaningful knowledge, and "[a]rticulated rationality was to be the mode of validation, not general acceptance based on pragmatic experience."[24] Consider the family structure. In the unconstrained vision, mere genetic affinity is not a reasonable basis for preferring one person rather than another. In the constrained visions, thousands of generations of biological and cultural evolution have selected social rules, norms, and institutions in which people love and care for their children before they love and care for others.

Philosophy, Politics, and Economics

Sowell has written broadly and taken an integrated approach to philosophy, politics, and economics. These are overlapping lines of inquiry concerning the way they treat social knowledge. For Sowell, trade-offs are inescapable, and positing a world without them does not do us much good. Scarcity, as well, is unavoidable. The especially quotable Sowell wrote that "[t]he first lesson of economics is scarcity," but "[t]he first lesson of politics is to disregard the first lesson of economics."[25] His understanding of why freedom works is not due to unrealistic assumptions about businesspeople and their motivations or cynicism about politicians and their sincerity. He used to offer an A to anyone in his classes who could find anywhere in Adam Smith's work where he wrote nice things about businessmen. Smith hesitated with his praise but was unstinting in his criticism of "the sophistry of merchants." Instead, he argued that political choices do not work as well as economic freedom because of the *systemic* characteristics that give people the incentives they face.

Sowell is a realist when it comes to political economy and on-the-ground decision-making. Politicians, he argues, rarely look past the next election because they have very weak incentives to do so. Furthermore, the fact that people are *human* means that everyone shares the cognitive biases interventionists delight in pointing out.[26] As Brennan and Freiman put it in their evaluation of political authority and the conditions that have to be met for it to be justified,

> the assumption of voter competence is even more doubtful than the assumption of consumer competence. *A priori,* we would expect that every flaw in consumers [would] be worse in voters because the expected cost of an uninformed and biased consumption choice is even higher than an uninformed and biased voting choice.[27]

Politicians easily mislead voters as a result of the "high costs of voter knowledge."[28] In Sowell's framework, this is not a cognitive bias to condemn but a fact of the political decision-making process to understand and draw out the implications.

Conclusion

The philosopher David Schmidtz once told one of us that as famous as he is, Adam Smith is still underrated. The same, we think, is true of Thomas Sowell. As "appreciated" as he might be, Thomas Sowell is still underappreciated by economists, other social scientists, and historians across the humanities. Thomas Sowell has a long list of admirers within economics and without. Most of us know—or at least were introduced to—Sowell from his popular writing. He has served the popular cause of the public understanding of the dismal science eloquently and articulately. His work deserves a more extensive academic hearing as well. Though trained as an economist—and as an economist who remained a Marxist even after taking a course from Milton Friedman, so an economist who does not change his mind for light and transient causes—Sowell has written extensively on politics, philosophy, education, history, and even child development. He has been embraced by the Right and largely dismissed by the Left for his efforts. As a scholar working in the constrained vision and tradition of Adam Smith, Friedrich Hayek, Edmund Burke, Milton Friedman, and James M. Buchanan, Sowell leaves an intellectual legacy waiting to be thoroughly mined and fully appreciated.

Acknowledgments: Connor Sutton provided valuable research assistance. In addition, we benefited from discussions with David Carden and Jacob Carden, who were working on their Black History Month projects about Sowell for Red Mountain Community School during the early stages of this project.

17

Julian Simon

Irreplaceable Economist, Irreplaceable Man

Robert M. Whaples

JULIAN SIMON FELT underappreciated. Simon, whose book *The Ultimate Resource* (1981) effectively punctured Malthusian[1] worries about population growth and natural resource scarcity, began his autobiography by noting that "a novelty of this book among scientific autobiographies is that it is not written by a person who is a success," calling himself a "professional outcast, a failure," and lamenting that "most of my best scientific work has gone for naught." He lamented, "I have never (I mean literally *never,* truly an amazing statistic) had a single standard mark of professional respect (let alone honor) in my academic professions," observing that he had never held office in a professional association or been asked to referee a paper for a top journal in economics, demography, or statistics.[2] Near the end of the autobiography, Simon recounted that when administrators at the University of Maryland tried to hire him, the Department of Economics twice rejected the offer, so he was appointed to a position in the College of Business and Management.

Although Simon has been substantially underappreciated, few would reach his extreme conclusion about this fact. He did, after all, publish articles in top professional journals, including the *American Economic Review*, the *Journal of Political Economy*, the *Quarterly Journal of Economics*, the *Review of Economics and Statistics*, the *Review of Economic Studies*, and *Econometrica*.[3] And recognition has come after his death, including the Institute for the Study of Labor's annual Julian L. Simon Lecture to honor his work in population

---

Robert Whaples is professor of economics at Wake Forest University and editor of *The Independent Review.*

economics and the University of Illinois's Julian Simon Memorial Faculty Scholar Endowment.

Simon's Life and Career Before Academia

Simon (1932–98) graduated from Harvard University, which he attended on an ROTC scholarship; served in the United States Navy; and then entered the advertising business. His experience in the real world of business contributed to his realistic view of the economy.[4]

> Around this time, there appeared several books with themes like that of *The Hidden Persuaders* by Vance Packard that warned of the enormous power of "Madison Avenue" to propagandize and influence people's buying and their ways of life. Academics such as . . . John Kenneth Galbraith frequently wrote about the power of advertising over people as if it can have the powers of a Svengali. Clearly, these people had never attempted to actually convince people to buy a commercial product with advertising; if they had, they would have known how difficult it is to do so.[5]

Simon earned an MBA and a PhD in business economics from the University of Chicago. Never one to hide his own failures, he advertised the "Pain of Failing a Ph.D. Oral Exam" in the *American Economist.*[6] The truth is that Simon's economics coursework amounted to only three or four quarter-length courses, all in the School of Business at Chicago, rather than in its famed Department of Economics. The first question in his oral examination was elementary, concerning consumer surplus, but when he was asked to demonstrate the concept geometrically, he put quantity on the vertical axis and price on the horizontal axis—something students learn not to do in the first couple weeks of introductory courses on the subject. "I lost my moorings, and my mind began to float away."[7] Simon passed the exam on his second attempt and went on to show that someone with enough common sense and a keen eye for cold, hard facts could make major contributions to a field in which he sometimes had a slippery grasp of formal theory. Better to humbly admit one's errors than to be one of those who were "harmfully wrong" in their "contemporary analyses and . . . consequent forecasts for the future," who "arrogantly relied on their supposedly superior intellects and therefore scanted on the examination of the available evidence," as were John Maynard Keynes and Paul Samuelson.[8]

Following graduate school, Simon entered the mail-order business, developing a healthy wariness of and appreciation for regulations while running his own firm. When he sold a booklet titled "How to Make Your Will," which was accompanied by a blank form and written by a professional lawyer, the Federal Trade Commission shut him down, charging that it was against the law for him to dispense legal advice. Later, he achieved excellent results selling a catalog of materials for home brewing but was again shut down. "The law permitted people to make wine at home and seemed to permit people to make a limited quantity of beer as well. But the federal alcohol authorities—probably at the behest of the commercial brewers—carried on a sporadic campaign of harassment against the sellers of such books."[9] Simon again ran afoul of regulators when he ran misleading pharmaceutical ads. Admitting his culpability, he decided to publish *How to Start and Operate a Mail-Order Business*[10] and then turned to full-time writing and research as an academic.

Simon the Polymath

At the beginning of his academic career while at the University of Illinois, Simon published a wide range of studies related to advertising and marketing. Typical examples are an article in which he examined the rationale for newspapers' price discrimination in setting advertising rates, using the results of a questionnaire he had mailed to daily newspapers;[11] an examination of economies of scale in advertising; and studies that estimated the elasticity of demand for liquor and for cigarettes. Simon's early academic research went in numerous directions—including an economic analysis of where libraries should store their books, an empirical analysis of the effect of income on suicide, and a two-page paper that ultimately had a profound impact on public policy: "An Almost Practical Solution to Airline Overbooking."[12]

Arguably, Simon should have omitted the word "almost" from his title. The plan has been widely adopted and speaks for itself.

> Perhaps the reader has suffered a fit of impotent rage at being told that he could not board an aeroplane for which he held a valid ticket. The explanation is clear, and no angry letter to the president of the airline will rectify the mistake, for mistake it was not. The airline gambles on a certain number of cancellations, and therefore sometimes sells more tickets than there are seats. Naturally there are sometimes more seat claimants than seats. The solution is simple. All that need happen when there is overbooking is that an airline agent distributes among the ticket-holders an envelope and a bid form, instructing each person to write down the lowest sum of money he is willing to accept in return for waiting for the next flight. The lowest bidder is paid in cash and given a ticket for the next flight. All other passengers board the plane and complete the flight to their destination. All parties benefit, and no party loses.[13]

Simon speculated that this commonsense solution wasn't adopted because "such an auction does not seem decorous," but the primary reason was probably government regulations, which were swept away when an economist, Alfred Kahn, was appointed chair of the Civil Aeronautics Board in 1977 and allowed airlines to follow Simon's advice.

Population Questions and *The Ultimate Resource*

By the end of the 1960s, Simon had begun to focus his attention on population issues, retooling himself as a demographer. His attention was drawn to the field by worries, which he shared with many others at the time, about overpopulation. But his research led him to the opposite conclusion, that, especially in the long run, rising population was a key *source* of rising prosperity.[14]

This decade of research culminated in a pathbreaking book, *The Ultimate Resource*,[15] which was warmly greeted by most economists but reviled by advocates of population control. In the book, Simon reframed the natural resource "problem" and the population "problem," using sound economics. The natural resource problem isn't that we're "running out"; it is, more basically, scarcity, and scarcity can be usefully measured using prices. Is the problem of natural resource scarcity getting worse? No. Not even close. As Simon documented again and again, the inflation-adjusted (real) price of natural resources—from iron to oil to lead to coal—had been *falling,* not rising, in the long run. Likewise, the long-run price of food—including staples such as wheat and corn—was falling and per capita food production was rising.[16]

To his credit, Simon intuited that the rising natural resource prices of the 1970s were an anomaly. Accordingly, he focused on the long run: decades, centuries, millennia. Ever provocative, Simon tweaked readers by arguing that natural resources aren't merely abundant; they are "infinite." He didn't mean infinite in the sense that God is infinite, but rather in the sense that there is so much that we will never run out. (It's not clear that he realized this, but the word "finite" derives from the Latin *finire*, which means "to finish"—and Simon essentially argued that the process of producing natural resources would never reach an end.) We certainly haven't run out in the years since Simon wrote. Thomas Covert, Michael Greenstone, and Christopher Knittel showed, for example, that proven reserves of both petroleum and natural gas have more than doubled since 1980. They concluded that the "historical record indicates that the supply of fossil fuels has consistently *increased* over time."[17]

The population problem isn't "too many people." The problem, as Simon explained it, has always been that children are very costly to parents, whereas most of the material benefits from them come when they are adults, and many of these benefits go to people other than their parents. Putting the natural resources and population together, his argument can be summarized very simply: Prices are determined by supply and demand; as goods become scarcer, their prices increase; as prices increase, we look for substitutes, better methods of production, and better methods of conserving those goods. There is abundant empirical evidence that, in the long run, mankind has been made better off for having faced increased scarcity because we have been successful in reducing it. Rising population isn't a problem; rather, it's evidence that a problem has been solved: population rises *because* the discoveries and cooperation of man allow and encourage it to occur. Even more important, greater population *allows* us to solve more problems. Thus, the ultimate resource isn't energy or minerals or metals. The ultimate resource is the creative power of humankind. The final sentence of *The Ultimate Resource* pulls everything together: "The ultimate resource is people—skilled, spirited, and hopeful people who will exert their wills and imaginations for their own benefit, and so, inevitably, for the benefit of us all."[18]

Unfortunately, there is a catch in this sentence. "The better future does not happen 'automatically' and without effort."[19] Not every set of social and economic arrangements makes good use of human drive and ingenuity. Simon indicated that only one has a good track record—the capitalist market system: "The extent to which the political-social-economic system provides personal freedom from government coercion is a crucial element in the economics of resources and population. Skilled persons require an appropriate social and economic framework that provides incentives for working hard and taking risks, enabling their talents to flower and come to fruition. The key elements of such a framework are economic liberty, respect for property, and fair and sensible rules of the market that are enforced equally for all."[20] "No government decision maker can come close to the efficiency of millions of individual buyers and investors who go comparison shopping."[21]

The Bet

Some people belittle numbers. Henry David Thoreau claimed that an "honest man has hardly need to count more than his ten fingers or in extreme cases he may add his ten toes."[22] Antoine de Saint-Exupéry's Little Prince says, "Grown-ups like numbers. When you tell them about a new friend, they never ask questions about what really matters. They never ask: 'What does his voice sound like?' 'What games does he like best?' 'Does he collect butterflies?' They ask: 'How old is he?' 'How many brothers does he have?' . . . 'How much money does his father make?'"[23] Ironically, Julian Simon showed that people of all ages can benefit from simply looking at reliable statistics that capture such things as prices, populations, and plentitude. Even people who, as Saint-Exupéry would have it, collect butterflies—people like Stanford University lepidopterist Paul Ehrlich.

Tired of the fawning attention given to Ehrlich, author of *The Population Bomb* (1968), and his unfulfilled gloom-and-doom predictions, Simon famously challenged him to put his money where his mouth was.[24] In the pages of the *Social Science Quarterly*, Simon asked, "How often does a prophet have to be wrong before we no longer believe that he or she is a true prophet?" and goaded Ehrlich into a wager on resource scarcity as demonstrated by the trend in raw material prices. They settled on a bet covering $1,000 worth of five metals (a $200 contract for each metal). If the inflation-adjusted price of the metals rose from 1980 to 1990, Simon would pay the difference; if the prices went down, Ehrlich would pay the difference to Simon.[25] In monetary terms, Simon bore almost all the risk—at most he could win $1,000 (if the prices all fell to zero), but his potential losses were unbounded. And he gave Ehrlich a blank check by letting him pick the five commodities. As you've probably heard, Ehrlich lost the bet about as spectacularly as possible. The prices of all five of the commodities fell. Jointly, they fell by a remarkable 36 percent.[26]

Simon had no way of knowing that commodity prices would fall so sharply during the 1980s. Over many recent ten-year periods, the prices of natural resources have risen; in many other periods, they have fallen. But it was fitting that Ehrlich lost this particular bet so convincingly.[27] He (and his collaborators John Holdren and John Harte) failed to do their homework, choosing to bet on copper, chromium, nickel, tin, and tungsten on the basis of little more than gut instincts and random guesses. The price of copper was abnormally high at the start of the bet because of temporary factors, including strikes in Chile and political disruptions in Zaire and Zimbabwe. Simple economic reasoning suggests that the price would drop after these temporary supply reductions ended. More important, it's fitting that Ehrlich lost the bet because his other, better-known, and emphatic predictions were so profoundly wrong as well.

Conclusion

Perhaps Julian Simon has been underrated because, out of step with the economics of his age, formal theorizing was never his forte.[28] As an economist—and as a demographer—Simon was basically self-taught. However, he was an exceptional marketer and storyteller, and the story he told, firmly anchored in irrefutable facts, simply made sense. Turning aside Keynes's truism that "in the long run we're all dead," Simon showed, instead, that in the long run we're all richer—and the trend is unlikely to end because we have established a system that effectively harnesses human ingenuity for the good of all.

Subsequent history has been kind to Simon's optimism. Simon didn't merely win "the bet." His broad predictions that human prosperity would continue to rise have been proven correct. The largest decline in extreme poverty in human history has occurred during the four decades since Simon published *The Ultimate Resource.* The World Bank estimated that the number of people living in extreme poverty (living on less than $1.90 per day in 2011 dollars, which is approximately $2.54 in 2023 dollars) fell from 1.91 billion in 1981 to 648 million in 2019[29]—despite an increase in global population from 4.5 billion to 8 billion. The poorest 5 percent of Americans today have incomes that are likely higher than all but 95 percent of the 117 billion people who have ever lived.[30]

What could derail such economic progress in the future? The contributors to *Future: Economic Peril or Prosperity?* considered a range of possibilities—rising levels of debt, creeping government power, and simple complacency, among others—but were mostly optimistic that the upward trend will continue.[31] Robert Atkinson argued that over the past two decades, many Americans have abandoned their faith in economic growth, warning that "unless we restore increasing per-capita income growth to the center of economic policy, relative U.S. power will shrink, income growth and poverty reduction will slow, and public funding available to achieve important goals will remain inadequate."[32] Brink Lindsay warned of an "anti-Promethean" backlash—a "broad-based cultural turn away from those forms of technological progress that extend and amplify human mastery over the physical world."[33]

However, Simon's explanation of the population "problem"—that children are very costly to parents, whereas most of the material benefits from them come when they are adults and many of these benefits go to people other than their parents—has taken on new meaning today. In recent years, fertility rates around the world have collapsed. Two-thirds of the world's population now lives in countries where the total fertility rate is below the replacement level,[34] and the percentage of American adults who say that having children is very important to them plummeted from 59 percent to 30 percent between 1998 and 2023.[35] A recent survey of economists drives home a looming fear—that the world's population is growing too slowly and is likely to decline within a few decades. The survey asked whether economists agreed or disagreed with the statement that "[t]he economic benefits of an expanding world population outweigh the economic costs." When asked in 2000, 64 percent of economists "disagreed" with the proposition while only 36 percent "agreed" or "agreed with provisos." Most economists rejected Simon's idea that global population growth is good in economic terms. However, the tide has turned. When surveyed in 2021, 58 percent agreed or partly agreed and only 42 disagreed.[36]

Economists are gradually coming to Simon's provocative conclusion that the existence of more people is a good thing. It saddens me that reaching this conclusion has taken so long and that so many men and women of childbearing age have decided that children are too much of a burden to bear. Simon reported having an epiphany around 1969 when traveling to Washington, DC, to discuss a project intended to lower fertility in less-developed countries. There, he saw a sign for the Iwo Jima Highway and remembered reading about a eulogy delivered over the dead on the battlefield at Iwo Jima, in which a chaplain said "something like 'How many who would have been a Mozart or a Michelangelo or an Einstein have we buried here?' And then I thought," continued Simon, "Have I gone crazy? What business do I have trying to help arrange it that fewer human beings will be born, each one of whom might be a Mozart or a Michelangelo or an Einstein—or simply a joy to his or her family and community, and a person who will enjoy life?"[37] That is, perhaps, the greatest insight of Simon's brilliant but underappreciated mind. Simon—husband, father, scholar, teacher—who wrote during a period of great pessimism, much like ours today, recognized that every life is irreplaceable and full of infinite potential.

18

Karl Mittermaier

Economic Theory vs. Reality

Michael C. Munger

> *Of course, it would not be necessary to consider presuppositions at all if our science were daily revealing new truths of great intellectual beauty or of great beneficence to mankind. But when the existing paradigms have been explored down to almost the last niche and still sensible men feel there is much room for improvement, then we cannot afford to ignore the philosophy of science.*
>
> —Karl Mittermaier[1]

KARL MITTERMAIER WAS born in Germany in 1938 and was a child raised in the turmoil of war. He was related to the prominent nineteenth-century German legal theorist and antiquarian Karl Joseph Anton Mittermaier. After World War II, at the age of eleven, young Karl and his family left the increasing dangers of Soviet-controlled East Berlin for South Africa. But he was forever marked by his experience of the centrality of the state and the environment of rules in his approach to political economy.

He graduated from the University of Cape Town in 1963 with a BA and began teaching at the University of the Witwatersrand in Johannesburg in 1967. A productive scholar and congenial colleague, Mittermaier was much more interested in scholarship and writing than he was in publication, and he was cautious about saying that anything was finished lest it be dated and

---

Michael C. Munger is senior fellow and former coeditor of *The Independent Review* at Independent Institute and professor of political science, economics, and public policy and director of the Philosophy, Politics, and Economics Program at Duke University.

narrow. This combination of a sense of his intellectual importance in tension with modesty was a central feature of Mittermaier's career. Michael Stettler put it this way:

> Highly respected by his colleagues and setting himself the highest intellectual standards, his academic path was nonetheless not conventional by current norms, caring little for publishing, but still writing for his own satisfaction, and so some of his work is being put to print posthumously. In 1977 he completed a long dissertation, which however was never submitted for examination. When in 1986 he produced a long occasional paper, the Head of Department submitted it to the higher degrees committee, with Boland and Leijonhufvud acting as external examiners. He was awarded a PhD for it, and the book was under contract for publication, but Mittermaier shelved it, thinking that the additions recommended [a case study of Eastern Europe] by the publisher would date the book and detract from its merits.[2]

From 1967 until 2002, Mittermaier met classes on what we would call "history of thought" and "philosophy of science" with a focus on economics. The Wits economics department was ecumenical, to say the least, given that it was chaired for much of Mittermaier's time there by Ludwig Lachmann, whose story is interesting on its own.[3] Faculty were allowed, even encouraged, to stake out heterodox positions, and Mittermaier was particularly taken by Lachmann's views, meeting with him often until Lachmann's death in 1990, though Mittermaier himself did not share Lachmann's view of the severe requirements of accepting subjectivity in preferences and expectations.

Models and Things

A number of scholars have said, in different contexts, "All models are bad. But some models are bad in an interesting way."[4] But, useful or not, *models are models*, not the phenomenon *being modeled*. This problem of confusing the model of a thing for the thing itself was a lifelong preoccupation for Karl Mittermaier.

Consider the common equating of Adam Smith's contribution in *The Wealth of Nations* with his succinct formulation involving "an invisible hand."[5] At the outset, this sounds discordant to modern ears because we all know that Smith advanced a theory of "the" invisible hand, not "an" invisible hand. This is the sort of thing that drove Mittermaier crazy because Smith never actually developed a theory of "the invisible hand" at all but instead had a much more flexible and nuanced view. As Emma Rothschild pointed out, the uses of "invisible hand" in Smith (there are only three!) are quite different and were clearly intended sardonically; the pagan belief in "the invisible hand of Jupiter" was not actually a force in Smith's cosmology.[6]

Mittermaier found the "invisible hand" model as a summary of Smith not just inadequate but absurd:

> It seems clear (at least to me) that Smith did not, in any of the three cases [of the "invisible hand" figure], use the words aphoristically, as is the rule nowadays. They may not have been altogether incidental to his intentions, but they were nevertheless in the nature of throw-away expressions. Had Smith been asked what exactly his invisible-hand doctrine was, he would surely have been puzzled by the question.[7]

His most important monograph, in my view (informed by others who are more familiar with his work), was a book posthumously published by Bristol University Press with the intercession of his spouse, Isabella Mittermaier, and two colleagues, Michael Stettler and Christopher Torr.[8] Daniel Klein of George Mason University also wrote a chapter in the book.[9]

One might read between the lines that Karl's passing, at nearly eighty, in 2016 removed the last obstacle to publication of the book. In any case, the central argument of the book is that there is a needless, and frankly harmful, divergence between economic dogmatism (abstract theory) and pragmatism (policy advice). Economic theory, at least the kind worth reading and considering, focuses on understanding the spontaneous orders that emerge into what is known as "commercial society," whereas policy advice accepts the efficacy of planning and central direction as if economic theory did not exist.

The "invisible hand" is the order that arises as a consequence of human action but not as a result of human design or intention. "Natural" orders emerge spontaneously, as a result of decentralized activity, and "artificial" orders are designed, planned, or "laid on" by humans. That would mean that currency and language are "natural," even though they are social constructs and not biologically necessary, emerging spontaneously and consistently in the context of human interactions, without having a meeting or agreement that they will be selected or managed.

That, for Mittermaier, was where it got more complicated. An "invisible hand" might result from either an intended and planned or an unintended and spontaneous order. And we might wonder about the factors that would cause such an order to *emerge* and those that might cause it to *endure.* They might mix and match: emergence could be unintended or intended, and the maintenance or preservation of the order might be intended or unintended.[10] For a hand to be invisible—truly invisible—both the *emergence* and *survival* must be unintended. And yet such an order might organize much of the world around us, possibly without our having any substantial understanding of that order's origins or effects.

In the first chapter of the book, Christopher Torr gives the example of the Burning Man event held in the Nevada desert in the United States. The origin of the event was clearly intentional, or maybe intentionalish, given that founder Larry Harvey clearly had not the remotest conception of what would happen and what Burning Man would become. The rules and procedures adopted by the event organizers starting in 1996 (the event was largely self-organizing in the 1986–95 period) were general and foundational, providing broad latitude within which individuals could organize themselves. This planning, which is explicit, intentional, and intensive, is operating in the background. The ephemeral, city-like structure of Burning Man might appear to emerge spontaneously each year from the desert, but in fact the spontaneity is contingent on an active and intentional "visible hand" of setup and coordination.

That's why Mittermaier's question is so interesting and, frankly, so odd. Steeped in the Austrian tradition, longtime lunch companion of Ludwig Lachmann, Mittermaier was nonetheless raising deep questions about the model of markets as "what happens when the state does nothing." There appears to be a visible hand, operating invisibly behind, or logically prior to, the invisible hand of the market.

When someone wakes up in Paris and goes out for a baguette, they'll find a cheap, fresh, and remarkably delicious loaf at the boulangerie in the next block; it seems a marvel that this spontaneous arrangement of such a complex division of labor can just be taken for granted. But is it spontaneous, all the way down? Or are there visible, if subtle, rules and choices that operate at an *even deeper* level that empower and unfetter the emergent, highly organized system?

In Mittermaier's words:

> Since institutions vary so much from place to place and from period to period and since not all of them are conducive to an advantageous market order, the question arises how an arrangement of society which constitutes an invisible hand may come into being. Does it simply arise in the absence of the meddling hands or does someone have to turn his hand to the task? Do the rules of conduct which give rise to a spontaneous order arise spontaneously if governments do not interfere—or do governments and others have to bring them about deliberately? *There is a hand behind the invisible hand. The question is: Is that hand invisible too?*
>
> The answer to this question, we will say, shows whether a dogmatic or pragmatic view is held. "Yes" indicates a dogmatic point of view. "No" indicates a pragmatic point of view.[11]

In markets, the processes that economists describe about how prices are negotiated and goods and services are exchanged really do play out. But the curves that economists draw on blackboards, and the equations they type into computers, were for Mittermaier only models of markets and not markets themselves. It is not even clear that the models used to represent market processes reflected a good understanding of markets. To understand why, it is necessary to consider the core distinction Mittermaier tried to make between dogmatic and pragmatic perspectives of the world.

Dogmatism and Pragmatism

As discussed in the previous section, Mittermaier considered Lachmann a mentor and, in fact, a friend. But Mittermaier was not an Austrian, and he was quite explicit about his rejection of the "kaleidic" view of subjectivity associated with some Austrian thinkers.[12] The Austrian school, particularly the *a priori* or apodictic conclusions argued for by Ludwig von Mises (1949) and some of his followers, were unattractive to Mittermaier.

He saw the Austrians in general, and the Misesians in particular, as being "dogmatic" about economics, not in the sense that they were irrevocably committed to their positions, though that was often true, but rather because they were committed to the principles and dogma that their models were built on. That is, he saw Austrians as he saw most economists: the underlying dogmas might differ, but the dogmas themselves were advanced and adhered to regardless of the context. In short, they were committed to the models of the thing, not the thing.

Mittermaier favored pragmatism. As he put it:

> To some it may seem that the simple anti-government prescription is all that is needed while to others it may not be at all obvious that market order, as they understand it, would then come about automatically. We shall say that the former have a rather *dogmatic* view and the latter a more *pragmatic* view of the nature of market order.
>
> The pragmatist is likely to have misgivings, for instance, about the rather indulgent attitude of the dogmatist toward monopolies not enforced by government. "The only viable definition of monopoly is a grant of privilege from the government" [Rothbard 1970, 45]. The pragmatist may appreciate how difficult it is to put one's finger on monopolistic practices and yet not be persuaded that they do not exist or are entirely benign. . . . We live in an age not only of big government, but also of big business; an age of economic oligarchy in which government is only one of the oligarchs, albeit the chief one. Oligarchs are apt to come into conflict and to

> make use of whatever weapons are at hand. The dogmatic view on government and the indulgent attitudes towards all forms of combination not sanctioned by government are likely to prove handy weapons for the lesser oligarchs.[13]

It may be worth emphasizing that this was actually written in the 1980s, though it wasn't published until 2020; it has aged rather well, it seems. The notion that everything in private markets is voluntary and efficient, and everything in the public sector is coercive and inefficient, is in fact dogmatic.

Mittermaier pointed out that "dogmatists" see government as issuing mandatory edicts and enforcing those edicts using violence. Free associations and their sets of rules are voluntarily chosen by participants, and those participants are free to quit and go elsewhere and join other associations or patronize other businesses: "Whatever [the individual does in a private setting], he does voluntarily and that is all that is needed for the operation of the invisible hand."[14] Amusingly, Mittermaier noted as an aside that "Most dogfights we see are between dogmatists of different breeds."[15]

The pragmatist, as Mittermaier saw it, takes a step back and believes that some people, and perhaps many people, desire power over others:

> Organized government is simply the most convenient channel through which all manner of people force their will on others and, if a government does not oblige, they will find other ways of doing so. If every trade union, professional and trade association, agricultural union, cartel, and so on is to be regarded as engaging in governing activity in so far as it tries to coerce, then the dogmatic anti-intervention prescription is by no means as simple as it may at first appear to be.[16]

Of course, one might concede the point that dogmatic schema may be less than perfectly accurate but still wonder, "So what? What guides the pragmatist if principles are suspect?"

Mittermaier came down on the side of what he called "free-market pragmatism." But he admitted that he had "not yet shown in what sense free-market pragmatism is distinctly pragmatic. This will be rather difficult."[17] Still, it is possible to distinguish the two positions:

> The distinction between dogmatism and pragmatism in the realm of principles is [that] dogmatism is based on one or a few principles, regarded as fundamental, from which are deduced the properties of social and economic order as it should be. . . . Pragmatism in the realm of principles is based on ill-articulated notions of a well-ordered society from which are educed or extracted various principles in a process of articulation which progressively formulates these notions into ideal institutional compromises. . . .
>
> What makes a pragmatist in the realm of principles into a free-market pragmatist is the insistence that the ideal institutional compromise should include the principle of control by impersonal constraint, the principle of the invisible hand, as the agency of control by which social and economic order is maintained.[18]

Mittermaier recognized that this appears to be simply a lot of discussion to cover the fact that he sought to bring decentralized market processes in through the back door, given that, in fact, "the invisible hand" is thus established as a dogmatic principle. But he noted that there is a difference between imposing a dogmatic constraint to use the "invisible hand" *a priori* and tolerating no deviation, and adopting a Humean notion of convention, simply observing that societies that use private property as their organizing principle are happier and more prosperous. As David Hume put it:

> For when men, from their early education in society, have become sensible of the infinite advantages that result from it (property), and have besides acquir'd a new affection to company and conversation; and when they have observ'd, that the principal disturbance in society arises from those goods, which we call external, and from their looseness and easy transition from one person to another; they must seek for a remedy, by putting these goods, as far as possible, on the same footing with the fix'd and constant advantages of the mind and body. This can be done after no other manner, than by a convention enter'd into by all the members of the

> society to bestow stability on the possession of those external goods, and leave every one in the peaceable enjoyment of what he may acquire by his fortune and industry.[19]

Mittermaier recognized the value of economic dogmatists because he thought the pragmatic approach, though intellectually more sensible, was ineffective. He thought that young people who came to study economics would perceive that

> the world is full of burning questions and to them it must also seem that all the equilibrium theorists are fiddling like Nero. They come to humour equilibrium theory as stuff for passing examinations while they regard the Marxian analysis as the real stuff. When they reach this point, in all probability they are pounced upon by political predators dressed up as economic holy men. But political predators have it almost all their own way. Apart from some free-market dogmatists, there are very few in the ranks of economic theorists to gainsay them.[20]

Impact

It may be simply definitional that the impact of "underappreciated economists" is less than it *should* be, at least in the minds of those who do appreciate the contributions of scholars such as Mittermaier. The efforts of Michael Stettler and, of course, Karl's widow, Isabella Mittermaier, have resulted in the posthumous publication of several important works,[21] but the work now published deserves to be widely read.

Mittermaier's contributions center on two areas, each of which is significant. The first is the distinction between dogmatism and pragmatism, a distinction that articulates well with philosophy but that has not found much traction in economics.[22] The theories of economics, ranging from Marxism to constrained optimization in equilibrium, to praxeology, all use *a priori* theory as models to simplify a complex world. Mittermaier did not object to models, but he shared with Ronald Coase a concern for examining the economic world as it actually is.

The second contribution was institutional, and here Mittermaier took up a subject that has divided institutional and theoretical economics for more than a century. The context in which economic activity takes place, the "visible hand," is so important that the theorizing about the emergent "invisible hand" should always be seen as contingent, even idiosyncratic. I am myself, as a student of Douglass C. North, sympathetic to this view, but Mittermaier was writing about this perspective in the 1980s, before neo-institutionalism became mainstream.

Stettler argued that Mittermaier was seeking to reorient the way that economics was done, as an enterprise, an objective that is perhaps even more ambitious than the neo-institutionalist goal simply of getting the profession to account for institutions at all. Mittermaier was advocating for "the development of an alternative conceptual framework which could ultimately enable the economic theorist to use institutions as a means of empirical orientation."[23]

At the risk of oversimplifying, what Mittermaier was after was more along the lines of Elinor Ostrom, whom I have compared to Charles Darwin as a searcher for different species.[24] In Ostrom's case, the search was for examples of private institutions that solve common pool resource problems. For Mittermaier, the search was for the various niche species, or varieties of "market orders," each of which is adapted to local conditions and the product of a path-dependent process of generating institutions. The idea of a single, general "market order," which seems to be the goal of modern economics, is for all practical purposes never observed in practice. The goal of economics instead should be to consider "*a* market order," not "*the* market order." Each idiosyncratic market order is manifested as the set of market relations that emerge from the contingent history of times and places.

Calling this view heterodox is an understatement. Not only would Mittermaier's approach rule out a single monolithic equilibrium theory of constrained optimization; it would reject the Austrian view that assumes that a minimal, but ideal, set of enforcement institutions are operating in the background. Combining the attractions of pragmatism and the focus on institutions as being prior, and causal, would result in a very different "science of economics." I, for one, think that would be a very good thing.

19 Earl A. Thompson

Turning Economic Understandings Upside-Down

Joshua R. Hendrickson

IT IS HARD to imagine a more underappreciated economist than Earl Thompson. Perhaps one reason that he is underappreciated is that he never shied away from going against the conventional wisdom and making provocative arguments. Yet, no matter how provocative the argument, his thinking was always grounded in price theory. As Armen Alchian wrote in the foreword to the book Thompson wrote with Charles Hickson, "If you are not willing to run the high risk of having your present confident understanding turned upside down, you shouldn't read this book. I speak from prior personal experience with Thompson's publications. What appears upside down at first begins to look right-side-up—from the newly acquired but very lonely Thompsonian perspective."[1] This quote not only indicates Thompson's proclivity for going against the grain, but also how convincing his unconventional arguments could be. Thompson's arguments were not only unique, but significant. Throughout his career, Thompson made significant contributions to political economy, public choice, and monetary economics.

Earl Thompson was born in Los Angeles and attended UCLA as an undergraduate, where he credited Armen Alchian and William Allen, as well as their *University Economics* textbook, for turning his interest to economics.[2] Thompson went on to attend graduate school at Harvard and received his PhD at age twenty-three. After a brief stint as an assistant professor at Stanford, Thompson returned to UCLA, where he would spend the remainder of his career.

Joshua R. Hendrickson is professor of economics at the University of Mississippi.

As a young man, Thompson had hopes of being a professional baseball player. Recognizing that he was undersized relative to a lot of athletes he was competing with, Thompson thought that he needed to identify and exploit the weaknesses of his opponents to be successful.[3] No doubt this analytical skill aided him in identifying the weaknesses of other academics' arguments as well. Unfortunately for Thompson, but fortunately for the economics profession, an injury ended his athletic career.

Earl Thompson was also known for his unique style, personality, and unconventional working hours. After the Northridge earthquake hit on January 17, 1994, at 4:31 a.m., he found himself buried under a pile of books in his office.

At Thompson's funeral, his friend Rich Walton told the story of how they met. One evening, Walton showed up to teach his course on business law. When he arrived at his classroom, Thompson was holding a review session. Walton patiently waited for Thompson to finish. However, when Walton noticed that Thompson didn't seem to be wrapping up, Walton informed him that he had class to teach. Thompson apologized and inquired about the subject of the class. Walton replied that he was teaching business law, and Thompson immediately asked if Walton was a lawyer. When Walton responded in the affirmative, Thompson replied, "Well, that's interesting because I have an economic theory that will explain that the entire legal system is bulls**t." This quote is not only indicative of Thompson's reputation as someone unafraid to challenge conventional wisdom, but also marked the start of a long friendship between the two men. Furthermore, although stated provocatively, Thompson's argument was grounded in price theory and welfare economics. The idea was also part of one of the last projects he had been working on at the time of his death.

Earl Thompson was also an exceptional teacher. John Riley, whom Thompson helped to recruit to UCLA, said that whenever he asks alumni which faculty members they remember, Thompson's name is one of the most frequent responses. Riley attributes this to how economic theory became "a force of nature" in Thompson's classes.

Thompson passed away on July 29, 2010, in his office, no doubt working on a unique argument. He is survived by his wife, Velma, and his son, Bret. As important as any of the work described below, it is clear to anyone who has spoken to Bret that Earl Thompson was not only a great economist, but a great dad.

Public Finance

Thompson's early work focused on public finance. One of his early publications challenged the conventional wisdom on government debt.[4] In that paper, Thompson considered a model in which all taxes are lump sum taxes and the market for bonds is perfectly competitive. In doing so, he considered the effect of a debt-financed reduction in current taxes and made the following claims:

> One might think, following an American tradition begun by Hansen and carried on into practically every modern textbook discussion of fiscal policy, that an increase in the current aggregate consumption expenditures results from the increase in current aggregate disposable income from the current tax reduction involved in debt financing. But this thought would be basically fallacious, for it completely disregards the equal decrease in aggregate wealth due to the increased future tax liabilities. One might similarly think, following Patinkin or Tobin, for example, that debt financing by increasing the supply of government bonds would by definition increase the aggregate real wealth of the community. This hypothesis would also completely ignore the liability of future tax payments, a liability which is exactly equal in value to the new financial asset to each citizen when there are no distribution effects. Finally, one might think, following Modigliani or Tobin, for example, that the increased supply of government bonds would force a substitution of bonds for real assets and consequently increase the rate of interest on bonds. But this would also be fallacious, for, in the absence of distribution effects, the reduction in current taxes and equal increase in future tax liability increase the value of the demand for bonds at the

> original interest rate by an amount equal to the increase in the value of the supply of bonds.[5]

The astute reader will recognize this as a clear articulation of what is now referred to as Ricardian Equivalence. It is notable that this claim was made in print by Thompson seven years prior to the work of Barro, who is often credited with the idea in modern macroeconomics.[6]

Although we cannot know for certain the counterfactual, another early publication on public finance and the reaction to that paper seemed to alter and shape the work that Thompson pursued throughout the remainder of his career. In preparation for teaching a course on public finance in 1962, Thompson was trying to understand the US income tax system. It was during this time that Thompson realized that the income tax (and all its complications) could be explained as a tax on what he termed "coveted capital." In other words, Thompson defined "coveted capital" as capital that would be desired by potential foreign aggressors. If some capital is coveted, then investment in that type of capital creates a defense externality, in the sense that the investor obtains the private benefit while creating a social cost in the form of higher required defense expenditures to protect the capital. He then argued that the US income tax system, including its exemptions and deductions, could be explained by the desire to internalize the social cost associated with coveted capital.

Thompson presented the first draft of this idea in 1972 in American Economic Association meetings.[7] Among the discussants, the paper was not well-received. In his review of the paper, Henry Aaron wrote that "Thompson's [paper] is hopeless." Thompson himself later mentioned that John Kenneth Galbraith reached out to him after the conference to see if he wanted the summary of his paper removed from the *American Economic Review*'s "Papers and Proceedings" issue so that the review of the paper could also be excluded. Thompson was surprised by this reaction "given the lack of substance of the criticisms."[8] He subsequently published the paper in the *Journal of Political Economy* (so much for hopeless!).[9] But, more importantly, that experience motivated him to produce more work on the development of institutions and public policy as well as to examine whether other policies had similar motivations.

In subsequent work, Thompson outlined a theory of subsidies based on national defense.[10] His argument was that during times of war, certain goods are subject to wartime price controls. All else equal, one would expect that industries that experience price controls during wartime would underinvest in capital since the industry rationally expects such price controls during times of war. In order to offset that incentive for underinvestment, optimal policy would have the government give subsidies during peacetime to industries that are subjected to the costs associated with price controls during wartime.

Thompson's theory makes very specific predictions about the types of subsidies that one would expect to observe. In particular, since price controls would be expected to cause underinvestment in these industries, one should not expect the subsidies to outputs, but rather to inputs. In examining the pattern of subsidies in the US, Thompson found that industry subsidies do align with those industries subject to price controls during wartime *and* that those subsidies were concentrated in input producers for those industries. Furthermore, his back-of-the-envelope calculations showed that the magnitude of these subsidies were consistent with his model.

In addition, Thompson pointed out that, according to his model, not all wartime restrictions required peacetime subsidies. For example, during times of war, states often restrict the supply of consumer durables like cars in order to divert that productive capacity to other uses. This has the effect of temporarily reducing the supply of newly produced consumer durables. In the aggregate, consumers are therefore forced to extend the life of their durable goods. However, this implies that there is pent-up demand for consumer durables at the end of the war and the relative price of consumer durables rises. These higher prices in the aftermath of the war are sufficient to compensate producers for the costs associated with wartime restrictions. As a result, no subsidy is necessary. Consistent with his prediction, Thompson noted the absence of peacetime subsidies for consumer durables.

In subsequent work, Thompson began to examine historical analogues to his discussion of the modern income tax system. After all, the defense externality that he identifies is not unique to the modern world. Thus, one would expect that there were other institutional and policy responses to this externality prior to the use of taxes on income or capital. In joint work with Hickson, this led Thompson to examine the role of guilds. While the conventional wisdom in economics is that guilds are inefficient cartels designed to generate profits for members, Hickson and Thompson called this argument into question.[11] They did so by pointing out that these types of explanations for guilds are inconsistent with the evidence. For example, guilds often imposed maximum prices and minimum quality standards, which is consistent with optimal regulation of a monopoly. Furthermore, justifications for guilds based on arguments of political power are lacking. If merchant guilds had sufficient political power, then one would expect that they would use this power to restrict guilds of craftsmen since a cartel of craftsmen would increase the merchants' costs. However, merchant guilds and craftsmen guilds coexisted throughout Europe.

Hickson and Thompson proposed an alternative theory. They argued that guilds were an institutional solution to the defense externality. Although these guilds had rules that resembled optimal monopoly regulation, they did create a long-run entry restriction that served to limit the investment path in the same way as an *ad valorem* tax on capital. Guilds also provided a town with a source of soldiers. Given the lack of standing armies at the time, a city needed to be able to raise an army quickly in order to defend itself. It is important to note that, all else equal, some sort of requirement that young, able-bodied men would be required to serve in this defense role would necessarily reduce investments in human capital. In addition, since labor is mobile, desertion of the city could be an issue. The guild resolved this issue by creating the means to acquire human capital along with the promise of future income associated with guild membership. Hickson and Thompson also noted that apprenticeships were long and corresponded closely with the timeframe typically used for conscription in the modern world. Also, apprenticeships were denied on the grounds that the candidate was unfit for military service, but were not denied for reasons related to their ability to learn the relevant trade.[12]

Thompson's work on public finance also led him to study famous speculative asset bubbles. The conventional wisdom on asset bubbles has long been that such events are explained by the madness of crowds or irrational exuberance. However, Thompson and Hickson argue that famous asset bubbles like the South Sea Bubble and the Mississippi Bubble were the result of massive government debt consolidation schemes that turned debt into equity.[13] Although neither experiment created durable institutions capable of providing emergency financing, the experiments did benefit the existing monarchies and their domestic political allies in the short run.

Although these two historical bubbles were the product of massive government debt consolidation schemes, Thompson found that another famous bubble, the so-called Tulipmania, was a myth.[14] In particular, Thompson examined the evidence and found that the Dutch government had changed the terms of the futures contracts for tulip bulbs. The rule change gave the owner of the contract the *option* to purchase tulip bulbs at the stated price rather than the obligation associated with a futures contract. This change in the law resulted in a change in the interpretation of the available quoted prices. Rather than being a futures price, the quoted prices were now strike prices on an options contract. This meant that the actual price of the options contract was only a fraction of the quoted price. Thompson generated an alternative price series, which priced the future contract and then used the Black-Scholes model to estimate the implied price of the option contract. He showed that when this correction is made, there is no longer evidence of a price bubble.

Monetary Economics

Alongside this work on public finance and political economy, Thompson also made substantial contributions to monetary economics. Early on in his career, Thompson tackled the difficult problem of incorporating money into a competitive Arrow–Debreu-type model.[15] Studying money in the context of an Arrow–Debreu general equilibrium model is a longstanding problem for theorists since such models rely on a Walrasian auctioneer to choose the vector of prices that clear markets and the resulting equilibrium is Pareto efficient. The process of exchange is absent from the model. In the absence of exchange, it is unclear what role money would play in the model. In theory, money should improve the allocation of resources, but the perfectly competitive allocation is already Pareto efficient. Typical mechanisms of introducing money into the model include things like transaction costs. However, if transaction costs exist in equilibrium, then the model with money will produce a suboptimal equilibrium outcome. This implies the odd result that using money makes people worse off.

Thompson's model introduced a competitive supply of money into the model. His solution to the problem of introducing money was to argue that one could think of all other possible equilibria as including transactions costs, but that the equilibrium with money must result in the elimination of such transaction costs. Certain economic actors in the model have a sufficient reputation to issue their own money. Nonetheless, anyone issuing money faces the last period problem. If, at some point in the future, people are unwilling to accept this money, then backward induction implies that no one should accept that money today. The issuer needs to prevent that possibility. Thompson argues that one way to do that is for the issuer to promise to buy back the money for some fixed quantity of a commodity. With redeemable money of this type, there are complete markets, and the equilibrium outcome is optimal. Thompson's mechanism also resembles the world of competitive note issuance under a gold standard. Thus, his model can be used to understand how the gold standard works.

Thompson articulated several key results from the model. When banknotes are redeemable for gold, it is the supply and demand for gold that determine the price level. Since banknotes are redeemable for gold, an oversupply of banknotes will result in notes being redeemed for gold. Banks will never have an incentive to undersupply banknotes because doing so would mean forgoing profits. As a result, the supply of banknotes is entirely demand-determined. Thompson then used this result to demonstrate that a number of "puzzles" and controversies in monetary theory could be resolved using his model. In addition, he argued that business cycles and fluctuations in employment would be driven by changes in the supply and demand for gold. He used this result to argue that the Great Depression was caused by the increase in the demand for gold during the resumption of the gold standard in the interwar period. This explanation of the Great Depression has grown in popularity over time, albeit often without attribution to Thompson.

Thompson later extended this work in a couple of different directions. The first direction was one in which he compared and contrasted the economy under a competitive monetary system in which money is redeemable for some commodity with a fiat economy and an exogenous money supply.[16] He argued that the gold standard economy had a unique price level. However, the fiat economy was subject to multiple equilibria, one of which was stable and one unstable. For an economy in the unstable equilibrium, adverse shocks could result in a downward spiral of output and employment. Thompson used this result to point out that a potentially desirable characteristic of a positive secular rate of inflation is that it moves the economy away from the unstable equilibrium.

A second extension of his work was in his proposal for monetary policy reform. Thompson proposed that central banks adopt a labor standard, in which the central bank would act as though it is willing to buy and sell labor at a fixed nominal price.[17] In reality, there is no spot market for labor. Thus, the central bank cannot literally buy and sell labor for a fixed nominal price. However, Thompson proposed implementing this rule through indirect convertibility of the dollar into a fixed quantity of labor. The central bank would commit to a particular value of a wage index and offer to buy and sell gold associated with a fixed quantity of labor. For example, suppose that the central bank targets an average wage of $20 per hour and the current price of an ounce of gold is $2000. An ounce of gold can purchase one hundred hours of labor. At the end of the month, if the average wage is $21, then the central bank would have to pay $100 to anyone who purchased gold from the central bank (so that the ounce of gold still buys one hundred hours of labor). And anyone who had sold gold to the central bank would owe the central bank $100. The implications are as follows. First, when people anticipate the average wage to be higher than the central bank's target, they would have an incentive to buy gold from the central bank in order to earn an arbitrage profit. Thus, when the overall market expects wages to exceed the central bank's target, there will be net purchases of gold from the central bank. However, this implies that the central bank is engaging in open market sales of gold and therefore reducing the money supply. Symmetrically, when the market anticipates that wages are going to be lower than expected, they will sell gold to the central bank.

There are a couple of implications that follow from this proposal. First, this proposal outsources open market operations to the market based on the market's expectations. However, in doing so, open market operations are aligned with market expectations and thus push the average nominal wage back toward its target. Second, the stability of the nominal wage implies that the dollar purchases a fixed quantity of labor (i.e., if the average nominal wage remains at its target value of $20 per hour, this implies that the dollar always buys three minutes of labor). Fluctuations in the price level therefore reflect the state of the labor market. Over the long run, rising productivity would increase real wages through a declining price level.

It is also important to note that Thompson's contributions to understanding the gold standard did not stop with those early contributions. One long-running critique of the gold standard was in terms of how states typically behaved during wartime. The general pattern started with England, but by World War I had become the standard operating procedure. When wars began, states would suspend the convertibility of banknotes into gold but promise to restore the convertibility of banknotes into gold at the prewar parity after the war ended. The result of this policy is that the countries would experience inflation during the war. Following the conclusion of the war, the return to the prewar parity required a costly deflation. Many economists criticized this common practice for the costs it imposed on society.

While others condemned this as costly and irresponsible, Thompson offered a rationale for states adopting this behavior.[18] During wartime, states need emergency financing—or the ability to raise large sums of money in a short period of time. One way to do that is to resort, either directly or indirectly, to inflationary finance through an expansion of the central bank's balance sheet. However, for this to be successful, the expansion of the central bank's balance sheet must be an expansion in *real* terms.

Without the commitment to restore prewar parity, the public will expect the central bank to expand its balance sheet during the war and create inflation. Expectations of higher inflation will reduce the real rate of return from holding money and reduce money demand. The simultaneous increase in the money supply and reduction in money demand will tend to result in the price level rising faster than the increase in the money supply. However, with the commitment to return to the prewar parity, the general public has the expectation that any inflation experienced during the war will be offset by a corresponding deflation after the war. This serves to anchor long-run inflation expectations and prevent a reduction in money demand. The central bank's balance sheet thus expands in real terms and allows the state to more effectively finance its wartime spending. Thus, while the economic costs of deflation might be significant, these costs are evidently less than the benefits conveyed by the corresponding emergency finance. Thompson's view is supported by a comparison of the wartime finance strategies of the Bank of England and the early Riksbank.[19]

Fun Stuff

Along the way, Thompson also had some "fun" papers, by which I mean brief forays into a particular topic to provide a unique and provocative perspective or insight. These papers were those like "On Labor's Right to Strike," in which Thompson argues that under particular conditions the aggregate effect of a union strike would benefit capital owners. He then argues that the history of labor's right to strike and the prevalence of strikes actually seem to align with the idea that strikes benefit the owners of capital rather than conventional explanations that suggest the primary benefit is to the striking workers.[20] Thompson also wrote a paper in which he argued that Social Security is a policy for fixing malincentives of parents with respect to their children. In the absence of Social Security, Thompson argues that parents have an incentive to push their children toward excessive hard work and excessive savings in order to provide a means to support the parents in retirement. By raising the retirement consumption level, Social Security eliminates this particular malincentive. At the same time, the presence of Social Security has no effect on those parents capable of leaving bequests to their children. However, those parents already provide an optimal education to their children because they do not expect to rely on their children for financial support.[21]

Concluding Thoughts

Earl Thompson was a unique thinker. He was always willing to challenge the conventional wisdom, but such challenges were always grounded in price theory and the desire to understand the world *as it is*. He was responsible for a significant number of insights, including the first modern articulation of what we now refer to as Ricardian Equivalence, a monetary explanation of the Great Depression distinct from that of Milton Friedman and Anna Schwartz, an understanding of the political manipulation of the gold standard, and a theory of institutions for which the equilibrium result was subsequently shown to be the outcome of any evolutionary process when a stable hierarchy is present.[22] Thompson's work is brilliant. Even those inclined to disagree with his conclusions are forced to think carefully about his arguments. The more one reads Thompson, as Alchian said, the more one begins to come around to the Thompsonian way of thinking.

20

Robert D. Tollison

Underappreciated Economist

William F. Shughart II[1]

WHETHER OR NOT an economist is underappreciated depends on whose opinion is asked and how the scholar's influence is measured. Nowadays, the economics profession typically gauges influence by computing one of myriad standard "impact factors," such as raw citation counts or Google's h-index, which summarize the number of times or frequency with which a researcher's academic journal articles and books are cited by others working in the same field of study. But relying on such metrics risks conflating scholars engaging in what Thomas Kuhn calls "ordinary science"[2] (that is, efforts to consolidate and, perhaps, extend existing knowledge in modest directions) with truly paradigm-shifting scientific revolutions.

Less quantitative, more subjective methods of identifying "great" economists are available, the most recent being Cowen, who writes that,

> To qualify as "GOAT—the greatest economist of all time," I expect the following from a candidate. The economist must be original, of great historical import, serve as a creator and carrier of important ideas, have a hand in both theory and empirics, have a hand in both macro and micro, and be "not too wrong" on the substance of issues. Furthermore, the person also must be a pretty good economist! That is, if you sat down with the person and discussed economic issues, you would be in some way impressed.[3]

William F. Shughart II is distinguished research advisor and senior fellow at Independent Institute and J. Fish Smith Professor in Public Choice in the Jon M. Huntsman School of Business at Utah State University.

Nobel prizes began being awarded annually to one or more economists in 1969. Although certainly not controversy-free, the selection committee's choices synthesize members' objective and subjective evaluations of the candidates (the winners must be alive when notified in October) and their scholarship. Hence, many ways of identifying top economists are open. But this essay and the book in hand are about economists who are or have been underappreciated, thus ruling out Nobel laureates and other scholars who rank highly in the collective opinions of the economics profession, public intellectuals, or the population at large, such as Adam Smith and John Maynard Keynes.

When the editor of *The Independent Review*'s symposium on "underappreciated economists"[4] began soliciting contributions that would expand 2023's thirteen articles into a book-length volume, I immediately suggested writing an essay on my long-time mentor and coauthor Robert Tollison. Although I had edited a special issue of *Public Choice* in honor of Bob's sixty-fifth birthday[5] and published three later remembrances of him following his death in 2016,[6] much more could be said. Let's get to it.

Robert D. Tollison: His Life and Times

Bob Tollison was born in 1942 in Spartanburg, South Carolina. He played high-school basketball there and afterward began post-secondary studies at nearby Wofford College, where, as a Terrier, he ran up and down the hardwood floors for four more years. After graduating Phi Beta Kappa from Wofford with a BA degree in 1964, he immediately entered the University of Alabama's graduate program in economics, which had been recommended to him by a Wofford College faculty member. Although he earned an MA the following year, financed partly by a Woodrow Wilson Fellowship, he was not entirely happy in Tuscaloosa. Bob transferred to the PhD program at the University of Virginia, from which he graduated in 1969.

Bob laid the foundation for his prolific academic career during his Charlottesville years. That career had two main characteristics: incredibly creative intellectual energy (it is said that he wrote his doctoral dissertation over one summer "break") and the forging of lifelong relationships with his peers, professors, and (later) students. While still fulfilling the requirements for his terminal degree, he coauthored one of the first economic critiques of compulsory military conscription, which ultimately was published at a time when the United States was shifting from staffing the Army's ranks with young male draftees to today's all-volunteer force.[7] What is more significant, future (1986) Nobel laureate James Buchanan directed Bob's University of Virginia PhD dissertation. Tollison also benefited from exposure to UVA's other remarkable faculty members, including Gordon Tullock, Ronald Coase, Warren Nutter, and Charles Goetz, along with his fellow students, the careers of many of whom likewise were very successful. Along with the faculty colleagues and students with whom he forged productive relationships throughout his later academic career, the names of Bob's fellow UVA graduate students and professors pepper his extensive curriculum vitae.

Tollison was appointed as an assistant professor of economics at Cornell University after being awarded his PhD. His three years in Ithaca would be the longest period he would ever work full-time north of the Mason–Dixon Line. Bob took a leave of absence during his last year on Cornell's faculty (1972–1973) to serve as a senior staff economist on President Richard Nixon's Council of Economic Advisers. That was his first, but not last, experience in Washington, DC's public policy "swamp," or what he later called the "Belly of the Beast."[8]

Bob returned to academia as an associate professor of economics at Texas A&M in 1973; he was promoted to a full professorship and became head of the economics department there the following year. That was when our close personal relationship began.[9] I had returned to College Station in January 1975, after being discharged (honorably) from the US Navy the month before. (I enlisted in that branch of service to avoid conscription after receiving an MS from Texas A&M in December 1971.[10])

Bob departed College Station during his final year on the faculty (1976–1977) to become a visiting professor at the University of Miami's Law and Economics Center. He then returned to Virginia in the fall of 1977 as a professor of economics at Virginia Tech and Executive Director of the Center for Study of Public Choice,[11] posts in which he remained until 1981. After Ronald Reagan was elected to his first term in the White House in November 1980, the new president appointed Bob's UVA classmate James C. Miller III as chairman of the Federal Trade Commission. Miller soon convinced Tollison to become the director of the FTC's Bureau of Economics, a post to which Bob was confirmed by the US Senate.

Although Tollison and I lost track of one another in the fall of 1977 when I left College Station to finish my doctoral dissertation and teach for a year as a visiting instructor at the University of Arizona, my first permanent job was as a staff economist in the FTC's Bureau of Economics, assigned to its Orwellian Bureau of Competition, which began in the summer of 1978. Two and a half years later, soon after Bob himself had moved to the Commission, we reconnected during a fire drill at the office building in Foggy Bottom housing the Bureau of Economics. I became his "special assistant"; I might say that the rest is history, but much more was to come.

Tollison left the FTC in the summer of 1983, reentering academia as a named professor at Clemson University, just down the road from his Spartanburg, South Carolina, hometown. After only one year there, for personal reasons, he returned to Virginia and the Center for Study of Public Choice (then at George Mason), where he remained until 1998 when I enticed him to the University of Mississippi for five years (until 2003). Bob then rejoined Clemson's faculty, his final stop before the shocking news of his death reached me early on October 24, 2016.

The Breadth and Depth of Bob Tollison's Scholarship

Bob's many colleagues, coauthors, and students would be justified in saying that labeling him as "underappreciated" is hyperbole. After all, Bob was president of the Southern Economic Association (1984–1985) and served a then-standard two-year term as president of the Public Choice Society (1994–1996), both posts signifying the esteem he had earned amongst his academic peers. Nevertheless, Bob's reputation largely was confined to the Southeastern United States. He never published a bestselling book; he was not a "public intellectual," nor did he capture the public's attention like his more famous contemporary Steven Levitt—famous because of the tireless promotional efforts of Levitt's journalist coauthor Stephen Dubner.[12] Tollison was the original "freakonomist" because he "ask[ed] questions nobody else thought of and sometimes [found] answers that nobody else imagined."[13]

Bob was a proverbial fountainhead of novel contributions to the literature of economics. He ranged widely across his chosen field of study, grounded firmly in the rational choice model of human behavior, the history of economic thought, and comparative institutional analysis.[14] So many ideas bubbled up in his fertile brain that he could not possibly carry all of them to fruition by himself, thus explaining why he collaborated so frequently with other scholars.[15] As mentioned previously, insistence on empirical testing of the myriad hypotheses he framed likewise led Bob to seek coauthors schooled in the econometric methods of the day.[16]

Tollison's curriculum vitae is so long and eclectic that it's impossible to summarize his scholarly productivity adequately in a short essay. If the entries on Bob's CV were divided amongst ten (or more) other economists, all of them would earn promotion and tenure at their respective institutions of higher learning—and because of the intellectual honesty that Bob demanded of himself and his collaborators, they would never be accused of the fraud now rampant in the academy.

Bob published thirteen scholarly books, coauthored a widely adopted introductory economics textbook,[17] edited ("curated" is the new verb) twenty-two collective volumes, contributed chapters to numerous other edited works, and published more than four hundred peer-reviewed journal articles,[18] including a top five–ranked political science periodical.[19] He supplied public goods to his profession by contributing widely read (and cited) literature reviews on important topics like rent seeking, and he supervised roughly 150 doctoral dissertations at the institutions of higher learning where he hung his hat.[20] Owing to the constraints of space and readers' patience, I choose to emphasize three subfields of the economics literature that Bob pioneered: antitrust (competition) and regulatory policy; the economics of team sports (Bob called it "sportometrics"); and the economics of religion.

Antitrust and Regulation

Tollison's interest in the broad field of industrial organization grew out of his exposure to public choice reasoning during his late 1960s graduate school days at the University of Virginia. Influenced mightily by George Stigler's (1971) seminal journal article, and perhaps by his later experiences at the Council of Economic Advisors (CEA) and on two of President-Elect Ronald Reagan's

Transition Teams (the Environment and the Federal Trade Commission), Bob was well-positioned to be appointed as the director of the FTC's Bureau of Economics in 1981.

The conventional wisdom about antitrust and regulatory policies then and now is that the relevant laws and their enforcers are motivated to preserve competitive market conditions (prices aligned with production costs) by preventing private businesses from acquiring and exercising "market power," a term sometimes improperly conflated with "monopoly." Entrepreneurship spurs innovation (novel products, reductions in production and transaction costs) and the entry of rivals, drives prices down, and disciplines market power. Such "gales of creative destruction"[21] mean that corporations (even "big" ones), left to their own devices, find it hard to maintain whatever market power they enjoy *unless* they get help from the state.

Tollison saw few differences between antitrust law enforcement and the perhaps more familiar industry-specific regulation of prices and entry conditions (e.g., public utilities). Both are vulnerable to influence by well-organized, politically powerful special interests having stakes in policy processes and, in catering to such lobbying pressure, undermine rather than promote competition. Bob also recognized that explaining the origins and purposes of public policies toward business does not mean applying the economists' textbook model of perfect (pure) competition but studying real firms participating in actual markets and the flesh-and-blood human beings who promulgate and enforce the rules of the game.

All too often, antitrust policy blocks or subverts competition.[22] That is why Bob's still underappreciated work was and is important. It is worth emphasizing that Bob was *not* pro-business; he was pro-market.

Indeed, while on leave from Cornell's faculty at the CEA, Tollison published an important journal article exploring the factors influencing antitrust law enforcement activity.[23] The three coauthors—Long, Schramm, and Tollison—asked whether the cases instituted by the US Department of Justice alleging violations of the Sherman Act (1890)—the first antitrust statute enacted on the planet—could be explained by law enforcers' professed goal of minimizing social welfare losses in the economy. As they often are now, concerns for the public's interest then naively were thought to animate the origins and purposes of antitrust policymaking (as well as governmental regulatory interventions more generally). Long et al. reported evidence contradicting that claim.

In his leadership position at the Commission, Tollison involved many FTC staff economists in research projects probing myriad aspects of the agency's antitrust and consumer protection mandates. Most of the resulting papers were published in peer-reviewed academic journals;[24] many subsequently were collected in book form.[25] Bob inspired me and other then-bureaucrats, including President Reagan's assistant attorney general for antitrust,[26] to apply their insights to the governmental and private law enforcement processes.[27]

In broad-brush terms, the conclusion of that literature, which combines public choice reasoning with evidence documenting the influence of well-organized pressure groups on the public agencies responsible for enforcing the relevant laws, is that antitrust does not differ materially from conventional economic regulation of industry-specific prices and entry conditions. Combining the logic of collective action[28] with Gordon Tullock's rent-seeking insight[29] and Stigler's theory of economic regulation[30] leads to a more general interest-group theory of government[31] in which individuals and groups compete to obtain the favors granted by the state's exercise of its police powers (or to avoid the harm from being forced to finance those favors). Politicians, especially the powerful members of congressional oversight committees, mediate transfers of wealth between the winners and losers of antitrust law enforcement processes.[32]

Just because the antitrust laws apply to a wide range of business practices that supposedly impair the operations of free and open markets (mergers and acquisitions, for instance) does not mean that special interests, including the defendant's rivals, will not mobilize whenever and wherever the antitrust agencies are considering law enforcement actions that threaten the status quo.[33] Indeed, coalitions of rivals and other interested parties frequently instigate such lawsuits. Evidence from the by-now large literature following Long, Schramm, and Tollison[34] concluding that antitrust often fails to achieve its supposed goal of protecting consumers (the *only* goal consistent with congressional intent, according to Bork[35]) raises an obvious question: if consumers' welfare is not the top priority of the law enforcement process, what does explain the behavior of the Antitrust Division of the Department of Justice and the Federal Trade Commission?

Bob Tollison was among the first scholars to ask that question.[36] His still underappreciated answer, supported by evidence, is that interest groups shape antitrust law enforcement outcomes as they do in all other regulatory policy settings.[37]

Sportometrics

"Institutions matter" is a mantra of public choice economists and scholars interested in comparing the performances of distinctive legal regimes and economic systems. The rules of the game (incentives and constraints) governing the interactions of rational human actors are decisive in determining the observed outcomes.

College and professional sports supply ideal conditions ("natural experiments") for testing whether and how the rules of the game influence individual athletes' behaviors on the court, field, or "pitch" and the collective performances of the teams for which they play. Given his experiences as a starter at Wofford College, the lunchtime pickup basketball games he organized over the years among faculty colleagues and graduate students, and his lifelong interest in Clemson University's basketball and football programs, Bob Tollison was a pioneer in applying economic methods to the world of sports.

Bob's initial contribution to what he called "sportometrics" illustrates his innovative approach to comparative institutional analysis.[38] In the late 1970s, the Atlantic Coast Conference was experimenting with adding a third referee to its regular season basketball games. A key concern was that putting an extra pair of eyes on the court would cause more fouls to be called, fewer points to be scored, the paces of games to slow, and, consequently, fans to become less interested in ACC basketball contests. McCormick and Tollison assembled evidence to test those concerns. Hypothesizing that all else equal, rational players could respond to an additional referee by committing *fewer* fouls (because rules infractions were more likely to be detected), McCormick and Tollison reported a 34 percent reduction, on average, in the number of fouls called during ACC basketball games, thus undermining the critics.[39] Their evidence convinced other college programs and the professional National Basketball Association to mimic the ACC by adopting today's standard three-referee system.

Tollison's sportometrics research program subsequently was extended to study, *inter alia*, the purposes and effects of the cartelization and enforcement of the rules imposed by the National Collegiate Athletic Association aimed at preserving amateurism in college football,[40] the effects of property rights on athletic effort in the Olympic Games, and the behavioral impact on pitchers after Major League Baseball adopted in 1973 a designated hitter (DH) rule.[41] The American League implemented the rule that year, but the National League did not adopt it until 2022, thus generating the conditions for a natural experiment. Goff, Shughart, and Tollison conjectured that "insuring" AL pitchers against direct retaliation because they no longer appeared at the plate themselves would induce them to hit opposing batters more frequently than NL pitchers did.[42] The evidence supported that conjecture, which subsequently was confirmed.[43]

Bob Tollison was a serious scholar. But, for him, doing "*economics was synonymous with 'having fun*.'"[44] Sportometrics, which he fathered, is perhaps the best illustration of the exuberance he brought to his classroom teaching and the research ideas he shared generously with his many friends and collaborators.[45]

The Economics of Religion

Religious beliefs are examples of what economists call a "credence (perhaps meta-credence) good"—something whose quality (value to consumers) cannot be known before purchase or even afterward. Despite some anecdotal evidence from near-death experiences, no one ever has reported back from visiting Shakespeare's "undiscovered country." Although Bob Tollison as a South Carolinian adhered to the Presbyterian faith, his deep interest in economic history and the broad explanatory powers of price-theoretic methods led him to collaborate with two other Bobs (Ekelund and Hébert) to study the origins of the Roman Catholic Church and the evolution of its doctrines up through the Protestant Reformation.

That collaborative research program produced many journal articles and three books,[46] the first of which was Ekelund et al.[47] There, Ekelund, Tollison, Hébert, and two graduate-student coauthors treat the Catholic Church as a vertically integrated, multidivisional (M-form) firm (headquartered in

Rome) and then proceed to ask and answer questions about its sometimes puzzling dogmas, including opposition to usury (mainly when the Church was a borrower rather than a lender); priestly celibacy (preventing the births of children who might become heirs to Church property); aural confession (allowing priests to discover their flock's willingness to pay for absolution, which facilitated price discrimination); and the "invention" of purgatory as a waystation to heavenly salvation (thus generating revenue in return for priestly intercession on behalf of deceased loved ones not passing immediately through St. Peter's gates).

Those ideas were extended and fleshed out more fully in Ekelund, Hébert, and Tollison[48] and Ekelund and Tollison.[49] The latter volume examines Protestantism's competitive entry into the marketplace of Christianity and the Catholic Church's responses to the new rivalry, which the two Bobs see as being triggered by the Church's exercise of market power and excessive rent extraction from the faithful.

Few aspects of human behavior lie beyond the ambit of economic analysis. Although many scholars may consider religion to be "non-economic," Tollison and his coauthors contributed original, pathbreaking ways of thinking about religious beliefs and the institutions that govern access to the afterlife. Like much of Tollison's work, the skillful application of Chicago price theory to religion encouraged others to plow further and plant more seeds in a novel subfield.[50]

Summary and Conclusions

Bob Tollison's legacy comprises a colossal and wide-ranging corpus of scholarly work. This short essay only scratches the surface of his significant contributions to the literatures of public choice, antitrust and regulatory policy, the history of economic thought, economic history, sports, religion, and beyond—all grounded in neoclassical price theory and its rational actor model. Owing to his sociability (most of the time), fierce loyalty to his many colleagues and collaborators, and tireless dedication to his craft, he "was easy to like [and] easy to underestimate."[51]

Tollison was not a self-promoter; besides being recognized for teaching excellence at Virginia Tech and Clemson, he never won a national or international award for his scholarship. As is true in academia generally, the economics profession is sharply biased against scholars trained or employed in the American South. My bias herein is plain: Bob Tollison may be underappreciated as an economist globally, but not by me or others fortunate to have known him well.

21

The Underappreciated Political Economy of Charlotte Twight

Mikayla Novak

DISTRIBUTIONS ARE AN ineradicable aspect of human existence. It is unsurprising, then, to observe a distribution of appreciation of scholarly output emanating from the academy. Appreciation appears estimable using proxy indicators such as aggregate number of citations of scholarly works, as well as the bestowing of academic prizes and similar honors, all signaling recognition of novel and significant research contributions by individuals (and, to a lesser extent, research teams). Given the rise of interrelationships between social science and public policy, and the increasing demands upon academics to "publicly engage" in ways that transcend conventional research and teaching activities, traditional and social media mentions could be added to the list of "appreciation variables."

One need not delve too deeply into statistical evidence to reveal a distribution of scholarly appreciation within mainline political economy, an academic sub-discipline emphasizing how market economics, spontaneous order theorizing, and effective institutions underpin economic growth and material prosperity.[1] Ludwig von Mises, Friedrich A. Hayek, James M. Buchanan, and Elinor Ostrom represent the faces appearing on the figurative Mount Rushmore of mainline political economy, and whose scholarly contributions are likely to command the greatest recognition. Whereas historians of thought will likely nominate different figures, it is posited that the contributions of Frank Knight, Milton Friedman, Vincent Ostrom, Gordon Tullock, Ronald Coase, Israel Kirzner, Richard E. Wagner, and Peter Boettke would also appear

---

Mikayla Novak is senior fellow in the F. A. Hayek Program for Advanced Study in Philosophy, Politics, and Economics at the Mercatus Center at George Mason University.

well-appreciated among contemporary mainline political economists. However, this listing does not present the totality of academic figures who have contributed to mainline political economy. A great number of individuals not already listed could be roughly categorized as among those whose efforts have gone, for whichever reason, "underappreciated" in the grand scheme of all things academic.

Rating one's scholarly toil as underappreciated seems rather unfair. To clarify, consignment to underappreciation status is not necessarily assumed to occur because of a lack of effort by those who did not reach the apex of recognition, again as indicated by such measures as number of citations or number of awards received. If anything, it could be argued that the distributional tail of scholarly underappreciation has grown in modern times, as the exuberant growth in research activity competes for necessarily limited and divided human attention. Even so, moments of belated recognition remain achievable, even for the hitherto underappreciated, thanks to initiatives such as this volume. In this chapter, I seek to excavate and present the original scholarly works of Charlotte Twight, in the hope that her unique insights will be appreciated by new generations of scholars with an interest in mainline political economy.

The structure of this chapter is as follows. The next section briefly profiles the career of Charlotte Twight. Then, I summarize Twight's theory of political transaction cost manipulation, with an application to the rapidly developing surveillance state. This is followed by a discussion of Twight's description of American political economy as an exemplar of "participatory fascism," and how political exploitation of (real and imagined) crisis episodes have fostered an entrenchment of statist power. The chapter then concludes.

Charlotte Twight's Career

Charlotte Twight was born in New York City in March 1944. Just over two decades later, she received a bachelor of arts (*summa cum laude*) from California State University, Fresno.[2] Initially posted as a computer programmer in US Naval Command from 1966 to 1970, Twight was later admitted to the Washington State Bar in 1973. After attaining her JD degree in law from the University of Washington, Twight later attained a doctorate in economics in 1983 initially under the supervision of transaction cost economist Steven N. S. Cheung and, later, Robert Higgs.[3] Between the early 1970s and early 1980s she held a variety of junior academic posts, including as law lecturer at the University of Washington in 1975 and as a predoctoral teaching associate in the Department of Economics at the same institution between 1981 and 1983.[4]

Charlotte Twight later moved to Boise State University for more senior academic career opportunities. Twight commenced as assistant professor in the Department of Economics in 1986 and progressed up the ranks to become professor in 1991 and department chair for a two-year period (1994–96). Charlotte Twight was named the first Brandt Professor of Free Enterprise Capitalism in 2003 and retired in 2018. Twight maintained numerous professional affiliations during her career, including with the Independent Institute, Cato Institute, Institute for Humane Studies, and the Washington Bar Association.

Twight was the author of two books—*America's Emerging Fascist Economy* (1975) and *Dependent on D.C.* (2002)—and authored numerous scholarly articles. Her works appeared in outlets such as *Public Choice*, *Journal of Economic Behavior and Organization*, *Journal of Theoretical Politics*, *Constitutional Political Economy*, *Journal of Public Policy*, *The Independent Review*, and *Cato Journal*. The research interests of Twight have been broad-ranging and included political economy, public choice, and law and economics, and her published works covered topics as diverse as the legal and constitutional basis of government regulation, historical evolution of the regulatory state and its effects, the properties and implications of institutional change, and the growth of government.

Transaction Cost Manipulation: Twight's Micro-Foundation of Public Sector Expansion

Over the years economists, political scientists, and other scholars have identified numerous factors determining the growth of the public sector. Notable examples include Adolph Wagner's "law"[5] to the effect that industrialization would increase demands for public goods, that demographic changes could facilitate increasing revenue collection and governmental spending,[6] the median voter or interest groups play a determinative role in demands for more public sector activity,[7] or that globalization or technological change will lead to greater spending especially on redistributive activities.[8] These theories have been subject to extensive empirical testing, perhaps unsurprisingly with mixed results given the complex circumstances underpinning growth in the fiscal (and regulatory) profiles of government in various countries.

Twight suggests in her book *Dependent on D.C.* that these competing theoretical explanations focus upon "one aspect or another of the growth of government."[9] However, the theories are deficient in the sense that they do not provide a generalist account as to why government expands (both in scale and scope) in ways that both contravene constitutional stipulations and lack a certain popular legitimacy. Twight's explanation is that "manipulating costs of political decision making in order to achieve results initially *inconsistent* with actual public preferences has been a recurrent strategy in capturing and maintaining increased government authority."[10] A scholarly focus of Twight is upon *political transaction costs*, which are defined as "the costs of reaching and enforcing collective agreements that define the role and scope of government."[11]

Over the years, Twight identified an impressive array of political techniques relied upon by legislators and political administrators to *increase* the effective transaction costs faced by other political actors (such as ordinary citizen-voters) who may otherwise resist acts of governmental expansion.[12] The specific examples she articulated may be categorized as belonging in either one of two kinds of political transaction costs: "information costs," and "agreement and enforcement costs." Information costs refer to the costs of obtaining accurate information from official channels about policy specifications and their implications, as well as the costs borne by individuals when trying to evaluate the relative benefits and costs of private (or nonstate) alternatives to public policy proposals.[13] The phenomenon of fiscal illusion may be read as an example of how information costs of political exchange might be manipulated by strategic political agents.[14]

I now turn to Twight's agreement and enforcement costs. These are "the costs of *acting* on private perceptions of appropriate government functions and policies. Thus, in large measure, these strategies alter costs of reaching or enforcing political agreements pertaining to the scope of governmental authority and concomitant individual rights."[15] Agreement and enforcement costs include "deliberate increases in organizational costs . . . facing private citizens and other political actors in decisions influencing the role and scope of government."[16] There are many examples that Twight nominates for this category, with one of them being judicial rulings or adjustments to administrative law that have the effect of inducing a *de facto* (rather than *de jure*) expansion in discretionary political authority.

Twight's theory of transaction cost manipulation recognizes that institutions are likely to influence, in degree and kind, the transaction costs that are borne out politically. Indeed, the quality of the institutional environment is likely to influence the capacity of any given political actor (or set of actors) to shift political transaction costs onto their opponents. For example:

> When rent-seeking interest groups cause changes in the law that increase the transaction costs of political resistance by the taxpaying public, thereby reducing the already minimal incentives of rational voters to become informed and politically active, they increase the margin by which total societal costs may exceed the total benefits of particular fiscal programs. . . . This means that, when transaction-cost augmentation prevails, the net social cost is greater and hence efficiency less than what would be attained under an alternative *achievable* set of institutional rules.[17]

It is for these reasons that interest groups and certain other political actors look to "change the institutional rules of the game that establish transaction costs that constrain the rest of the voting public."[18] The nonconsensual shifts in the institutional order wrought by transaction cost manipulation are seen to violate contractarian standards of public agreement as the key criterion of political change.[19]

Another consideration is that ideological assertions could influence the extent of political acceptance (or the lack thereof) toward attempted transaction cost manipulations. Indeed, "endogenously determined transaction costs play a more central role than previously accorded them in models of ideological change. Through skillful shaping of such transaction costs, government actors can influence in systematic ways the degree of political opposition that they encounter in advancing their own policy objectives."[20] In an investigation of the growing role of government in US education financing and provision, Twight identifies that ideological shifts correspond with adaptation to new public sector institutions and practices by the masses.[21] It is also apparent that the ideological entrenchment of statist norms takes place as individuals refuse to publicly reveal their true sense of opposition to expanded government involvement, which is perhaps reflected by the relatively increasing political transaction costs of expressing dissent.[22]

The political transaction cost approach of Twight offers a unique explanation for the phenomenon of public sector growth. Crucially, it does so by explicitly bringing actors back into the conceptual and analytical pictures. This approach is seen as overcoming the deficiencies of structuralist explanations for governmental growth, which either tends to ignore the contributions of agents to such outcomes entirely or reduces the diversity of their roles by dint of representative agent modeling strategies.

As Twight frequently noted, growth in the scale and scope of modern government is unrelenting. A more recent example has been the development of the surveillance state. In *Dependent on D.C.*, Twight chronicles an array of techniques embraced by all levels of US government to collect personal information about each citizen, as well as nonpermanent residents, tourists, and so on. A crescendo of surveillance activity has occurred in the wake of the September 11, 2001, terrorist attacks. It is in this context that Twight observed that "searches and surveillance have proliferated, including ubiquitous video surveillance, the groping of travelers at airports, random roadblocks and searches on highways, and wholesale gathering and storage of people's phone calls, email messages, and Internet searches."[23] Newer developments such as the use of facial recognition technology and application of artificial intelligence maintain the expansion of the surveillance state.

Twight's scholarly contributions engaged with the rationale and effects of the surveillance state. Obtaining ready access to personal data provides government officials with immense leverage "for institutionalizing government control, individual dependence, and unprecedented threats to cherished American liberties."[24] This is argued to induce greater public compliance, not only because people are aware that they are being watched by anonymous bureaucrats but because individuals become fearful of the uncertain (and potentially pernicious) ways in which bureaucratic personnel will use one's personal, and often intimate, information.[25] In addition to Twight's concerns, issues have been raised over the prospects of the misuse of data in ways that discriminate, if not victimize, marginalized or unfavored sociopolitical groups, not to mention fundamental questions surrounding the security of information retained by governmental entities.

The most relevant aspect of Twight's contribution to the study of surveillance is a diagnosis as to what processes have facilitated the expansion of the surveillance state as we know it. Key to understanding this phenomenon is political transaction costs, particularly the manipulation of perceptions about the appropriateness and legitimacy of personal information collections by government. In this respect, "federal officials always provide an appealing reason for such intrusion into our private lives, however inadequate the reason or unconstitutional the intrusion."[26] Aside from the most vanilla of rationalizations, such as promoting efficiency in the management of public services, reasons used to help dull political resistance include fraud detection and elimination, and, more recently, repelling so-called "misinformation" and "domestic terrorism." Then there is the ultimate refrain of those figures who seek to justify state surveillance: "You have nothing to fear if you have nothing to hide."

Additional transaction cost manipulation techniques are identified by Twight to help fuel the expansion of population-wide surveillance capacity. Whereas isolated proposals to use new surveillance techniques (or the piecemeal application of existing techniques for a different purpose) may focus opposition, Twight also thinks that piecemeal expansions distract and lull the public into a false sense of security concerning the true extent of the surveillance state's domination over American lives.[27] To further hedge against strident opposition to surveillance state growth, Twight identifies instances where government agencies deploy "increasingly imperceptible means" of spying, recording, and reporting people's activities.[28] Examples include the multipurpose (but typically undisclosed) functionality of traffic cameras or the clandestine use of devices, apps, or spyware to capture cellphone content without consent.

The manipulation of political transaction costs that underpins the growth of the surveillance state has, for Twight, come at an immense cost. A primary cost of surveillance has been that of lost liberty itself, especially in the domains of personal and civil liberties, as most citizens appear to put up little resistance against new ways of monitoring the routine activities of everyday life. An increasingly notable aspect of the inducement to liberty-reduction by the surveillance state surrounds efforts to suppress freedom of assembly, expression, and speech, particularly of people who seek to peacefully dissent against unpopular government decisions.

Twight on the Death of Liberal Democracy: Poly-Crisis Facilitates Participatory Fascism

There is now a rich mainline political economy literature related to the causes and implications of crisis situations. One of the seminal texts in this regard is Robert Higgs's *Crisis and Leviathan* (1987). Charlotte Twight engaged with Higgsian crisis scholarship on several occasions. In a jointly written paper with Higgs, Twight recognized the existence of "ratcheting effects" that unfold during and after a crisis. "[N]ational emergencies invariably witness a transfer of economic rights from private citizens to government officials" that endures, with arguably "the most significant consequence of the emergency experience . . . [being] . . . the ideological change it fosters."[29] In addition to eroding the domain in which economic freedom is exercised, a danger of crisis-induced public sector expansionism is that the legal and policy instruments activated by political actors during the crisis period may be creatively repurposed, post-crisis, to respond (as H. L. Mencken would describe it) to the next (mostly imaginary) hobgoblin.

A later contribution of Twight's reinforces the intuitions of her earlier, coauthored contribution with Higgs by introducing political transaction costs onto the analytical scene. Indeed, "crisis in the form of war or depression is a powerful stimulus to transaction-cost augmentation, enabling government officials to do more of what they want to do with less resistance from the public."[30] A logical implication of this insight is that "[i]f 'crisis' is the ticket to expanded government authority, and if one favors expanded government authority, one has incentives to trump up crisis."[31] Twight effectively provides an explanatory account of what is contemporaneously identified as "poly-crisis," the simultaneous appearance of multiple forms of crisis at once that, in one sense, might prove unmanageable but, profoundly in the other, lays the basis for continuous political efforts to accumulate power and to dominate the terms and conditions of economic and social exchanges.[32] Using Twight's framework, poly-crisis is an endogenously devised situation of "transaction-cost-augmenting measures that make later contractions in government authority less likely."[33]

In the face of rampant public sector expansionism, political economists have often found themselves struggling to identify the prevailing economic–political regime that governs our world. Clean-line intellectual modalities of capitalism and socialism, or democracy and authoritarianism, seem increasingly ill-fitted to the complexified environments of today. Twight coined as early as 1975 a provocative categorization of political economy—labelled "participatory fascism"—to describe the developments she forensically studied during her career. Given that a fascist political economy "endows a group or 'collective' with rights," it follows that "[f]ascism deems the welfare of the nation to be its paramount concern."[34] The nominal exercise of economic agency, such as the acquisition and disposal of one's property, is tolerated by the state, but "[n]o economic sphere is immune from government control, for any economic activity that allegedly transcends public interests and affects the community at large is deemed a legitimate subject of state control."[35] Accordingly, economic interests need to remain watchful of sweeping political dictates not only affecting returns from allowable activities, but in determining what activities are permissible or not.

In *America's Emerging Fascist Economy*, Twight outlines numerous examples supporting her proposition that American political economy has assumed fascistic characteristics. One example has been the expansive interpretation of the Interstate Commerce Clause of the US Constitution. In this case, as in so many others discussed by Twight, legislative and administrative opportunism combined with these novel legal interpretations to greatly extend political authority over commercial activities. Expanded public sector powers were ratified in the face of feeble, or perhaps nonexistent, opposition, giving creative political actors room to deploy their newfound powers in a multiplicity of ways and in an unrestrained fashion. Although it is still largely the case that participation in "political ceremonies, proceedings, and engagements—most important, voting . . . engenders the sense that somehow the people control the government,"[36] under participatory fascism the capacity of these political practices to inhibit an expansion in the functions and powers of the state are limited at best.

Conclusion

A remarkable feature of Twight's scholarship is the consistent application of economic principles to legal and policy issues. In a 1993 interview published in a Boise State University magazine, Twight said, "If you are going to write and talk about political economy, you need to understand the economic effect of laws and regulations."[37] She added that "it's one thing to know about the statutory powers of the government; it's another to understand the law's economic effects on people. . . . Economics is at the heart of most policy issues."[38] At the heart of this approach is a focus upon the use of fiscal, legal, and regulatory techniques, coupled with ideological claims, for the purposes of raising the political transaction costs of opposition toward public sector expansion. Ongoing growth in the scale and scope of government in the US, and elsewhere, appears broadly consistent with Twight's theories.

Several studies have either directly adopted insights from Twight's scholarly literature or have conceptualized issues in a similar manner. For example, Holcombe illustrates how the economic, political, and social distance between political elite interests and nonelite citizen-voters is influenced by differential transaction costs of political exchange experienced by both groups.[39] Those fresh insights provide opportunities to build upon intellectual themes previously explored by Twight. It is also the case that continuing policy innovation provides a basis for applying Twight's analytical approaches to new circumstances. These thoughts lead me to suggest the following hypothesis: The rediscovery and reuse of transaction cost economics and politics is likely to be correlated with renewed appreciation of Twight's contributions toward the modern mainline political economy tradition.

22

Karen Vaughn

Building an Austrian Approach to Public Choice

Jayme Lemke

KAREN VAUGHN IS an academic entrepreneur and market process theorist whose contributions were formative in the building of the Austrian economics and public choice programs at George Mason University. This essay could easily be about her academic entrepreneurship alone, which is well appreciated by some, unknown to others, and absolutely critical to both the Austrian revival and the development of the Virginia school of public choice.[1] However, I intend to focus instead on the great merits of Vaughn's scholarly contributions and the benefits of including them more explicitly in the canon of important market process theorists of the late twentieth and early twenty-first centuries.

Vaughn developed her academic research under strict constraints relative to many of her peers. Not only did she invest enormous energies in building the Department of Economics at George Mason University; she was also a mother during a time when there was not much institutional understanding of how to structure an academic position to enable women to raise children and still do their best work.[2] As such, Vaughn was left to develop her research when she could between meetings and raising her children. In a 2020 interview, she described writing on a typewriter in her living room in fits and starts when her daughter was napping or during any other quiet moment she could find.[3]

In response to these trade-offs, Vaughn consciously chose quality over quantity in her academic pursuits. The result is a body of work that one of

---

Jayme Lemke is senior fellow in the F. A. Hayek Program for Advanced Study in Philosophy, Politics, and Economics at the Mercatus Center at George Mason University.

her former colleagues, economist Richard Wagner, described as containing "one of the highest ratios of meaningful to total verbiage of any economist currently practicing the craft."[4] Her first book, *John Locke: Economist and Social Scientist*, was an investigation of the economic influence of the ideas of John Locke published by the University of Chicago Press.[5] Her second book, *Austrian Economics in America: The Migration of a Tradition*, was an intellectual history of the development of market process theory in the twentieth century published by Cambridge University Press.[6] In addition, she wrote roughly thirty-five journal articles and book chapters in the fields of history of economic thought, economic methodology, Austrian economics, comparative economic systems, and public choice, most of them between 1972 and 2002.[7] My primary contention in this essay is that these works are underutilized both in the classroom and as a springboard for further research in Austrian political economy.

In an effort to persuade others to join me in correcting this oversight, I will highlight Vaughn's contributions in four areas: (1) the history of economic thought, (2) subjectivist economic methodology, (3) social change and learning, and (4) the political economy of morality. In the conclusion, I will offer brief remarks on how to build on Vaughn's research, hopefully sending you off with either a newfound or a renewed appreciation for the scholarship of Karen Vaughn.

History of Economic Thought

Vaughn's start was in history of economic thought. After focusing on the work of John Locke,[8] she shifted her attention to F. A. Hayek and other market process theorists after becoming interested in the field through interactions with Larry Moss and Israel Kirzner.[9] In addition to serving as president of the History of Economics Society (HES), she was editor of the *HES Bulletin*, which would later become the *Journal of the History of Economic Thought.*

Vaughn was a key contributor to the reevaluation of the socialist calculation debate that took place during the Austrian revival beginning in the 1970s: "Learning about the economic calculation debate was a revelation. There really was something wrong, not only with socialist economics but possibly with neoclassical economics as well. The next twenty-five years of my career, more or less, consisted of an exercise in figuring out exactly what was wrong with both."[10] Vaughn's argument emphasized that socialist models would never work because they fundamentally misunderstood that the actual operation of a market economy is dramatically different from the simplistic constructions found in equilibrium models. She saw this issue as going beyond the calculation debate itself—as if that weren't important enough—and speaking directly to the fact that something had gone deeply wrong in the discipline of economics.[11] In the course of explicating this argument, Vaughn offered what may be one of the clearest existing articulations of Hayek's criticisms of socialist calculation.

In addition to her work on the calculation debate, Vaughn explored and updated a wide range of controversies and theoretical developments originating in the Austrian tradition. She built on Hayek's theories of market process and social order, including on his interpretation of the Ricardo effect,[12] his contributions to the socialist calculation debate,[13] and his continual efforts to explain processes of social change and progress.[14] She was greatly inspired by Israel Kirzner, even when she did not agree with him. She challenged Kirzner's theory of entrepreneurial alertness on the grounds that he did not go "far enough in pointing to the implications of the creative nature of entrepreneurship"[15] and his views on equilibrium on the grounds that they were inconsistent with the idea of the market as a never-ending creative process.[16] She wrote about the unappreciated importance of Carl Menger's ideas, which she contended contained great potential for further development and consequently had played an important role in triggering the beginnings of the Austrian revival in the 1970s.[17]

Overall, Vaughn's research in the history of economic thought demonstrates the value of Kenneth Boulding's recommendation to stand on the shoulder of giants.[18] The ideas of the past are not merely historical curiosities but intellectual boosts that can help us push forward to a clearer understanding of the nature of our economic and political systems without having to constantly start over from scratch. Karen Vaughn succeeded both in building on the intellectual contributions of the past and in advancing those ideas in such a way that she herself could support those to follow.

Economic Methodology and Subjectivism

After meeting James M. Buchanan and eventually playing a critical role in negotiating the move of his research group to George Mason University, Vaughn became interested in what she recognized to be a uniquely important interpretation of cost. The idea of subjective cost is one that goes back to Menger and Friedrich von Wieser.[19] Despite the well-established nature of the *idea*, Buchanan argued—and Vaughn agreed—that the subjective nature of cost had not been fully integrated into the practice of economics. Rather, most economists agreed with subjective cost at an abstract level but failed to recognize its implications for economic theory and policy.

In addition to presenting an incredibly clear exposition of subjective cost and its significance for economic analysis—this theme of clarity is one that recurs throughout Vaughn's work—Vaughn got into the specifics of the way in which economic theory is abused when we fail to truly understand the subjective nature of cost. For instance, cost curves and a variety of other core neoclassical models presume that firms' opportunity costs can be fully captured by financial outlays—which may or may not come close to reflecting the actual value of the next best alternative. The same is true of indifference curves and production possibilities curves, both of which fail to capture the difference between the subjective, unmeasurable costs that influence choice and the objective changes in resource ownership that occur after a decision is made or a transaction executed.[20]

Vaughn also made an important argument about the implications of subjective cost for policy analysis. She argued that monetary outlays differ most from true (subjective) cost in the domain of economic policymaking, which by definition is a space where the market system is presumed to be a biased or incomplete reflection of values. Consequently, any model that uses monetary outlays to evaluate the efficiency of a policy intervention will be inherently flawed: "[T]he further we move away from purely competitive markets, and the more government decisions preempt market decisions, the less likely will policy based on models of markets in full equilibrium lead to accurate evaluation of alternatives and to outcomes desired by the policy makers."[21]

Vaughn's insights on subjective cost are extraordinarily important for scholars, bureaucrats, and activists who attempt to use monetary outlays to evaluate the performance of economic policies. Many in the policy process place great faith in cost-benefit analysis as a tool that can prevent the adoption of inefficient policies that will generate more harm than good. However, cost-benefit analysis departs from actual subjective valuation in many ways. Not only are any monetary values used subject to Vaughn's critique of the limited usefulness of monetary outlays in political spaces; the very choice of which factors are considered worth including in the cost-benefit analysis are determined by the subjective values of the *analyst* rather than by the individuals whose values are supposed to be under consideration. The same critique applies to the increasing pressure to develop measurable standards against which to evaluate the performance of aid agencies and other bureaucratic organizations.

The subjectivist critique leads directly to Vaughn's critique of welfare economics. Vaughn argues that subjectivist economists can "investigate the economic variables that are important to people" and "give analyses of the link between government policies and the economic consequences that flow from them" without abandoning their methodological principles.[22] Although more humble methods may not be able to give concrete answers—which, from Vaughn's perspective, would be largely illusory anyway—the understanding they can provide will be more honest and therefore more scientific: "It seems more a religious than a scientific exercise to identify what we want the outcome of people's actions to be in advance and then try to devise means to bring about our desired result. A scientific model should serve to help explain the world as it is, not serve as a reproach to a defective reality."[23] In making this argument, Vaughn continues a line of thought that began with Hayek's critique of scientism and continues with Buchanan's critique of the social welfare function. What Vaughn adds here, in my view, is both a way forward and the foundation for a critique that is specific to the practical influence of economics on political decision-making.

Social Learning and Reform

How social learning takes place and the possibility that a society could intentionally improve itself are questions of great interest in Vaughn's research.

In Vaughn's words, "How can man the dreamer channel his dreams into socially desirable ends?"[24]

There is a tension in nonviolent social reform between needing to preserve some degree of stability and the fact that institutional reform cannot occur until somebody breaks the existing rules: "Social change is a tension between human creativity and daring and human reluctance to disturb the known patterns of their lives."[25] This argument builds on two observations from the work of F. A. Hayek: (1) change and uncertainty are necessary ingredients for progress, and (2) systems that organize adaptation to change (such as the role prices play in the market system) are also essential in order to preserve enough social stability for people to be able to work toward that progress.

Vaughn argues for an evolutionary interpretation of Hayek's work as a starting point in the building of a theory of social change.[26] In Vaughn's interpretation, Hayek's vision of progress begins with the observation that every change creates a problem for somebody. Whether or not the problem is directly perceived, individuals—adapting their plans and strategies to resolve or work around the problem—begin to act according to a different set of rules from those they were following previously (again, whether those rules are explicit or tacit).[27] Once even one person begins to act according to a different set of social rules, others gain the opportunity to observe the existence of an alternative option and adapt their own plans and strategies accordingly.

Vaughn asks whether Hayekians can participate in social reform without feeling that they are committing the constructivist fallacy of using their own knowledge to supersede the knowledge that has been embedded in emergent institutions.[28] Although Hayek does not mince words in his critique of rational constructivism and the abuse of reason, Vaughn emphasizes the caveat that Hayek's critique is intended to apply to the forced implantation of social reforms. In reality, some element of design is essential if we are to avoid "consign[ing] intelligent men to evolutionary traps and dead ends within losing cultures."[29] However, the changes brought about by that design "must be gradual and at the margins" to avoid serious error and conflict.[30] As such, there is not such a contrast as there might seem between Hayek's critique of rational constructivism and Buchanan's constructive constitutional political economy. Rather, bringing Hayek's insights to the constitutional table could create opportunities for the development of a theory of *voluntary* reform as a productive alternative to the coercive radical change that was the subject of Hayek's critique.[31]

One way this argument can be interpreted is as an early theoretical foundation for the role of civil society and other voluntary organization building as an important component of the maintenance of a free society. This is one of many strands of thought in Vaughn's research that came to be picked up by later Austrian political economists, whether through her direct influence as an interlocutor and teacher or through her indirect influence as a program builder. Another concept that Vaughn connects to the Hayek–Buchanan line of research and that was picked up by later scholars is the idea of the ideological entrepreneur.[32] Vaughn defines the ideological entrepreneur as a person in the business of selling political consensus. As such, ideological entrepreneurs coordinate exchange in the political arena in the same way that economic entrepreneurs coordinate exchange in more traditional market spaces. These ideological entrepreneurs are often critical players in any process of political reform, and there is much yet to be learned by studying their actions both in theory and in practice.

Morality in a Free Society

Vaughn argues that even if understanding the moral and ideological reasons behind decision-making is not necessary to understand market exchange, this reluctance cannot be extended to our study of political decision-making without severely compromising the explanatory power of our theories. Moral considerations often play a larger role in our decision-making in political contexts, and rational calculation is problematic in a political context in a way it is not in market exchange. As such, in politics, people often do not have the ability to know—much less experience—the consequences of their actions. Moral commitments may then have a greater impact than other facets of expected cost.[33]

This relates to a core observation of public-choice economics: before solving a problem, a reasonable collective choice process will begin with asking whether the problem is worth solving. If the difficulty of navigating a collective problem-solving process exceeds what could be gained, it is better to simply leave the problem to individuals or smaller groups to deal with on their own as best they can. When people inevitably bring their moral codes to deliberations about acceptable constitutional agreements, those moral codes will become a key determinant of which constitutional rules will be most agreeable or even efficient—if such terminology is even appropriate for constitutional conversations.[34] Problems that once seemed worth solving may, under a new moral code, no longer be worth addressing and therefore no longer fall under the purview of collective choice-making processes at all. Enough moral change and a complete reevaluation of the constitutional order may be called for.

So, how should we proceed in understanding morality in a way that will be most useful in contributing to positive political economy and in helping us understand the moral codes that people bring to collective choice processes and how they shape the range of institutional possibilities?

> In charting this moral argument, we will have to take care to address the hard questions that too often have been sloughed over in the past. . . . There are always individual costs to any change in social structure, there are mean ends and noble ones, there are always injustices and accidents of fate. We live in an uncertain world which by its nature can never live up to any human conception of perfection. Hence, we need to develop a morality that accepts the fact of uncertainty, revels in it and places its faith in the ability of humans to plot a course through the unknown.[35]

In short, life in a free society may require concerted efforts to restrain our impulses to eliminate all imperfection. Sometimes life's a mess, and that's okay. If all problems seem worth solving, and frictions are never acceptable, more and more will be asked of collective decision-making processes until they become impossible to contain at a level that will limit concentration and eventual abuse of power.

Vaughn suggests that Kirzner's work on entrepreneurship is a useful starting point from which to understand the morality of the market:

> By centering his moral inquiries on the role of entrepreneurship as creativity and discovery rather than on the role of

> prices in bringing about allocative efficiency in the marketplace, he has started from the central attribute of capitalism. I have long harbored the optimistic belief that if people truly understood the nature of the market process, they would find it to be a system that embodies some of our most cherished moral sentiments.[36]

This was an intuition that would go on to be supported by work such as Virgil Henry Storr and Ginny Seung Choi's inquiry into the morality of the market and the crucial role that market systems play in disciplining bad behavior and in helping people develop their moral intuitions.[37]

Conclusion

Karen Vaughn's account of her own career trajectory is a story of following curiosity wherever it might lead, even in the face of great uncertainty.[38] Her dissatisfaction with the explanations of neoclassical economics and with the status of debates in market process theory motivated a great deal of her work in Austrian economics, public choice, and history of economic thought. In short, Vaughn's career was driven by critical thought, curiosity, and perhaps even a dash of a stubborn unwillingness to accept an inferior status quo in the face of an opportunity to make something better.

There are several directions in which Vaughn's research have yet to be extended:

1. In the field of history of thought, Bruce Caldwell suggested in a 2023 panel discussion[39] that it was high time for a new history of the Austrian school that could pick up where Vaughn's 1994 book left off. In addition to intellectually tracing the origins of the ideas that have been most fruitful in the modern Austrian program, there is a great deal of intellectual and programmatic history that simply has yet to be written down.
2. In the field of economic methodology, the appropriate role of subjectivism and equilibrium analysis in modern economics is far from settled. Vaughn's focus on the impact of these methods on policy suggests a way forward in specifically addressing contemporary

methods in economics and policy analysis and how the subjectivist critique does or does not apply.

3. With respect to social learning and reform, there is an enormous amount of both theoretical and applied work to be completed on how to think about social change in an evolutionary context. This could include the development of complexity theory,[40] laboratory experiments, or the elaboration of theories developed by Vaughn through the study of real-world cases of social reform.
4. Finally, although economics has tried its best to reduce morality to measurable survey responses, Vaughn's research calls for an inquiry into morality that investigates more carefully its origins, evolution, and relevance to political decision-making.

To truly follow Vaughn's example, these research projects should be approached with curiosity and a willingness to adapt and change course through the learning process. The fields of history of economic thought, Austrian economics, and public choice owe a great debt to the work and scholarship of Karen Vaughn, and there is still a great deal more to learn.

Acknowledgments: I wish to thank Peter Boettke and other colleagues at George Mason University for introducing me to the scholarship of Karen Vaughn. However, mostly, I would like to thank Karen for her wisdom and generosity. Any errors of interpretation are my own.

23

Viviana Zelizer

Relational Exchange and Association

Stefanie Haeffele and Jessica Carges

VIVIANA A. ZELIZER, sociologist and pioneer of the economic sociology field, has made significant contributions to economics and arguably should be more thoroughly recognized by the discipline.[1] Her work explores the cultural, social, and moral aspects of money and exchange, providing context and explanation to patterns of real-world activity that otherwise may seem to defy economic theory. Scholars and students would benefit from reading her work and pursuing research that advances her approach, which shares much in common with the mainline political economy tradition articulated by Peter Boettke.

Mainline political economy, as explained in Boettke, Haeffele, and Storr, is research that advances at least three propositions: that "(1) there are limits to the benevolence that individuals can rely on and therefore they face cognitive and epistemic limits as they negotiate the social world, but (2) formal and informal institutions guide and direct human activity, and, so (3) social cooperation is possible without central direction."[2] Such research focuses on understanding how fallible humans find ways to live together in society despite their differences in experiences, goals, values, and preferences. It does not just focus on efficient resource allocation under scarcity but, instead, on exchange and the institutions within which exchange takes place.[3]

Stefanie Haeffele is senior fellow in the F. A. Hayek Program for Advanced Study in Philosophy, Politics, and Economics at the Mercatus Center at George Mason University. Jessica Carges is research fellow in the F. A. Hayek Program for Advanced Study in Philosophy, Politics, and Economics at the Mercatus Center at George Mason University.

Classical economists Adam Smith and Max Weber proposed that good social science integrates both economic and noneconomic dimensions of social life—including culture, morality, and interpersonal relations—to fully understand economic processes. For instance, Weber described how religious and cultural attitudes shape economic activity.[4] As such, he is seen as a major figure in the disciplines of economics and sociology. In *The Theory of Moral Sentiments*, Smith focused on how sympathy and social relations influence our actions and understanding of morality.[5] Although many saw this work as distinct from and contradictory to his political economy, others persuasively argued that Smith's works provide a connected and integrated account of associational life.[6] Likewise, more contemporary economists such as F. A. Hayek and Vernon Smith combine insights from psychology and social philosophy to better understand the complex world around us.[7] Elinor Ostrom argued that multiple methods are needed to collect and study the varied ways in which humans cooperate with one another.[8] And Deirdre McCloskey emphasized the shift in societal beliefs about commerce as a significant factor in the exponential progress seen since the Industrial Revolution. Ideas matter, and they shape economics.[9]

Viviana Zelizer, in following in this tradition, advances a framework for understanding otherwise perplexing human phenomena. She seeks to examine "how connected people incorporate available culture and interpersonal relations into their daily negotiation of economic activity. In doing so, all of us incessantly reshape the economy at the small scale and the large."[10] Her work explores the complex relational patterns of people, bringing the interconnectedness of social relations and economic activity to the foreground of analysis. Specifically, Zelizer's wide-ranging work includes analyzing how valuations of human life are calculated via the life insurance market in *Morals and Markets* (1979); how society shifted from treating children as economic assets to treating them as priceless in *Pricing the Priceless Child* (1985); the formation of "special monies," used to earmark legal tender for different activities and social relations, in *The Social Meaning of Money* (1994); the intersection of economic activity and intimate relations, such as the household, couples, the provision of personal care, and the legal disputes that arise from these relations, in *The Purchase of Intimacy* (2005); and the complex relational connections that shape exchange, known as circuits of commerce, in *Economic Lives* (2011).

Her unique contributions push economic understanding forward by illuminating the complex realties of real-world exchange relationships and adding nuance to preexisting economic models. She makes confounding interactions look intuitive and straightforward while adding needed substance to the tools of economics. This, we think, makes her worthy of study and appreciation as an economist of the mainline political economy tradition.

This essay proceeds as follows. In the next section, we summarize Zelizer's critiques of preexisting economic models. Then we briefly explore her theoretical advancements before adding concluding thoughts.

Pushing Against Preexisting Models

Viviana Zelizer identified three common perspectives adopted by scholars concerning economic and social processes: the "separate spheres," "hostile worlds," and "nothing-but" viewpoints.[11] The "separate spheres" concept describes two separate arenas of human life, one arena with rational economic calculation and the other with personal relations and sentiments. For instance, many scholars see markets as amoral spaces and moral development as something that occurs outside the market, in family, friendships, and community.[12]

Consider money neutrality in the quantity theory of money—the idea that changes in the stock of money impact only nominal, not real, economic variables. Although money is primarily a common medium of exchange, distortions can affect various types of exchange differently. This non-neutrality can occur when money holds more meaning than just as a medium of exchange. Zelizer argued that

> money is not one thing but many things. It turns out that how the money is earned, by whom, what it is spent on, when, and for whom often matters as much as—or more than—how much money is involved in the transaction. At stake is not just the quantity of money, but its quality; and that quality is variable.[13]

Zelizer discussed the various ways that people earmark monies for special purposes.[14] Parents, for example, often set aside money for their children to attend college and deem it inappropriate to dip into those reserves even when they are struggling financially. Or think of how money put in a communal "swear jar" is often used only for activities or goods the entire group can enjoy. There are also different moral evaluations of money.[15] Income earned by performing certain activities may be deemed inappropriate or dirty. Contested money, or blood money, may result in people returning the funds or spending it on charity as a way of cleaning it. Additionally, government interventions may not be used in the way they were originally intended. For instance, tax refunds and government stimulus checks are often put into savings or used to pay down debts instead of to boost consumption.[16] Understanding how people obtain, value, and spend money has implications for policy. Zelizer concluded, "As soon as we recognize the inexorable social and moral differentiation of money, then it becomes clear that money will always be shaped by institutions and people's social relations. In other words, money is not a social engine, but rather a malleable social product."[17]

The "hostile worlds" concept explains that if these two separate arenas interact, the result is contamination. The paired concepts of separate spheres and hostile worlds are how many social scientists view and understand economic and social processes. The efficient market, driven by self-interested, profit-maximizing behavior, is viewed as a separate sphere from the world of sentiments, such as family, customs and culture, and love and friendships. When the two worlds interact, particularly when markets are introduced to the world of sentiment, contamination and corruption results. Selling of blood or organs, intimate relations, and other so-called repugnant goods and services is viewed as unethical. Further, this view means that social and moral character must be buttressed against the forces of the everyday market, which rewards selfish behavior at expense of the collective.[18]

The concept of separate spheres and hostile worlds permeates not only economics, sociology, and other social sciences, but also many people's daily life. For example, Zelizer points out that couples make it clear to both themselves and others that they are not exchanging sex for economic rewards and that "courts, for example, regularly rule that economic transactions between spouses must count as free gifts rather than quid pro quo exchanges—at least until the moment of divorce."[19] Terms such as "sugar daddies" and "gold diggers" point to the social disdain felt toward engaging in relations, and especially marriage, for money. Yet people can choose to marry for love when they have their own resources and careers, children receive allowances from their parents, and child support payments are common after divorce. Money is tangled in our social relations, and many forms seem not to corrupt but rather to ease tensions.

For instance, from a hostile worlds perspective, taking care of children may seem like an activity best left outside the market. And indeed, many parents stay home to tend to their children or rely on family and friends to help. However, many parents pay for day-care services, hire full-time nannies, or pool resources with other parents to pay for childcare. Zelizer noted, "When it comes to care outside of households, you might expect it to be steely, brisk, and efficient, thus a contradiction in terms."[20] Instead, she finds that "people caring outside of households do establish warm personal ties, often involving extensive intimacy."[21] The women who care for other parents' children often help out beyond their contractual obligations, treating the children as if they were their own and forming close bonds with both the children and the parents.[22]

Advancing social scientific analysis beyond the separate spheres and hostile world concepts is important because it moves the study of economic processes beyond "the dichotomy between serious economic phenomena, such as firms, corporations, or financial markets, and supposedly inconsequential, sentimental economies, such as households, microcredits, local money communities, immigrant ROSCAs (rotations savings and credit associations), pawning, gifts, or remittances."[23] These understudied arenas are often treated as trivial, but Zelizer insists that even minor transactions can have macroeconomic effects. Zelizer concentrated on small-scale monetary processes, such as family gifts, and explored the meanings people attach to money.[24] In other works, she explored how college students from diverse financial backgrounds relate and exchange with one another and how money served as a way of connection during the pandemic.[25]

She argued against the common view that commodification and money corrupt social relations. Instead, she illustrated that "monetary phenomena consist of and depend on social practices."[26] She ultimately concluded:

> Why did I choose to focus on families, welfare, and gifts? These are areas where, according to the traditional di-

> chotomy between the market and personal relations, either money should not have entered at all or rationalization should have wrought the largest changes, homogenizing core personal and social relations and commodifying sentiment in family, friendship, charity, death. My research shows instead that it is very hard work to suppress the active creative power of supposedly vulnerable social relations.[27]

Social scientists who do not subscribe to the separate spheres / hostile worlds dichotomy can still hold a rather reductionist view of economic processes and phenomena. Zelizer describes this view as "nothing-but." The "nothing-but" concept contains myriad accounts of the world to understand social activity, which includes "nothing but rationally organized markets, nothing but power, nothing but culture."[28] Culture, outside of a broader institutional context, does not have much explanatory power; as a "nothing-but" explanation, it is more of a tautology: it is what it is. Instead, integrating culture into economic processes can provide meaning within the institutional contexts in which exchange takes place. It can animate the different entrepreneurial spirits of communities.[29] And it can help explain why interventions may stick in some societies and not in others.[30]

The nothing-but concept is also common among many economists in the way they view and understand economic processes; rational choice theory and economic models can explain not only economic concepts but also concepts typically thought of as outside the market space. Economists can be "imperialists by nature. [They] view the rational choice model as the uniquely correct way to explain and interpret human behavior and . . . apply it without apology to questions once thought to be the exclusive province of other disciplines."[31] Zelizer explained that "for economic reductionists, personal relations of caring, friendship, sexuality, or parent-child ties become special cases of advantage seeking individual choice under conditions of constraint—in short, of economic rationality."[32] Viewed this way, sentiment and relational ties are baked into preference sets and are not worthy of further inquiry, taking the subjectivity of preferences to an extreme.

Take, for example, life insurance. One may look at the existence of life insurance through a nothing-but approach and determine it must be within people's preference sets and any fluctuations in amounts purchased are based on various trade-offs and relative price changes. This rational choice explanation is no doubt correct but lacks nuance as to how life insurance evolved within society. Instead, Zelizer showed how changing societal beliefs, aided by clever marketing campaigns, resulted in people feeling obligated to purchase life insurance to make sure their loved ones could afford their funerals and maintain their lives without them. Life insurance went from being repugnant, as profiting off a loved one's death, to a socially obligatory form of inheritance.[33]

Advancing Beyond Preexisting Models

Although models can be useful abstractions to help us understand the world, and rational choice theory can be a powerful tool for understanding complex phenomena, Zelizer's work illuminates how the nothing-but approach to social science is lacking. And her framework does not simply add on to the standard neoclassical models or rational choice theory. To Zelizer, "economic processes should not be set in opposition to extraeconomic cultural and social forces but understood as one special category of social relations."[34] Her research breaks free from the common concepts of separate spheres, hostile worlds, and nothing-but analysis. She recognizes that "economic phenomena, although partly autonomous, are interdependent with a system of meanings and structures of social relations."[35] And for Zelizer, social relations are not simply flatlined networks but rather resemble rich ethnographic relationships. She contends that "ethnography reveals a great deal of negotiation of meaning and the actual production of cultural meaning."[36]

Zelizer's alternative is the "connected-lives" approach. Zelizer recognizes the interconnected nature of markets and social relations, and the importance of understanding how subjective meanings influence both. She describes how "by promoting clearer descriptions and explanations, a connected-lives approach to the intersection of economic activity and personal relations, including intimacy, prods scholars, lawmakers, and policy experts to identify normatively superior combinations."[37] As such, she follows in the line of Adam Smith, Max Weber, Elinor Ostrom, and others in the mainline political economy tradition.[38]

Take, for example, the rapid decline in child labor in the United States between 1870 and 1930.[39] Whereas conventional economic theory reveals how the decline in child labor during this period was largely due to a change in the trade-offs between education and work, Zelizer reveals how "cultural guidelines profoundly shaped and directed the process of social change by differentiating legitimate from illegitimate occupations for children and distinguishing licit from illicit forms of child money."[40] She details a complex process of negotiation that spanned more than fifty years between the view that children are useful wage earners and the view that children are "economically useless but emotionally priceless."[41] A new social understanding of what was appropriate work for children emerged, and the relationship between work and morality gradually strengthened. As Zelizer noted,

> As twentieth-century American children became defined by their sentimental, noneconomic value, child work could no longer remain "real" work; it was only justifiable as a form of education or as sort of game. The useful labor of the nineteenth-century child was replaced by educational work for the useless child. While child labor had served the household economy, child work would benefit primarily the child.[42]

This explanation animates the minimalist story told by standard economic reasoning, pinpointing the shifts in culture, social relations, and subjective meaning that pushed parents to invest in their children's future.

Further, Zelizer's development of "circuits of commerce" comes from the connected-lives approach.[43] Circuits of commerce include areas in which economic transactions are embedded within particular social ties rather than being clearly categorized within firms, bureaus, or other formal organizational structures. Zelizer compiled a list of common characteristics:

> (a) distinctive social relations among specific individuals; (b) shared economic activities carried on by means of those special relations; (c) creation of common accounting systems for evaluating economic exchanges, for example, special forms of monies; (d) shared understandings concerning the mean-

> ing of transactions within the circuit, including their moral valuation; and (e) a boundary separating members of the circuit from nonmembers, with some control over transactions crossing the boundary.[44]

Circuits are not found everywhere in economic life but specifically where a network of people are connected by shared and distinctive cultural meanings that shape economic transactions, media, and social relations. Zelizer described circuits as comparable to Ostrom's (1990) common pool resources,[45] but distinct because only circuits "draw attention to the fact that exchange is invariably conducted in particularized social and cultural settings."[46] Examples of such circuits include remittances, reward systems, caring connections, clusters within corporations, and local monies.[47] Other examples include the markets for art[48] and for fashion models.[49]

These circuits are deeply embedded and intertwined with social relations, cultural narratives, and the meanings participants ascribe to activities and products (such as status, prestige, etc.). In order to understand the meaning people attach to their actions and the relational work involved in circuits, qualitative methodologies such as interviews, ethnography, and archival work are most often utilized. The use of methodologies outside the conventional econometric analysis adds nuance, detail, and increased understanding to make sense of complex phenomena.[50]

Circuits of commerce are a framework for understanding local, bottom-up activity that crosses economic and social arenas. They further advance research in private money and accounting systems as well as collective action and the commons. These types of self-governance show how individuals and communities can live together in novel and cooperative ways.[51]

Conclusion

Viviana Zelizer has pushed against prevailing theories of money and economic exchange that attempt to isolate economic behavior and has advanced an integrated, connected-lives approach to studying human association. In doing so, her work animates the complicated and messy economic and social lives of real-world people. Over time, life insurance has become an acceptable and even obligatory purchase, children have gone from productive inputs to priceless investments, and special monies permeate our personal accounting. Her accounts explain how social, moral, and cultural shifts led to these economic phenomena. Further, circuits of commerce provide a framework for understanding bottom-up exchange outside of formal organizations such as the firm and bureaucracies.

Students and scholars interested in understanding the rich and perplexing social world around us and, particularly, how everyday people find ways to live cooperatively, would benefit greatly from learning of Zelizer's work. Indeed, if more economists would integrate social relations, cultural considerations, and subjective meanings into their analysis, they, like Zelizer, could bring topics that are commonly overlooked in economics into the foreground. Social phenomena such as the market for intimacy, children and commerce, the caring economy, family labor, migrant circuits, and so on would all benefit from further inquiry. Fully appreciating Zelizer's work is a great step in that direction.

24

Don Lavoie

The Failures of Socialist Central Planning

Peter J. Boettke

DON LAVOIE DIED in 2001 at the age of fifty from pancreatic cancer. I mention this sad fact because I sincerely believe that had he not had this untimely death, there would be no need for me to write this essay. All readers of *The Independent Review* would have known Lavoie's work. He would have continued to influence students for a generation or two with his teaching and mentorship. And he would have completed his methodological book and his social theory treatise. Lavoie would have become a household name among scholars in the humanities and the social sciences, especially among classical liberals and libertarian intellectuals.

As it is, Lavoie died before the age of social media fully kicked in. We do not have a good record of his lectures on YouTube, and many of his publications remain behind the paywalls of scholarly journals.[1] His two main books, *Rivalry and Central Planning: The Socialist Calculation Debate Revisited* and *National Economic Planning: What Is Left?*, became since their publication in the 1980s prohibitively difficult to obtain until the Mercatus Center republished them. But Lavoie made serious contributions to Austrian economics and to the analysis of comparative economic systems that were recognized within the mainstream of economic and political science scholarship. In addition, Lavoie made serious contributions, which I will talk about, in the disciplines of philosophy of science, computer science, and social theory.

Peter J. Boettke is distinguished university professor of economics and philosophy, George Mason University, and director of the F. A. Hayek Program for Advanced Study in Philosophy, Politics, and Economics at the Mercatus Center at George Mason University.

For those who were mentored by him during their doctoral education, his influence was far more than his written work and spoken words. He set a standard of scholarship and demanded that you live up to that. By the time I entered graduate school in 1984, it was already the common practice for PhD students to submit three essays for their dissertation. These essays could be connected by a common theme, but they need not be. These essays also could be coauthored with faculty members or one's peers in the graduate student cohort. What then was an emerging common practice is now the standard practice in PhD programs from Harvard University and the Massachusetts Institute of Technology down to the least prestigious schools. Lavoie refused to go along with this trend. He insisted that his students write a coherent book for their dissertation project and that they produce it as a single authored work. He was an exacting taskmaster in terms of both quality of argument and effective writing. Chapters would return with either red or green—mostly red—markings and directions on each and every page. When he finally agreed that your chapter was in shape, it was in publish-ready shape. Lavoie remained a constant source of inspiration and encouragement throughout my career.

But it is important to stress that Lavoie was never *just* an economist; he was always much more. And he was an outstanding teacher of philosophy and social theory. He saw the economics of the Austrian school within a broader social theory framework, which he worked hard to articulate as an alternative to the Frankfurt school.

In the spring of 2001, Lavoie received his diagnosis, and within six months he passed away. There were no extensive videotaped interviews, there were no completed books in methodology and social theory, and there would be no more students to learn under his mentorship. His influence was carried forward in the work of his students, namely Emily Chamlee-Wright, Steve Horwitz, David Prychitko, and Virgil Storr. I dedicated my book *The Struggle for a Better World* to Lavoie and his students.[2] But Don Lavoie remains an underappreciated scholar, and I would like to reverse that fate for my teacher, mentor, and friend.

Socialist Calculation

Lavoie earned his PhD in economics in 1981 from New York University. That same year, he began teaching at George Mason University, where he would remain for the next twenty years. His dissertation would eventually be published as *Rivalry and Central Planning* by Cambridge University Press. In his revisionist account, Lavoie forcefully concluded that "[Ludwig von Mises's initial] challenge was never met."[3] Thus, socialist economists, despite their efforts in formal theory to design systems of planning, still needed to address the question: How can resources be rationally allocated without recourse to money prices?

In order to derive that conclusion, Lavoie centered his analysis on how the debate was diverted by the preoccupation with static equilibrium modeling, rather than wrestling with the process by which economic coordination through time is achieved. Lavoie began his analysis with a detailed discussion of Karl Marx and the Marxist critique of capitalism. In the late nineteenth and early twentieth centuries, socialism had a particular meaning that was well understood. Its program was tied to the abolition of private ownership in the means of production and the substitution of a comprehensive central plan for the chaotic tug and pull of market activity characterized by prices and profits and losses. The goal was to rationalize production and generate a burst of productivity so that the socialist future would deliver humanity from the "Kingdom of Necessity" to the "Kingdom of Freedom." Lavoie's subtle and charitable interpretation of Marxism and the revolutionary project is critical to understanding the initial impetus for Ludwig von Mises to offer his challenge.

Lavoie walked the reader through Mises's challenge that without private ownership in the means of production, rational economic calculation would become impossible to do, and why this argument is so decisive in its criticism of the socialist project. Not only would socialism by construction eliminate the relative money prices that emerge in the market for the means of production; it would also as a result eliminate profit-and-loss statements. Without these tools of commercial life that serve as "aids to the human mind," there would be no economic compass. Production would be just so many steps in the dark, the opposite of the promised rationalization. And, as Lavoie demonstrated, Mises applied his critical analysis to both the traditional Marxian mechanics of substituting labor units for prices and the plan to substitute production for direct use rather than exchange. In addition, Mises anticipated various counters to his challenge and, in Lavoie's rendering, provided the correct response. Absent the functional role played by relative prices and profit-and-loss accounting, economic decision makers would have no way to sort from the array of technologically feasible projects those that are economically viable. Such sorting is necessary to eliminate systemic waste in the social system of production. A rational plan must be able to produce more with less, not less with more. That socialism eliminates by construction the very means to engage in rational planning means that it is rendered an incoherent program that promises much but will deliver little by way of economic progress in its operation.

To understand the subsequent evolution of the debate, it was important that Lavoie establish that Mises's argument concerned the dynamic market process, rather than invoking some image of a perfectly competitive economy. Instead of a static depiction of the economy in which economic forces have all completed their job and equilibrium prices reflect the optimality conditions, Mises was presenting a depiction of the market process in which the economic forces are hard *at work* as prices guide future decisions, profits lure entrepreneurs to direct their attention toward some ventures and away from others, and losses discipline economic actors for making the wrong assessment and judgment about investment and methods of production. Economic actors operate in a world of deep uncertainty and must learn to cope with their ignorance and the reality that time's arrow runs in only one direction. Mistakes are costly, but the market process is one of constant adaptation and readaptation to the constantly changing circumstances. This requires economic decision makers to adjust their behavior on multiple margins in order to coordinate their activities with those of others and pursue productive specialization and realize peaceful social cooperation.

Unfortunately, the debate was diverted into statics. Economists had demonstrated in the late 1890s that if socialism was to achieve its purpose, it would have to realize the same optimality conditions that were obtained in the model of general competitive equilibrium. This was known as "formal similarity," and it was widely recognized by all those trained in neoclassical economics. Optimality conditions and the technical coefficients had to be aligned so that prices reflected the full opportunity costs and least-cost methods of production were being utilized. Resources, at this point, would be allocated to their highest-valued use. That is the very definition of rational exchange and production. The socialist project was, we must always remember, linked to the *rationalization* of production and, with that, a transformation of social relations throughout society.

Lavoie demonstrated with his detailed examination of the models of market socialism, and his elaboration of the responses articulated not only by Mises but also by F. A. Hayek and Lionel Robbins, that the clash was one of alternative paradigms within neoclassical economics—one focused on equilibrium states and the other focused on the processes that bring about a tendency toward those equilibrium states. In equilibrium, the functional significance of rivalrous competition disappears, but so does a recognition of the critical importance of the institutional infrastructure within which economic life takes place. The challenges raised by Mises, Hayek, and Robbins were not answered but evaded by diverting the conversation into the theoretical possibility of a solution when all the knowledge required to achieve the formal similarity is in the hands of the benevolent and omniscient planner.

The Austrians' rejoinder to the market socialist led to the refinement of their theory of the entrepreneurial market process by Mises, Hayek, and then Israel Kirzner. *Rivalry and Central Planning* thus took on the role of not only a thorough overview of the debate but also a subtle and sophisticated rendering of the Austrian theory of the market process and the knowledge-generating process of rivalrous competition. Lavoie's book was a professional success, no doubt aided by the timing of its publication. By 1985, word had unambiguously spread throughout the international scientific establishment of economics that the Soviet economy was in shambles. Meanwhile, real, existing socialist regimes across the world were undertaking steps to make themselves decidedly less socialist. Mikhail Gorbachev had begun perestroika, Hungary and Poland had begun privatization, and reforms were well underway in Deng Xiaoping's China. As economists witnessed the collapse of socialism and the apparent triumph of a new era of global liberalism, many wondered why socialism had failed so utterly. Lavoie, in his novel presentation of Mises's and Hayek's more than fifty-year-old arguments, gave them an answer.

National Economic Planning: What Is Left? was a companion volume of Lavoie's that was also published in 1985. A subset of this book is directed at the policy discussions then alive in the United States concerning "industrial policy" to counter the declining industrial sector during the 1980s in middle America. But Lavoie was never a "policy economist," so the book, while providing a detailed criticism of the proposals by Robert Reich and Felix Rohatyn, devoted considerable space to refining what Lavoie dubbed the "knowledge problem" and how the entrepreneurial market process offered effective ways to address this fundamental problem that all systems of exchange, production, and distribution must confront, whereas government planning in all its varieties does not.

In developing this argument, Lavoie drew not only on Mises and Hayek but also on an adjacent figure who operated within their larger circle of midcentury liberal intellectuals—the chemist-turned-philosopher Michael Polanyi[4] and the "growth of knowledge" literature in the philosophy of science. There were two reasons for this intellectual move. First, Polanyi himself had emerged as a strong critic of the socialist experiments during the first half of the twentieth century and had moved from being a world-renowned physical chemist to a philosopher of science as a result of the corruption of science by the totalitarian regimes of the 1930s and 1940s. Science in a free society operated differently from science in a planned society, and scientific inquiry was also a crucial enterprise for the maintenance and progress of a free society. Science had to be safeguarded from corruption, and scientific inquiry must be respected for what it delivers for social progress. To achieve both, Polanyi sought to explain the inner workings of science. In his examination of how scientific inquiry works, Polanyi drew attention to the tacit dimension in science and in the marketplace and to the spontaneous order characteristic of both of these human endeavors. His argument aligned with Hayek's discussions of the use of knowledge in society. Second, like Mises and Hayek before him, Lavoie understood that methodology mattered, and it mattered not only in determining what questions were valuable to ask in science but also in what answers were considered acceptable. The formalistic and positivistic ethos of modern economics blocked an understanding among economists of the points Lavoie was raising in his books. So, even while working on these twin books dissecting the problems with socialism and economic planning large and small, he was deeply engaged with the philosophy of science literature and seeking to put the modern Austrian school of economics on firmer philosophical foundations.

Philosophy of Science

Lavoie had to turn to philosophy of science to try to get his scientific peers in economics to ask different questions and accept different answers. The way he did that was to do an accounting of developments in the philosophy of science since World War II. The methodological self-understanding of economists was significantly out of date. Philosophers had moved beyond the positivist vision of science for at least a generation when Lavoie started his career. Not only Polanyi but also Thomas Kuhn had changed our image of scientific progress. The "growth of knowledge" literature was a start for Lavoie, and Imre Lakatos's notion of scientific research programs would be a good way to frame methodological discussion in economics.

Lavoie's quest, however, was to draw a tight connection between the philosophy of science and the practice of economics by the Austrian economists. To do this, he did a simple philosophical trajectory analysis. Go back to Mises's philosophical influences in his understanding of the differences between the human sciences and the natural sciences. Lavoie revisited Mises's original writings in methodology, first encountering Mises's student Alfred Schütz and then, pushing further back, Edmund Husserl, who provided the philosophical justification for theoretical inquiry. There were others whom Mises mentioned, such as Wilhelm Dilthey, who Mises thought provided the philosophical justification for the method of history and the cultural sciences in general. Once at the root thinkers, Lavoie then drew the trajectory to where that literature ended up by the 1980s. Lavoie landed on philosophical hermeneutics and the writings of Hans-Georg Gadamer, in particular his treatise *Truth and Method*.[5]

Lavoie's move had nothing to do with intellectual fashion, nor was it an effort to soften Mises's harsh methodological pronouncements for a new era; instead, it was an honest and sincere tracing out of the footnotes in Mises to where the current state of the literature was on the foundational arguments Mises had relied upon when making his defense of the uniqueness of the sciences of human action. To Mises, economics was every bit a science as physics; it just followed different epistemological procedures. We are who we study, which gives us unique insight. Our subject is complex phenomena, which presents unique challenges to any effort at the control required in the "model and measure" view of economic science. Where did that line of argument go in the philosophy of science, and where did methodology of the social sciences in particular go after Mises wrote? It led to the "interpretive turn" in the social sciences.

Lavoie's interpretive turn would challenge the hegemony of mainstream methodology in economics. Lavoie wrote many papers in the philosophy of science, and he edited a volume titled *Economics and Hermeneutics* (1991), but because of his illness he never was able to complete his intended book on the interpretive dimension in economics, which promised to introduce "economists to ideas about the nature of human understanding from contemporary hermeneutical philosophy. Its purpose is to translate hermeneutics into a language more accessible to the economist, and to suggest many of the profound implications this philosophy may have for modern economics."[6] As with Deirdre McCloskey's *The Rhetoric of Economics* (1985) and subsequent methodological musings, Lavoie's work might not have changed the practice of day-to-day economists, but it would have, as with McCloskey, made Lavoie's name permanently imprinted in the field of the philosophy and methodology of economics. The appreciation of his project, and what he was hoping to accomplish, would have grown with his commitment to its promotion. His untimely death prevented that path from being followed. A work not produced is a work not read and talked about. That is what happened with Lavoie. I would like readers to go back and read his papers, and read them in light of how I have framed this as an attempt to update Mises and demonstrate the relevance for a proper grounding of the sciences of human action in a post-positivist era.

As mentioned earlier, Lavoie had focused his analytical attention on "the knowledge problem," and thus he was concerned deeply not only with the economics of the discovery, dissemination, and utilization of knowledge but also with the nature of knowledge itself—its technical and practical dimensions, its articulate and inarticulate forms. For Lavoie, as an Austrian subjectivist, a major puzzle was to study how the institutions in a society served as guideposts to enable us to escape the trap of solipsism and enjoy the benefits of social cooperation. Rather than some atomistic conception of our confrontation with nature and with others, Lavoie drew attention to intersubjectivity of the tools and practices that serve as "aids to the human mind" so we may coordinate our activities with those of others, so we may live together far better than we ever could in isolation. Lavoie didn't just come at this from the angle of the socialist calculation debate, nor purely from the philosophy of science perspective. He had a deep connection to these questions through computer science and his early career as a computer programmer.

Computer Science

One of the first books Lavoie made me read when I came to graduate school was Hubert Dreyfus's *What Computers Can't Do* (1972). "Strange," you might say; I certainly did. I was there to study economics and why socialism doesn't work—it was Lavoie's survey paper on the calculation debate, which I read during my senior year in college, that originally caught my attention. But I soon learned to appreciate what Lavoie was trying to get at.

Lavoie had graduated from Worcester Polytechnic Institute in 1973 with a BS in computer science and begun a career as a programmer. He had successfully programmed a computer to mimic Bach in playing music. But not jazz. That matters. Like Dreyfus, Lavoie had doubts about what we might call hard artificial intelligence (AI). This was relevant for the calculation argument because, with the development of computing technology, there emerged a new confidence that the problem Mises had identified could finally be overcome. The supercomputer could do the job in a matter of minutes, if not seconds, whereas the market, with its clumsy methods of relative price adjustments and profit-and-loss statements, would take forever in comparison. Lavoie wrote a series of papers between 1986 and 1990 carefully arguing that computers could never solve the planner's knowledge problem.[7] First, the calculation problem was never a computational complexity problem; it was a problem of the contextual nature of knowledge. The knowledge utilized in the market is knowledge of time and place. Outside of that context, the knowledge does not exist. It is not that it is difficult to access; it is that it is nowhere to be found because it was never generated. Second, much of this knowledge is not only contextual and emergent but also tacit in nature. It is the type that cannot be gathered as a statistic.

If Lavoie had lived longer, I am sure he also would have stressed that the market process, characterized as one of adaptation and readaptation to constantly changing circumstances, presents to us as what is called a "wicked learning environment"—one in which the parameters are relatively free. What computers can do is process information in "kind learning environments"—those in which the parameters are fixed. In such a world, the algorithms that are finite and known (even if absurdly numerous) just need to be sorted with speed. Computers can do that—for example, in playing chess. But in those "wicked environments," the adaptations and adjustments require a skillful adjudication between a variety of past experiences and imagined responses, and through some combinatorial thinking, creative and novel adaptations emerge to tackle the problem at hand—for example, in playing soccer. Computers can expertly play chess, but they only badly and without much agility play soccer. Is that a technological question, or is it an essential element associated with comparing action in a world of fixed parameters with action in a world of free parameters? Lavoie's argument was that this was not just a technological issue but essentially one related to the nature of the knowledge to be utilized by the actors to effectively execute their plans. A world of creativity and novelty, or, in other words, a world of entrepreneurship, cannot be reduced to algorithms.[8]

In his work on computing technology, Lavoie drew attention to the property rights system evident in object-oriented programming, the way knowledge is utilized in complex computer networks, the entrepreneurial alertness and creativity demonstrated in the imagining of future computational markets by programmers, and most interestingly, given our earlier discussion, the necessitated shift in perspective toward AI once a spontaneous order approach is pursued. Traditional AI was dominated by an "expert systems" approach, which treated intelligence as an algorithmic and mechanical process. But, Lavoie stressed, this is not "intelligence"; intelligence in the market process perspective is related to learning, creativity, and imagination. So, rather than an expert systems approach to AI, the alternative approach builds on work in neural network theory. This alternative approach goes by the name "emergent AI."

Social Theory

The Austrian economists in Vienna were all educated within the context of the School of Law at the University of Vienna. Their first degrees were in some hybrid of jurisprudence and political science. It was in their second degree that they might specialize in technical economics. They saw themselves as students of civilization. That is both a radically different background from their scientific counterparts in the United Kingdom and the United States and a training that would be most difficult to shake off, even in the era of scientism. Lavoie embraced his role as a social theorist grounded in economics. His social theory was worked out in the context of the grand debate over socialism. No doubt, this debate had technically positive economic components to it, but it also would inevitably touch on the major components of normative political economy and social philosophy.

In *National Economic Planning*, Lavoie devoted an entire chapter to laying out his vision of a radical libertarian society in the wake of the failure of socialism to escape the militaristic and totalitarian trap. "What was wrong with the Russian revolution," Lavoie wrote, "was the very direction in which it was trying to go, while what was wrong with the American one was that its leaders did not carry it far enough in the right direction in which it pointed them. Our task now, therefore, is to complete the American revolution." Lavoie concluded by stating, "Unlike the failed Marxist utopia of Planning, the Jeffersonian Market-guided society is a workable ideal, an ideal that when properly understood is far more consistent with the humanitarian and internationalistic values of the Left."[9]

Lavoie in this chapter also explained that vestiges of a mercantilist system of special privileges, and not a *laissez-faire* economy, were the root cause of our nation's shame in the massacre of Native Americans, the enslavement of blacks, and the restrictions of the rights of women. It was monopoly control over money and credit that produced the Great Depression. It was the violation of property rights by favored business elites that led to pollution, and it was the mercantilist policies of protection for the monied elites that led to our perpetual involvement in foreign wars. Free-market capitalism, Lavoie argued, would deliver us from this fate of playing into the hands of the citadels of power. The creative powers of a free civilization are the greatest threat to the ideology of power and privilege. The spontaneous forces of the market process will deliver to humanity peace and prosperity if they are permitted to operate freely.

The alternative radical ideology of planning produces the militaristic state. "The theory of planning was, from its inception, modeled after feudal and militaristic organizations. Elements of the Left tried to transform it into a radical program, to fit into a progressive revolutionary vision. But it doesn't fit. Attempts to implement this theory invariably reveal its true nature. The practice of planning is nothing but the militarization of the economy."[10] Our hope for a just and humane world must, Lavoie argued, move in the direction of true, radical, free markets.

This passion for a just world grounded in respect for persons and property, which would afford dignity to all and recognize their fundamental human rights, is evident throughout Lavoie's writings. His forays into philosophical hermeneutics led him to consider the ideal speech community as an example of the free interaction of individuals resulting in the growth of knowledge through mutual learning. Lavoie was romantic about ideal philosophical inquiry. Mutual respect and learning, and thus the possibility of a fusion of horizons, was possible in a "good conversation." The rules that would frame such a conversation could perhaps provide a demonstration to us of the rules that should govern all our social interactions. Lavoie's libertarianism was "dialogical" because it wasn't deductive, and it wasn't utilitarian. It was, instead, gentle and humane, grounded in our mutual respect and desire to learn from one another. The endless stream of fresh and new knowledge exhibits creativity and novelty, and we discover better ways to cooperate with one another, better ways to produce, to tinker on margins that result in life-changing innovations. Like Michael Polanyi, Lavoie saw the relationship between the progress we see in the free inquiry of science, the prosperity of a free economy, and the justice of a free society.

As with the book on methodology, Lavoie had long planned to publish a book on social theory, titled *Understanding Political Economy*, which, sadly, we are also denied because of his untimely death. In an undated memo, he described this work as follows:

> Working on a book entitled Understanding Political Economy which involves a fairly comprehensive critique and re-interpretation of the Austrian school of economics, especially Menger, Mises, Lachmann, Kirzner, and Hayek. It will refer extensively to Marxism, especially the school of critical theory, and its leading contemporary representative, Jürgen Habermas, in an attempt to show that some of the key philosophical aims of critical theory are better achieved in the Austrian approach to economics than they are in Marx's own economics.

Again, had this book been on our shelves, Lavoie would have been read more widely and remembered more deeply than has been the case. As it is, the most coherent statement we have is chapter 7 in *National Economic Planning: What Is Left?*, but that was published before his thinking had matured and been refined by his sojourns in philosophy, computer science, and cultural studies. Given where the intellectual world has gone in the years since his death, it is easy to see just how ahead of his time Lavoie was in social theory as well.

Conclusion

This essay has a rather straightforward purpose—give a sweeping overview of the work of Don Lavoie, who I believe is significantly underappreciated, so readers today may take the time to read his work, learn from it, and grow in their appreciation of it. I have spoken of the loss the intellectual world had as a result of Lavoie's death at the young age of fifty. I want to end on a more personal note. Don's death meant that a loving husband and devoted father of three young children was gone. A dear friend was lost. A dedicated teacher and mentor to so many. Don Lavoie was a good man. It is tragic when anyone dies young; it is especially tragic when it is someone who gave so much to his family and community. I was asked to speak at his memorial on behalf of all who were Don's students. It was very hard for me to first find the appropriate words and to then deliver them that day.[11]

In the years since, I have developed a unique and deep bond with my cohort of Don's students: Steve Horwitz (who also, sadly, has passed), Dave Prychitko, Emily Chamlee-Wright, and Virgil Storr. In a real sense, they are my intellectual brothers and sister, and Don was our doctoral father. Don's voice has been kept alive for me all these years through them, in their lectures, in their writings, and most of all in their kindness, gentleness, and humanity toward others. Don wanted us to be the sort of scholars he could be proud of. He was a romantic about the scholarly life, and he had exacting standards that one had to match to be accepted into his circle. I just hope that I have been able to give you a glimpse of this Lavoie training in this essay, and that when you do sit down to read him, and read him carefully, you will see what I am talking about. Before meeting him, I had never met anyone who took so much joy in the act of reading, of learning in discussion, and in the pure pleasure in figuring things out. Don the man, Don the teacher, Don the scholar played a huge positive role in my life. It is my sincere hope that in reading this essay, you have gained a sense of who he was and why he was so important to his students, to Austrian economics, and to the social theory project of true radical liberalism.

Notes

Introduction: Unsung Heroes by Robert M. Whaples

1. Vernon L. Smith, "Adam Smith, Sociality, and Classical Liberalism," *The Independent Review* 28, no. 1 (Summer 2023): 117.

2. Kenneth E. Boulding, "Economics as a Moral Science," *American Economic Review* 59, no. 1 (March 1969): 1.

3. William L. Davis, Bob G. Figgins, David Hedengren, and Daniel B. Klein, "Economics Professors' Favorite Economic Thinkers, Journals, and Blogs (Along with Party and Policy Views)," *Econ Journal Watch* 8, no. 2 (May 2011): 126–46.

Chapter 1: Alexander Hamilton by Richard M. Salsman

1. Michael Lind, "A New Hamiltonianism," *Boston Review*, June 13, 2012; Stephen S. Cohen and J. Bradford DeLong, *Concrete Economics: The Hamilton Approach to Economic Growth and Policy* (Harvard Business Review Press, 2016); Thomas DiLorenzo, *Hamilton's Curse: How Jefferson's Arch Enemy Betrayed the American Revolution—and What It Means for Americans Today* (Three Rivers Press, 2009); Lawrence W. White, "Alexander Hamilton, a Second-Hand Dealer in Retrograde Mercantilist Ideas," *FEE Stories*, September 6, 2016; Brion McClanahan, *How Alexander Hamilton Screwed Up America* (Regnery History, 2017). See Salsman (2016a) for a critique of Cohen and DeLong (2016). Knott (2002) provides illuminating history on fluctuations in Hamilton's posthumous reputation and links them mostly to changes in American ideology and economic development.

2. Edward C. Lunt, "Hamilton as a Political Economist," *Journal of Political Economy* 3, no. 3 (1895): 305, 309–10.

3. William Nester, *The Hamiltonian Vision, 1789–1800: The Art of American Power During the Early Republic* (Potomac Books, 2012).

4. Elsewhere, I've provided a comprehensive account of Hamilton's wide-ranging thought and works (Salsman 2017a), but here I focus only on his economics.

5. Edward G. Bourne, "Alexander Hamilton and Adam Smith," *Quarterly Journal of Economics* 8 (1894); Peter McNamara, *Political Economy and Statesmanship: Smith, Hamilton, and the Foundation of the Commercial Republic* (Northern Illinois University Press, 1998); Samuel Fleischacker, "Adam Smith's Reception Among the American Founders,

1776–1790," *William and Mary Quarterly* 59, no. 4 (2002): 897–924; Michael P. Federici, "Hamilton's Political Economy," in *The Political Philosophy of Alexander Hamilton* (Johns Hopkins University Press, 2012); Glory M. Liu, *Adam Smith's America: How a Scottish Philosopher Became an Icon of American Capitalism* (Princeton University Press, 2022).

6. Hamilton likely read Hume's essays "Of Commerce," "Of Money," "Of Interest," "Of the Balance of Trade," "Of the Jealousy of Trade," "Of Taxes," and "Of Public Credit" (Hume [1752, 1777] 1985). The best source for all of Hamilton's likely sources in researching and writing his Treasury reports is Harold C. Syrett, who provides comprehensive introductory notes to each report as editor of *The Papers of Alexander Hamilton* (Syrett 1962–87).

7. Alexander Hamilton, "The Continentalist no. 4," in *The Papers of Alexander Hamilton*, Harold C. Syrett, ed., 27 vols. (Columbia University Press, 1962–87), https://founders.archives.gov/content/volumes#Hamilton. Hamilton was certainly no "nationalist" in the modern meaning of the term—a statist-imperialist committed to subordinating individuals (and foreigners) to the state. By "national," Hamilton meant "continental." He hoped liberty could be enjoyed by all the states together and then extended westward (he endorsed the Louisiana Purchase in 1803). See also Holloway (2015) for a refutation of the (similar) charge that Hamilton was a would-be progressive eager to impose statist measures.

8. William D. Grampp, *Economic Liberalism: The Beginnings* (Random House, 1965).

9. John R. Nelson Jr., "Alexander Hamilton and American Manufacturing: A Reexamination," *Journal of American History* 65, no. 4 (1979): 972.

10. Michael Chan (2004, 207) refuted "the prevailing scholarly view that Hamilton, like the Founders generally, lacked a deep concern about slavery." In truth, "ending slavery was one of his abiding concerns." "Hamilton's political principles were not Hobbesian but consistent with the views of more traditional natural law theorists." He "understood that the natural rights of man imposed a corresponding duty to end slavery." As for political economy, Hamilton endorsed "compensated emancipation" to preclude ongoing injustice, discord, and violence.

11. Richard M. Salsman, "The U.S. Founding: Washington's Allies and Opponents," *Reason Papers* 38, no. 2 (2016): 89–99.

12. Alexander Hamilton, "Letter to Robert Morris," in *The Papers of Alexander Hamilton*, 2:604–35.

13. Alexander Hamilton, "Report on a Plan for the Further Support of Public Credit," in *The Papers of Alexander Hamilton*, 18:102–3.

14. Hamilton, "Letter to Robert Morris," in *The Papers of Alexander Hamilton*, 2:635.

15. For a pro and con debate on Hamilton's view of public debt, see Gordon (1997), DiLorenzo (2009), and Salsman (2017b).

16. Alexander Hamilton, "Report Relative to a Provision for the Support of Public Credit," in *The Papers of Alexander Hamilton*, 6:106–7.

17. Richard M. Salsman, "The Golden Rule of Public Finance and Prospects for Its Revival," chap. 16 in *A Fiscal Cliff: New Perspectives on the U.S. Federal Debt Crisis*, John Merrifield and Barry W. Poulson, eds. (Cato Institute, 2020).

18. Alexander Hamilton, "Final Version of the Second Report on the Further Provision Necessary for Establishing Public Credit (Report on a National Bank)," in *The Papers of Alexander Hamilton*, 7:331.

19. Richard M. Salsman, *Breaking the Banks: Central Banking Problems and Free Banking Solutions* (American Institute for Economic Research, 1990).

20. Hamilton (1788, 477, 482) made this clear in *Federalist* no. 35: "There is no part of the administration of government that requires extensive information and a thorough knowledge of the principles of political economy so much as the business of taxation. The man who understands those principles best will be least likely to resort to oppressive expedients or sacrifice a particular class of citizens to the procurement of revenue." "[T]he most productive system of finance will always be the least burthensome." Tariffs should not reach "an injurious excess" nor entail "exorbitant duties on imported articles," which "would beget a general spirit of smuggling, which is always prejudicial to the fair trader, and eventually to the revenue itself."

21. Douglas A. Irwin, "Revenue or Reciprocity? Founding Feuds over Early U.S. Trade Policy," Working Paper No. 15144 (National Bureau of Economic Research, 2009), 1–2.

22. Indeed, when Jefferson and Madison were US presidents sequentially (1801–17), they imposed trade embargoes and other discriminatory-punitive measures on Britain and helped fund its war foe, Napoleon (by the 1803 Louisiana Purchase); the policies heightened US–British hostilities and led to the War of 1812–14 (which the US nearly lost because the duo previously gutted military spending).

23. Alexander Hamilton, "Draft of Washington's Farewell Address," in *The Papers of Alexander Hamilton*, 20:284–85.

24. Robert E. Wright, *Hamilton Unbound: Finance and the Creation of the American Republic* (Greenwood Press, 2002).

25. Alexander Hamilton, *The Federalist* no. 12, in *The Papers of Alexander Hamilton*, 4: 347.

26. Hamilton, "Final Version of the Report on the Subject of Manufactures," in *The Papers of Alexander Hamilton*, vol. 2.

27. Hamilton, "Report Relative to a Provision for the Support of Public Credit," in *The Papers of Alexander Hamilton*, 6:65–110; Hamilton, "Final Version of the Second Report on the Further Provision Necessary for Establishing Public Credit (Report on a National Bank)," in *The Papers of Alexander Hamilton*, 7:305–42; Hamilton, "Final Version of the Report on the Establishment of a Mint," in *The Papers of Alexander Hamilton*, 7:570–607.

28. Hamilton, "Final Version of the Report on the Subject of Manufactures," in *The Papers of Alexander Hamilton*, 10:254–56.

29. Ibid., 254.

30. Jeff Wilser, *Alexander Hamilton's Guide to Life* (Three Rivers Press, 2016), 21.

31. Frank Taussig, *State Papers and Speeches on the Tariff* (Harvard University Press, 1892), iv.

32. Ron Chernow's biography of Hamilton rightly includes an index subentry that is phrased "as capitalist prophet" (Chernow 2004, 801) and cites twenty-five pages.

Chapter 2: Harriet Martineau by David M. Levy and Sandra J. Peart

1. In her autobiography, Martineau wrote with joy that her work was read by a young Princess Victoria (Martineau 1877, 2:118–19). See Levy and Peart (2022) for additional details about Martineau's difficult personal life.

2. "Miss Martineau made a very different and clever attempt [from that of J. S. Mill and J. R. McCulloch], more than thirty years ago, to spread a knowledge of political economy in a series of tales entitled 'Illustrations of Political Economy.' The tales are very interesting and readable, and the doctrines clearly inculcated and sound. But like many other moral tales, they have not been so much read as they deserved, nor have they been read by the classes in whom we are concerned" Jevons ([1866] 1981, 7:51).

3. See Sandra J. Peart, "HES Presidential Address: We're All 'Persons' Now: Classical Economists and Their Opponents on Marriage, the Franchise, and Socialism," *Journal of the History of Economic Thought* 31, no. 1 (2009): 3–20. Martineau was number 42 in the 1830–38 *Gallery of Illustrious Literary Characters* (Maclise and Maginn 1873). The two other named political economists were William Godwin, number 53, and Francis Place, number 66. The editor of the collected gallery, William Bates, suggested that the puzzling "Tydus-Pooh-Pooh," number 17, was a racialized caricature of political economist and linguist John Bowring (Maclise and Maginn 1873, 46), being attacked for his translations and advocacy of free trade in vocabulary, issues independent of what we discuss.

4. David M. Levy, "Some Normative Aspects of the Malthusian Controversy," *History of Political Economy* 10 (Summer 1978): 271–85.

5. This world was idealized as late as Charles Darwin's denunciation of contraception (Peart and Levy 2008).

6. Martineau explained her procedure at the outset; see Martineau (1832, xi). To give some idea of her own estimation of her importance to the contemporary discussion, Martineau told a correspondent on January 2, 1864, that her "Martyr Age of the United States" (Martineau 1838) "created" J. S. Mill's interest in the case (Martineau 2007, 5:47).

7. Deborah Ann Logan, *The Hour and the Woman: Harriet Martineau's "Somewhat Remarkable" Life* (Northern Illinois University Press, 2002), 24.

8. Demerara, now Guyana, in August 1823 was the scene of one of the most massive uprisings in history. For an account of the rebellion, see Costa (1994). Seymour Drescher (2009, 256) wrote that "the death of this freeborn native Englishman [John Smith] was converted into decisive evidence that the brutal suppression of the rebellion had been an assault on native-born Christian Britons as well as overseas Christian West Indians. Missionary Smith was the abolitionists' Archimedian fulcrum, which enabled them to raise popular contention in the New World to the level of the Old World. His death allowed the rebels to be identified not just as fellow men and brothers, but as fellow freedom-loving Christians. The Demerarans had reacted to their unnatural deprivation as would any freeborn Briton."

9. Harriet Martineau, *Demerara,* vol. 2, in *Illustrations of Political Economy* (Charles Fox, 1833), 23–24.

10. Ibid., 2:69–70. Martineau observed such a link between effort and income in the American South when task wages were used as education, to teach the link between effort and reward during the period when formal methods of education were outlawed (Martineau

1837, 2:157–58). In their study of slavery in the United States some 150 years later, Robert Fogel and Stanley Engerman discovered the payments that linked wages to output that Martineau had predicted in *Demerara* (Fogel and Engerman 1974, 239–42).

11. Adam Smith, *An Inquiry into the Nature and Causes of the Wealth of Nations,* edited by W. B. Todd (Liberty Fund, 1981), 388.

12. Martineau told her reader, "[M]y having published 'Demerara' was the main reason why they wished me to visit them. They desired me to see their 'peculiar institution' for myself: they would show me the best and the worst instances of its working; and their hope was—so they declared,—that I should publish exactly what I saw" (Martineau 1877, 2:19).

13. Harriet Martineau, *Society in America,* 3 vols. (Saunders and Otley, 1837), 2:112.

14. Ibid., 2:118.

15. See, for example, Darity (1998); Goldsmith, Hamilton and Darity (2007); Herring and Nynes (2017).

16. The first students at Wilberforce University, founded in 1856, included the children of enslaved mothers and their father-owners (McGinnis 1941). We owe the reference to William Darity.

17. Martineau, *Society in America*, 2:325–26.

18. See Carlyle (1881, 437–48) for his extremely offensive words about Martineau.

19. *The Pro-Slavery Argument* (1852), published after *Uncle Tom's Cabin,* collected and republished the earlier attacks on Martineau after her visit. None of the responses denied her charge of sexual usage.

20. For instance, Alfred Marshall referred to Martineau as a "parasite" (Marshall 1890, 63).

21. For a recent examination of the significance and value of travelers' tales, see Morgan (2022). Daniel Kuehn's (2023) examination of Warren Nutter's travels and the NBER Soviet growth study is particularly relevant because Rutledge Vining was both the important defender of the NBER practice as one of hypothesis discovery and a senior colleague of Nutter at the Thomas Jefferson Center at Virginia (Levy and Peart 2020).

22. Steven J. Micheletti et al., "Genetic Consequences of the Transatlantic Slave Trade in the Americas," *American Journal of Human Genetics* 107 (August 6, 2020): 273.

23. Robert Fogel (1989, 391–92): "I was also startled to discover the numerous ways in which masters relied on rewards to elicit labor—a device I had assumed was almost entirely absent since David Hume, Adam Smith, John E. Cairnes, and most of the other economic writers had identified this lack as the fatal flaw in slavery as an economic system."

24. Gunnar Myrdal, *An American Dilemma: The Negro Problem and Modern Democracy* (Harper & Brothers, 1944), 1075; Maribel Morey, *White Philanthropy: Carnegie Corporation's An American Dilemma and the Making of a White World Order* (University of North Carolina Press, 2021), 219.

25. William A. Darity Jr., ed., "Introduction: The Odyssey of Abram Harris from Howard to Chicago," in *Race, Radicalism, and Reform: Selected Papers of Abram L. Harris* (Transaction Publishers, 1989): 1–34; Julianne Malveaux, "Missed Opportunity: Sadie Tanner Mossell Alexander and the Economics Profession," *American Economic Review* 81, no. 2 (1991): 307–10.

26. David M. Levy and Sandra J. Peart, *Towards an Economics of Natural Equals: A Documentary History of the Early Virginia School* (Cambridge University Press, 2020).

27. Thomas Carlyle, "Occasional Discourse on the Negro Question," *Fraser's Magazine for Town and Country* 40 (December 1849): 671.

28. Martineau, *Society in America*, 2:222.

Chapter 3: Knut Wicksell by Diana W. Thomas

1. Knut Wicksell, "A New Principle of Just Taxation," in *Classics in the Theory of Public Finance*, edited by Richard A. Musgrave and Alan T. Peacock (Macmillan, 1967), 74.

2. Lionel Robbins, *A History of Economic Thought: The LSE Lectures* (Princeton University Press, 2000); Stephen G. Medema and Warren Samuels, *The History of Economic Thought: A Reader* (Routledge, 2003); Bo Sandelin and Hans-Michael Trautwein, *A Short History of Economic Thought* (Taylor & Francis, 2014).

3. Bertil Ohlin (1926, 507) poked fun at John Maynard Keynes for not being aware of Wicksell's book *Geldzins und Güterpreise.* Quoting Keynes in his memorial to Marshall, Ohlin wrote: "'It was an odd state of affairs that one of the most fundamental parts of monetary theory should, for about a quarter of a century, have been available to students nowhere except embedded in the form of question and answer before a Government Commission interested in a transitory practical problem.' If this surprise is justified, from Mr. Keynes' standpoint, what shall we say of the surprise felt in many quarters that a very full and comprehensive analysis has remained practically unknown among writers on monetary problems in Great Britain, only because it happened to be published in German?"

4. Bertil Ohlin, "Obituary: Knut Wicksell (1851–1926)," *Economic Journal* 36, no. 143 (1926): 503–12.6; Emil Sommarin, "Das Lebenswerk von Knut Wicksell," *Zeitschrift für Nationalökonomie* 2, no. 2 (1930): 221–67; Carl G. Uhr, "Knut Wicksell: A Centennial Evaluation," *American Economic Review* 41, no. 5 (1951): 829–60.

5. Uhr, "Knut Wicksell," 833.

6. Sommarin, "Das Lebenswerk von Knut Wicksell," 228.

7. Ohlin, "Obituary: Knut Wicksell (1851–1926)," 510.

8. Uhr, "Knut Wicksell," 842.

9. Ibid.

10. Ibid., 848.

11. Ibid., 852.

12. Wicksell, "A New Principle of Just Taxation," 72.

13. Ibid., 89.

14. Ibid., 89–90.

15. Lars Jonung, trans., "Knut Wicksell's Unpublished Manuscripts: A First Glance," *European Economic Review* 32, nos. 2–3 (1988): 509.

16. Wicksell, "A New Principle of Just Taxation," 108.

17. Ibid., 91.

18. Richard Wagner, "The Calculus of Consent: A Wicksellian Retrospective," *Public Choice* 65 (1988): 158.

19. Marianne Johnson, "Wicksell's Social Philosophy and His Unanimity Rule," *Review of Social Economy* 68, no. 2 (2010): 187–204.

20. David Gordon, "Justice and Redistributive Taxation: James Buchanan versus Ludwig von Mises," *Review of Austrian Economics* 8, no. 1 (1994): 117–31.

21. James M. Buchanan, "Rent Seeking, Noncompensated Transfers, and Laws of Succession," *Journal of Law and Economics* 26, no. 1 (1983): 71–85.

22. Joaquim Silvestre, "Wicksell, Lindahl and the Theory of Public Goods," *Scandinavian Journal of Economics* 105, no. 4 (2003): 527–53.

23. Wicksell, "A New Principle of Just Taxation," 87.

24. James M. Buchanan, "Wicksell on Fiscal Reform: Comment," *American Economic Review* 42, no. 4 (1952): 599–602.

25. Wicksell, "A New Principle of Just Taxation," 75.

Chapter 4: Thorstein Veblen by Robert M. Whaples

1. William L. Davis, Bob G. Figgins, David Hedengren, and Daniel B. Klein, "Economics Professors' Favorite Economic Thinkers, Journals, and Blogs (Along with Party and Policy Views)," *Econ Journal Watch* 8, no. 2 (May 2011): 126–46.

2. The ten history of economics textbooks that I have amassed (many of them passed down from older members of my department) vary considerably in the space given to Veblen. This ranges from a few brief mentions in two of them to a 29-page chapter on the high end. The median coverage is 8.5 pages and 1.7 percent of the textbook.

3. My argument is that appreciation of Veblen is narrow, not that it is shallow. The depth of appreciation for Veblen is reflected, for example, in the fact that *The Theory of the Leisure Class* has more than thirty thousand Google Scholar citations.

4. Davis, Figgins, Hedengren, and Klein, "Economics Professors' Favorite Economic Thinkers, Journals, and Blogs (Along with Party and Policy Views)."

5. Charles Camic, *Veblen: The Making of an Economist Who Unmade Economics* (Harvard University Press, 2020), 2.

6. Robert B. Ekelund Jr. and Robert F. Hébert, *A History of Economic Theory and Method* (Waveland Press, 2014), 480.

7. One of Schumpeter's footnotes says (dismissively?) that "Veblen's work was practically all in economic *sociology*" (p. 795, emphasis added). It is striking that a recent "definitive" work on Veblen is by a sociologist, Charles Camic.

8. Alfonso Giuliani, "Thorstein Bunde Veblen (1857–1929)," in Gilbert Faccarello and Heinz D. Kurz, eds., *Hand on the History of Economic Analysis*, vol. 1, *Great Economists Since Petty and Boisguilbert* (Edward Elgar, 2016), 375.

9. Two history of economic thought textbooks written by classical liberal authors give Veblen greater than average coverage. Skousen (2001 [2022]) emphasizes Veblen's unusual personality, with subsections titled "The Life of Veblen, the Oscar Wilde of Economics" and "Marital Troubles at Stanford," for example. Ekelund and Hébert (1997 [2014]) dig down into Veblen's ideas at great length—taking them seriously, though explaining their shortcomings with considerable insight. Veblen's face is one of the eight portraits on the cover of their book.

10. Camic, *Veblen*, 65.

11. Ibid., 185.

12. Ekelund and Hébert, *A History of Economic Theory and Method*, 482.

13. Dorfman (1934 [1972]) provides extensive coverage of Veblen as a teacher: "Judged by conventional standards he was the world's worst teacher" (250). Students complained, among other things, that he only gave out C's, that he seemed to care little for consistency, that his speech was slow, "indolent," and monotone, that he "lectured into his lap" (250), that he was "too lazy to clarify his ideas and that his attitude was 'try and find out what I mean if you can'" (249).

14. W. W. Rostow, *Theorists of Economics Growth: From Hume to the Present* (Oxford University Press, 1990), 125.

15. Lewis H. Haney, *History of Economic Thought: A Critical Account of the Origin and Development of the Economic Theories of the Leading Thinkers in the Leading Nations* (Macmillan, 1949), 723.

16. Eric Hoffer, *The True Believer: Thoughts on the Nature of Mass Movements* (Harper and Row, 1966), 60.

17. Ekelund and Hébert, *A History of Economic Theory and Method*, 481, quoting Veblen's student and fellow institutionalist Wesley Mitchell.

18. In *The Engineers and the Price System* (1921 [2001], 102), Veblen went so far as to say that "immediately and unremittingly, the technicians and their advice and surveillance are essential to any work whatever in those great primary industries on which the country's productive systems turn. . . . And it is obvious that so soon as they shall draw together, in a reasonably inclusive way, and take common counsel as to what had best be done, they are in a position to say what work shall be done and to fix the terms on which it is to be done. In short, so far as regards the technical requirements of the case, the situation is ready for a self-selected, but inclusive, Soviet of technicians to take over the economic affairs of the country and to allow and disallow what they may agree on."

19. Louis Johnston and Samuel H. Williamson, "What Was the U.S. GDP Then?," MeasuringWorth, 2024, https://www.measuringworth.com/datasets/usgdp.

20. Thorstein Veblen, *The Theory of the Leisure Class* (Augustus M. Kelley, 1991), 230, 236. When I teach the economics of entrepreneurship, my students read biographies of entrepreneurs—many of them from Veblen's era. These biographers generally demonstrate that leading entrepreneurs *were* the "Carusos" that Schumpeter (1911 [1934], 82) analyzes—full of organizational genius and insights about how to put resources into higher valued uses. They earned profits by making life better for their customers and giving better deals than their competitors. Perhaps more importantly, these biographers show that many of them strived to live out the virtues that Veblen says captains of industry disdain—such as thrift, humility, and gratitude—rather than being predatory. Some entrepreneurs of this era—such as Charles Yerkes (Franch 2006), who built much of Chicago's mass transit system and was a major donor to Veblen's University of Chicago—clearly fit Veblen's description. But just as many—including John D. Rockefeller Sr., who supplied the bulk of the donations to build the University of Chicago into a premier institution—don't. For example, Ron Chernow describes the economies that Rockefeller practiced so that his children wouldn't become

spoiled drones: "Rockefeller never tired of preaching economy and whenever a package arrived at home, he made a point of saving the paper and string. . . . It was a far cry from Thorstein Veblen's image of the spoiled leisure class" (1998, 124). "Rockefeller belied Thorstein Veblen's generalization that rich men possessed 'an instinctive repugnance for the vulgar forms of labor,' for he always believed in the dignity of manual labor" and enjoyed it himself (Chernow 1998, 403). Veblen's take on actual captains of industry seems amateurish and clumsy.

21. I wish I had space to discuss other important themes in Veblen that may be of value to classical liberal economists, especially his thoughts on the instincts (Veblen 1914 [1964]). For a short, accessible overview of Veblen's broader thinking see Prasch (2013).

22. Stuart Chase, "Foreword," in *The Theory of the Leisure Class* (Modern Library, 1934), xiv.

23. Adam Smith argued that people place considerable emphasis on "status" too, but Smith's review was far more benign that Veblen's. He focused on the value-adding "desire both to be respectable and to be respected" (1759 [1982], 62) rather than the zero-sum desire to outrank others.

24. Thorstein Veblen, "Christian Morals and the Competitive System," *International Journal of Ethics* 20, no. 2 (1910): 177, emphasis added.

25. Ibid., 15, emphasis added.

26. It is worth noting that at the time of this writing, the most valuable corporation in the world is named Nvidia. Bowie (2024) explains that the name was "rationalized by the company's aspiration to make jealousy-inducing products, and it must have helped that it sounded sort of like 'video' to boot," as the company's chips were originally used primarily in video games. An employee of the company noted to me that their logo—which evokes an eye—is colored green: green-eyed envy.

27. However, the envy that Veblen focuses on doesn't appear to be as malevolent and destructive as much of the envy discussed by Schoeck (1966).

28. The idea that there was once a peaceable stage of human history, for example, is belied by estimates that the percent of people dying violent deaths began high and has decreased across the millennia (Pinker 2011).

29. Veblen, *The Theory of the Leisure Class*, 25, emphasis added.

30. Ibid., 291.

31. Ibid., 31.

32. Ibid.

33. Ibid., 30, 32.

34. Ibid., 33, emphasis added.

35. Ibid., 103.

36. Ibid., 36.

37. Ibid., 204.

38. Ibid., 84, emphasis added.

39. Ibid., 110, emphasis added.

40. Thorstein Veblen, *The Instinct of Workmanship and the State of the Industrial Arts* (Augustus M. Kelley, 1964), 31.

41. Ibid., 43.

42. Ibid., 43. "Count it as the greatest sin to prefer life to honor and for the sake of living to lose what makes life worth living." (My ability to understand the passage is no evidence of quasi-scholarly conspicuous leisure, thanks to the internet.) Camic (2020, 85) notes that during his pre-college and college programs as a student at Carleton, "Veblen enrolled every term in the classical track" and therefore learned a lot of Latin. He also points out that much of what Veblen would have read extolled the virtuous lives of the ancients, excoriating the "leisure class" of the ancient world.

43. Ibid., 112.

44. Ibid., 132.

45. Ibid., 155.

46. Ibid., 156.

47. Ibid., 110, emphasis added.

48. Perhaps because we are fearful that doing so would blur the boundaries between economics and psychology, as one reader noted. But if Veblen is correct that "the propensity for emulation is probably the strongest and most alert and persistent of the *economic* motives proper," then these boundaries need to be crossed.

49. According to the Higher Education Research Institute's annual survey of first-year college students, the fraction saying that being financially well-off is an "essential" or "very important" goal rose from 44.5 percent in 1967 to 84.5 percent in 2022 (Taylor 2024).

50. See Forbes.com, "The World's Real-Time Billionaires," https://www.forbes.com/real-time-billionaires/#220b975c3d78.

51. John Kenneth Galbraith, *The Affluent Society* (New American Library, 1958), 72.

52. Ibid., 74.

53. See Robert Whaples, "Why Didn't Galbraith Convince Us That America Is an Affluent Society?," *The Independent Review* 24, no. 4 (2020): 579–92.

54. Ibid., 582.

55. Another influential follower of Veblen during the postwar period was James Duesenberry, a professor at Harvard University and member of the Council of Economic Advisors. He uses the mathematical assumption that the utility of one's consumption expenditures depends upon the ratio of one's own consumption expenditures to those of one's associates. Sounding like Veblen, but without the edge and the envy, Duesenberry (1949, 28, 31) argues that "ours is a society in which one of the principal social goals is a higher standard of living." This goal is "instilled in every individual's mind by the socialization process. . . . The goal becomes essential to the maintenance of self-esteem," which is "a basic drive in every individual." In this manner, "our social goal of a high standard of living, then, converts the drive for self-esteem into a drive to get high quality goods."

56. Robert Frank, *Luxury Fever: Why Money Fails to Satisfy in an Era of Excess* (Free Press, 1999), 183.

57. Ibid., 198.

58. Robert Frank, "Should Public Policy Respond to Positional Externalities?," *Journal of Public Economics* 92 (2008): 1777–86.

59. Jack Hirshleifer, "The Expanding Domain of Economics," *American Economic Review* 75, no. 6 (1985): 58–59.

60. See Benny Moldovanu, Aner Sela, and Xianwen Shi, "Contests for Status," *Journal of Political Economy* 115, no. 2 (2007): 338–63.

61. See Leonardo Bursztyn, Bruno Ferman, Stefano Fiorin, Martin Kanz, and Gautam Rao, "Status Goods: Experimental Evidence from Platinum Credit Cards," *Quarterly Journal of Economics* 133, no. 3 (2018): 1561–95; Ilyana Kuziemko, Ryan W. Buell, Taly Reich, and Michael I. Norton, "'Last-Place Aversion': Evidence and Redistributive Implications," *Quarterly Journal of Economics* 129, no. 1 (2014): 105–50.

62. See Desiree Desierto and Mark Koyama, "The Political Economy of Status Competition: Sumptuary Laws in Preindustrial Europe," *Journal of Economic History* 84, no. 2 (2024): 479–516.

63. Hirshleifer, "The Expanding Domain of Economics."

64. Robert William Fogel, *The Fourth Great Awakening and the Future of Egalitarianism* (University of Chicago Press, 2000), 188–90.

65. Robert Whaples, "Where Do the Poorest Americans Stand in the Income Distribution among All People Ever Born?" *The Independent Review* 27, no. 1 (2022): 155–59.

66. Veblen, *The Theory of the Leisure Class*, 84.

67. Rob Henderson, "'Luxury Beliefs' That Only the Privileged Few Can Afford," *Wall Street Journal*, February 10–11, 2024, C3.

68. Matthew 23:5, NABRE.

69. Veblen (1910) also reminds us of the true radicalness of Christianity, which elevates renunciation and humility—voluntarily accepting less and a lower status than others—as among the highest virtues.

Chapter 5: Frank Fetter by Matthew McCaffrey

1. J. Douglas Brown, "Memorial: Frank Albert Fetter, 1863–1949," *American Economic Review* 39, no. 5 (1949): 979.

2. Fetter was also influenced to a lesser extent by other traditions, including German Historicism and Old Institutionalism, both of which he appreciated and learned from, but criticized (e.g., Hodgson 2008). In politics Fetter also had varying influences, from classical liberalism to progressive-era social reformism.

3. See, for example, Murray N. Rothbard, "Introduction," in *Capital, Interest, and Rent: Essays in the Theory of Distribution* (Institute for Humane Studies, 1977), 1–23; Jeffrey M. Herbener, "Frank A. Fetter: A Forgotten Giant," in *15 Great Austrian Economists*, edited by R. G. Holcombe (Ludwig von Mises Institute, 1999), 123–41; Joseph T. Salerno, "The Place of Mises's *Human Action* in the Development of Modern Economic Thought," *Quarterly Journal of Austrian Economics* 2, no. 1 (1999): 35–65.

4. Stanley E. Howard and Edwin W. Kemmerer, "Frank Albert Fetter: A Birthday Note," *American Economic Review* 33, no. 1 (1943): 230–35.

5. Matthew McCaffrey, "Pure Theory and Progressive Liberalism: Frank Fetter and the Austrian Economists," *Journal of Institutional Economics* 15, no. 3 (2019): 469–86; Matthew

McCaffrey, "The Long Rehabilitation of Frank Fetter," *Quarterly Journal of Austrian Economics* 24, no. 3 (2021): 467–95.

6. Herbener, "Frank A. Fetter."

7. Frank A. Fetter, *Capital, Interest, and Rent: Essays in the Theory of Distribution*, edited by M. N. Rothbard (Institute for Humane Studies, 1977).

8. Jeffrey M. Herbener, "Frank A. Fetter: A Forgotten Giant," in *15 Great Austrian Economists*, edited by R. G. Holcombe (Ludwig von Mises Institute, 1999), 123–41.

9. Cf. McCaffrey (2021) in References for some examples of new research streams that rely explicitly on Fetter's work.

10. Peter Lewin and Steven E. Phelan, "Firms, Strategies, and Resources: Contributions from Austrian Economics," *Quarterly Journal of Austrian Economics* 2, no. 2 (1999): 3–18.

11. Jeffrey M. Herbener, "Introduction," in *The Pure Time-Preference Theory of Interest*, edited by J. Herbener (Ludwig von Mises Institute, 2011), 11–58.

12. Matthew McCaffrey, "Good Judgment, Good Luck: Frank Fetter's Neglected Theory of Entrepreneurship," *Review of Political Economy* 28, no. 4 (2016): 504–22.

13. Gerald P. O'Driscoll Jr., "Frank A. Fetter and 'Austrian' Business Cycle Theory," *History of Political Economy* 12, no. 4 (1980): 542–57.

14. See, for example, Frank A. Fetter, *The Principles of Economics, with Applications to Practical Problems* (The Century Co., 1904); Frank A. Fetter, *Economic Principles* (The Century Co., 1915); Frank A. Fetter, *Capital, Interest, and Rent: Essays in the Theory of Distribution*, edited by M. N. Rothbard (Institute for Humane Studies, 1977).

15. See Joseph Dorfman, *The Economic Mind in American Civilization* (n.p., 1949), 360–65.

16. Frank A. Fetter, "Present State of Economic Theory in the United States of America," FAF, Box 12, Folder: Miscellaneous Writings, 1926.

17. Ibid.

18. Mason Gaffney, "Neo-classical Economics as a Stratagem Against Henry George," in *The Corruption of Economics*, edited by M. Gaffney and F. Harrison (Shepheard-Walwyn, 1994), 78.

19. This is to say nothing of the Keynesian revolution that began in the 1930s, which faced a much-weakened opposition from Austrians and other subjectivists, who in the 1920s had been struggling to integrate different and sometimes incompatible price theories. This hindered their ability to present a strong, unified front (Salerno 1999).

20. Joseph T. Salerno, "The Place of Mises's *Human Action* in the Development of Modern Economic Thought," *Quarterly Journal of Austrian Economics* 2, no. 1 (1999): 35–65.

21. Frank A. Fetter, "Value and the Larger Economics, II: Value Giving Way to Welfare," *Journal of Political Economy* 31, no. 6 (1923): 587.

22. Ludwig von Mises, *Memoirs* (Ludwig von Mises Institute, 2009), 98.

23. Frank A. Fetter, "The Definition of Price," *American Economic Review* 2, no. 4 (1912): 783–813.

24. Frank A. Fetter, "Price Economics Versus Welfare Economics," *American Economic Review* 10, no. 3 (1920): 467–87; Frank A. Fetter, "Price Economics Versus Welfare Economics: Contemporary Opinion," *American Economic Review* 10, no. 4 (1920): 719–37.

25. Frank A. Fetter, "Value and the Larger Economics, I: Rise of the Marginal Doctrine," *Journal of Political Economy* 31, no. 5 (1923): 587–605; Frank A. Fetter, "Value and the Larger Economics, II: Value Giving Way to Welfare," *Journal of Political Economy* 31, no. 6 (1923): 790–803.

26. Frank A. Fetter, "Present State of Economic Theory in the United States of America." FAF, Box 12, Folder: Miscellaneous Writings, 1926.

27. Frank A. Fetter, "The Definition of Price," *American Economic Review* 2, no. 4 (1912): 783–813.

28. Ibid., 784.

29. Ibid.

30. Ibid.

31. Ibid.

32. Some writers provided no clear definition of price, including Friedrich von Wieser and Léon Walras.

33. Fetter, "The Definition of Price," 813.

34. Ibid., 804–5.

35. Ibid., 794.

36. Joseph T. Salerno, "Fetter on the Meaning of Price, Market, and Equilibrium," in *Liberty Matters: Frank Fetter and the Austrian Tradition in the United States* (Online Library of Liberty, 2019), 9, emphasis in original, https://oll.libertyfund.org/publications/liberty-matters/matthew-mccaffrey-frank-fetter-austrian-economics.

37. Fetter, "The Definition of Price," 795–96, 79–98.

38. Fetter, "Price Economics"; "Price Economics Versus Welfare Economics: Contemporary Opinion."

39. Fetter, "Price Economics," 467.

40. Ibid.

41. Fetter, "Price Economics Versus Welfare Economics: Contemporary Opinion," 737.

42. Fetter, "Price Economics," 472–74.

43. Carl Menger, *Principles of Economics* (Libertarian Press, 1994).

44. Carl Menger, "The Social Theories of Classical Political Economy and Modern Economic Policy," *Cosmos + Taxis* 13, no. 3 (2016): 473–88.

45. See Joseph T. Salerno, "Böhm-Bawerk's Vision of the Capitalist Economic Process: Intellectual Influences and Conceptual Foundations," *New Perspectives on Political Economy* 4, no. 2 (2008): 87–112.

46. Fetter, "Price Economics," 486; "Price Economics Versus Welfare Economics: Contemporary Opinion," 729; "Value and the Larger Economics, I," 600.

47. Fetter is quick to praise the public-spiritedness of Marshall and Taussig and suggests that both men wanted to advance a welfare economics. Yet they relapsed into price economics because of their methodological views, which were inconsistent with a richer subjectivist approach to welfare.

48. Fetter, "Price Economics Versus Welfare Economics: Contemporary Opinion," 719.

49. Postwar economics did, of course, produce an enormous body of work on welfare economics. Importantly though, the fundamental theorems of welfare economics depend on

assumptions—well-defined preferences, price taking, perfect information, etc.—that Fetter would consider to be price economics in new garb.

50. Fetter, "Value and the Larger Economics, I"; Frank A. Fetter, "Value and the Larger Economics, II: Value Giving Way to Welfare," *Journal of Political Economy*. 31, no. 6 (1923): 790–803.

51. Fetter, "Value and the Larger Economics, II," 790–91.

52. Joseph T. Salerno, "The Place of Mises's *Human Action* in the Development of Modern Economic Thought," *Quarterly Journal of Austrian Economics* 2, no. 1 (1999): 57.

53. Fetter, "Value and the Larger Economics, II."

54. Frank A. Fetter, "Present State of Economic Theory in the United States of America," FAF, Box 12, Folder: Miscellaneous Writings, 1926.

55. Matthew McCaffrey, "Pure Theory and Progressive Liberalism: Frank Fetter and the Austrian Economists," *Journal of Institutional Economics* 15, no. 3 (2019): 469–86.

56. Fetter, "Present State of Economic Theory in the United States of America."

57. Ibid.

58. Ibid.

59. Ibid.

60. Ibid.

61. Ibid.

62. Frank A. Fetter, "Overhead Costs," unpublished manuscript, FAF, Box 4, Folder: Overhead Costs.

63. Frank H. Knight, "Marginal Utility Economics," in *Encyclopaedia of the Social Sciences*, edited by Edwin R. A. Seligman (Macmillan, 1935), 5: 357–63.

64. Jacob Viner, *Lectures in Economics 301*, edited by D. A. Erwin and S. G. Medema (Transaction Publishers, 2013), 57–60.

65. Ludwig von Mises, *The Historical Setting of the Austrian School of Economics* (Ludwig von Mises Institute, 2007), 19; Friedrich A. Hayek, "The Austrian School of Economics," in *The Collected Works of F. A. Hayek*, vol. 4: *The Fortunes of Liberalism*, edited by Peter G. Klein (Liberty Fund, 1992), 52.

66. Joseph T. Salerno, "The Rebirth of Austrian Economics in Light of Austrian Economics," *Quarterly Journal of Austrian Economics* 5, no. 4 (Winter 2002): 115.

Chapter 6: Clark Warburton by Thomas F. Cargill

1. John Maynard Keynes, *The General Theory of Employment, Interest and Money* (Palgrave McMillian, 1936).

2. The Great Contraction period of the decline from 1929 to 1933 ended the large capital inflow into Germany that had supported Germany's economy after November 1923 when hyperinflation was brought under control. The sudden cessation of this capital inflow generated economic and financial distress in Germany and provided Hitler and the Nazi Party the opportunity to assume leadership of Germany.

3. Franco Modigliani, "The Monetarist Controversy or Should We Forsake Stabilization Policies?," *American Economic Review* 67 (March 1977): 1.

4. Michael Bordo and Anna J. Schwartz, "Clark Warburton: Pioneer Monetarist," *Journal of Monetary Economics* 5 (January 1979): 43–65.

5. Thomas F. Cargill, "Clark Warburton and the Development of Monetarism Since the Great Depression," *History of Political Economy* 11 (Fall 1979): 425–49.

6. Clark Warburton, *Depression, Inflation and Monetary Policy: Selected Papers, 1945–1953* (Johns Hopkins Press, 1966).

7. Based on conversations with Warburton at his home office while collecting information and documentation for a review of Warburton's work published in 1979 (Cargill, "Clark Warburton and the Development of Monetarism Since the Great Depression").

8. Friedrich A. Lutz and Lloyd W. Mints, *Readings in Monetary Theory* (American Economic Association, 1951).

9. Fels (1949) was one of the few economists that criticized Warburton's views in any detail.

10. During the 1970s, I made many presentations on Warburton's contributions, and after one presentation, someone who had worked in Washington, DC, in the 1950s and 1960s remarked that he was unaware Warburton had published so many papers that anticipated the monetarists and Keynesian debates; in fact, he stated that he and others regarded Warburton as a nut.

11. Robert E. Weintraub, "Congressional Supervision of Monetary Policy," *Journal of Monetary Economics* 4 (April 1978): 341–62.

12. Ben Bernanke, "Remarks by Governor Ben S. Bernanke at the Conference to Honor Milton Friedman's Ninetieth Birthday," Federal Reserve, November 8, 2002, https://www.federalreserve.gov/boarddocs/speeches/2002/20021108.

13. Bernanke did not mention Warburton in his tribute to Friedman and Schwartz. This is understandable in part and arguably appropriate, but one can counter by pointing out that since Bernanke's comments focused on the Great Depression and the Federal Reserve's role, it would have been historically appropriate to mention Warburton in a manner that would not detract from Friedman's remarkable contributions. Friedman and Schwartz had no problem in doing so.

14. Milton Friedman and Anna J. Schwartz, *A Monetary History of the United States: 1867–1960* (Princeton University Press, 1963), xxii.

15. Cargill, "Clark Warburton and the Development of Monetarism Since the Great Depression." This paper was presented at a Federal Reserve Bank of San Francisco seminar in November 1978, and Friedman, who had been awarded the 1976 Nobel Prize in Economics, was the discussant.

16. Michael Bordo and Anna J. Schwartz, "Clark Warburton: Pioneer Monetarist," *Journal of Monetary Economics* 5 (January 1979): 43–65.

17. Thomas M. Humphrey, "Role of Non-Chicago Economists in the Evolution of the Quantity Theory in America 1930–1950," *Southern Economic Journal* 38 (July 1971): 12–18.

18. Richard Seldon, "Stable Money Growth," in *In Search of a Monetary Constitution*, edited by Leland Yeager (Harvard University Press, 1962); Richard Seldon, "Monetarism," in *Modern Economic Thought*, edited by Sidney Weintraub (University of Pennsylvania Press, 1977).

19. George S. Tavlas, "Some Further Observations on the Monetary Economics of Chicagoans and Non-Chicagoans," *Southern Economic Journal* 42 (April 1976): 685–92.

20. Paul B. Trescott, "Discovery of the Money Income Relationship in the United States: 1921–1944," *History of Political Economy* 14, no. 1 (1982): 65–88.

21. Thomas F. Cargill, "A Tribute to Clark Warburton, 1896–1979," *Journal of Money, Credit, and Banking* 13, no 1 (1981): 89–93.

Chapter 7: Ursula K. Hicks by Marianne Johnson

1. A. C. Pigou, "Reviewed Work: *The Taxation of War Wealth* by J. R. Hicks, Ursula K. Hicks, and L. Rostas," *Economic Journal* 51, nos. 202–3 (1941): 299.

2. Simeon Leland, "Reviewed Work: *The Finance of British Government, 1920–1936* by Ursula K. Hicks," *Journal of Political Economy* 48, no. 2 (1940): 265–66.

3. C. D. Harbury, "Reviewed Work: *Public Finance, Planning and Economic Development: Essays in Honour of Ursula Hicks*, edited by Wilfred L. David," *Economic Journal* 84, no. 333 (1974): 226.

4. Robert Cord, *The Palgrave Companion to LSE Economics* (Palgrave Macmillan, 2018).

5. See John G. Head, *Public Goods and Public Welfare* (Duke University Press, 1974); Steven G. Medema, "It's Fundamental: Welfare Theorems, Market Failures, and the Turn from 'Public Finance' to 'Public Economics,'" CHOPE Working Paper No. 2022-09, 2022.

6. Joyce Jacobson, "Ursula Hicks," in *A Biographical Dictionary of Women Economists*, edited by R. Dimand, M. Dimand, and E. Forget (Edward Elgar, 2000), 215.

7. Kirsten Madden and Robert Dimand, eds., *Routledge Handbook of the History of Women's Economic Thought* (Routledge, 2019); Giandomenica Becchio, *A History of Feminist and Gender Economics* (Routledge, 2020); Cléo Chassonnery-Zaïgouche, Evelyn Forget, and John Singleton, "Women and Economics: New Historical Perspectives," *History of Political Economy* 54 (Supplement, 2022): 1–16; Ann Mari May, *Gender and the Dismal Science* (Columbia University Press, 2022).

8. Several sources provide detailed biographical information on Hicks, including David (1976), Brilliant (2019), Jacobson (2000), and Thomas (2020).

9. Ursula K. Hicks, *The Finance of British Government 1920–1936* (Oxford University Press, 1938).

10. In addition to Robbins, LSE faculty at the time included Friedrich Hayek, R. G. D. Allen, James Meade, Ronald Coase, Abba Lerner, and Nicholas Kaldor. LSE was known for providing somewhat better opportunities for women students and faculty, particularly as compared with Cambridge University (Marcuzzo and Sanfilippo 2008; Lipsey 2020).

11. John and Ursula Hicks's letters from these years are published in Marcuzzo and Sanfilippo (2008).

12. Because of space constraints, I focus on Hicks's contributions to public finance. Her work in economic development received some attention by Lucy Brilliant (2019); see also David (1976). A more extensive and systematic analysis of her work is warranted.

13. Ursula K. Hicks, "Reviewed Work: *Central and Local Finance in Germany and England* by Mabel Newcomer," *Economic Journal* 48, no. 190 (1938): 287.

14. Ursula K. Hicks, "Reviewed Works: *Miti e Paradossi Della Guitstizia Tributaria by L. Einaudi; Personal Income Taxation* by Henry C. Simons," *Economic Journal* 48, no. 192 (1938): 719.

15. Hicks, *The Finance of British Government 1920–1936*. Wilfred David (1976, xi) explained Hicks's approach connected "positive public finance . . . a theoretical subdiscipline of economic science" with "normative public finance," which required knowledge of the sociopolitical and historical context.

16. Ursula K. Hicks, *Public Finance* (Nisbet & Co., 1947).

17. Ursula K. Hicks, *British Public Finances: Their Structure and Development, 1880–1952* (Oxford University Press, 1954), ix.

18. Hicks, *Public Finance.*

19. Hicks, *British Public Finances*, 1.

20. Hicks, *Public Finance*, xi.

21. Hicks, *British Public Finances*, 2.

22. Hicks, *Public Finance*, 2.

23. Ibid.

24. Consider, for example, Hicks on "government . . . as the fourth factor of production. It would not be right to associate the many liberal and democratic economists (such as Einaudi) who followed this tradition, with the excesses of the Fascist Corporative State, but the connection is clear" (Hicks 1965, 149). See also Hicks (1972, 364): "[I]t is pleasant to meet a line of argument which refuses to accept a policy prescription which is assumed to be made exogenously, presumably by a benevolent despot, who is prepared to do just what the economists say, just because it is logical, unless it is also politically and socially relevant to real conditions."

25. John R. Hicks, "Introductory: LSE and the Robbins Circle," in *Money, Interest and Wages*, edited by J. R. Hicks (Harvard University Press, 1982), 3.

26. Roger Backhouse (2017) documented some of the difficulties the editors of the *Review of Economic Studies* faced in exchanging drafts of papers between the United Kingdom and the United States during the 1940s and 1950s, given the frequent interruptions caused by war, paper shortages, strikes, and mail disruptions.

27. Ursula K. Hicks, "Reviewed Work: *Principles of Public Finance* by Hugh Dalton," *Economica* 22, no. 88 (1955): 360.

28. Ursula K. Hicks, "Reviewed Work: *Central and Local Finance in Germany and England* by Mabel Newcomer," *Economic Journal* 48, no. 190 (1938): 287. See also Hicks's review of a later edition of Dalton's *Principles of Public Finance* ([1922] 1954): "the first book in this country to put public finance in the wider background which is universally acknowledged to be its right, and to give due weight to the expenditure side of the budget" (Hicks 1955, 360).

29. Ursula K. Hicks, "On Teaching Public Finance," *Oxford Economic Papers* 13, no. 2 (1961): 124.

30. Ursula K. Hicks, "Reviewed Work: *The Shifting and Incidence of Taxation* by Otto von Mering," *Economica* 12, no. 45 (1945): 41.

31. Hicks, *Public Finance*, 159.

32. Ursula K. Hicks, "Reviewed Work: *Theorie und Praxis der Modernen Einkommenbesteurerung* by F. Neumark," *Economic Journal* 59, no. 235 (1949): 432.

33. See Webb 1934; Hicks 1946a, 1946b.

34. Hicks, "Reviewed Work: *Theorie und Praxis der Modernen Einkommenbesteurerung* by F. Neumark."

35. Hicks, "Reviewed Work: *The Shifting and Incidence of Taxation* by Otto von Mering," 41.

36. Ursula K. Hicks, "Reviewed Work: *Post-War Taxation and Economic Progress* by H. M. Groves," *Economic Journal* 57, no. 226 (1947): 204.

37. Ursula K. Hicks, "Reviewed Work: *Fiscal Theory and Political Economy* by J. M. Buchanan," *Economic Journal* 75, no. 297 (1965): 149.

38. Ibid., 149; see also Ursula K. Hicks, "Musgrave's 'Public Finance,'" *FinanzArchiv* 20, no. 3 (1959–60).

39. See Hicks 1946a, 1946b, 1947b, 1965, 1972.

40. Ursula K. Hicks, "Reviewed Work: *Sweden: The Middle Way* by W. M. Childs," *Economic Journal* 47, no. 186 (1937): 342–45.

41. See Hicks 1938c, 1949.

42. The founding document of the *Review of Economic Studies* can be found on the journal's website at http://www.restud.com/about/history.

43. Wilfred L. David, ed., "Introduction," in *Public Finance, Planning, and Economic Development: Essays in Honour of Ursula Hicks* (Macmillan, 1976), xiv.

44. Nahid Aslanbeigui and Guy Oakes, "The Editor as Scientific Revolutionary: Keynes, The Economic Journal, and the Pigou Affair, 1936–1938," *Journal of the History of Economic Thought* 29, no. 1 (2007); Michael Szenberg and Lall Ramrattan, *Secrets of Economics Editors* (MIT Press, 2014); Ann Mari May, Mary G. McGarvey, Yana van der Meulen Rodgers, and Mark Killingsworth, "Critiques, Ethics, Prestige, and Status: A Survey of Editors," *Eastern Economic Journal* 47, no. 2 (2021): 295–318. Editorial power includes "managing the production of knowledge: framing research and publication agendas; commissioning, editing, and sometimes ghost-writing contributions that fall within favored agendas; rejecting or neutralizing those that do not; tracking the execution of research policies; and servicing personnel" (Aslanbeigui and Oakes 2007, 44).

45. "U. Hicks to H. Johnson, June 21, 1949," Harry Johnson Papers, cited in D. E. Moggridge, *Harry Johnson: A Life in Economics* (Cambridge University Press, 2008), 104.

46. "U. Hicks to P. Samuelson, October 25, 1949," Paul A. Samuelson Papers [PASP], David M. Rubenstein Rare Book and Manuscript Library, Duke University, Box 62.

47. "U. Hicks to P. Samuelson, September 15, 1947," PASP Box 62.

48. "U. Hicks to P. Samuelson, June 3, 1947," PASP Box 62.

49. "U. Hicks to W. Stolper, October 16, 1941," PASP Box 71; see also Roger Backhouse, *Founder of Modern Economics: Paul A. Samuelson* (Oxford University Press, 2017).

50. Ronald Coase, "The Marginal Cost Controversy," *Economica* 13, no. 51 (1946): 169–82; "U. Hicks to P. Samuelson, October 25, 1949," PASP Box 62.

51. Harold Hotelling, "The General Welfare in Relation to Problems of Taxation and of Railway and Utility Rates," *Econometrica* 6, no. 3 (1938): 242.

52. Brett Frischmann and Christiaan Hogendorn, "Retrospectives: The Marginal Cost Controversy," *Journal of Economic Perspectives* 29, no. 1 (2015): 193–206.

53. Nancy Ruggles, "The Welfare Basis of the Marginal Cost Pricing Principle," *Review of Economic Studies* 17, no. 1 (1949); Nancy Ruggles, "Recent Developments in the Theory of Marginal Cost Pricing," *Review of Economic Studies* 17, no. 2 (1949–50).

54. Ruggles, "Recent Developments in the Theory of Marginal Cost Pricing," 120, emphasis in original.

55. "U. Hicks to P. Samuelson, January 2, 1950," PASP Box 62.

56. "U. Hicks to P. Samuelson, June 3, 1947," PASP Box 62.

57. "U. Hicks to P. Samuelson, August 7, 1947," PASP Box 62.

58. "U. Hicks to H. Johnson, March 25, 1955," Harry Johnson Papers, Hanna Holborn Gray Special Collections Research Center, University of Chicago Library, Box 32, Folder *RES,* reproduced in Moggridge, *Harry Johnson*, 106.

59. O. D. Hart and G. E. Mizon, "50th Anniversary of the Review of Economic Studies," *Review of Economic Studies* 50, no. 4 (1983): 583; G. E. Mizon and K. W. S. Roberts, "Editorial," *Review of Economic Studies* 53, no. 2 (1986): 171–72; Jim Thomas, "Ursula Kathleen Hicks: The First Woman Editor of a Major Economics Journal," *LSE Blogs*, December 3, 2020, https://blogs.lse.ac.uk/lsehistory/2020/12/03/ursula-kathleen-hicks-the-first-woman-editor-of-a-major-economic-journal.

60. Jacobson, "Ursula Hicks."

61. Thomas, "Ursula Kathleen Hicks."

62. David, "Introduction," ix.

Chapter 8: W. H. Hutt by Art Carden and Ilia Murtazashvili

1. C. S. Lewis, "On Reading Old Books," in *God in the Dock: Essays on Theology and Ethics*, Kindle (HarperOne, 2014), 201.

2. For more on the principles of a just and humane society, see James R. Otteson, *Honorable Business: A Framework for Business in a Just and Humane Society* (Oxford University Press, 2019).

3. Thomas W. Hazlett, "Razing Keynes: An Economist for the Long Run," in *W. H. Hutt: An Economist for the Long Run*, ed. Morgan O. Reynolds (Gateway Editions, 1986), 11. This paragraph is drawn from the end of Magness, Carden, and Murtazashvili, "Coercion Against Coordination: W. H. Hutt on Collective Bargaining and the Strike-Threat System."

4. Diane Gilcreast, "Lectureship Honors Economist W. H. Hutt," *University News*, October 25, 1989.

5. W. H. Hutt, "To Edwin Cannan," December 28, 1927, Reference 1029, 152-156, Edwin Cannan Papers, London School of Economics Archives.

6. John Davenport, "A Heretical View of Labor Unions," *Fortune*, February 1974.

7. Russell Lewis, "Summary of the Economics of the Colour Bar by W. H. Hutt," in *Apartheid-Capitalism or Socialism?* (Institute of Economic Affairs, 1986), 4–5.

8. Charles W. Baird, "The Varieties of 'Right to Work.' An Essay in Honor of W. H. Hutt," *Managerial and Decision Economics* 9, no. Special Issue (1988): 39.

9. W. H. Hutt, *The Theory of Collective Bargaining: A History, Analysis and Criticism of the Principal Theories Which Have Sought to Explain the Effects of Trade Unions and Employers' Associations upon the Distribution of the Product of Industry* (The Free Press, 1930); W. H. Hutt, *The Economics of the Colour Bar* (Institute of Economic Affairs, republished by the Ludwig von Mises Institute, 1964); W. H. Hutt, *The Strike-Threat System: The Economic Consequences of Collective Bargaining* (Arlington House, 1973).

10. W. H. Hutt, "The Factory System of the Early 19th Century," *Economica*, no. 16 (March 1926): 78–93.

11. Hutt, "To Edwin Cannan," December 28, 1927.

12. Ibid.

13. W. H. Hutt, "Trade Unions: The Private Use of Coercive Power," *Review of Austrian Economics* 3, no. 1 (1990): 116, 120.

14. Jennifer Roback, "W. H. Hutt's the Economics of the Colour Bar," *Managerial and Decision Economics* 9, no. 5 (1988): 65–70; Jennifer Roback, "Racism as Rent Seeking," *Economic Inquiry* 27, no. 4 (1989): 661–81.

15. John B. Egger, "The Contributions of W. H. Hutt," *Review of Austrian Economics* 7, no. 1 (1994): 107–38.

16. W. H. Hutt, "Misgivings and Casuistry on Strikes," *Modern Age*, Fall 1968, 353.

17. Roback, "W. H. Hutt's the Economics of the Colour Bar," 3.

18. Hutt, *Strike-Threat System*, 46.

19. Ibid., 172.

20. Ibid., 182.

21. Ibid., 47.

22. Ibid., 51.

23. W. H. Hutt, "The 'Power' of Labour Unions," in *The Unfinished Agenda: Essays on the Political Economy of Government Policy in Honour of Arthur Seldon*, edited by Martin J. Anderson (Institute of Economic Affairs, 1986), 44.

24. Ibid., 59.

25. Ibid., 59–60.

26. W. H. Hutt, *Economists and the Public: A Study of Competition and Opinion* (Transaction Publishers, 1936), 257.

27. Hutt, "The 'Power' of Labour Unions," 60; Baird, "The Varieties of 'Right to Work.' An Essay in Honor of W. H. Hutt," 37.

28. Morgan O. Reynolds, "An Interview with W. H. Hutt," in *W. H. Hutt: An Economist for the Long Run*, edited by Morgan O. Reynolds (Gateway Editions, 1986), 17–48.

29. Reynolds, "An Interview with W. H. Hutt," 40.

30. W. H. Hutt, "Every Man a Capitalist," *Policy Review*, no. 22 (1982): 141.

31. W. H. Hutt, "Autobiography" (typescript, undated), Hoover Institution, 81.

32. Reynolds, "An Interview with W. H. Hutt," 43.

33. Douglass C. North, John Joseph Wallis, and Barry R. Weingast, *Violence and Social Orders: A Conceptual Framework for Interpreting Recorded Human History* (Cambridge University Press, 2009).

34. Gary W. Cox, Douglass C. North, and Barry R. Weingast, "The Violence Trap: A Political-Economic Approach to the Problems of Development," *Journal of Public Finance and Public Choice* 34, no. 1 (2019): 3–19.

35. W. H. Hutt, "The Complexities of South Africa," in *The African Nettle: Dilemmas of an Emerging Continent*, edited by Frank S. Meyer (John Day, 1965), 171.

36. Christopher J. Coyne, *After War: The Political Economy of Exporting Democracy* (Stanford University Press, 2008); Christopher J. Coyne, "The Politics of Bureaucracy and the Failure of Post-War Reconstruction," *Public Choice* 135, nos. 1–2 (2008): 11–22; Christopher J. Coyne, *Doing Bad by Doing Good: Why Humanitarian Action Fails* (Stanford University Press, 2013); Christopher J. Coyne, "Reconstructing Weak and Failed States: Foreign Intervention and the Nirvana Fallacy," *Foreign Policy Analysis* 2, no. 4 (2006): 343–60.

37. W. H. Hutt, "To Z. K. Matthews," January 20, 1961, http://uir.unisa.ac.za/handle/10500/4176/discover; Phillip W. Magness, Art Carden, and Ilia Murtazashvili, "'The Danger of Deplorable Reactions:' W. H. Hutt on Liberalism, Populism, and the Constitutional Political Economy of Racism," *The Independent Review* 26, no. 4 (2022): 533–52.

38. W. H. Hutt, *Politically Impossible. . .? An Essay on the Supposed Electoral Obstacles Impeding the Translation of Economic Analysis into Policy or Why Politicians Do Not Take Economic Advice* (Institute of Economic Affairs, republished by the Ludwig von Mises Institute, 1971); Adam Smith, *Theory of Moral Sentiments and Essays on Philosophical Subjects* (Alex Murray & Son, 1869), 207–8, https://oll.libertyfund.org/titles/theory-of-moral-sentiments-and-essays-on-philosophical-subjects.

39. James M. Buchanan, "Economists and the Gains from Trade," *Managerial and Decision Economics* 9, no. 5 (1988): 6.

40. Ibid., 10.

41. Hutt, *Theory of Collective Bargaining*, 41–42.

42. Ibid., 41–42.

43. Hutt, "The Complexities of South Africa," 160.

44. Ibid., 161, 168–69.

45. Ibid., 166–67.

46. "Prof W. H. Hutt; Obituary," *The Times*, June 25, 1988, link.gale.com/apps/doc/A117384005/AONE?u=naal_sam&sid=ebsco&xid=2a22643c.

47. John Maynard Keynes, *The General Theory of Employment, Interest, and Money* (Harvest/Harcourt, 1936), 383.

Chapter 9: Friedrich A. Lutz by Lachezar Grudev

1. William Silber, *Volcker: The Triumph of Persistence* (Bloomsbury Press, 2013), 17.

2. Paul A. Volcker and Christine Harper, *Keeping At It: The Quest for Sound Money and Good Government* (Public Affairs, 2018), 17.

3. Silber, *Volcker*, 34.

4. Verena Veit-Bachmann, "Friedrich A. Lutz: Leben und Werk," in *Währungsordnung und Inflation: Zum Gedenken an Friedrich A. Lutz (1901–1975)*, edited by Viktor J. Vanberg (Mohr Siebeck, 2003), 14–15.

5. Bruce Caldwell, "The Chicago School, Hayek, and Neoliberalism," in *Building Chicago Economics: New Perspectives on the History of America's Most Powerful Economics Program*, edited by Robert Van Horn, Philip Mirowski, and Thomas A. Stapleford (Cambridge University Press, 2011), 303.

6. Muriel Dal-Pont Legrand and Harald Hagemann, "Lutz and Equilibrium Theories of the Business Cycle," *Œconomia* 3, no. 2 (2013): 249.

7. Hans O. Lenel, "Zum Gedenken an Friedrich A. Lutz," *ORDO—Jahrbuch für die Ordnung von Wirtschaft und Gesellschaft* 27, no. 1 (1976): 3–4; Silber, *Volcker*, 17.

8. Nils Goldschmidt, "Walter Eucken's Place in the History of Ideas," *Review of Austrian Economics* 26, no. 2 (2013); Stefan Kolev and Ekkehard A. Köhler, "Transatlantic Roads to Mont Pèlerin: 'Old Chicago' and Freiburg in a World of Disintegrating Orders," *History of Political Economy* 54, no. 4 (2022); Wendula Gräfin von Klinckowstroem, *Walter Eucken: Ein Leben für Menschenwürde und Wettbewerb* (Mohr Siebeck, 2023).

9. Friedrich A. Lutz, *Politische Überzeugungen und nationalökonomische Theorie: Zürcher Vorträge* (Political Beliefs and National Economic Theories), edited by Alfred Bosch and Reinhold Veit (Mohr Siebeck, 1971), 62–63.

10. Hauke Janssen, *Nationalökonomie und Nationalsozialismus: Die deutsche Volkswirtschaftslehre in den dreißiger Jahren des 20. Jahrhunderts* (Metropolis, 2012).

11. Veit-Bachmann, "Friedrich A. Lutz: Leben und Werk," 11–12.

12. Lutz to Eucken, October 2, 1934. The cited letters between Lutz and Eucken are from the Walter Eucken Archive at Thüringer Universitäts-und Landesbibliothek Jena, University of Jena.

13. Christof Rühl, "The Transformation of the Business Cycle Theory: Hayek, Lucas and a Change in the Notion of Equilibrium," in *Money and Business Cycles: The Economics of F. A. Hayek*, vol. 1, edited by Marina Colonna and Harald Hagemann (Edward Elgar, 1994), 168–202; Klaus-Rainer Brintzinger, *Die Nationalökonomie an den Universitäten Freiburg, Heidelberg und Tübingen, 1918–1945* (Peter Lang, 1996), 45–46; Lachezar Grudev, "Friedrich A. Lutz' Epistemological and Methodological Messages During the German-Language Business Cycle Debate," *Journal of Contextual Economics—Schmollers Jahrbuch* 139, no. 1 (2019).

14. Friedrich A. Hayek, "Interview by Armen A. Alchian. 'Tape: Alchian I, Side One: Tape Date: November 11, 1978,'" in *Nobel Prize–Winning Economist: Friedrich A. von Hayek* (Regents of the University of California, 1983), 362, completed under the auspices of the Oral History Program, University of California, Los Angeles, https://archive.org/details/nobelprizewinninoohaye/mode/2up.

15. Leonidas Zelmanovitz, "Vera Smith: The Contrarian View," Library of Economics and Liberty, 2019, https://www.econlib.org/library/Columns/y2019/ZelmanovitzSmithV.html.

16. Howard S. Ellis, *German Monetary Theory 1905–1933* (Harvard University Press, 1937).

17. Hayek, "Interview by Armen A. Alchian," 362.

18. Friedrich A. Hayek, "The Economics of the 1930s as Seen from London," in *Contra Keynes and Cambridge: The Collected Works of F. A. Hayek*, vol. 9, edited by Bruce Caldwell (University of Chicago Press, 1995), 49.

19. Lachezar Grudev, "Emigration with a Pulled Handbrake: Friedrich A. Lutz's Internal Methodenstreit," Center for the History of Political Economy at Duke University Working Paper Series, 2021, https://ssrn.com/abstract=3858831.

20. For more about the Grand Seminars at LSE, see Howson (2011) and Caldwell and Klausinger (2022).

21. Klinckowstroem, *Walter Eucken*, 172–74.

22. Judith Syga-Dubois, *Wissenschaftliche Philanthropie und transatlantischer Austausch in der Zwischenkriegszeit: Die sozialwissenschaftlichen Förderprogramme der Rockefeller-Stiftungen in Deutschland* (Böhlau, 2019), 636; Grudev, "Emigration with a Pulled Handbrake," 22–23.

23. Friedrich A. Lutz, "Das Grundproblem der Geldverfassung (The Fundamental Problem of the Monetary Constitution)," in *Geld und Währung: Gesammelte Abhandlungen*, edited by Karl Friedrich Maier (Mohr Siebeck, 1962), 99–102.

24. Grudev, "Emigration with a Pulled Handbrake," 19–20.

25. Martin Shubik Papers, "Notes, Economic Theory; Prof. F. Lutz (Fall 1949–Spring 1950)" Folder, Box 2, Economists' Papers Archive, David M. Rubenstein Rare Book and Manuscript Library, Duke University.

26. Veit-Bachmann, "Friedrich A. Lutz: Leben und Werk"; Grudev, "Emigration with a Pulled Handbrake."

27. Friedrich A. Lutz, "The Interest Rate and Investment in a Dynamic Economy," *American Economic Review* 35, no. 5 (1945): 811–30.

28. Friedrich A. Lutz, "The Criterion of Maximum Profits in the Theory of Investment," *Quarterly Journal of Economics* 60, no. 1 (1945): 56–77.

29. Friedrich A. Lutz, *International Monetary Mechanism: The Keynes and White Proposals*, International Finance Section, Department of Economics and Social Institutions, Princeton University, 1943.

30. See, for example, Friedrich A. Lutz, "The Case for Flexible Exchange Rates," *Banca Nazionale del Lavoro Quarterly Review* 7, no. 31 (1954): 175–83.

31. Veit-Bachmann, "Friedrich A. Lutz: Leben und Werk," 22.

32. Lenel, "Zum Gedenken an Friedrich A. Lutz"; Veit-Bachmann, "Friedrich A. Lutz: Leben und Werk."

33. Perry Mehrling, "An Interview with Paul A. Volcker," *Macroeconomic Dynamics* 5, no. 3 (2001): 435.

34. Franz Ritzmann, "Professor Dr. Friedrich A. Lutz," in *Rektoratsrede und Jahresbericht 1975/76* (University of Zurich, 1976), 79–81; Klaus-Rainer Brintzinger, *Die Nationalökonomie an den Universitäten Freiburg, Heidelberg und Tübingen, 1918–1945* (Peter Lang, 1996).

35. Mark Blaug, *Economic Theory in Retrospect* (Cambridge University Press, 2003), 547.

36. Rudolf Richter, "Die Geldpolitik im Spiegel der wissenschaftlichen Diskussion," in *Fünfzig Jahre Deutsche Mark: Notenbank und Währung in Deutschland seit 1948*, edited by Deutsche Bundesbank (C. H. Beck, 1998), 561–608; Gianni Toniolo, *Central Bank Cooperation at the Bank for International Settlements, 1930–1973* (Cambridge University Press, 2005).

37. American Economic Association, *Readings in Monetary Theory: Selected by a Committee of the American Economic Association* (Richard D. Irwin, 1951); Veit-Bachmann, "Friedrich A. Lutz: Leben und Werk."

38. Friedrich A. Lutz and Douglas C. Hague, eds., *The Theory of Capital: Proceedings of a Conference Held by the International Economic Association* (Macmillan, 1961).

39. Harold Hagemann, "Zur Einführung: Friedrich A. Lutz (1901–1975)," in *Grundtexte zur Freiburger Tradition der Ordnungsökonomik*, edited by Nils Goldschmidt and Michael Wohlgemut (Mohr Siebeck, 2008), 273–78.

40. Carol M. Connell, *Reforming the World Monetary System: Fritz Machlup and the Bellagio Group* (Pickering & Chatto, 2013).

41. Friedrich A. Lutz, *The Problem of International Liquidity and the Multiple-Currency Standard*, International Finance Section, Department of Economics and Social Institutions, Princeton University, 1966.

42. Bruce Caldwell and Hansjörg Klausinger, *Hayek: A Life 1899–1950* (University of Chicago Press, 2022), 642–43.

43. Ronald M. Hartwell, *A History of the Mont Pelerin Society* (Liberty Fund, 1995), 145–46, 151–56; Matthias Schmelzer, *Freiheit für Wechselkurse und Kapital: Die Ursprünge neoliberaler Währungspolitik und die Mont Pèlerin Society* (Metropolis, 2010), 74–76.

Chapter 10: Eric Hoffer by Alberto Mingardi

1. Friedrich August von Hayek, *A New Statement of the Liberal Principles of Justice and Political Economy*, vol. I, *Rules and Order*, edited by Jeremy Shearmur (University of Chicago Press, 2022), 30.

2. Bethell (2017, 171) actually suggests that "Hoffer paid little attention to thinkers such as Milton Friedman or Friedrich Hayek, and at times viewed economic explanations as beside the point." He then offers a quote by Hoffer from *The True Believer*, in which the latter scorns the view that economic motivation is the only driver of human actions.

3. Karl Mannheim, *Man and Society in an Age of Reconstruction: Studies in Modern Social Structure* (Routledge & Kegan, 1960), 61.

4. Hannah Arendt, *The Origins of Totalitarianism* (Harcourt Brace & Company, 1973), 317.

5. A similar thesis had been advanced before by Emil Lederer (*The Threat of the Classless Society* [Norton, 1940]), who saw the crumbling of a pluralistic stratification of society into an amorphous mass as the turning-point towards totalitarianism.

6. Judith Shklar, "Hannah Arendt as a Pariah," in *Political Thought & Political Thinkers* (University of Chicago Press, 1998), 369.

7. E. V. Walter, "'Mass Society': The Late Stages of an Idea," *Social Research* 31, no. 4 (1964): 410.

8. The classic locus for that is José Ortega y Gasset, *The Revolt of the Masses* (W. W. Norton, [1929] 1994).

9. Edward Shils, "Mass Society and Its Culture," *Daedalus* 89, no. 2 (1960): 288. Interestingly, Shils had been the translator of Mannheim ([1935] 1960).

10. The so called "long nineteenth century" changed the demographics of Europe dramatically. The population doubled, child mortality started to decline, and life expectancy to increase. In Victorian England, the population rose from fourteen million in the 1830s to thirty-two million in 1901. "Mass society" is in a sense a strictly descriptive locution.

11. Eric Hoffer, *The Passionate State of Mind and Other Aphorisms* (Hopewell Publications, 2006), 13.

12. Tom Bethell, *Eric Hoffer: The Longshoreman Philosopher* (Hoover Institution Press, 2017), 24.

13. James D. Koerner, *Hoffer's America* (Library Press, 1973), 3.

14. Ibid., 58.

15. Ibid., 9.

16. Bethell, *Eric Hoffer*, 39–40.

17. Ibid., chap 3.

18. Koerner, *Hoffer's America*, 19.

19. Bethell, *Eric Hoffer*, 97–112.

20. Koerner, *Hoffer's America*, 20.

21. Mark E. Thompson, "Eric Hoffer and the Significance of Reading," *Reading Horizons: A Journal of Literacy and Language Arts* 20, no. 11 (1979): 69.

22. Calvin Tomkins, *Eric Hoffer: An American Odyssey* (Dutton, 1970), 2.

23. Tom Shachtman, *American Iconoclast: The Life and Times of Eric Hoffer* (Hopewell Publications, 2011), 54.

24. Bethell, *Eric Hoffer*, 69.

25. Ibid., 70.

26. Ibid., 115.

27. Ibid., 120.

28. Ibid., 23. Hoffer was not flattered by being identified as "Ike's favorite author" and commented that the fact simply proved to him that "any child" could read his book (Tomkins 1970, 71).

29. Shachtman, *American Iconoclast*, 11–12.

30. Eric Hoffer, *The Temper of Our Time* (Hopewell Publications, 2008), 94.

31. Ibid., 67.

32. Eric Hoffer, *Reflections on the Human Condition* (Hopewell Publications, 2006), 3.

33. For an overview of who reads and cites Hoffer today, see Anthony Rausch, "Longshoreman Philosopher: Where Is Eric Hoffer Now?" *Qeios* (2023), doi:10.32388/6MD7H1.

34. Tom Stoppard, *The Real Thing* (Faber & Faber, 1983), 33.

35. Hoffer, *Reflections on the Human Condition*, 32.

36. George Will, "A Young 75 Years Old," *Washington Post*, January 15, 1978.

37. Bethell, *Eric Hoffer*, 116.

38. Shachtman, *American Iconoclast*, 71.

39. Alan Kahan, *Freedom from Fear: An Incomplete History of Liberalism* (Princeton University Press, 2023).

40. Ludwig von Mises, *Omnipotent Government. The Rise of the Total State and Total War* (Yale University Press, 1944).

41. Eric Hoffer, *The True Believer* (Harper & Row, 1966), 25. The source (Hermann Rauschning, *Hitler Speaks* [G. P. Putnam's Sons, 1940], 134) has since been called into question.

42. Ibid., x.

43. Ibid., 22.

44. Ibid., 31.

45. Ibid., 33. Both Tocqueville's quotations come from *L'Ancien Regime et la Revolution*.

46. Hoffer, *The Temper of Our Time*, 24.

47. Hoffer, *The True Believer*, 16. To use a more contemporary jargon, Hoffer is speaking of people who have external locus of control—who believe that their existence is shaped by external factors.

48. Ibid., 21.

49. Hoffer, *Reflections on the Human Condition*, 16.

50. "When a mass movement begins to attract people who are interested in their individual careers, it is a sign that it has passed its vigorous stage" (Hoffer, *The True Believer*, 22).

51. Hoffer, *Reflections on the Human Condition*, 59.

52. Hoffer, *True Believer*, 126.

53. Hoffer, *The Temper of Our Time*, 83.

54. See, for example, Jonathan Haidt, *The Righteous Mind: Why Good People Are Divided by Politics and Religion* (Vintage Books, 2012).

55. Eric Hoffer, *Working and Thinking on the Waterfront* (Hopewell Publications, 2009), 103.

56. Eric Hoffer, *The Ordeal of Change* (Hopewell Publications, 2006), 2.

57. Ibid., 4.

58. Ibid., 6.

59. Ibid., 4–5.

60. Edmund Phelps, *Mass Flourishing: How Grassroots Innovation Created Jobs, Challenge, and Change* (Princeton University Press, 2013), 36.

61. Hoffer, *The Ordeal of Change*, 25.

62. Eric Hoffer, *Working and Thinking on the Waterfront* (Hopewell Publications, 2009), 101.

63. Hoffer, *The Ordeal of Change*, 44–45.

64. Hoffer, *The Temper of Our Time*, 64.

65. Eric Hoffer, *Before the Sabbath* (Hopewell Publications, 2009), 4.

66. Hoffer, *The Ordeal of Change*, 71, 72.

67. Ibid., 57, 61.

68. Ibid., 27.

69. Ibid., 26.

70. Deirdre N. McCloskey, *Bourgeois Equality: How Ideas, Not Capital or Institutions, Enriched the World* (University of Chicago Press, 2016).

71. Ibid., 27.

72. Hoffer, *Working and Thinking on the Waterfront*, 4. It is indeed a time in which a culture for which "thrift consists as much in making good use of things as in preserving them" and hence an imperative to "make as good use as possible of time, and never to waste any" ("I have a rule that I always follow: never remain idle") emerged. Leon Battista Alberti, *The Family in Renaissance Florence* (University of South Carolina Press, [1433–34] 1969), 171–72.

73. Hoffer, *The Ordeal of Change*, 27.

74. Ibid., 27.

75. Ibid., 25.
76. Hoffer, *Working and Thinking on the Waterfront*, 29.
77. Hoffer, *The Ordeal of Change*, 36.
78. Ibid., 33.
79. Hoffer, *The Temper of Our Time*, 100.
80. Ibid., 61–74.

Chapter 11: Kenneth Boulding by Yahya Alshamy and Christopher J. Coyne

1. For detailed biographies of Boulding, see Kerman (1974), Mott (2000), and Scott (2015).
2. Michael Szenberg, "Kenneth E. Boulding: 1910–1993: In Memoriam," *American Economist* 37, no. 2 (1993): 3.
3. Kenneth Boulding, "The Place of the 'Displacement Cost' Concept in Economic Theory," *Economic Journal* 42, no. 165 (1932): 137–41.
4. Sylvia Nasar, "Kenneth Boulding, an Economist, Philosopher and Poet, Dies at 83," *New York Times*, March 20, 1993, https://www.nytimes.com/1993/03/20/obituaries/kenneth-boulding-an-economist-philosopher-and-poet-dies-at-83.html.
5. Kenneth Boulding, "Introduction to the Collected Papers of Kenneth E. Boulding: Volume 1," in *Kenneth E. Boulding: Collected Papers*, vol. 1, edited by Fred Glahe (Colorado Associated University Press, 1971), viii.
6. Robert L. Heilbroner, "Kenneth Boulding, *Collected Papers*: A Review Article," *Journal of Economic Issues* 9, no. 1 (1975): 77.
7. Ibid., 79.
8. Quoted in Nasar, "Kenneth Boulding, an Economist, Philosopher and Poet, Dies at 83."
9. Robert Scott, *Kenneth Boulding: A Voice Crying in the Wilderness* (Palgrave Macmillan, 2015).
10. Kenneth Boulding, *The Image: Knowledge in Life and Society* (Ann Arbor Paperbacks, 1956), 6, 54, 55.
11. Ibid., 59
12. Ibid., 55.
13. Ibid., 64.
14. Ibid., 75.
15. Ibid., 76.
16. Israel Kirzner, *Perception, Opportunity, and Profit: Studies in the Theory of Entrepreneurship* (University of Chicago Press, 1979), 142.
17. Kenneth Boulding, *Beyond Economics: Essays on Society, Religion, and Ethics* (University of Michigan Press, 1968), 146.
18. Peter J. Boettke and David L. Prychitko, "Mr. Boulding and the Austrians: Boulding's Contribution to Subjectivist Economics," in *Joseph A. Schumpeter: Historian of Economics*, edited by Laurence S. Moss (Routledge, 1996).
19. Kenneth Boulding, "The Power of Nonconflict," *Journal of Social Issues* 33, no. 1 (1977): 22–33, 32.

20. Ibid., 32.

21. Thomas C. Schelling, *Arms and Influence* (Yale University Press, 1966).

22. Kenneth Boulding, *Stable Peace* (University of Texas Press, 1978), 64.

23. Kenneth Boulding, "Moving from Unstable to Stable Peace," in *Breakthrough: Emerging New Thinking—Soviet and Western Scholars Issue a Challenge to Build a World Beyond War*, edited by Anatoly Gromyko and Martin Hellman (Walker & Company, 1988), 160.

24. Boulding, *Stable Peace*, 25.

25. Kenneth Boulding, *Beyond Economics: Essays on Society, Religion, and Ethics* (University of Michigan Press, 1968), 43–54.

26. Kenneth Boulding, *Three Faces of Power* (Sage, 1989), 17.

27. Ibid., 25.

28. Ibid., 27.

29. Ibid., 29.

30. Ibid., 55.

31. Ibid., 55.

32. Robert L. Heilbroner, "Kenneth Boulding, *Collected Papers*: A Review Article," *Journal of Economic Issues* 9, no. 1 (1975): 73–79.

33. Peter J. Boettke, "Where Did Economics Go Wrong? Modern Economics as a Flight from Reality," *Critical Review* 11, no. 1 (1997): 11–64.

34. Peter J. Boettke, *Living Economics: Yesterday, Today, and Tomorrow* (Independent Institute, 2012).

35. Peter J. Boettke, Stefanie Haeffele-Balch, and Virgil Henry Storr, *Mainline Economics: Six Nobel Lectures in the Tradition of Adam Smith* (Mercatus Center at George Mason University, 2016), 4.

Chapter 12: Bruno Leoni by Michael C. Munger

1. Bruno Leoni, *Freedom and the Law* (Van Nostrand/Princeton, 1961, commissioned by William Volker Fund; Liberty Fund, Inc., reprinted in expanded 3rd edition, 1991), 22.

2. For an excellent review of these contributions, see Aranson 1988 in References.

3. It is possible that Leoni's various contributions did not fit together very well, but he believed they did. Yet we have no substantial statement in his words of how this articulation was accomplished.

4. For background on "institutions," see North (1990). For Leoni's particular view of legal institutions as a "fifth factor of production," see Boettke and Candela (2015). See also Hasnas (2024) for a theory that incorporates Leoni's approach.

5. Alberto Mingardi, "Bruno Leoni and the Search for Certainty in Law," *Law and Liberty*, November 7, 2018, https://lawliberty.org/classic/bruno-leoni-and-the-search-for-certainty-in-law.

6. See Bradsher (2017).

7. Mingardi, "Bruno Leoni and the Search for Certainty in Law."

8. Antonio Masala, "Leoni, Hayek, and 'Il Politico,'" *Il Politico* 87, no. 2 (2022): 5–22.

9. Leoni also showed considerable interest in Public Choice, writing about *The Calculus of Consent* (Buchanan and Tullock 1962) immediately after it appeared (Leoni 1963) and arguing, though not very successfully, to have the Public Choice approach adopted in Italian political science departments (Empoli 1993).

10. Max Hartwell, *History of the Mont Pelerin Society* (Liberty Fund, 1995), 149–51.

11. I used a number of Italian newspaper archives to piece together this account. The primary sources can be found at *La Stampa* (1967).

12. For some reason, Olivetti's name is often written as "Magola," but that's not right. Perhaps the "d" looked like an "o l" in some font, or in handwriting?

13. Osvaldo Quero, thirty-nine at the time of these events, lived at 83 via Cavour. He was married to Rosina (thirty-five at the time), and they had two children, Riccardo (nine) and Mauro (seven). He worked as a printer at Rotogravure Capretti in Via Villar, and made around 180,000 lire ($300 US 1967, $2,800 today) per month.

14. These "quotes" are from reconstructions in newspaper accounts and should not be taken literally. They are at best conjectural contemporary history.

15. Again, these "quotes" cannot be trusted. The writing style of the newspapers where this account was described is more *National Enquirer* than *New York Times*.

16. "The reason why the fake kidnapping letter was signed 'I sardi' (the Sardinians) is twofold: (1) Leoni came from a Sardinian family; (2) the Sardinians were famous for kidnapping rich people in the 1960s (and 1970s)" (Alberto Mingardi, personal correspondence with the author).

17. "Condannate in appello a 24 anni Quero, l'uccisore del prof. Leoni," *La Stampa*, 1970, http://www.archiviolastampa.it/component/option,com_lastampa/task,search/mod,avanzata/action,viewer/Itemid,3/page,5/articleid,0131_01_1970_0120_0005_4813499.

18. Hartwell, *History of the Mont Pelerin* Society, 149–53.

19. F. A. Hayek, *The Market and Other Orders* in *Collected Works of F. A. Hayek*, edited by Bruce Caldwell, vol. 15 (University of Chicago Press, 2014), 167, emphasis added.

20. Antonio Masala, "Bruno Leoni and the Austrian Tradition," from the session on "Libertarianism: Intellectual History and Applications," presented at the Austrian Economics Research Conference. Originally recorded 23 March 2013 at the Ludwig von Mises Institute in Auburn, Alabama, https://mises.org/podcasts/aerc-2013/bruno-leoni-and-austrian-tradition. Because there were no papers or concrete references where Leoni's ideas could be referenced, he was often discussed in conversation but not cited in research. "People were speaking about Leoni's ideas, but there was no reference; it was not possible to say, 'Okay, Leoni said this, in this paper.' Leoni's ideas were circulating, but it was not possible to give a reference" Masala (2014; 3'44").

21. Ibid.

22. The opposite could also be true, however: the state could expand if such limits were not taken seriously. See, e.g., Bassani and Lottieri (2021).

23. Masala, "Bruno Leoni and the Austrian Tradition."

24. That Latin phrase always makes me think of verse 25 from the Book of James, Chapter 1, in the Christian Bible: "But whoever looks intently into the perfect law that gives freedom,

and continues in it—not forgetting what they have heard, but doing it—they will be blessed in what they do" (New International Version).

25. Murray N. Rothbard, "Review of *Freedom and the Law*," *New Individualist Review* 1, no. 1 (1961): 188.

26. Ibid.

27. See Masala 2014; Mingardi 2018a, 2018b; and Zywicki 2015 in References for more details.

28. Bruno Leoni, *Freedom and the Law*, 3rd edition (Liberty Fund, 1991), 83; cited in Todd Zywicki, "Bruno Leoni's Legacy and Continued Relevance," *Journal of Private Enterprise* 30, no. 1 (2015): 131–41.

29. Reviewed by Todd Zywicki, "The Rise and Fall of Efficiency in the Common Law: A Supply-Side Analysis," *Northwestern Law Review* 97, no. 4 (2003): 1551–96.

Chapter 13: Edith Penrose by Richard N. Langlois

1. Alan M. Rugman and Alain Verbeke, "A Final Word on Edith Penrose," *Journal of Management Studies* 41, no. 1 (2004): 205.

2. John Kay, "The Story of Flight," *International Review of Applied Economics* 38, nos. 1–2 (2024): 99.

3. Richard N. Langlois, *The Corporation and the Twentieth Century: The History of American Business Enterprise* (Princeton University Press, 2023).

4. Angela Penrose, *No Ordinary Woman: The Life of Edith Penrose* (Oxford University Press, 2017); Perran Penrose and Christos Pitelis, "Edith Elura Tilton Penrose: Life, Contributions and Influence," in Christos Pitelis, ed., *The Growth of the Firm: The Legacy of Edith Penrose* (Oxford University Press, 2002), 17–36.

5. This was far from the only tragedy in Edith's life. Both of her younger brothers became Air Force pilots and were killed in air crashes, one of them in combat. Her first son with Ernest Penrose would die at age eighteen months.

6. Margit von Mises, *My Years with Ludwig von Mises* (Arlington House, 1976), 55–56.

7. Edith T. Penrose, *The Economics of the International Patent System* (Johns Hopkins University Press, 1951).

8. Clement Levallois, "Why Were Biological Analogies in Economics 'a Bad Thing'? Edith Penrose's Battles Against Social Darwinism and McCarthyism," *Science in Context* 24, no. 4 (2011): 465–85.

9. Penrose, *No Ordinary Woman*, 120.

10. Edith T. Penrose, "The Growth of the Firm—a Case Study: The Hercules Powder Company," *Business History Review* 34, no. 1 (1960): 1–23.

11. Fritz Machlup, *Essays on Economic Semantics* (Prentice-Hall, 1963).

12. Edith T. Penrose, *The Theory of the Growth of the Firm* (Oxford University Press, Fourth Edition, 2009), 13.

13. Ibid., 21–22.

14. Ibid., 48.

15. Ibid., 60.

16. Ibid., 97.

17. Penrose generated a business history of Hercules Powder, which was originally to have been part of *TGF*, but it was left out for reasons of length and published separately in *Business History Review* in 1960. Interestingly, *TGF* never refers to Hercules let alone draws on examples from the firm.

18. Penrose, "The Growth of the Firm—a Case Study: The Hercules Powder Company."

19. Penrose, *The Theory of the Growth of the Firm*, 101.

20. William J. Baumol, "On the Theory of Expansion of the Firm," *American Economic Review* 52, no. 5 (1962): 1078–87; Oliver E. Williamson, "The Economics of Discretionary Behavior: Managerial Objectives," in *A Theory of the Firm* (Prentice Hall, 1964).

21. Robin Marris, *The Economic Theory of "Managerial" Capitalism* (Macmillan, 1966).

22. Hirofumi Uzawa, "The Penrose Effect and Optimum Growth," *Economic Studies Quarterly* 19, no. 1 (1968): 1–14.

23. Joe S. Bain, *Industrial Organization* (John Wiley & Sons, 1959).

24. Richard E. Caves, *American Industry: Structure, Conduct, Performance* (Prentice–Hall, 1964).

25. Michael E. Porter, *Competitive Strategy* (The Free Press, 1980).

26. Birger Wernerfelt, "A Resource-Based View of the Firm," *Strategic Management Journal* 5, no. 2 (1984): 171–80.

27. Nicolai J. Foss, "Edith Penrose: Economics and Stategic Management," in Christos Pitelis, ed., *The Growth of the Firm: The Legacy of Edith Penrose* (Oxford University Press, 2002), 147–64; Alan M. Rugman and Alain Verbeke, "Edith Penrose's Contribution to the Resource-Based View of Strategic Management," *Strategic Management Journal* 23, no. 8 (2002): 769–80.

28. Jay Barney, "Firm Resources and Sustained Competitive Advantage," *Journal of Management* 17, no. 1 (1991): 99–120.

29. Foss, "Edith Penrose," 158.

30. Alfred D. Chandler Jr., "The Beginnings of 'Big Business' in American Industry," *Business History Review* 33, no. 1 (1959): 1–31.

31. Christopher D. McKenna, "Writing the Ghost-Writer Back In: Alfred Sloan, Alfred Chandler, John McDonald and the Intellectual Origins of Corporate Strategy," *Management & Organizational History* 1, no. 2 (May 2006): 107–26.

32. Alfred D. Chandler Jr., *Strategy and Structure: Chapters in the History of the Industrial Enterprise* (MIT Press, 1962), 453.

33. Alfred D. Chandler Jr., *The Visible Hand: The Managerial Revolution in American Business* (Belknap Press, 1977), 489.

34. I fully agree with Brian Loasby's opinion that Richardson (1972) "must be a close contender with Young's (1928) exposition of increasing returns for the title of the best article ever written on industrial organization" (Loasby 2002, p. 52).

35. G. B. Richardson, "The Organisation of Industry," *Economic Journal* 82, no. 327 (1972): 888.

36. Ronald H. Coase, "The Nature of the Firm," *Economica* 4, no. 16 (1937): 386–405.

37. Ronald H. Coase, "Industrial Organization: A Proposal for Research," in Victor R. Fuchs, ed., *Economic Research: Retrospect and Prospect*, vol. 3, *Policy Issues and Research Op-*

portunities in Industrial Organization (Columbia University Press for the National Bureau of Economic Research, 1972), 63.

38. Richardson, "The Organization of Industry," 895.

39. Brian J. Loasby, "The Significance of Penrose's Theory for the Development of Economics," in Christos Pitelis, ed., *The Growth of the Firm: The Legacy of Edith Penrose* (Oxford University Press, 2002), 45–59.

40. Dynamic capabilities are "the firm's ability to integrate, build, and reconfigure internal and external competences to address rapidly changing environments" (Teece, Pisano and Shuen 1997, p. 516).

41. Richard N. Langlois, "Rationality, Institutions, and Explanation," in Richard N. Langlois, ed., *Economics as a Process: Essays in the New Institutional Economics* (Cambridge University Press, 1986), 240–41.

42. Fritz Machlup, "Theories of the Firm: Marginalist, Behavioral, Managerial," *American Economic Review* 57, no. 1 (1967): 1–33.

43. Armen A. Alchian, "Uncertainty, Evolution, and Economic Theory," *Journal of Political Economy* 58, no. 3 (1950): 211–21.

44. Milton Friedman, "The Methodology of Positive Economics," in *Essays in Positive Economics* (University of Chicago Press, 1953), 22.

45. Edith T. Penrose, "Biological Analogies in the Theory of the Firm," *American Economic Review* 42, no. 5 (1952): 812.

46. Sidney G. Winter, "Satisficing, Selection, and the Innovating Remnant," *Quarterly Journal of Economics* 85, no 2 (1971): 245.

47. Richard M. Cyert and James G. March, *A Behavioral Theory of the Firm* (Prentice-Hall, 1963); James G. March and Herbert A. Simon, *Organizations* (John Wiley and Sons, 1958).

48. Herbert A. Simon, "Rational Choice and the Structure of the Environment," *Psychological Review* 63, no. 2 (1956): 129–38.

49. Richard R. Nelson and Sidney G. Winter, *An Evolutionary Theory of Economic Change* (Harvard University Press, 1982), 15.

50. Steven D. Levitt, John A. List, and Chad Syverson, "Toward an Understanding of Learning by Doing: Evidence from an Automobile Assembly Plant," *Journal of Political Economy* 121, no. 4 (2013): 643–81.

51. Richard R. Nelson and Sidney G. Winter, "Evolutionary Theorizing in Economics," *Journal of Economic Perspectives* 16, no. 2 (Spring 2002): 30.

52. It is one of many charming Penrosean paradoxes that, whereas evolutionary economists would reinvent a concept of economic capabilities fundamentally similar to her own, she herself remained hostile to evolutionary theorizing in economics (as her 1952 comment suggests), possibly because she linked it to Social Darwinism (Levallois 2011).

53. Oliver E. Williamson, "The Vertical Integration of Production: Market Failure Considerations," *American Economic Review* 61, no. 2 (1971): 112–23; Oliver E. Williamson, *Markets and Hierarchies: Analysis and Antitrust Implications* (The Free Press, 1975).

54. Joseph T. Mahoney and Jackson Nickerson, "Oliver Williamson: A Hero's Journey on the Merits," *Journal of Institutional Economics* 18, no. 2 (2022): 196–97.

55. Oliver E. Williamson, *The Economics of Discretionary Behavior: Managerial Objectives in a Theory of the Firm* (Prentice Hall, 1964).

56. Ronald H. Coase, "The Nature of the Firm," *Economica* 4 (1937): 390.

57. David J. Teece, "Economies of Scope and the Scope of the Enterprise," *Journal of Economic Behavior & Organization* 1, no. 3 (September 1980): 223–47; David J. Teece, "Towards an Economic Theory of the Multiproduct Firm," *Journal of Economic Behavior & Organization* 3, no. 1 (March 1982): 39–63. According to David Teece (private communication), it was his citation of Penrose that called Wernerfelt's (1984) attention to *TGF.* Teece was aware of George Richardson's 1960 book *Information and Investment*, which bore no influence from Penrose (Richardson 2002, p. 37), but he was long unaware of Richardson's 1972 article.

58. Edith T. Penrose, *The Theory of the Growth of the Firm*, 3rd ed. (Oxford University Press, 1995), x.

59. Edith T. Penrose, *The Theory of the Growth of the Firm*, 4th ed. (Oxford University Press, 2009), 9.

60. Perran Penrose and Christos Pitelis, "Edith Elura Tilton Penrose: Life, Contributions and Influence," in Christos Pitelis, ed., *The Growth of the Firm: The Legacy of Edith Penrose* (Oxford University Press, 2002), 19.

61. Richard N. Langlois and Roger G. Koppl, "Fritz Machlup and Marginalism: A Reevaluation," *Methodus* 3, no. 2 (December 1991): 86–102.

62. Brian J. Loasby, "The Significance of Penrose's Theory for the Development of Economics," in Christos Pitelis, ed., *The Growth of the Firm: The Legacy of Edith Penrose* (Oxford University Press, 2002), 51–52.

Chapter 14: Warren Nutter by Phillip W. Magness

1. David M. Levy and Sandra J. Peart, "Soviet Growth and American Textbooks: An Endogenous Past," *Journal of Economic Behavior & Organization* 78, nos. 1–2 (2011): 110–25.

2. Ibid.

3. G. Warren Nutter, "Some Observations on Soviet Industrial Growth," *American Economic Review* 47, no. 2 (1957): 618–30; G. Warren Nutter, Israel Borenstein, and Adam Kaufman, "Growth of Industrial Production in the Soviet Union," *NBER Books*, 1962.

4. Henry Hazlitt, "Communist Crack-Up," *Newsweek*, May 27, 1957.

5. Rendigs Fels, *The Challenge to the American Economy* (n.p., 1961), 11–12, excerpted in Levy and Peart, "Soviet Growth and American Textbooks," 121.

6. Jo Anne Cavallo and Walter E. Block, *Libertarian Autobiographies: Moving Toward Freedom in Today's World* (Springer, 2023), 172.

7. David M. Levy and Sandra J. Peart, "G. Warren Nutter's 'Traveler's Tale of the Soviet Economy': A Witness to the Actual World," *Review of Austrian Economics* 28, no. 4 (2015): 397–404.

8. Ibid.

9. For more on Vining's role at UVA, see Richard Wagner, "Rutledge Vining and the Virginia Political Economy That Might Have Been," Working Paper, 2024, https://papers.ssrn.com/sol3/papers.cfm?abstract_id=4730231.

10. This incident has become noteworthy in recent years after Duke University historian Nancy MacLean's 2017 book *Democracy in Chains* misidentified Nutter as an associate of the "Massive Resisters" in an attempt to discredit his work at UVA. In both her book and subsequent lectures, MacLean depicts the Parents Committee for Emergency Schooling (PCES) as a heroic foil to the Byrd machine, recounting how it "cobbl[ed] together temporary schooling in church basements, home family rooms, and clubhouses" rather than partaking in "Massive Resistance" (p. 63). The stunning historical incompetence of MacLean's larger thesis, and of her specific charges against Nutter, becomes apparent from the fact that she did not realize that Nutter and his wife Jane played a leading role in setting up the PCES, the very same group she praises as an alternative to Byrd.

11. G. Warren Nutter and James M. Buchanan, "The Economics of Universal Education," Thomas Jefferson Center for Political Economy, 1959.

12. Milton Friedman, "The Role of Government in Education," in Robert Solo, ed., *Economics and the Public Interest* (Rutgers University Press, 1955).

13. Nancy MacLean's book *Democracy in Chains* depicts Nutter and Buchanan as collaborative partners with the Byrd machine, based on a misreading of evidence as well as a citation error in an earlier work by historian James Hershman who incorrectly reported that the Nutter–Buchanan paper had been published by segregationist newspaper editor James J. Kilpatrick. In reality, Kilpatrick's correspondence indicates that he had not seen the Nutter–Buchanan paper prior to its publication in a different outlet. See Phillip W. Magness, Art Carden, and Vincent Geloso, "James M. Buchanan and the Political Economy of Desegregation," *Southern Economic Journal* 85, no. 3 (2019): 715–41.

14. Thomas Jefferson Center for Political Economy, "Report on the Virginia Plan for Universal Education," Occasional Paper No. 2, 1965.

15. G. Warren Nutter, "A Traveler's Tale of the Soviet Economy," September 1956. Manuscript located at the Dwight D. Eisenhower Presidential Library. Acknowledgment and thanks to David M. Levy, who provided me with a copy.

16. Nutter, Borenstein, and Kaufman, *Growth of Industrial Production in the Soviet Union*, 9–11, 13.

17. Ibid., 18.

18. Ibid., 46.

19. "Nutter to Buckley, May 3, 1967," William F. Buckley Papers, Yale University.

20. G. Warren Nutter, "Economic Aspects of Freedom," in *Liberty Under Law, Anarchy, Totalitarianism* (American Bar Association, 1969).

Chapter 15: Israel M. Kirzner by Rosolino Candela

1. Israel M. Kirzner, "How Markets Work: Disequilibrium, Entrepreneurship and Discovery," IEA Hobart Paper no. 133 (Institute of Economic Affairs, 1997).

2. Israel M. Kirzner, "Advertising," *Freeman* 22, no. 9 (1972): 515–28.

3. Israel M. Kirzner, "Some Ethical Implications for Capitalism of the Socialist Calculation Debate," *Social Philosophy and Policy* 6, no. 1 (1988): 165–82; Israel M. Kirzner, *The Collected Works of Israel M. Kirzner: Discovery, Capitalism and Distributive Justice* (Liberty

Fund, 2016); Israel M. Kirzner, "The Ethics of Pure Entrepreneurship: An Austrian Perspective," *Review of Austrian Economics* 32, no. 2 (2019): 89–99.

4. Robin Douhan, Gunnar Eliasson, and Magnus Henrekson, "Israel M. Kirzner: An Outstanding Austrian Contributor to the Economics of Entrepreneurship," *Small Business Economics* 29, nos. 1–2 (2007): 213–23.

5. Israel M. Kirzner, "The Alert and Creative Entrepreneur: A Clarification," *Small Business Economics* 32, no. 2 (2009): 145–46.

6. Ibid., 146.

7. Joseph A. Schumpeter, *The Theory of Economic Development: An Inquiry into Profits, Capital, Credit, Interest, and the Business Cycle* (Harvard University Press, 1934).

8. Don Lavoie, "The Discovery and Interpretation of Profit Opportunities: Culture and the Kirznerian Entrepreneur," in *The Culture of Entrepreneurship*, edited by Brigette Berger (Institute for Contemporary Studies, 1991), 39.

9. Israel M. Kirzner, *The Collected Works of Israel M. Kirzner: Discovery, Capitalism and Distributive Justice* (Liberty Fund, 2016), 109, emphasis in original. See also Kirzner's "Classical Economics and the Entrepreneurial Role" in *Perception, Opportunity, and Profit* (Kirzner 1979, 37–52).

10. See, for example, Kenneth J. Arrow and Gerard Debreu, "Existence of an Equilibrium for a Competitive Economy," *Econometrica* 22, no. 3 (1954): 265–90.

11. Kenneth J. Arrow, "Toward a Theory of Price Adjustment," in *The Allocation of Economic Resources: Essays in Honor of Bernard Francis Haley* (Stanford University Press, 1959), 46.

12. Israel M. Kirzner, *The Collected Works of Israel M. Kirzner: The Economic Point of View* (Liberty Fund, 2009), 83.

13. See in particular Kirzner (1967b), as well as Kirzner (1967a, 1971).

14. History of Economics Society, "Distinguished Fellow," at https://historyofeconomics.org/awards-and-honors/distinguished-fellow.

15. Israel M. Kirzner, *Competition and Entrepreneurship* (University of Chicago Press, 1973), 35, emphasis in original.

16. Schumpeter, *The Theory of Economic Development*; Joseph A. Schumpeter, *Capitalism, Socialism, and Democracy*, 2nd ed. (Harper & Brothers, 1947); see also Murray N. Rothbard, "Breaking Out of the Walrasian Box: The Cases of Schumpeter and Hansen," *Review of Austrian Economics* 1, no. 1 (1987): 97–108.

17. Schumpeter, *The Theory of Economic Development*, 64.

18. Schumpeter, *Capitalism, Socialism, and Democracy*, 83.

19. Kirzner, *Perception, Opportunity, and Profit*, 119.

20. Baumol also was the 2003 recipient of the International Award for Entrepreneurship and Small Business Research.

21. William J. Baumol, "Entrepreneurship: Productive, Unproductive, and Destructive," *Journal of Political Economy* 98, no. 5 (1990): 894.

22. Peter J. Boettke and Christopher J. Coyne, "Entrepreneurship and Development: Cause or Consequence?," *Advances in Austrian Economics* 6 (2003): 67–88.

23. See, for example, David Daokui Li, Junxin Feng, and Hongping Jiang, "Institutional Entrepreneurs," *American Economic Review* 96, no. 2 (2006): 358–62; Magnus Henrekson and Tino Sanandaji, eds., *Institutional Entrepreneurship* (Edward Elgar, 2012); Zeynab Aeeni, Mahmoud Motavaseli, Kamal Sakhdari, and Ali Mobini Dehkordi, "Baumol's Theory of Entrepreneurial Allocation: A Systematic Review and Research Agenda," *European Research on Management and Business Economics* 25, no. 1 (2019): 30–37.

24. Eric Jones, *The European Miracle: Environments, Economies, and Geopolitics in the History of Europe and Asia*, 3rd ed. (Cambridge University Press, 2003).

25. Nathan Rosenberg and L. E. Birdzell Jr., *How the West Grew Rich: The Economic Transformation of the Industrial World* (Basic Books, 1986), 87; Jones, *The European Miracle*, 6.

26. Baumol, "Entrepreneurship: Productive, Unproductive, and Destructive," 897.

27. See Rosolino A. Candela, Peter J. Jacobsen, and Kacey Reeves, "Malcom McLean, Containerization and Entrepreneurship," *Review of Austrian Economics* 35, no. 4 (2022): 445–65.

28. Harold Demsetz, "The Neglect of the Entrepreneur," in *Entrepreneurship*, edited by Joshua Ronen (Lexington Books, 1983), 279.

29. Harold Demsetz, "Toward a Theory of Property Rights," *American Economic Review* 57, no. 2 (1967): 359.

30. For example, see also Demsetz (1983b, 382–83).

31. Israel M. Kirzner, *Perception, Opportunity, and Profit: Studies in the Theory of Entrepreneurship* (University of Chicago Press, 1979), 104.

32. Israel M. Kirzner, "The Perils of Regulation: A Market Process Approach," in *Discovery and the Capitalist Process* (University of Chicago Press, 1985), 139–40.

33. Ibid., 144–45.

34. Ibid., 135.

35. See also Shughart (2014).

36. Israel M. Kirzner, "The Ethics of Pure Entrepreneurship: An Austrian Perspective," *Review of Austrian Economics* 32, no. 2 (2019): 89–99.

37. Thomas Piketty, *Capital in the Twenty-First Century* (Harvard University Press, 2014).

38. Kirzner, *The Collected Works of Israel M. Kirzner: Discovery, Capitalism and Distributive Justice*, 16.

39. John Locke, *Second Treatise of Government* (Hackett, 1980).

40. Robert Nozick, *Anarchy, State, and Utopia* (Basic Books, 1974).

41. Kirzner, *The Collected Works of Israel M. Kirzner: Discovery, Capitalism and Distributive Justice*, 109.

42. F. A. Hayek, "The Dilemma of Specialization," in *Studies in Philosophy, Politics and Economics* (University of Chicago Press, 1967), 123.

43. Israel M. Kirzner, *The Meaning of Market Process: Essays in the Development of Modern Austrian Economics* (Routledge, 1992), 53, emphasis in original.

Chapter 16: Thomas Sowell by Art Carden and Brian C. Albrecht

1. Amazon.com, "Best Sellers in Economics," https://www.amazon.com/gp/bestsellers/books/2581/ref=pd_zg_hrsr_books, accessed April 28, 2023.

2. William L. Davis, Bob Figgins, David Hedengren, and Daniel B. Klein, "Economics Professors' Favorite Economic Thinkers, Journals, and Blogs (Along with Party and Policy Views)," *Econ Journal Watch* 8, no. 2 (2011): 126.

3. Retrieved from Google Scholar April 28, 2023.

4. Deirdre Nansen McCloskey and Art Carden, *Leave Me Alone and I'll Make You Rich: How the Bourgeois Deal Enriched the World* (University of Chicago Press, 2020); cf. Art Carden, Phillip W. Magness, John Meadowcroft, and Ilia Murtazashvili, "Slavery," 2022, prepared for the *Edward Elgar Encyclopedia of Public Choice.*

5. Thomas Sowell, *Ethnic America: A History* (Basic Books, 1981), 184.

6. Thomas Sowell, *Race and Culture: A World View* (Basic Books, 1994), 74.

7. Ibid., 75.

8. Ibid., 186.

9. Sowell, *Ethnic America,* 193.

10. Cf. Sowell, *Intellectuals and Society* (2009).

11. Sowell, *Race and Culture*, 3ff.

12. See Guiso, Sapienza, and Zingales (2006) and Alesina and Giuliano (2015) for literature reviews.

13. Available at https://reason.com/1981/12/01/the-best-book-on-general-econo.

14. Thomas Sowell, *Knowledge and Decisions* (Basic Books, 1996), xii.

15. Ibid., xxi.

16. Adam Smith, *The Theory of Moral Sentiments*, 6th ed., 1790, https://www.adamsmithworks.org/documents/asw-edition, 6:2:42.

17. See Leonard (2016) for discussions.

18. Quinn Slobodian, *Globalists: The End of Empire and the Birth of Neoliberalism* (Harvard University Press, 2018), 28.

19. Sowell, *Race and Culture*, 23.

20. Ibid., 26.

21. Thomas Sowell, *A Conflict of Visions: Ideological Origins of Political Struggles* (Basic Books, 2007), 3.

22. Ibid., 3.

23. Ibid., 37.

24. Ibid., 37, 40.

25. Thomas Sowell, *Is Reality Optional? And Other Essays* (Hoover Institution Press, 1993), 131.

26. Cf. Mario Rizzo and Glen Whitman, *Escaping Paternalism* (Cambridge University Press, 2019); Jason Brennan and Christopher Freiman, "Why Paternalists Must Endorse Epistocracy," *Journal of Ethics and Social Philosophy* 21, no. 3 (2022): 329, 335–36.

27. Brennan and Freiman, "Why Paternalists Must Endorse Epistocracy," 336.

28. Sowell, *Knowledge and Decisions*, 136.

Chapter 17: Julian Simon by Robert M. Whaples

1. Unlike most scholars, Simon (1981b, 177) read Malthus correctly. Malthus realized, as Simon put it, that "human beings are very different from flies or rats. When faced with . . . limits . . . people can alter their behavior so as to accommodate to that limit. Unlike plants and animals, people are capable of foresight and may abstain from having children from 'fear of misery.'" He quoted Malthus's insight that "impelled to the increase of his species by an equally powerful instinct, reason interrupts his career, and asks him whether he may not bring beings into the world, for whom he cannot provide the means of support." See Hammond (2020) for a clear explanation of why "Malthus was not a Malthusian."

2. Julian Simon, *A Life Against the Grain: The Autobiography of an Unconventional Economist* (Transaction, 2002), xii–xiii, emphasis in original.

3. He also published in *Science* and in top journals in his other disciplines, including *Demography, Population Studies,* and the *American Statistician.* In addition, he published books with prestigious presses including Princeton University Press and the University of Chicago Press—and published numerous op-eds in the *Wall Street Journal.*

4. Additional real-world experience during his school years included encyclopedia salesman, caddy, cost accountant, drugstore clerk, sign painter, brewery worker, tin-can factory worker, technical writer, freelance magazine writer, grass-seed factory worker, and cab driver (see http://juliansimon.com/vita.html).

5. Simon, *A Life Against the Grain,* 169.

6. Julian Simon, "The Pain of Failing a Ph.D. Oral Exam, and an Unfortunate Confusion in Economic Thought," *American Economist* 24, no. 2 (1980).

7. Ibid., 44.

8. Simon, *A Life Against the Grain,* 88.

9. Ibid., 194.

10. See Simon 1965b, which was updated through five editions.

11. Julian Simon, "The Cause of the Newspaper Rate Differential: A Subjective-Demand-Curve Analysis," *Journal of Political Economy* 57, no. 5 (1965).

12. Julian Simon, "An Almost Practical Solution to Airline Overbooking," *Journal of Transport Economics and Policy* 2, no. 2 (1968). The idea arose spontaneously in Simon's mind. John Blundell recalled the following: "At a dinner party in the late 1950s, a young lady commented that her job as an airline employee was wonderful except for one thing. The airline overbooked and then relied on staff like her to move people on to other flights. She was told to choose those in the armed forces and the elderly. Why? Because both were easily recognised, and market research showed that neither was likely to complain. Instantly, Julian said: 'That's crazy. They should use an auction process to discover who is the most prepared to wait'" (Blundell 1998).

13. Simon, "An Almost Practical Solution to Airline Overbooking," 201.

14. Simon (1989) even concluded that population growth would eventually reduce the likelihood of war: population growth leads to technological progress, reducing the importance of land for economic prosperity, and thereby the benefits of trying to annex other nations' territory.

15. Julian Simon, *The Ultimate Resource* (Princeton University Press, 1981).

16. Simon updated and expanded the reach of these findings in *The State of Humanity,* the central assertion of which (Simon 1995, 7) was that "almost every absolute change, and the absolute component of almost every economic and social change or trend, points in a positive direction, as long as we view the matter over a reasonably long period of time." The book includes fifty-eight chapters by leading scholars including Nobel laureate Theodore Schultz and future Nobel winner Robert Fogel. The contributors were a veritable who's who among economic historians, including Terry Anderson, Jeremy Atack, Stanley Engerman, Michael Haines, Robert Higgs, Stanley Lebergott, Peter Lindert, Robert Margo, Joel Mokyr, and Jeffrey Williamson. Simon continued to update and broaden these findings until the end of his life in *The Ultimate Resource 2* (1996) and *It's Getting Better All the Time: 100 Greatest Trends of the Last 100 Years* (Moore and Simon 2000).

17. Thomas Covert, Michael Greenstone, and Christopher R. Knittel, "Will We Ever Stop Using Fossil Fuels?," *Journal of Economic Perspectives* 30, no. 1 (2016): 117–38. Quotation from abstract, at https://www.aeaweb.org/articles?id=10.1257/jep.30.1.117, emphasis added.

18. Simon, *The Ultimate Resource*, 348.

19. Julian Simon, *The State of Humanity* (Blackwell, 1995), 21.

20. Ibid., 26.

21. Simon, *The Ultimate Resource*, 119.

22. Henry David Thoreau, *Walden* (Bramhall House, 1951), 106.

23. Antoine de Saint-Exupéry, *The Little Prince* (Harcourt, 2000), 10.

24. The following two paragraphs are drawn from my review (Whaples 2014) of Paul Sabin's *The Bet* (2013).

25. Julian Simon, "Environmental Disruption or Environmental Improvement?," *Social Science Quarterly* 62, no. 1 (1981): 38.

26. The nominal price of the metals inched up to $1003.93, but the overall price level rose by 58 percent, so the real price of the metals fell by approximately 36 percent (Tupy and Pooley 2022, 185).

27. Not everyone agrees that it is fitting that Simon won the bet. Emmett and Grabowski (2022, 1, emphasis added) concluded that Simon was "lucky," that "with *careful* portfolio construction, Ehrlich should win this bet more often than not." Others, including Perry (2010), Tupy and Pooley (2022), and scholars cited in Emmett and Grabowski (2022), agree with my conclusion.

28. *The Great Breakthrough and Its Cause* (Simon 2000) was published after Simon's death. It presents a veritable monocausal explanation for the explosion of standards of living in the past few centuries: rising population. "If the world's population had not grown at all since (say) 10,000 years ago, or if population had not grown as fast as it did over the millennia, the material condition of humanity could not have progressed to its present state by now" (Simon 2000, 14). However, the book's "theoretical framework" chapter has none of the mathematical modeling favored by economists. The "very-long-run full-adjustment model" and others in the chapter are a series of arrows rather than what most economists consider to be a true model.

29. Our World in Data, "World Population Living in Extreme Poverty, 1820 to 2015," https://ourworldindata.org/grapher/world-population-in-extreme-poverty-absolute; World Bank, *Poverty and Shared Prosperity 2022: Correcting Course* (World Bank, 2022), 7.

30. Robert Whaples, "Where Do the Poorest Americans Stand in the Income Distribution Among All People Ever Born?," *The Independent Review* 27, no. 1 (2022): 155–59.

31. Robert Whaples, Christopher J. Coyne, and Michael C. Munger, eds., *Future: Economic Peril or Prosperity?* (Independent Institute, 2016).

32. Robert D. Atkinson, "The Abandonment of Growth and the Decline of the West," *The Independent Review* 27, no. 2 (2022): 202.

33. Brink Lindsay, "The Anti-Promethean Backlash," *The Permanent Problem* (Substack), November 15, 2022, https://brinklindsey.substack.com/p/the-anti-promethean-backlash.

34. Our World in Data, "The Global Fertility Rate Has Continued to Decline to 2.3 Births per Woman," 2022, https://ourworldindata.org/world-population-update-2022.

35. Aaron Zitner, "Poll Shows Shift in What Americans Value," *Wall Street Journal*, March 28, 2023, A4.

36. Doris Geide-Stevenson and Alvaro La Parra Perez, "Consensus Among Economists 2020: A Sharpening of the Picture," Research Gate, 2021, https://www.researchgate.net/profile/Alvaro-La-Parra-Perez/publication/357526861_Consensus_among_economists_2020_A_sharpening_of_the_picture/links/62a23ce3416ec50bdb1995ea/Consensus-among-economists-2020-A-sharpening-of-the-picture.pdf.

37. Simon, *The Ultimate Resource*, 9–10. In discussing conservation, Simon (1981a, 144) noted the importance of "one of a kind or close to it" resources that we value—"examples include the Mona Lisa . . . and Muhammad Ali." In keeping with Simon's epiphany during his trip to Washington, one wonders whether only Ali was "one of a kind." What about Smokin' Joe Frazier or Chuck Wepner . . . or every human being who has ever been conceived? Is any individual more unique or irreplaceable than any other?

Chapter 18: Karl Mittermaier by Michael C. Munger

1. Epigraph: Karl Mittermaier, *The Hand Behind the Invisible Hand: Dogmatic and Pragmatic Views on Free Markets and the State of Economic Theory* (Bristol University Press, 2020), 21.

2. Michael Stettler, "An Introduction to Karl Mittermaier and His Philosophy of Economics," *Journal of Contextual Economics* 139, no. 1 (2019): 124.

3. See, e.g., Peter J. Boettke, "Ludwig Lachmann and His Contributions to Economic Science," *Advances in Austrian Economics* 1 (1994): 229–32.

4. See Truran 2013 in References for a summary.

5. Adam Smith, *An Inquiry into the Nature and Causes of the Wealth of Nations* (Modern Library, 1994).

6. Emma Rothschild, "Adam Smith and the Invisible Hand," *American Economic Review* 84, no. 2 (1994): 319–22.

7. Karl Mittermaier, "The Invisible Hand and Some Thoughts on the Non-Existent in What We Study," Paper (Second International Workshop on Methodology of Economics,

Cambridge University, 1994), reprinted in *Journal of Contextual Economics* 139, no. 1 (2019): 138.

8. Mittermaier, *The Hand Behind the Invisible Hand.*

9. See also Daniel B. Klein, "Karl Mittermaier and the Hands of Classical Liberalism," *Economic Affairs* 40, no. 2 (2020): 209–19.

10. Michael C. Munger, "Hayek's Political Insights: Emergent Orders and Laid-on Laws," in *Advances in Austrian Economics: Revisiting Hayek's Political Economy*, edited by Peter Boettke and Virgil Storr (Emerald, 2016).

11. Mittermaier, *The Hand Behind the Invisible Hand*, 25–26, emphasis in original.

12. Stettler, "An Introduction to Karl Mittermaier and His Philosophy of Economics."

13. Mittermaier, *The Hand Behind the Invisible Hand*, 24, emphasis in original.

14. Ibid., 24.

15. Ibid., 136.

16. Ibid., 25.

17. Ibid., 135.

18. Ibid., 139.

19. David Hume, "Of the Origin of Justice and Property," in *A Treatise of Human Nature* (n.p., 1739), available online at https://davidhume.org/texts/t/3/2/2.

20. Mittermaier, *The Hand Behind the Invisible Hand*, 204.

21. Karl Mittermaier, "Menger's Aristotelianism," *Cambridge Journal of Economics* 42, no. 2 (2018): 577–94; Mittermaier, "The Invisible Hand and Some Thoughts on the Non-Existent in What We Study"; Mittermaier, *The Hand Behind the Invisible Hand.*

22. See, for example, Richard Rorty, *Consequences of Pragmatism* (University of Minnesota Press, 1982).

23. Karl Mittermaier, "Unpublished manuscript," quoted in Stettler, "An Introduction to Karl Mittermaier and His Philosophy of Economics," 131.

24. Michael C. Munger, "Endless Forms Most Beautiful and Most Wonderful: Elinor Ostrom and the Diversity of Institutions," *Public Choice* 143, no. 3 (2010): 263–68.

Chapter 19: Earl A. Thompson by Joshua R. Hendrickson

1. Earl A. Thompson and Charles R. Hickson, *Ideology and the Evolution of Vital Institutions: Guilds, the Gold Standard and International Cooperation* (Kluwer Academic Publishers, 2001), xiii.

2. Earl A. Thompson, "Alchian as a Teacher and an Economist," *International Society for New Institutional Economics* 3, no. 2 (2001): 11–13.

3. Thompson's thoughts on this aspect of his athletic career were recounted by his former student, Edward Mehrez, at Earl's funeral, a recording of which was provided to the author by Earl's son Bret.

4. Earl A. Thompson, "Debt Instruments in Both Macroeconomic Theory and Capital Theory," *American Economic Review* 57, no. 5 (1967).

5. Ibid., 1198–99.

6. Robert J. Barro, "Are Government Bonds Net Wealth?," *Journal of Political Economy* 82, no. 6 (1974): 1095–1117.

7. Earl A. Thompson, "The Taxation of Wealth and the Wealthy," *American Economic Review Papers and Proceedings* 62, no. 1–2 (1972): 329 –30.

8. Earl A. Thompson, "What Globalization Is Really All About," in *Business and Economics Society International – Anthology* (n.p., 2002), 2.

9. Earl A. Thompson, "Taxation and National Defense," *Journal of Political Economy* 82, no. 4 (1974): 755–82.

10. Earl A. Thompson, "An Economic Basis for the 'National Defense' Argument for Aiding Certain Industries," *Journal of Political Economy* 87, no. 1 (1979): 1–36.

11. Charles R. Hickson and Earl A. Thompson, "A New Theory of Guilds and European Economic Development," *Explorations in Economic History* 28 (1991): 127–68.

12. Ibid.

13. Earl A. Thompson and Charles R. Hickson, "Predicting Bubbles," *Global Business and Economics Review* 8, nos. 3–4 (2006): 217–46.

14. Earl A. Thompson, "The Tulipmania: Fact or Artifact?," *Public Choice* 130 (2006): 99–114.

15. Earl A. Thompson, "The Theory of Money and Income Consistent with Orthodox Value Theory," in G. Horwich and P. Samuelson, eds., *Trade, Stability, and Macroeconomics: Essays in Honor of Lloyd Metzler* (Academic Press, 1974), 427–53.

16. Earl A. Thompson, "A Reformulation of Macroeconomic Theory," UCLA Working Paper no. 91, 1977.

17. Earl A. Thompson, "Free Banking Under a Labor Standard," *The Role of Gold in Domestic and International Monetary Systems*, II, Annex B Report to Congress of the US Gold Commission, US G.P.O., March 1982, 502–4.

18. Earl A. Thompson, "The Gold Standard: Causes and Consequences," in David Glasner, ed., *Encyclopedia of Business Cycles and Depressions* (Garland Publishing, 1995), 267–72.

19. Joshua R. Hendrickson, "The Riksbank, Emergency Finance, Policy Experimentation, and Sweden's Reversal of Fortune," *Journal of Economic Behavior and Organization* 171 (2020): 312–32.

20. Earl A. Thompson, "On Labor's Right to Strike," *Economic Inquiry* 28 (1980): 640–53.

21. Earl A. Thompson, "From Social Security to Social Insecurity: The Genius of Democratic Politics," *Global Business and Economics Review* 9, no. 1 (2007): 1–7.

22. Earl A. Thompson and Roger L. Faith, "A Pure Theory of Strategic Behavior and Social Institutions," *American Economic Review* 71, no. 3 (1981): 366–80.

Chapter 20: Robert D. Tollison by William F. Shughart II

1. Department of Economics and Finance, Jon M. Huntsman School of Business, Utah State University, Logan, UT 84322-3565, USA; william.shughart@usu.edu. I thank Mark Crain and Michael Munger for their helpful comments on an earlier version.

2. Thomas S. Kuhn, *The Structure of Scientific Revolutions*, 4th ed. (University of Chicago Press, 2012).

3. Tyler Cowen, *GOAT: Who Is the Greatest Economist of All Time and Why Does it Matter?* (n.p., 2024), 8, https://goatgreatesteconomistofalltime.ai/en. For a review, see Whaples (2024).

4. *The Independent Review* 28, no. 2 (Fall 2023).

5. William F. Shughart II (ed.), "Essays in Honor of Robert D. Tollison," *Public Choice* 142, nos. 3–4 (2010).

6. William F. Shughart II, "A Personal Remembrance," *Southern Economic Journal* 83, no. 3 (2017): 630–36; William F. Shughart II, "Rest in Peace, Bob Tollison," *Public Choice* 171, nos. 1–2 (2017): 1–5; William F. Shughart II, "Robert D. Tollison, In Memoriam," *The Independent Review* 22, no. 1 (2017): 153–57.

7. Ryan C. Amacher, James C. Miller III, Mark Pauly, Robert D. Tollison, and Thomas D. Willet, *The Economics of the Military Draft* (General Learning Press, 1973); also see Robert D. Tollison, "The Political Economy of the Military Draft," *Public Choice* 9 (1970): 67–78.

8. Robert D. Tollison, "Antitrust in the Reagan Administration: A Report from the Belly of the Beast," *International Journal of Industrial Organization* 1, no. 1 (1983): 211–21.

9. I have written about my graduate school days several times before, the most recent occasion being Shughart (2025). The PhD students in economics at Texas A&M in the mid to late 1970s included Mark Crain, Robert McCormick, Thomas Deaton, David Saurman, me, and many others too numerous to name. For analyses of Tollison's scholarship highlighting the contributions of coauthors to his productive career (up to circa 2009), see Crain and Crain (2010). If I were more modest, I wouldn't mention that I rank first on the coauthor list, having collaborated with Bob on sixty-eight of his publications.

10. An executive order issued by President Richard Nixon the prior year had eliminated draft deferments for graduate students. Consequently, I joined more than 850,000 other young men (born between 1944 and 1950) in the first-ever military draft lottery, held on December 1, 1970. It turns out that the mechanical process for selecting draftees (based on their birthdays) was not random but biased significantly towards young men born in the last six months of the calendar years comprising the draft pool, especially my birth month of December. See Emery (2022), who writes that, except for "October, each month from the second half of the year saw over half of its dates called within the first 195 numbers—December had a striking 26 out of 31 days called while March skated by with only one-third of its days being called."

11. Buchanan, Coase, and Tullock had departed Charlottesville following the central administration's failure to support creating an interdisciplinary academic program at the Thomas Jefferson Center for Political Economy and denying Tullock promotion to full professor three times. (The University of Virginia thus earned the distinction of failing to keep two future Nobel laureates, Buchanan and Coase.) After a year or so in the wilderness (Buchanan at UCLA, Tullock at Rice University), the "Virginia School" reconstituted itself in Blacksburg in what was then (and still is) called the Center for Study of Public Choice, which subsequently moved to George Mason University in Fairfax. See Levy and Peart (2010) for more details.

12. Steven D. Levitt and Stephen J. Dubner, *Freakonomics: A Rogue Economist Explores the Hidden Side of Everything*, revised and expanded edition (William Morrow, 2020).

13. *Freakonomics* blurb attributed to the *Atlanta Journal-Constitution*.

14. In his remembrance of the late Robert Ekelund, Thornton (2024), accurately in my view, credits Ekelund and Tollison (1981) with launching what is now known as the "new institutional economics." See also Ekelund and Tollison (1997).

15. Crain and Crain (2010) counted 524 Tollison coauthors at the time; the total surely rose afterward. Bob's productive career continued for six more years; his final book-length contribution (Ekelund, Jackson, and Tollison 2017) was published posthumously.

16. Bob was old-school technology-wise. He drafted manuscripts in ballpoint pen, pencil, and occasionally a red felt tip; his "chicken-scratching" must have exasperated most typists. Only late in life was he able to compose or respond to emails, usually sending messages no longer than two sentences. Bob preferred telephoning his collaborators.

17. Robert B. Ekelund Jr. and Robert D. Tollison, *Economics* (Little, Brown, 1986). The text went through seven editions over the next two decades, the last being Ekelund, Tollison, and Ressler (2006).

18. Nicole V. Crain and W. Mark Crain, "Determinants of Publication Productivity: An Empirical Analysis," *Public Choice* 142, nos. 3–4 (2010): 265–77; W. Mark Crain and Nicole V. Crain, "Robert's Rules for a Knowledge-Creating Society," *Public Choice* 171, nos. 1–2 (2017): 29–32.

19. Robert D. Tollison and Thomas D. Willett, "An Economic Theory of Mutually Advantageous Issue Linkages in International Negotiations," *International Organization* 33, no. 4 (1979): 425–49.

20. Robert D. Tollison, "Rent Seeking: A Survey," *Kyklos* 35, no. 4 (1982): 575–602.

21. Joseph A. Schumpeter, *Capitalism, Socialism, and Democracy*, 3rd edition (Harper & Row, 2008).

22. William J. Baumol and Janusz A. Ordover, "Use of Antitrust to Subvert Competition," *Journal of Law and Economics* 28, no. 2 (1985): 247–65.

23. William F. Long, Richard Schramm, and Robert D. Tollison, "The Determinants of Antitrust Activity," *Journal of Law and Economics* 16, no. 2 (1973): 351–64.

24. See, e.g., William F. Shughart II and Robert D. Tollison, "The Positive Economics of Antitrust Policy: A Survey Article," *International Review of Law and Economics* 5, no. 1 (1985): 39–57.

25. Robert J. Mackay, James C. Miller III, and Bruce Yandle, (eds.), *Public Choice and Regulation: A View from Inside the Federal Trade Commission* (Hoover Institution Press, 1987).

26. William F. Baxter, "The Political Economy of Antitrust," in Robert D. Tollison (ed.), *The Political Economy of Antitrust: Principal Paper by William Baxter* (Lexington Books, 1980), 3–49.

27. William F. Shughart II, *Antitrust Policy and Interest-Group Politics* (Quorum Books, 1990); Fred S. McChesney and William F. Shughart II (eds.), *The Causes and Consequences of Antitrust: The Public-Choice Perspective* (University of Chicago Press, 1995).

28. Mancur Olson, *The Logic of Collective Action: Public Goods and the Theory of Groups* (Harvard University Press, 1965).

29. Gordon Tullock, "The Welfare Costs of Tariffs, Monopolies, and Theft," *Western Economic Journal* 5 (1967): 224–32.

30. George J. Stigler, "The Economic Theory of Regulation," *Bell Journal of Economics and Management Science* 2, no. 1 (1971): 3–21.

31. Robert E. McCormick and Robert D. Tollison, *Politicians, Legislation, and the Economy: An Inquiry into the Interest-Group Theory of Government* (Martinus Nijhoff, 1981).

32. Roger L. Faith, Donald R. Leavens, and Robert D. Tollison, "Antitrust Pork Barrel," *Journal of Law and Economics* 15 (1982): 329–42.

33. Richard B. McKenzie and William F. Shughart II, "Is Microsoft a Monopolist?," *The Independent Review* 3, no. 2 (1998): 165–97.

34. William F. Long, Richard Schramm, and Robert D. Tollison, "The Determinants of Antitrust Activity," *Journal of Law and Economics* 16, no. 2 (1973): 351–64.

35. Robert H. Bork, *The Antitrust Paradox: A Policy at War with Itself* (Basic Books, 1978).

36. Robert D. Tollison, "Antitrust in the Reagan Administration: A Report from the Belly of the Beast," *International Journal of Industrial Organization* 1, no. 1 (1983): 211–21; Robert D. Tollison, "Public Choice and Antitrust," *Cato Journal* 4, no. 3 (1985): 905–16.

37. William F. Shughart II, *Antitrust Policy and Interest-Group Politics* (Quorum Books, 1990); William F. Shughart II, "On the Virginia School of Antitrust: Competition Policy, Law and Economics, and Public Choice," *Public Choice* 191, nos. 1–2 (2022), 1–19; William F. Shughart II, "Antitrust Agonistes," *Journal of Law, Economics & Policy* 17, no. 3 (September 2022): 646–72; Fred S. McChesney and William F. Shughart II, "Public Choice Theory and Antitrust Policy," *Public Choice* 142, nos. 3–4 (2010): 385–406.

38. Brian L. Goff and Robert D. Tollison (eds.), *Sportometrics* (Texas A&M University Press, 1990).

39. Robert E. McCormick and Robert D. Tollison, "Crime on the Court," *Journal of Political Economy* 92, no. 2 (1984): 223–35.

40. Arthur A. Fleisher III, Brian L. Goff, William F. Shughart II, and Robert D. Tollison, "Crime or Punishment? Enforcement of the NCAA Cartel," *Journal of Economic Behavior and Organization* 10, no. 4 (1988): 433–51; Arthur A. Fleisher III, Brian L. Goff, and Robert D. Tollison, *The National Collegiate Athletic Association: A Study in Cartel Behavior* (University of Chicago Press, 1992).

41. William F. Shughart II and Robert D. Tollison, "Going for the Gold: Property Rights and Athletic Effort in Transitional Economies," *Kyklos* 46, no. 2 (1993): 263–72.

42. Brian L. Goff, William F. Shughart II, and Robert D. Tollison, "Batter Up! Moral Hazard and the Effects of the Designated Hitter Rule on Hit Batsmen," *Economic Inquiry* 35, no. 3 (1997): 555–61.

43. J. C. Bradbury, *The Baseball Economist: The Real Game Exposed* (Plume/Penguin, 2007).

44. Robert B. Ekelund Jr., "Memories of Bob Tollison: Memories of a Friendship," *Public Choice* 171, nos. 1–2 (2017): 40, original emphasis.

45. Raymond D. Sauer, "Robert D. Tollison: Father of Sportometrics, Friend and Colleague," *Public Choice* 171, nos. 1–2 (2017): 67–71.

46. For a useful summary, see Ekelund (2013).

47. Robert B. Ekelund Jr., Robert F. Hébert, Robert D. Tollison, Gary M. Anderson, and Audrey B. Davidson, *Sacred Trust: The Medieval Church as an Economic Firm* (Oxford University Press, 1996).

48. Robert B. Ekelund Jr., Robert F. Hébert, and Robert D. Tollison, *The Marketplace of Christianity* (MIT Press, 2006).

49. Robert B. Ekelund Jr. and Robert D. Tollison, *Economic Origins of Roman Christianity* (University of Chicago Press, 2011).

50. See, e.g., Paul Seabright, *The Divine Economy: How Religions Compete for Wealth, Power, and People* (Princeton University Press, 2024).

51. Michael C. Munger, "Robert D. Tollison: A Remembrance," *Public Choice* 171, nos. 1–2 (2017): 65.

Chapter 21: Charlotte Twight by Mikayla Novak

1. Peter J. Boettke, *Living Economics: Yesterday, Today, and Tomorrow* (Independent Institute, 2012).

2. Encyclopedia.com, "Twight, Charlotte Augusta 1944–," n.d., https://www.encyclopedia.com/arts/educational-magazines/twight-charlotte-augusta-1944.

3. I thank Robert Higgs for providing this information (personal correspondence, March 27, 2024).

4. Charles K. Rowley and Friedrich Schneider, *The Encyclopedia of Public Choice* (Kluwer Academic Publishers, 2004).

5. Adolph Wagner, "Three Extracts on Public Finance," in *Classics in the Theory of Public Finance*, edited by Richard Musgrave and Alan T. Peacock (Macmillan, 1958), 1–16.

6. James B. Kau and Paul H Rubin, "The Size of Government," *Public Choice* 37, no. 2 (1981): 261–74.

7. Allan H. Meltzer and Scott F. Richard, "A Rational Theory of the Size of Government," *Journal of Political Economy* 89, no. 5 (1981): 914–27; Mancur Olson, *The Rise and Decline of Nations: Economic Growth, Stagflation, and Social Rigidities* (Yale University Press, 1982).

8. Dani Rodrik, "Why Do More Open Economies Have Bigger Governments?," *Journal of Political Economy* 106 no. 5 (1998): 997–1032; Tyler Cowen, "Does Technology Drive the Growth of Government?" Paper presented to Mont Pelerin Society Stockholm General Meeting, June 2009.

9. Charlotte A. Twight, *Dependent on D.C.: The Rise of Federal Control over the Lives of Ordinary Americans* (Palgrave, 2002), 17.

10. Charlotte A. Twight, "Designing Dependence," *The Freeman: Ideas on Liberty* 52, no. 5 (2002): 10.

11. Charlotte A. Twight, "Channeling Ideological Change: The Political Economy of Dependence on Government," *Kyklos* 46, no. 4 (1993): 500. For the sake of clarity, the political interpretation of transaction costs contrasts against well-known economic transaction costs, with the latter described as the "negotiation and enforcement costs specifically attributable to the multiparty character of market exchange" (Twight 1996, 300).

12. Space constraints preclude me from replicating the lengthy listings and tables presented by Twight (1988, 1994).

13. Charlotte A. Twight, "Government Manipulation of Constitutional-Level Transaction Costs: A General Theory of Transaction-Cost Augmentation and the Growth of Government," *Public Choice* 56, no. 2 (1988): 131–52.

14. See, e.g., Richard E. Wagner, "Revenue Structure, Fiscal Illusion, and Budgetary Choice," *Public Choice* 25, no. 1 (1976): 45–61.

15. Charlotte A. Twight, "Political Transaction Cost Manipulation: An Integrating Theory," *Journal of Theoretical Politics* 6, no. 2 (1994): 202.

16. Charlotte A. Twight, "Federal Control over Education: Crisis, Deception, and Institutional Change," *Journal of Economic Behavior & Organization* 31, no. 3 (1996): 302.

17. Michael A. Crew and Charlotte A. Twight, "On the Efficiency of Law: A Public Choice Perspective," *Public Choice* 66, no. 11 (1990): 22–23.

18. Ibid., 23–24.

19. Charlotte A. Twight, "Constitutional Renegotiation: Impediments to Consensual Revision," *Constitutional Political Economy* 3, no. 1 (1992): 89–112.

20. Charlotte A. Twight, "Channeling Ideological Change: The Political Economy of Dependence on Government," *Kyklos* 46, no. 4 (1993): 500.

21. Robert Higgs, *Crisis and Leviathan: Critical Episodes in the Growth of American Government* (Oxford University Press, 1987).

22. Timur Kuran, *Private Truths, Public Lies: The Social Consequences of Preference Falsification* (Harvard University Press, 1995).

23. Charlotte A. Twight, "Through the Mist: American Liberty and Political Economy, 2065," *The Independent Review* 20, no. 3 (2016): 428.

24. Twight, "Designing Dependence," 237.

25. Ibid., 238–39.

26. Ibid., 238.

27. Ibid., 239.

28. Ibid., 428.

29. Robert Higgs and Charlotte Twight, "National Emergency and the Erosion of Private Property Rights," *Cato Journal* 6, no. 3 (1987): 747–72.

30. Twight, "Federal Control over Education," 304.

31. Ibid.

32. Adam Tooze, "Welcome to the World of Polycrisis," *Financial Times*, October 29, 2022.

33. Twight, "Federal Control over Education," 304.

34. Charlotte Twight, *America's Emerging Fascist Economy* (Arlington House Publishers, 1975), 14.

35. Ibid., 16.

36. Robert Higgs, "Once More, with Feeling: Our System Is Not Socialism, but Participatory Fascism," Independent Institute blog, October 30, 2012, https://blog.independent.org/2012/10/30/once-more-with-feeling-our-system-is-not-socialism-but-participatory-fascism.

37. Bob Evancho, "The Politics of Economics," *Boise State University Focus*, Summer 1993, 32, https://scholarworks.boisestate.edu/cgi/viewcontent.cgi?article=1051&context=focus.

38. Ibid.

39. Randall G. Holcombe, *Political Capitalism: How Economic and Political Power Is Made and Maintained* (Cambridge University Press, 2018); Randall G. Holcombe, *Following Their Leaders: Political Preferences and Public Policy* (Cambridge University Press, 2023).

Chapter 22: Karen Vaughn by Jayme Lemke

1. Bruce Caldwell, "JHET Interviews: Karen Vaughn," *Journal of the History of Economic Thought* 43, no. 3 (2021): 450–73.

2. Admittedly, economics departments are still struggling with this today (see Goldin 2021). When I asked Vaughn about her experiences as a woman in academia in a 2020 interview, she considered herself to have generally been treated fairly or even to have had a leg up by virtue of the extreme scarcity of women. She did recount some instances in which she either experienced or observed sexism during her career, including a future department chair who implied she should be grateful to have secretarial support because the department usually expected women—but not men—to do their own typing. Her response "was to dismiss these people as not worth my attention and just plow on" (Lemke and Vaughn 2020).

3. Jayme Lemke and Karen Vaughn, "Jayme Lemke and Karen Vaughn on Women in Economics," *Hayek Program Podcast,* March 26, 2020, https://www.mercatus.org/hayekprogram/hayek-program-podcast/jayme-lemke-and-karen-vaughn-women-economics.

4. From the blurb on the back of a collection of Vaughn's articles (Vaughn 2021c).

5. Karen Vaughn, *John Locke: Economist and Social Scientist* (University of Chicago Press, 1980).

6. Karen Vaughn, *Austrian Economics in America: The Migration of a Tradition* (Cambridge University Press, 1994).

7. A bibliography of Vaughn's work is available as an online supplement through the *Journal of the History of Economic Thought* (Caldwell 2021).

8. Vaughn, *John Locke: Economist and Social Scientist.*

9. Caldwell, "JHET Interviews: Karen Vaughn," 455–58.

10. Karen Vaughn, "Economic Calculation Under Socialism: The Austrian Contribution," *Economic Inquiry* 18, no. 4 (1980): 535–54; Vaughn, *Austrian Economics in America*; Karen Vaughn, *Essays on Austrian Economics and Political Economy* (Mercatus Center at George Mason University, 2021), 3.

11. Vaughn, "Economic Calculation Under Socialism."

12. Laurence S. Moss and Karen I. Vaughn, "Hayek's Ricardo Effect: A Second Look," *History of Political Economy* 18, no. 4 (1986): 545–65.

13. Vaughn, "Economic Calculation Under Socialism."

14. See in References: Vaughn 1994; 1999; [2017] 2021d; [1999] 2021e.

15. Karen Vaughn, "Profit, Alertness, and Imagination," in *Essays on Austrian Economics and Political Economy* (Mercatus Center at George Mason University, 2021), 75.

16. Karen Vaughn, "Hayek's Implicit Economics: Rules and the Problem of Order," *Review of Austrian Economics* 11, no. 1 (1999): 142.

17. Karen Vaughn, "The Mengerian Roots of the Austrian Revival," *History of Political Economy* 22, no. S1 (1990): 379–407; Vaughn, *Austrian Economics in America*.

18. Kenneth E. Boulding, "After Samuelson, Who Needs Adam Smith?," *History of Political Economy* 3, no. 2 (1971): 225–37.

19. Karen Vaughn, "Does It Matter That Costs Are Subjective?," *Southern Economic Journal* 46, no. 3 (1980): 702.

20. Ibid., 706.

21. Ibid., 711.

22. Karen Vaughn, "Should There Be an Austrian Welfare Economics?," in *Essays on Austrian Economics and Political Economy* (Mercatus Center at George Mason University, 2021), 150.

23. Karen Vaughn, "Economic Policy for an Imperfect World," *Southern Economic Journal* 62, no. 4: (1996): 838.

24. Karen Vaughn, "Can Democratic Society Reform Itself? The Limits of Constructive Change," in *Essays on Austrian Economics and Political Economy* (Mercatus Center at George Mason University, 2021), 194.

25. Ibid., 193.

26. Ibid. See also in References: Vaughn [1984] 2021b; [2017] 2021d; [1999] 2021e.

27. Vaughn, "Hayek's Implicit Economics."

28. Vaughn, "Can Democratic Society Reform Itself?," 191.

29. Ibid., 201.

30. Ibid.

31. Ibid., 197.

32. Ibid., 202.

33. Karen Vaughn, "The Limits of Homo Economicus in Public Choice and in Political Philosophy," *Analyse & Kritik* 10, no. 2 (1988): 164.

34. Ibid., 176–78.

35. Vaughn, "Can Democratic Society Reform Itself?," 204.

36. Vaughn, "Profit, Alertness, and Imagination," in *Essays on Austrian Economics and Political Economy,* 79.

37. Virgil Henry Storr and Ginny Seung Choi, *Do Markets Corrupt Our Morals?* (Palgrave Macmillan, 2019).

38. Lemke and Vaughn, "Jayme Lemke and Karen Vaughn on Women in Economics"; Caldwell, "JHET Interviews: Karen Vaughn"; Vaughn, *Essays on Austrian Economics and Political Economy,* 1–9.

39. Peter J. Boettke, Karen I. Vaughn, Bruce Caldwell, Jayme Lemke, and Viktor Vanberg, "*Essays on Austrian Economics and Political Economy* Book Panel," *Hayek Program Podcast,* February 22, 2023, https://www.mercatus.org/hayekprogram/hayek-program-podcast/essays-austrian-economics-and-political-economy-book-panel.

40. Karen Vaughn, "Hayek's Theory of the Market Order as an Instance of the Theory of Complex, Adaptive Systems," in *Essays on Austrian Economics and Political Economy* (Mercatus Center at George Mason University, 2021), 174.

Chapter 23: Viviana Zelizer by Stefanie Haeffele and Jessica Carges

1. Zelizer's prominence in her field is apparent. She is the Lloyd Cotsen '50 Professor of Sociology at Princeton University and has held positions at Columbia University and Rutgers University. Her research consists of six authored books, one edited volume, and more than seventy-five articles and book chapters. She was elected the first chair of the economic sociology section of the American Sociological Association in 2001, and in 2003, the section named its annual book prize in her honor. Zelizer also was elected to the American Academy of Arts and Sciences and the American Philosophical Society in 2007, received an honorary doctorate from Sciences Po University in Paris in 2019, and has earned numerous awards for her research over the course of her career. See Zelizer's biography and current curriculum vitae at https://sociology.princeton.edu/people/viviana-zelizer.

2. Peter J. Boettke, Stefanie Haeffele, and Virgil Henry Storr, *Mainline Economics: Six Nobel Lectures in the Tradition of Adam Smith* (Mercatus Center at George Mason University, 2016), 4.

3. James M. Buchanan, "What Should Economists Do?" *Southern Economic Journal* 30, no. 3 (1964): 213–22.

4. Max Weber, *The Protestant Ethic and the Spirit of Capitalism: And Other Writings* (Penguin Classics, 2002).

5. Adam Smith, *The Theory of Moral Sentiments* (Liberty Fund, 1982).

6. Vernon L. Smith, "The Two Faces of Adam Smith," *Southern Economic Journal* 65, no. 1 (1998): 1–19.

7. See Boettke, Haeffele, and Storr, *Mainline Economics*.

8. See Amy R. Poteete, Marco A. Janssen, and Elinor Ostrom, *Working Together: Collective Action, the Commons, and Multiple Methods in Practice* (Princeton University Press, 2010).

9. Deirdre McCloskey, *The Bourgeois Virtues: Ethics for an Age of Commerce* (University of Chicago Press, 2006); Deirdre McCloskey, *Bourgeois Dignity: Why Economics Can't Explain the Modern World* (University of Chicago Press, 2010).

10. Viviana Zelizer, *Economic Lives: How Culture Shapes the Economy* (Princeton University Press, 2011), 11.

11. Ibid., 5.

12. See Storr and Choi 2019 for a review of this stance.

13. Viviana Zelizer, "A Dollar Is a Dollar Is Not a Dollar: Unmasking the Social and Moral Meanings of Monies," *Los Angeles Review of Books*, June 15, 2017, https://lareviewofbooks.org/article/a-dollar-is-a-dollar-is-not-a-dollar-unmasking-the-social-and-moral-meanings-of-money.

14. Viviana Zelizer, *The Social Meaning of Money* (Basic Books, 2017).

15. Ibid.

16. Sarah Halpern-Meekin, Kathryn Edin, Laura Tach, and Jennifer Sykes, *It's Not Like I'm Poor: How Working Families Make Ends Meet in a Post-Welfare World* (University of California Press, 2015); Zelizer, "A Dollar Is Not a Dollar"; Laurent Belsie, "Most Stimulus Payments Were Saved or Applied to Debt," *National Bureau of Economic Research: The Digest*,

no. 10 (2020): https://www.nber.org/digest/oct20/most-stimulus-payments-were-saved-or-applied-debt.

17. Zelizer, "A Dollar Is Not a Dollar."

18. Virgil Henry Storr and Ginny Seung Choi, *Do Markets Corrupt Our Morals?* (Palgrave Macmillan, 2019).

19. Viviana Zelizer, *Economic Lives: How Culture Shapes the Economy* (Princeton University Press, 2011), 152; see also Viviana Zelizer, *The Purchase of Intimacy* (Princeton University Press, 2005).

20. Zelizer, *The Purchase of Intimacy*, 181.

21. Ibid., 182.

22. Ibid.

23. Zelizer, *Economic Lives*, 386–87.

24. Zelizer, *The Social Meaning of Money.*

25. Zelizer, "Pandemic Money Puzzles," in *The Euro at 20: The Future of Our Money*, edited by Johannes Beermann (Penguin Random House, 2022); Viviana Zelizer, "How and Why Social Relations Matter for Economic Lives," in *Living Better Together: Social Relations and Economic Governance in the Work of Ostrom and Zelizer*, edited by Stefanie Haeffele and Virgil Henry Storr (Palgrave Macmillan, 2023).

26. Zelizer, *Economic Lives*, 390.

27. Ibid., 393.

28. Ibid., 5.

29. Weber, *The Protestant Ethic and the Spirit of Capitalism*; Virgil Henry Storr, *Understanding the Culture of Markets* (Routledge, 2012).

30. Peter J. Boettke, Christopher J. Coyne, and Peter T. Leeson, "Institutional Stickiness and the New Development Economics," *American Journal of Economics and Sociology* 67, no. 2 (2008): 331–58.

31. Robert H. Frank, "Book Review: The Economic Mind: The Social Psychology of Economic Behavior by Adrian Furnhamand and Alan Lewis," *Journal of Economic Literature* 25, no. 3 (1987): 1307.

32. Zelizer, *Economic Lives*, 387.

33. Viviana A. Zelizer, *Morals and Markets: The Development of Life Insurance in the United States* (Columbia University Press, 1979).

34. Zelizer, *Economic Lives*, 367.

35. Ibid., 367.

36. Ibid., 390; see Poteete, Janssen, and Ostrom, *Working Together.*

37. Zelizer, *Economic Lives*, 360.

38. Boettke, Haeffele, and Storr, *Mainline Economics.*

39. Viviana A. Zelizer, *Pricing the Priceless Child: The Changing Social Value of Children* (Basic Books, 1985).

40. Viviana A. Zelizer, "Pricing the Priceless Child: The Changing Social Value of Children," in *The New Economic Sociology: A Reader*, edited by Frank Dobbin (Princeton University Press, 2004), 155.

41. Ibid., 136.

42. Ibid., 153.
43. Zelizer, *Economic Lives.*
44. Ibid., 304.
45. Ibid., 347.
46. Olav Velthuis, *Talking Prices: Symbolic Meanings of Prices on the Market for Contemporary Art* (Princeton University Press, 2005), 57. The connections between, and the usefulness of combining, the work of Zelizer and Ostrom is explored in a recent edited volume (Haeffele and Storr 2023).
47. See Zelizer 2000, 2002, 2004a, 2005, 2011 in References.
48. Velthuis, *Talking Prices.*
49. Ashley Mears, *Pricing Beauty: The Making of a Fashion Model* (University of California Press, 2011).
50. See Poteete, Janssen, and Ostrom, *Working Together*; Emily Chamlee-Wright, *The Cultural and Political Economy of Recovery: Social Learning in a Post-Disaster Environment* (Routledge, 2010).
51. Stefanie Haeffele and Virgil Henry Storr, eds., *Living Better Together: Social Relations and Economic Governance in the Work of Ostrom and Zelizer* (Palgrave Macmillan, 2023).

Chapter 24: Don Lavoie by Peter J. Boettke

1. There is a lecture, recorded at George Mason University, on Marxism and central planning from the early 1980s ("The Failure of Central Planning (Don Lavoie) – The Turney Collection," https://youtu.be/ehLq-da3hkQ), and Chris Sciabarra has recently released audiotapes of three of Lavoie's talks dealing with immigration ("Don Lavoie Lectures, 1980–1981: Immigration," https://youtu.be/1nolgPIsoWY) and the failure of socialism ("Don Lavoie Lectures, 1980–1981: Planned Chaos – The Failure of Socialism," https://youtu.be/fBZ85cTxE-A) and a discussion with Bertell Ollman on libertarianism and Marxism ("Don Lavoie Lectures, 1980–1981: Freedom: Libertarian vs. Marxist Perspective, with Bertell Ollman," https://youtu.be/ba2R-UNljGc). Also see this Mercatus Center video about how Lavoie changed the debate about socialism and central planning ("How Don Lavoie Changed the Debate About Socialism and Central Planning," https://youtu.be/PIqBGVU-VKks).
2. Peter J. Boettke, *The Struggle for a Better World* (Mercatus Center at George Mason University, 2021).
3. Don Lavoie, *Rivalry and Central Planning: The Socialist Calculation Debate Reconsidered* (Cambridge University Press, 1985), 183.
4. See Michael Polanyi, *The Logic of Liberty* (University of Chicago Press, 1951) and *Personal Choice* (University of Chicago Press, 1958).
5. Hans-Georg Gadamer, *Truth and Method* (Continuum, 1960).
6. This is from a description of forthcoming projects drawn from his last updated curriculum vitae, from March 2001.
7. See, e.g., Don Lavoie, "The Market as a Procedure for the Discovery and Conveyance of Inarticulate Knowledge," *Comparative Economic Studies* 28 (Spring 1986): 1–19; Don Lavoie, "Computation, Incentives and Discovery: The Cognitive Function of Markets in

Market Socialism," *Annals of the American Academy of Political and Social Science* 507 (January 1990): 72–79.

8. See a description of what Lavoie began pursuing in the fall of 1989 at http://www.philsalin.com/hth/hth.html. And this article from *Reason* explains how far Lavoie was ahead of the curve in this regard: https://reason.com/video/2020/10/07/before-the-web-the-1980s-dream-of-a-free-and-borderless-virtual-world.

9. Don Lavoie, *National Economic Planning: What Is Left?* (Ballinger, 1985), 238.

10. Ibid., 230.

11. Peter J. Boettke, "Remembering Don Lavoie (1951–2001): A Student's Perspective," *Review of Austrian Economics* 15, no. 1 (2002): 103–5.

References

Introduction: Unsung Heroes by Robert M. Whaples

Boulding, Kenneth E. 1969. "Economics as a Moral Science." *American Economic Review* 59, no. 1 (March): 1–12.

Davis, William L., Bob G. Figgins, David Hedengren, and Daniel B. Klein. 2011. "Economics Professors' Favorite Economic Thinkers, Journals, and Blogs (along with Party and Policy Views)." *Econ Journal Watch* 8, no. 2 (May): 126–45.

Smith, Vernon L. 2023. "Adam Smith, Sociality, and Classical Liberalism." *The Independent Review* 28, no. 1 (Summer): 117–22.

Chapter 1: Alexander Hamilton by Richard M. Salsman

Bourne, Edward G. 1894. "Alexander Hamilton and Adam Smith." *Quarterly Journal of Economics* 8: 328–44.

Chan, Michael. 2004. "Alexander Hamilton on Slavery." *Review of Politics* 66, no. 2: 207–31.

Chernow, Ron. 2004. *Alexander Hamilton.* Penguin Books.

Cohen, Stephen S., and J. Bradford DeLong. 2016. *Concrete Economics: The Hamilton Approach to Economic Growth and Policy.* Harvard Business Review Press.

DiLorenzo, Thomas. 2009. *Hamilton's Curse: How Jefferson's Arch Enemy Betrayed the American Revolution—and What It Means for Americans Today.* Three Rivers Press.

Federici, Michael P. 2012. "Hamilton's Political Economy." Chap. 6 in *The Political Philosophy of Alexander Hamilton.* Johns Hopkins University Press.

Fleischacker, Samuel. 2002. "Adam Smith's Reception Among the American Founders, 1776–1790." *William and Mary Quarterly* 59, no. 4: 897–924.

Gordon, John Steele. 1997. *Hamilton's Blessing: The Extraordinary Life and Times of Our National Debt.* Walker and Company.

Grampp, William D. 1965. *Economic Liberalism: The Beginnings.* Random House.

Hamilton, Alexander. 1781a [April]. "Letter to Robert Morris." In Syrett 1962–87, 2:604–35.

———. 1781b [August]. "The Continentalist no. 4." In Syrett 1962–87, 2:669–74.

———. 1787 [November]. *Federalist* no. 12. In Syrett 1962–87, 4:346–52.

———. 1788 [January]. *Federalist* no. 35. In Syrett 1962–87, 4:476–82.

———. 1790a [January]. "Report Relative to a Provision for the Support of Public Credit." In Syrett 1962–87, 6:65–110.

———. 1790b [December]. "Final Version of the Second Report on the Further Provision Necessary for Establishing Public Credit (Report on a National Bank)." In Syrett 1962–87, 7:305–42.

———. 1791a [January]. "Final Version of the Report on the Establishment of a Mint." In Syrett 1962–87, 7:570–607.

———. 1791b [December]. "Final Version of the Report on the Subject of Manufactures." In Syrett 1962–87, 10:230–340.

———. 1795 [January]. "Report on a Plan for the Further Support of Public Credit." In Syrett 1962–87, 18:56–129.

———. 1796 [July]. "Draft of Washington's Farewell Address." In Syrett 1962–87, 20:265–88.

Holloway, Carson. 2015. "Alexander Hamilton and American Progressivism." *First Principles,* no. 52. The Heritage Foundation.

Hume, David. [1752, 1777] 1985. *Essays Moral, Political, and Literary.* Edited by Eugene F. Miller. Liberty Fund.

Irwin, Douglas A. 2009. "Revenue or Reciprocity? Founding Feuds over Early U.S. Trade Policy." Working Paper 15144. National Bureau of Economic Research.

Knott, Stephen F. 2002. *Alexander Hamilton and the Persistence of Myth.* University of Kansas Press.

Lind, Michael. 2012. "A New Hamiltonianism." *Boston Review.* June 13.

Liu, Glory M. 2022. *Adam Smith's America: How a Scottish Philosopher Became an Icon of American Capitalism.* Princeton University Press.

Lunt, Edward C. 1895. "Hamilton as a Political Economist." *Journal of Political Economy* 3, no. 3: 289–310.

McClanahan, Brion. 2017. *How Alexander Hamilton Screwed Up America.* Regnery History.

McNamara, Peter. 1998. *Political Economy and Statesmanship: Smith, Hamilton, and the Foundation of the Commercial Republic.* Northern Illinois University Press.

Nelson, John R. Jr. 1979. "Alexander Hamilton and American Manufacturing: A Reexamination." *Journal of American History* 65, no. 4: 971–95.

Nester, William. 2012. *The Hamiltonian Vision, 1789–1800: The Art of American Power During the Early Republic.* Potomac Books.

Rand, Ayn. 1967. *Capitalism: The Unknown Ideal.* New American Library.

Salsman, Richard M. 1990. *Breaking the Banks: Central Banking Problems and Free Banking Solutions.* American Institute for Economic Research.

———. 2016a. "Review of *Concrete Economics: The Hamiltonian Approach to Economic Growth and Policy.*" At https://eh.net/book_reviews/concrete-economics-the-hamiltonian-approach-to-economic-growth-and-policy.

———. 2016b. "The U.S. Founding: Washington's Allies and Opponents." *Reason Papers* 38, no. 2: 89–99.

———. 2017a. "America at Her Best Is Hamiltonian." *Objective Standard* 12, no. 1: 12–42.

———. 2017b. "Early American Debate: Hamilton Versus Jefferson." In *The Political Economy of Public Debt: Three Centuries of Theory and Evidence*, 58–75. Edward Elgar.

———. 2020. "The Golden Rule of Public Finance and Prospects for Its Revival." Chap. 16 in *A Fiscal Cliff: New Perspectives on the U.S. Federal Debt Crisis.* Edited by John Merrifield and Barry W. Poulson. Cato Institute.

Syrett, Harold C., ed. 1962–87. *The Papers of Alexander Hamilton.* 27 vols. Columbia University Press. At https://founders.archives.gov/about/Hamilton.

Taussig, Frank. 1892. *State Papers and Speeches on the Tariff.* Harvard University Press.

White, Lawrence H. 2016. "Alexander Hamilton, a Second-Hand Dealer in Retrograde Mercantilist Ideas." *FEE Stories.* September 6. Foundation for Economic Education.

Wilser, Jeff. 2016. *Alexander Hamilton's Guide to Life.* Three Rivers Press.

Wright, Robert E. 2002. *Hamilton Unbound: Finance and the Creation of the American Republic.* Greenwood Press.

Chapter 2: Harriet Martineau by David M. Levy and Sandra J. Peart

Carlyle, Thomas. 1849. "Occasional Discourse on the Negro Question." *Fraser's Magazine for Town and Country* 40 (December): 670–79.

———. 1881. *Reminiscences.* Edited by James Anthony Froude. Harper & Brothers.

Costa, Emelia Viotti da. 1994. *Crowns of Glory, Tears of Blood: The Demerara Slave Rebellion of 1823.* Oxford University Press.

Darity, William A. Jr. 1998. "Intergroup Disparity: Economic Theory and Social Science Evidence." *Southern Economic Journal* 64, no. 4 (April): 805–26.

———, ed. 1989. "Introduction: The Odyssey of Abram Harris from Howard to Chicago." In *Race, Radicalism, and Reform: Selected Papers of Abram L. Harris*, 1–34. Transaction Publishers.

Drescher, Seymour. 2009. *Abolition: A History of Slavery and Antislavery.* Cambridge University Press.

Fogel, Robert William. 1989. *Without Consent or Contract: The Rise and Fall of American Slavery.* W. W. Norton.

Fogel, Robert William, and Stanley L. Engerman. 1974. *Time on the Cross: The Economics of American Negro Slavery.* W. W. Norton.

Goldsmith, Arthur H., Darrick Hamilton, and William Darity Jr. 2007. "From Dark to Light: Skin Color and Wages Among African-Americans." *Journal of Human Resources* 12: 701–38.

Herring, Cedric, and Anthony Nynes. 2017. "Race, Skin Tone, and Wealth Inequality in America." In *Color Struck: How Race and Complexion Matter in the "Color-Blind Era."* Edited by Lori Latrice Martin, Hayward Derrick Horton, Cedric Herring, Venra M. Keith, and Melvin Thomas, 1–18. Rotterdam: Sense.

Jevons, W. S. [1866] 1981. "The Importance of Diffusing a Knowledge of Political Economy. Lecture delivered at Owens College, Manchester, October 12, 1866." In *Papers and Correspondence of William Stanley Jevons.* Vol. 7. Edited by R. C. D. Black, 37–54. Macmillan.

Kuehn, Daniel. 2023. "'Marco Polo Economics' and Narrative in the NBER Soviet Growth Study." *History of Political Economy* 55, no. 3: 471–96.

Levy, David M. 1978. "Some Normative Aspects of the Malthusian Controversy." *History of Political Economy* 10 (Summer): 271–85.

Levy, David M., and Sandra J. Peart. 2020. *Towards an Economics of Natural Equals: A Documentary History of the Early Virginia School.* Cambridge University Press.

———. 2022. "Harriet Martineau (1802–1876)." In *The Essential Women of Liberty.* Edited by Donald J. Boudreaux and Aeon Skoble, 17–29. Fraser Institute.

Logan, Deborah Ann. 2002. *The Hour and the Woman: Harriet Martineau's "Somewhat Remarkable" Life.* Northern Illinois University Press.

Maclise, Daniel, and William Maginn. 1873. *A Gallery of Illustrious Literary Characters.* Edited by William Bates. Chatto and Windus.

Malveaux, Julianne. 1991. "Missed Opportunity: Sadie Tanner Mossell Alexander and the Economics Profession." *American Economic Review* 81, no. 2: 307–10.

Marshall, Alfred. 1890. *Principles of Economics.* Macmillan.

Martineau, Harriet. 1832. *Life in the Wilds.* Vol. 1 in *Illustrations of Political Economy.* Charles Fox.

———. 1833. *Demerara.* Vol. 2 in *Illustrations of Political Economy.* Charles Fox.

———. 1837. *Society in America.* 3 vols. Saunders and Otley.

———. 1838. "The Martyr Age of the United States." *London and Westminster Review.*

———. 1877. *Harriet Martineau's Autobiography with Memorials by Maria Weston Chapman.* 3 vols. Smith, Elder & Co.

———. 2007. *The Collected Letters of Harriet Martineau.* 5 vols. Edited by Deborah Anna Logan. Pickering & Chatto.

McGinnis, Frederick A. 1941. *A History and an Interpretation of Wilberforce University.* Brown.

Micheletti, Steven J., Kasia Bryc, Samantha G. Ancona Esselmann, William A. Freyman, Meghan E. Moreno, G. David Poznik, Anjali J. Shastri, 23andMe Research Team, Sandra Beleza, and Joanna L. Mountain. 2020. "Genetic Consequences of the Transatlantic Slave Trade in the Americas." *American Journal of Human Genetics* 107 (August 6): 265–77.

Morey, Maribel. 2021. *White Philanthropy: Carnegie Corporation's An American Dilemma and the Making of a White World Order.* University of North Carolina Press.

Morgan, Mary. 2022. "Travelers' Tales: Their Values and Virtues." *History of Political Economy* 54, no. 3: 571–82.

Myrdal, Gunnar. 1944. *An American Dilemma: The Negro Problem and Modern Democracy.* Harper & Brothers.

Newman, Leonard. 1944. "Opposition to Lincoln in the Elections of 1864." *Science and Society* 8, no. 4: 305–27.

Peart, Sandra J. 2009. "2008 HES Presidential Address: We're All 'Persons' Now: Classical Economists and Their Opponents on Marriage, the Franchise, and Socialism." *Journal of the History of Economic Thought* 31, no. 1: 3–20.

Peart, Sandra J., and David M. Levy. 2008. "Darwin's Unpublished Letter at the Bradlaugh-Besant Trial: A Question of Divided Expert Judgment." *European Journal of Political Economy* 24, no. 2: 343–53.

The Pro-slavery Argument; as Maintained by the Most Distinguished Writers on the Southern States, Containing the Several Essays, on the Subject, of Chancellor Harper, Governor Hammond, Dr. Simms, and Professor Dew. 1852. Walker, Richards.

Smith, Adam. [1776] 1981. *An Inquiry into the Nature and Causes of the Wealth of Nations.* Edited by W. B. Todd. Liberty Fund.

Vining, Rutledge. 1949. "Koopmans on the Choice of Variables to Be Studied and the Methods of Measurement." *Review of Economics and Statistics* 31:77–86.

Woodson, Carter G. 1918. "The Beginning of the Miscegenation of the Whites and the Blacks." *Journal of Negro History* 3, no. 4: 335–53.

Chapter 3: Knut Wicksell by Diana W. Thomas

Åkerman, Johan. 1933. "Knut Wicksell, A Pioneer of Econometrics." *Econometrica* 1, no. 2: 113–18.

Buchanan, James M. 1952. "Wicksell on Fiscal Reform: Comment." *American Economic Review* 42, no. 4: 599–602.

———. 1983. "Rent Seeking, Noncompensated Transfers, and Laws of Succession." *Journal of Law and Economics* 26, no. 1: 71–85.

Gordon, David. 1994. "Justice and Redistributive Taxation: James Buchanan Versus Ludwig von Mises." *Review of Austrian Economics* 8, no. 1: 117–31.

Johnson, Marianne. 2010. "Wicksell's Social Philosophy and His Unanimity Rule." *Review of Social Economy* 68, no. 2: 187–204.

Jonung, Lars. 1988. "Knut Wicksell's Unpublished Manuscripts: A First Glance." *European Economic Review* 32, nos. 2–3: 503–11.

Lundahl, Mats. 2015. "Population Growth and Diminishing Returns: Knut Wicksell on the Causes of Poverty." In *Seven Figures in the History of Swedish Economic Thought,* 55–83. Palgrave Macmillan.

Medema, Stephen G., and Warren Samuels. 2003. *The History of Economic Thought: A Reader.* Routledge.

Ohlin, Bertil. 1926. "Obituary: Knut Wicksell (1851–1926)." *Economic Journal* 36, no. 143: 503–12.

Robbins, Lionel. 2000. *A History of Economic Thought: The LSE Lectures.* Princeton University Press.

Sandelin, Bo, and Hans-Michael Trautwein. 2014. *A Short History of Economic Thought.* Taylor & Francis.

Silvestre, Joaquim. 2003. "Wicksell, Lindahl and the Theory of Public Goods." *Scandinavian Journal of Economics* 105, no. 4: 527–53.

Sommarin, Emil. 1930. "Das Lebenswerk von Knut Wicksell." *Zeitschrift für Nationalökonomie* 2, no. 2: 221–67.

Uhr, Carl G. 1951. "Knut Wicksell: A Centennial Evaluation." *American Economic Review* 41, no. 5: 829–60.

Wagner, Richard. 1988. "The Calculus of Consent: A Wicksellian Retrospective." *Public Choice* 65: 153–66.

Wicksell, Knut. [1896] 1967. "A New Principle of Just Taxation." In *Classics in the Theory of Public Finance,* edited by Richard A. Musgrave and Alan T. Peacock, 72–118. Macmillan.

———. [1896] 1992. *Finanztheoretische Untersuchungen: Nebst Darstellung und Kritik des Steuerwesens Schwedens.* Thoemmes Press.

Chapter 4: Thorstein Veblen by Robert M. Whaples

Bowie, James I. 2024. "Nvidia's Quirky Logo Reveals Just How Much the Company Has Changed." Fast Company. https://www.fastcompany.com/91135380/nvidias-quirky-logo-reveals-just-how-much-the-company-has-changed.

Bursztyn, Leonardo, Bruno Ferman, Stefano Fiorin, Martin Kanz, and Gautam Rao. 2018. "Status Goods: Experimental Evidence from Platinum Credit Cards." *Quarterly Journal of Economics* 133, no. 3: 1561–95.

Camic, Charles. 2020. *Veblen: The Making of an Economist Who Unmade Economics.* Harvard University Press.

Charles, Kerwin Kofi, Erik Hurst, and Nikolai Roussanov. 2009. "Conspicuous Consumption and Race." *Quarterly Journal of Economics* 124, no. 2: 425–67.

Chase, Stuart. 1934. "Foreword." In Veblen, Thorstein, *The Theory of the Leisure Class.* Modern Library.

Chernow, Ron. 1998. *Titan: The Life of John D. Rockefeller Sr.* Random House.

Davis, William L., Bob G. Figgins, David Hedengren, and Daniel B. Klein. 2011. "Economics Professors' Favorite Economic Thinkers, Journals, and Blogs (Along with Party and Policy Views)." *Econ Journal Watch* 8, no. 2 (May): 126–46.

Desierto, Desiree, and Mark Koyama. 2024. "The Political Economy of Status Competition: Sumptuary Laws in Preindustrial Europe." *Journal of Economic History* 84, no. 2: 479–516.

Dorfman, Joseph. [1934] 1972. *Thorstein Veblen and His America*, seventh edition. Augustus M. Kelley.

Duesenberry, James S. 1949. *Income, Saving, and the Theory of Consumer Behavior.* Harvard University Press.

Ekelund, Robert B. Jr., and Robert F. Hébert. 1997 [2014]. *A History of Economic Theory and Method.* Waveland Press.

Fogel, Robert William. 2000. *The Fourth Great Awakening and the Future of Egalitarianism.* University of Chicago Press.

Franch, John. 2008. *Robber Baron: The Life of Charles Tyson Yerkes.* University of Illinois Press.

Frank, Robert H. 1987. *Choosing the Right Pond: Human Behavior and the Quest for Status.* Oxford University Press.

———. 2000. *Luxury Fever: Weighing the Costs of Excess.* Princeton University Press.

———. 2008. "Should Public Policy Respond to Positional Externalities?" *Journal of Public Economics* 92: 1777–86.

Galbraith, John Kenneth. 1958. *The Affluent Society.* New American Library.

Giuliani, Alfonso. 2016. "Thorstein Bunde Veblen (1857–1929)." In Gilbert Faccarello and Heinz D. Kurz, editors. *Hand on the History of Economic Analysis, Volume 1, Great Economists Since Petty and Boisguilbert.* Edward Elgar.

Hamermesh, Daniel. 2017. *Beauty Pays: Why Attractive People Are More Successful.* Princeton University Press.

Haney, Lewis H. 1911 [1949]. *History of Economic Thought: A Critical Account of the Origin and Development of the Economic Theories of the Leading Thinkers in the Leading Nations.* Macmillan.

Heilbroner, Robert L. 1953. *The Worldly Philosophers.* Simon and Schuster.

Henderson, Rob. 2024. "'Luxury Beliefs' That Only the Privileged Few Can Afford." *Wall Street Journal*, February 10/11, 2024, C3.

Hirshleifer, Jack. 1985. "The Expanding Domain of Economics." *American Economic Review* 75, no. 6: 53–68.

Hoffer, Eric. 1951 [1966]. *The True Believer: Thoughts on the Nature of Mass Movements.* Harper and Row.

Johnston, Louis, and Samuel H. Williamson. 2024. "What Was the U.S. GDP Then?" MeasuringWorth, https://www.measuringworth.com/datasets/usgdp.

Kuziemko, Ilyana, Ryan W. Buell, Taly Reich, and Michael I. Norton. 2014. "'Last-Place Aversion': Evidence and Redistributive Implications." *Quarterly Journal of Economics* 129, no. 1: 105–50.

Leibenstein, Harvey. 1950. "Bandwagon, Sob, and Veblen Effects in the Theory of Consumers' Demand." *Quarterly Journal of Economics* 62, no. 2:183–207.

Moldovanu, Benny, Aner Sela, and Xianwen Shi. 2007. "Contests for Status." *Journal of Political Economy* 115, no. 2: 338–63.

Pinker, Steven. 2011. *The Better Angels of Our Nature: Why Violence Has Declined.* Viking.

Prasch, Robert. 2013. "Insights from Thorstein Veblen." In G. Page West III and Robert M. Whaples, editors. *The Economic Crisis in Retrospect.* Edward Elgar Publishing.

Rostow, W. W. 1990. *Theorists of Economics Growth: From Hume to the Present.* Oxford University Press.

Schoeck, Helmut. 1966. *Envy: A Theory of Social Behaviour.* Liberty Fund.

Schumpeter, Joseph A. 1912 [1934]. *The Theory of Economic Development.* Harvard University Press.

———. 1954. *History of Economic Analysis.* Oxford University Press.

Smith, Adam. 1759 [1980]. *The Theory of Moral Sentiments.* Edited by D. D. Raphael and A. L. Macfie. Liberty Fund

Skousen, Mark. 2001 [2022]. *The Making of Modern Economics: The Lives and Ideas of the Great Thinkers.* Routledge.

Taylor, Timothy. 2024. "What Are the Objectives of First-Year College Students?" https://conversableeconomist.com/2024/04/11/what-are-the-objectives-of-first-year-college-students.

Veblen, Thorstein. [1899] 1991. *The Theory of the Leisure Class.* Augustus M. Kelley.

———. 1904. *The Theory of Business Enterprise.* Charles Scribner's Sons.

———. 1910. "Christian Morals and the Competitive System." *International Journal of Ethics* 20, no. 2: 168–185

———. [1914] 1964. *The Instinct of Workmanship and the State of the Industrial Arts.* Augustus M. Kelley.

———. 1918. *The Higher Learning in America: A Memorandum on the Conduct of Universities by Business Men.* B. W. Huebsch.

———. [1921] 2001. *The Engineers and the Price System.* Batoche Books.

Whaples, Robert. 2020. "Why Didn't Galbraith Convince Us That America Is an Affluent Society?" *The Independent Review* 24, no. 4: 579–92.

———. 2022. "Where Do the Poorest Americans Stand in the Income Distribution Among All People Ever Born?" *The Independent Review* 27, no. 1: 155–59.

———. 2023. "Julian Simon: Irreplaceable Economist, Irreplaceable Man." *The Independent Review* 28, no. 2: 271–80.

Chapter 5: Frank Fetter by Matthew McCaffrey

Brown, J. Douglas. 1949. "Memorial: Frank Albert Fetter, 1863-1949." *American Economic Review* 39, no. 5: 979–81.

Dorfman, Joseph. 1949. *The Economic Mind in American Civilization.* N.p., 360–65.

Fetter, Frank A. Unpublished. "Overhead Costs." FAF, Box 4, Folder: Overhead Costs.

———. 1904. *The Principles of Economics, with Applications to Practical Problems.* The Century Co.

———. 1912. "The Definition of Price." *American Economic Review* 2, no. 4: 783–813.

———. 1915. *Economic Principles.* The Century Co.

———. 1920a. "Price Economics Versus Welfare Economics." *American Economic Review* 10, no. 3: 467–87.

———. 1920b. "Price Economics Versus Welfare Economics: Contemporary Opinion." *American Economic Review* 10, no. 4: 719–37.

———. 1923a. "Value and the Larger Economics, I: Rise of the Marginal Doctrine." *Journal of Political Economy* 31, no. 5: 587–605.

———. 1923b. "Value and the Larger Economics, II: Value Giving Way to Welfare." *Journal of Political Economy* 31, no. 6: 790–803.

———. 1926. "Present State of Economic Theory in the United States of America." FAF, Box 12, Folder: Miscellaneous Writings.

———. 1977. *Capital, Interest, and Rent: Essays in the Theory of Distribution*. Edited by Murray N. Rothbard. Institute for Humane Studies.

Gaffney, Mason. 1994. "Neo-classical Economics as a Stratagem Against Henry George." In *The Corruption of Economics*. Edited by Mason Gaffney and Fred Harrison. Shepheard–Walwyn, 29–163.

Hayek, Friedrich A. 1992. "The Austrian School of Economics." In *The Collected Works of F. A. Hayek, Volume 4: The Fortunes of Liberalism*. Edited by Peter G. Klein. Liberty Fund, 42–60.

Herbener, Jeffrey M. 1999. "Frank A. Fetter: A Forgotten Giant." In *15 Great Austrian Economists*. Edited by R. G. Holcombe. Ludwig von Mises Institute, 123–41.

———. 2011. "Introduction." In *The Pure Time-Preference Theory of Interest*. Edited by Jeffrey Herbener. Ludwig von Mises Institute, 11–58.

Hodgson, Geoffrey M. 2008. "Editorial Introduction to 'Capital' by Frank A. Fetter." *Journal of Institutional Economics* 4, no. 1: 127–37.

Howard, Stanley E., and Edwin W. Kemmerer. 1943. "Frank Albert Fetter: A Birthday Note." *American Economic Review* 33, no. 1: 230–35.

Knight, Frank H. 1935. "Marginal Utility Economics." In *Encyclopaedia of the Social Sciences*. Edited by Edwin R. A. Seligman. Macmillan. 5: 357–63.

Lewin, Peter, and Steven E. Phelan. 1999. "Firms, Strategies, and Resources: Contributions from Austrian Economics." *Quarterly Journal of Austrian Economics* 2, no. 2: 3–18.

McCaffrey, Matthew. 2016. "Good Judgment, Good Luck: Frank Fetter's Neglected Theory of Entrepreneurship." *Review of Political Economy* 28, no. 4: 504–22.

———. 2019. "Pure Theory and Progressive Liberalism: Frank Fetter and the Austrian Economists." *Journal of Institutional Economics* 15, no. 3: 469–86.

———. 2021. "The Long Rehabilitation of Frank Fetter." *Quarterly Journal of Austrian Economics* 24, no. 3: 467–95.

Menger, Carl. 1994. *Principles of Economics*. Libertarian Press.

———. 2016. "The Social Theories of Classical Political Economy and Modern Economic Policy." *Cosmos + Taxis* 13, no. 3: 473–88.

Mises, Ludwig von. 2007. *The Historical Setting of the Austrian School of Economics*. Ludwig von Mises Institute.

O'Driscoll, Gerald P., Jr. 1980. "Frank A. Fetter and 'Austrian' Business Cycle Theory." *History of Political Economy* 12, no. 4: 542–57.

Rothbard, Murray N. 1977. "Introduction." In *Capital, Interest, and Rent: Essays in the Theory of Distribution*. Institute for Humane Studies, 1–23.

Salerno, Joseph T. 1999. "The Place of Mises's *Human Action* in the Development of Modern Economic Thought." *Quarterly Journal of Austrian Economics* 2, no. 1: 35–65.

———. 2002. "The Rebirth of Austrian Economics—in Light of Austrian Economics." *Quarterly Journal of Austrian Economics* 5, no. 4 (Winter): 115.

———. 2008. "Böhm-Bawerk's Vision of the Capitalist Economic Process: Intellectual Influences and Conceptual Foundations." *New Perspectives on Political Economy* 4, no. 2: 87–112.

———. 2019. "Fetter on the Meaning of Price, Market, and Equilibrium." In *Liberty Matters: Frank Fetter and the Austrian Tradition in the United States*. Online Library of Liberty, 9–12. Available at: https://oll.libertyfund.org/publications/liberty-matters/matthew-mccaffrey-frank-fetter-austrian-economics.

Viner, Jacob. 2013. *Lectures in Economics 301*. Edited by D. A. Erwin and S. G. Medema. Transaction Publishers.

Chapter 6: Clark Warburton by Thomas F. Cargill

American Economic Association. 1951. *Readings in Monetary Theory*. Blakiston.

Bernanke, Ben. 2002. "Remarks by Governor Ben S. Bernanke at the Conference to Honor Milton Friedman's Ninetieth Birthday." https://www.federalreserve.gov/boarddocs/speeches/2002/20021108.

Bordo, Michael, and Anna J. Schwartz. 1979. "Clark Warburton: Pioneer Monetarist." *Journal of Monetary Economics* 5 (January): 43–65.

Cargill, Thomas F. 1979. "Clark Warburton and the Development of Monetarism Since the Great Depression." *History of Political Economy* 11 (Fall): 425–49.

———. 1981. "A Tribute to Clark Warburton, 1896–1979." *Journal of Money, Credit, and Banking* 13, no 1: 89–93.

Fels, Rendigs. 1949. "Warburton vs. Hansen and Keynes." *American Economic Review* 39 (September): 923–29.

Friedman, Milton, and Anna J. Schwartz. 1963. *A Monetary History of the United States: 1867–1960*. Princeton University Press.

Humphrey, Thomas M. 1971. "Role of Non-Chicago Economists in the Evolution of the Quantity Theory in America 1930–1950." *Southern Economic Journal* 38 (July): 12–18.

Keynes, John Maynard. 1936. *The General Theory of Employment, Interest and Money*. Palgrave McMillian.

Modigliani, Franco. 1977. "The Monetarist Controversy or Should We Forsake Stabilization Policies." *American Economic Review* 67 (March): 1–19.

Seldon, Richard. 1962. "Stable Money Growth." *In Search of a Monetary Constitution*. Edited by Leland Yeager. Harvard University Press.

———. 1977. Monetarism. *Modern Economic Thought*. Edited by Sidney Weintraub. University of Pennsylvania Press.

Tavlas, George S. 1976. "Some Further Observations on the Monetary Economics of Chicagoans and Non-Chicagoans." *Southern Economic Journal* 42 (April): 685–92.

Trescott, Paul B. 1982. "Discovery of the Money Income Relationship in the United States: 1921–1944." *History of Political Economy* 14, no. 1: 65–88.

Warburton, Clark. 1946. "The Misplaced Emphasis in Contemporary Business Fluctuation Theory." *Journal of Business* 19, no. 4: 199–220.

———. 1966. *Depression, Inflation and Monetary Policy: Selected Papers, 1945–1953.* Johns Hopkins Press.

Weintraub, Robert E. 1978. "Congressional Supervision of Monetary Policy." *Journal of Monetary Economics* 4 (April): 341–62.

Chapter 7: Ursula K. Hicks by Marianne Johnson

Aslanbeigui, Nahid, and Guy Oakes. 2007. "The Editor as Scientific Revolutionary: Keynes, *The Economic Journal,* and the Pigou Affair, 1936–1938." *Journal of the History of Economic Thought* 29, no. 1: 15–48.

Backhouse, Roger. 2017. *Founder of Modern Economics: Paul A. Samuelson.* Oxford University Press.

Becchio, Giandomenica. 2020. *A History of Feminist and Gender Economics.* Routledge.

Brilliant, Lucy. 2019. "Ursula Hicks' and Vera Lutz's Contributions to Development Finance." In *Routledge Handbook of the History of Women's Economic Thought.* Edited by K. Madden and R. Dimand, 341–57. Routledge.

Chassonnery-Zaïgouche, Cléo, Evelyn Forget, and John Singleton. 2022. "Women and Economics: New Historical Perspectives." *History of Political Economy* 54 (Supplement): 1–16.

Coase, Ronald. 1946. "The Marginal Cost Controversy." *Economica* 13, no. 51: 169–82.

Cord, Robert. 2018. *The Palgrave Companion to LSE Economics.* Palgrave Macmillan.

Dalton, Hugh. [1922] 1954. *Principles of Public Finance.* George Routledge & Sons.

David, Wilfred L. 1976. "Introduction." In *Public Finance, Planning, and Economic Development: Essays in Honour of Ursula Hicks.* Edited by Wilfred L. David, ix–xvi. Macmillan.

Frischmann, Brett, and Christiaan Hogendorn. 2015. "Retrospectives: The Marginal Cost Controversy." *Journal of Economic Perspectives* 29, no. 1: 193–206.

Harbury, C. D. 1974. "Reviewed Work: *Public Finance, Planning and Economic Development: Essays in Honour of Ursula Hicks.* Edited by Wilfred L. David." *Economic Journal* 84, no. 333: 224–26.

Hart, O. D., and G. E. Mizon. 1983. "50th Anniversary of the *Review of Economic Studies.*" *Review of Economic Studies* 50, no. 4: 583.

Head, John G. 1974. *Public Goods and Public Welfare.* Duke University Press.

Hicks, John R. 1982. "Introductory: LSE and the Robbins Circle." In *Money, Interest and Wages,* edited by J. R. Hicks, 3–10. Harvard University Press.

Hicks, Ursula K. 1937. "Reviewed Work: *Sweden: The Middle Way* by W. M. Childs." *Economic Journal* 47, no. 186: 342–45.

———. 1938a. *The Finance of British Government 1920–1936.* Oxford University Press.

———. 1938b. "Reviewed Work: *Central and Local Finance in Germany and England* by Mabel Newcomer." *Economic Journal* 48, no. 190: 287–89.

———. 1938c. "Reviewed Works: *Miti e Paradossi Della Guitstizia Tributaria* by L. Einaudi; *Personal Income Taxation* by Henry C. Simons." *Economic Journal* 48, no. 192: 719–21.

———. 1945. "Reviewed Work: *The Shifting and Incidence of Taxation* by Otto von Mering." *Economica* 12, no. 45: 41.

———. 1946a. "National and Local Finance." *Economic Journal* 56, no. 224: 609–22.

———. 1946b. "The Terminology of Tax Incidence." *Economic Journal* 56, no. 221: 38–50.

———. 1947a. *Public Finance.* Nisbet & Co.

———. 1947b. "Reviewed Work: *Post-War Taxation and Economic Progress* by H. M. Groves." *Economic Journal* 57, no. 226: 202–5.

———. 1949. "Reviewed Work: *Theorie und Praxis der Modernen Einkommenbesteuerung* by F. Neumark." *Economic Journal* 59, no. 235: 430–32.

———. 1954. *British Public Finances: Their Structure and Development, 1880–1952.* Oxford University Press.

———. 1955. "Reviewed Work: *Principles of Public Finance* by Hugh Dalton." *Economica* 22, no. 88: 360–61.

———. 1959–60. "Musgrave's 'Public Finance.'" *FinanzArchiv* 20, no. 3: 464–67.

———. 1961. "On Teaching Public Finance." *Oxford Economic Papers* 13, no. 2: 123–31.

———. 1965. "Reviewed Work: *Fiscal Theory and Political Economy* by J. M. Buchanan." *Economic Journal* 75, no. 297: 148–49.

———. 1972. "Problems of Public Choice." *FinanzArchiv/Public Finance Analysis* 31, no. 2: 363–66.

Hotelling, Harold. 1938. "The General Welfare in Relation to Problems of Taxation and of Railway and Utility Rates." *Econometrica* 6, no. 3: 242–69.

Jacobson, Joyce. 2000. "Ursula Hicks." In *A Biographical Dictionary of Women Economists,* edited by R. Dimand, M. Dimand, and E. Forget, 211–15. Edward Elgar.

Klein, Lawrence R., and Herman Rubin. 1947. "A Constant-Utility Index of the Cost of Living." *Review of Economic Studies* 15, no. 2: 84–87.

Leland, Simeon. 1940. "Reviewed Work: *The Finance of British Government, 1920–1936* by Ursula K. Hicks." *Journal of Political Economy* 48, no. 2: 265–71.

Lipsey, Richard. 2020. "Who's Who and What's What at the LSE, Then and Now?" *History of Political Economy* 52, no. 5: 947–61.

Madden, Kirsten, and Robert Dimand, eds. 2019. *Routledge Handbook of the History of Women's Economic Thought.* Routledge.

Marcuzzo, Maria Cristina, and Eleonora Sanfilippo. 2008. "Dear John, Dear Ursula (Cambridge and LSE, 1935): Eighty-Eight Letters Unearthed." In *Markets, Money and Capital: Hicksian Economics for the Twenty-First Century.* Edited by Roberto Scazzieri, Amartya Sen, and Stefano Zamagni, 72–91. Cambridge University Press.

May, Ann Mari. 2022. *Gender and the Dismal Science.* Columbia University Press.

May, Ann Mari, Mary G. McGarvey, Yana van der Meulen Rodgers, and Mark Killingsworth. 2021. "Critiques, Ethics, Prestige, and Status: A Survey of Editors." *Eastern Economic Journal* 47, no. 2: 295–318.

Medema, Steven G. 2022. "It's Fundamental: Welfare Theorems, Market Failures, and the Turn from 'Public Finance' to 'Public Economics.'" CHOPE Working Paper No. 2022-09.

Mizon, G. E., and K. W. S. Roberts. 1986. "Editorial." *Review of Economic Studies* 53, no. 2: 171–72.

Moggridge, D. E. 2008. *Harry Johnson: A Life in Economics.* Cambridge University Press.

Musgrave, Richard A. 1959. *The Theory of Public Finance.* McGraw Hill.

Pigou, A. C. 1941. "Reviewed Work: *The Taxation of War Wealth* by J. R. Hicks, Ursula K. Hicks, and L. Rostas." *Economic Journal* 51, nos. 202–3: 297–99.

Prest, Alan R. 1960. *Public Finance in Theory and Practice.* Quadrangle Books.

Ruggles, Nancy. 1949. "The Welfare Basis of the Marginal Cost Pricing Principle." *Review of Economic Studies* 17, no. 1: 29–46.

———. 1949–50. "Recent Developments in the Theory of Marginal Cost Pricing." *Review of Economic Studies* 17, no. 2: 107–26.

Szenberg, Michael, and Lall Ramrattan. 2014. *Secrets of Economics Editors.* MIT Press.

Thomas, Jim. 2020. "Ursula Kathleen Hicks: The First Woman Editor of a Major Economics Journal." *LSE Blogs,* December 3. At https://blogs.lse.ac.uk/lsehistory/2020/12/03/ursula-kathleen-hicks-the-first-woman-editor-of-a-major-economic-journal.

Webb, Ursula K. 1934. "Taxation and Production: The Wicksell Analysis." *Review of Economic Studies* 2, no. 1: 18–30.

Chapter 8: W. H. Hutt by Art Carden and Ilia Murtazashvili

Baird, Charles W. 1988. "The Varieties of 'Right to Work.' An Essay in Honor of W. H. Hutt." *Managerial and Decision Economics* 9 (Special Issue): 33–43.

Buchanan, James M. 1988. "Economists and the Gains from Trade." *Managerial and Decision Economics* 9, no. 5: 5–12.

Cox, Gary W., Douglass C. North, and Barry R. Weingast. 2019. "The Violence Trap: A Political-Economic Approach to the Problems of Development." *Journal of Public Finance and Public Choice* 34, no. 1: 3–19.

Coyne, Christopher J. 2006. "Reconstructing Weak and Failed States: Foreign Intervention and the Nirvana Fallacy." *Foreign Policy Analysis* 2, no. 4: 343–60.

———. 2008a. *After War: The Political Economy of Exporting Democracy*. Stanford University Press.

———. 2008b. "The Politics of Bureaucracy and the Failure of Post-War Reconstruction." *Public Choice* 135, no. 1–2: 11–22.

———. 2013. *Doing Bad by Doing Good: Why Humanitarian Action Fails*. Stanford University Press.

Davenport, John. 1974. "A Heretical View of Labor Unions." *Fortune*. February.

Egger, John B. 1994. "The Contributions of W. H. Hutt." *Review of Austrian Economics* 7, no. 1: 107–38.

Gilcreast, Diane. 1989. "Lectureship Honors Economist W. H. Hutt." *University News*. October 25.

Hazlett, Thomas W. 1986. "Razing Keynes: An Economist for the Long Run." In *W. H. Hutt: An Economist for the Long Run*. Edited by Morgan O. Reynolds, 11–16. Gateway Editions.

Hutt, W. H. "Autobiography." Typescript, Undated. Hoover Institution.

———. 1926. "The Factory System of the Early 19th Century." *Economica*, no. 16 (March): 78–93.

———. 1927. "To Edwin Cannan," December 28. Reference 1029, 152–56. Edwin Cannan Papers, London School of Economics Archives.

———.1930. *The Theory of Collective Bargaining: A History, Analysis and Criticism of the Principal Theories Which Have Sought to Explain the Effects of Trade Unions and Employers' Associations upon the Distribution of the Product of Industry*. The Free Press.

———. 1936. *Economists and the Public: A Study of Competition and Opinion*. Transaction Publishers.

———. 1961. "To Z. K. Matthews," January 20. http://uir.unisa.ac.za/handle/10500/4176/discover.

———. 1964. *The Economics of the Colour Bar*. Institute of Economic Affairs. Republished by the Ludwig von Mises Institute.

———. 1965. "The Complexities of South Africa." In *The African Nettle: Dilemmas of an Emerging Continent*, edited by Frank S. Meyer, 157–74. John Day.

———. 1968. "Misgivings and Casuistry on Strikes." *Modern Age*, Fall.

———. 1971. *Politically Impossible. . . ? An Essay on the Supposed Electoral Obstacles Impeding the Translation of Economic Analysis into Policy or Why Politicians Do Not*

Take Economic Advice. Institute of Economic Affairs. Republished by the Ludwig von Mises Institute.

———. 1973. *The Strike-Threat System: The Economic Consequences of Collective Bargaining*. Arlington House.

———. 1982. "Every Man a Capitalist." *Policy Review*, no. 22: 141.

———. 1986. "The 'Power' of Labour Unions." In *The Unfinished Agenda: Essays on the Political Economy of Government Policy in Honour of Arthur Seldon*. Edited by Martin J. Anderson, 39–64. Institute of Economic Affairs.

———. 1990. "Trade Unions: The Private Use of Coercive Power." *Review of Austrian Economics* 3, no. 1: 109–20.

Keynes, John Maynard. 1936. *The General Theory of Employment, Interest, and Money*. Harvest/Harcourt.

Lewis, C. S. 2014. "On Reading Old Books." In *God in the Dock: Essays on Theology and Ethics*. Kindle., 200–207. HarperOne.

Lewis, Russell. 1986. "Summary of the Economics of the Colour Bar by W. H. Hutt." In *Apartheid-Capitalism or Socialism?*, 1–20. Institute of Economic Affairs.

Magness, Phillip W., Art Carden, and Ilia Murtazashvili. 2022. "'The Danger of Deplorable Reactions:' W. H. Hutt on Liberalism, Populism, and the Constitutional Political Economy of Racism." *The Independent Review* 26, no. 4: 533–52.

North, Douglass C., John Joseph Wallis, and Barry R. Weingast. 2009. *Violence and Social Orders: A Conceptual Framework for Interpreting Recorded Human History*. Cambridge University Press.

Otteson, James R. 2019. *Honorable Business: A Framework for Business in a Just and Humane Society*. Oxford University Press.

Reynolds, Morgan O. 1986. "An Interview with W. H. Hutt." In *W. H. Hutt: An Economist for the Long Run*. Edited by Morgan O. Reynolds, 17–48. Gateway Editions.

Roback, Jennifer. 1988. "W. H. Hutt's the Economics of the Colour Bar." *Managerial and Decision Economics* 9, no. 5: 65–70.

———. 1989. "Racism as Rent Seeking." *Economic Inquiry* 27, no. 4: 661–81.

Smith, Adam. 1869. *Theory of Moral Sentiments and Essays on Philosophical Subjects*. Alex Murray & Son. https://oll.libertyfund.org/titles/theory-of-moral-sentiments-and-essays-on-philosophical-subjects.

The Times. 1988. "Prof W. H. Hutt; Obituary," June 25 edition. Accessed July 6, 2023. link.gale.com/apps/doc/A117384005/AONE?u=naal_sam&sid=ebsco&xid=2a22643c.

Chapter 9: Friedrich A. Lutz by Lachezar Grudev

American Economic Association. 1951. *Readings in Monetary Theory: Selected by a Committee of the American Economic Association* (Chairs of the Selection Committee for this volume: Friedrich A. Lutz and Lloyd W. Mints). Richard D. Irwin.

Blaug, Mark. [1962] 2003. *Economic Theory in Retrospect.* Cambridge University Press.

Brintzinger, Klaus-Rainer. 1996. *Die Nationalökonomie an den Universitäten Freiburg, Heidelberg und Tübingen, 1918–1945.* Peter Lang.

Caldwell, Bruce. 2011. "The Chicago School, Hayek, and Neoliberalism." In *Building Chicago Economics: New Perspectives on the History of America's Most Powerful Economics Program.* Edited by Robert Van Horn, Philip Mirowski, and Thomas A. Stapleford, 301–14. Cambridge University Press.

Caldwell, Bruce, and Hansjörg Klausinger. 2022. *Hayek: A Life 1899–1950.* University of Chicago Press.

Connell, Carol M. 2013. *Reforming the World Monetary System: Fritz Machlup and the Bellagio Group.* Pickering & Chatto.

Dal-Pont Legrand, Muriel, and Harald Hagemann. 2013. "Lutz and Equilibrium Theories of the Business Cycle." *Œconomia* 3, no. 2: 241–62.

Ellis, Howard S. [1934] 1937. *German Monetary Theory 1905–1933.* Harvard University Press.

Goldschmidt, Nils. 2013. "Walter Eucken's Place in the History of Ideas." *Review of Austrian Economics* 26, no. 2: 127–47.

Grudev, Lachezar. 2019. "Friedrich A. Lutz' Epistemological and Methodological Messages During the German-Language Business Cycle Debate." *Journal of Contextual Economics—Schmollers Jahrbuch* 139, no. 1: 1–27.

———. 2021. "Emigration with a Pulled Handbrake: Friedrich A. Lutz's Internal Methodenstreit." Center for the History of Political Economy at Duke University Working Paper Series. At https://ssrn.com/abstract=3858831.

Hagemann, Harald. 2008. "Zur Einführung: Friedrich A. Lutz (1901–1975)." In *Grundtexte zur Freiburger Tradition der Ordnungsökonomik.* Edited by Nils Goldschmidt and Michael Wohlgemuth, 273–78. Mohr Siebeck.

Hartwell, Ronald M. 1995. *A History of the Mont Pelerin Society.* Liberty Fund.

Hayek, Friedrich A. 1983. "Interview by Armen A. Alchian. 'Tape: Alchian I, Side One: Tape Date: November 11, 1978.'" In *Nobel Prize–Winning Economist: Friedrich A. von Hayek,* 362–88. Completed under the auspices of the Oral History Program, University of California, Los Angeles. Regents of the University of California. At https://archive.org/details/nobelprizewinninoohaye/mode/2up.

———. [1963] 1995. "The Economics of the 1930s as Seen from London." In *Contra Keynes and Cambridge: The Collected Works of F. A. Hayek*. Vol. 9. Edited by Bruce Caldwell, 49–73. University of Chicago Press.

Hicks, John R. 1939. *Value and Capital: An Inquiry into Some Fundamental Principles of Economic Theory*. Clarendon Press.

Howson, Susan. 2011. *Lionel Robbins*. Cambridge University Press.

Janssen, Hauke. [1998] 2012. *Nationalökonomie und Nationalsozialismus: Die deutsche Volkswirtschaftslehre in den dreißiger Jahren des 20. Jahrhunderts*. Metropolis.

Klinckowstroem, Wendula Gräfin von. 2023. *Walter Eucken: Ein Leben für Menschenwürde und Wettbewerb*. Mohr Siebeck.

Kolev, Stefan, and Ekkehard A. Köhler. 2022. "Transatlantic Roads to Mont Pèlerin: 'Old Chicago' and Freiburg in a World of Disintegrating Orders." *History of Political Economy* 54, no. 4: 745–84.

Lange, Oskar. 1939. "Saving and Investment: Saving in Process Analysis." *Quarterly Journal of Economics* 53, no. 4: 620–22.

Lenel, Hans O. 1976. "Zum Gedenken an Friedrich A. Lutz." *ORDO—Jahrbuch für die Ordnung von Wirtschaft und Gesellschaft* 27, no. 1: 3–5.

Lerner, Abba. 1939. "Saving and Investment: Definitions, Assumptions, Objectives." *Quarterly Journal of Economics* 53, no. 4: 611–19.

Lutz, Friedrich A. 1927. *Der Kampf um den Kapitalbegriff in der neuesten Zeit: Inaugural-Dissertation an der Eberhards-Karls-Universität Tübingen* (The Recent Battle over the Notion of Capital). Eugen Göbel.

———. 1932. *Das Konjunkturproblem in der Nationalökonomie* (The Business Cycle Problem in Economics). Gustav Fischer.

———. 1938. "The Outcome of the Saving-Investment Discussion." *Quarterly Journal of Economics* 52, no. 4: 588–614.

———. 1940: "The Structure of Interest Rates." *Quarterly Journal of Economics* 55, no. 1: 36–63.

———. 1943. *International Monetary Mechanism: The Keynes and White Proposals*. International Finance Section, Department of Economics and Social Institutions, Princeton University.

———. 1945a. "The Criterion of Maximum Profits in the Theory of Investment." *Quarterly Journal of Economics* 60, no. 1: 56–77.

———. 1945b. "The Interest Rate and Investment in a Dynamic Economy." *American Economic Review* 35, no. 5: 811–30.

———. 1954. "The Case for Flexible Exchange Rates." *Banca Nazionale del Lavoro Quarterly Review* 7, no. 31: 175–83.

———. [1936] 1962. "Das Grundproblem der Geldverfassung (The Fundamental Problem of the Monetary Constitution)." In *Geld und Währung: Gesammelte Abhandlungen*. Edited by Karl Friedrich Maier, 28–102. J. C. B. Mohr (Paul Siebeck).

———. 1956. *Zinstheorie*. Tübingen: J. C. B. Mohr (Paul Siebeck). English translation. 1967. *The Theory of Interest*. D. Reidel.

———. 1961. "The Essentials of Capital Theory." In *The Theory of Capital: Proceedings of a Conference Held by the International Economic Association*. Edited by Friedrich A. Lutz and Douglas C. Hague, 3–17. Macmillan.

———. 1966. *The Problem of International Liquidity and the Multiple-Currency Standard*. International Finance Section, Department of Economics and Social Institutions, Princeton University.

———. 1971. *Politische Überzeugungen und nationalökonomische Theorie: Zürcher Vorträge* (Political Beliefs and National Economic Theories). Edited by Alfred Bosch and Reinhold Veit. J. C. B. Mohr (Paul Siebeck).

Lutz, Friedrich A., and Douglas C. Hague, eds. 1961. *The Theory of Capital: Proceedings of a Conference Held by the International Economic Association*. Macmillan.

Lutz, Friedrich A., and Vera Lutz. 1951. *The Theory of Investment of the Firm*. Princeton University Press.

Mehrling, Perry. 2001. "An Interview with Paul A. Volcker." *Macroeconomic Dynamics* 5, no. 3: 434–60.

Richter, Rudolf. 1998. "Die Geldpolitik im Spiegel der wissenschaftlichen Diskussion." In *Fünfzig Jahre Deutsche Mark: Notenbank und Währung in Deutschland seit 1948*. Edited by Deutsche Bundesbank, 561–608. C. H. Beck.

Ritzmann, Franz. 1976. "Professor Dr. Friedrich A. Lutz." In *Rektoratsrede und Jahresbericht 1975/76*, 79–81. University of Zurich.

Rühl, Christof. 1994. "The Transformation of the Business Cycle Theory: Hayek, Lucas and a Change in the Notion of Equilibrium." In *Money and Business Cycles: The Economics of F. A. Hayek*. Vol. 1. Edited by Marina Colonna and Harald Hagemann, 168–202. Edward Elgar.

Schmelzer, Matthias. 2010. *Freiheit für Wechselkurse und Kapital: Die Ursprünge neoliberaler Währungspolitik und die Mont Pèlerin Society*. Metropolis.

Silber, William. 2013. *Volcker: The Triumph of Persistence*. Bloomsbury Press.

Syga-Dubois, Judith. 2019. *Wissenschaftliche Philanthropie und transatlantischer Austausch in der Zwischenkriegszeit: Die sozialwissenschaftlichen Förderprogramme der Rockefeller-Stiftungen in Deutschland*. Böhlau.

Toniolo, Gianni. 2005. *Central Bank Cooperation at the Bank for International Settlements, 1930–1973*. Cambridge University Press.

Veit-Bachmann, Verena. 2003. "Friedrich A. Lutz: Leben und Werk." In *Währungsordnung und Inflation: Zum Gedenken an Friedrich A. Lutz (1901–1975)*. Edited by Viktor J. Vanberg, 9–43. Mohr Siebeck.

Volcker, Paul A., and Christine Harper. 2018. *Keeping At It: The Quest for Sound Money and Good Government*. Public Affairs.

Zelmanovitz, Leonidas. 2019. "Vera Smith: The Contrarian View." *Library of Economics and Liberty*. At https://www.econlib.org/library/Columns/y2019/Zelmanovitz-SmithV.html.

Chapter 10: Eric Hoffer by Alberto Mingardi

Alberti, Leon Battista. [1433–34] 1969. *The Family in Renaissance Florence*. University of South Carolina Press.

Arendt, Hannah. [1951] 1973. *The Origins of Totalitarianism*. Harcourt Brace & Company.

Bethell, Tom. 2017. *Eric Hoffer: The Longshoreman Philosopher*. Hoover Institution Press.

Cole, Peter. 2014. "The Right's Working-Class Philosopher." *Jacobin*. February 2, https://jacobin.com/2014/09/the-rights-working-class-philosopher.

Haidt, Jonathan. 2012. *The Righteous Mind: Why Good People Are Divided by Politics and Religion*. Vintage Books.

Hayek, Friedrich August von. [1973] 2021. *Law, Legislation and Liberty: A New Statement of the Liberal Principles of Justice and Political Economy. Vol. I. Rules and Order*. Edited by Jeremy Shearmur. University of Chicago Press.

Hoffer, Eric. [1951] 1966. *The True Believer*. Perennial Library, Harper & Row.

———. [1955] 2006. *The Passionate State of Mind and Other Aphorisms*. Hopewell Publications.

———. [1963] 2006. *The Ordeal of Change*. Hopewell Publications.

———. [1973] 2006. *Reflections on the Human Condition*. Hopewell Publications.

———. [1967] 2008. *The Temper of Our Time*. Hopewell Publications.

———. [1969] 2009. *Working and Thinking on the Waterfront*. Hopewell Publications.

———. [1979] 2009. *Before the Sabbath*. Hopewell Publications.

Kahan, Alan. 2023. *Freedom from Fear: An Incomplete History of Liberalism*. Princeton University Press.

Koerner, James D. 1973. *Hoffer's America*. Library Press.

Lederer, Emil. 1940. *The Threat of the Classless Society*. Norton.

Mannheim, Karl. [1935] 1960. *Man and Society in an Age of Reconstruction: Studies in Modern Social Structure*. Routledge & Kegan.

McCloskey, Deirdre N. 2016. *Bourgeois Equality: How Ideas, Not Capital or Institutions, Enriched the World*. University of Chicago Press.

Mises, Ludwig von. 1944. *Omnipotent Government: The Rise of the Total State and Total War*. Yale University Press.

Ortega y Gasset, José. [1929] 1994. *The Revolt of the Masses*. W. W. Norton.

Phelps, Edmund. 2013. *Mass Flourishing: How Grassroots Innovation Created Jobs, Challenge, and Change*. Princeton University Press.

Rausch, Anthony. 2023. "Longshoreman Philosopher: Where Is Eric Hoffer Now?" *Qeios*. doi:10.32388/6MD7H1.

Rauschning, Hermann. 1940. *Hitler Speaks*. G. P. Putnam's Sons.

Shachtman, Tom. 2011. *American Iconoclast: The Life and Times of Eric Hoffer*. Hopewell Publications.

Shils, Edward. 1960. "Mass Society and Its Culture." *Daedalus* 89, no. 2: 288–314.

Shklar, Judith. [1983] 1998. "Hannah Arendt as a Pariah." Now in idem, *Political Thought & Political Thinkers*. University of Chicago Press, 1998, 361–375.

Stoppard, Tom. [1982] 1983. *The Real Thing*. Faber & Faber.

Thompson, Mark E. 1979. "Eric Hoffer and the Significance of Reading." *Reading Horizons: A Journal of Literacy and Language Arts* 20, no. 1: 69–71.

Tomkins, Calvin. 1970. *Eric Hoffer: An American Odyssey*. Dutton.

Walter, E. V. 1964. "'Mass Society': The Late Stages of an Idea." *Social Research* 31, no. 4: 391–410.

Will, George. 1978. "A Young 75 Years Old." *Washington Post*. January 15.

Chapter 11: Kenneth Boulding by Yahya Alshamy and Christopher J. Coyne

Boettke, Peter J. 1997. "Where Did Economics Go Wrong? Modern Economics as a Flight from Reality." *Critical Review* 11, no. 1: 11–64.

———. 2012. *Living Economics: Yesterday, Today, and Tomorrow*. Independent Institute.

Boettke, Peter J., Stefanie Haeffele-Balch, and Virgil Henry Storr. 2016. *Mainline Economics: Six Nobel Lectures in the Tradition of Adam Smith*. Mercatus Center at George Mason University.

Boettke, Peter J., and David L. Prychitko. 1996. "Mr. Boulding and the Austrians: Boulding's Contribution to Subjectivist Economics." In *Joseph A. Schumpeter: Historian of Economics*. Edited by Laurence S. Moss, 250–59. Routledge.

Boulding, Kenneth. 1932. "The Place of the 'Displacement Cost' Concept in Economic Theory." *Economic Journal* 42, no. 165: 137–41.

———. 1956. *The Image: Knowledge in Life and Society*. Ann Arbor Paperbacks.

———. 1962. *Conflict and Defense: A General Theory*. Harper & Brothers.

———. 1968. *Beyond Economics: Essays on Society, Religion, and Ethics*. University of Michigan Press.

———. 1971. "Introduction to the Collected Papers of Kenneth E. Boulding: Volume 1." In *Kenneth E. Boulding: Collected Papers,* vol. 1, edited by Fred Glahe, vii–xi. Colorado Associated University Press.

———. 1977. "The Power of Nonconflict." *Journal of Social Issues* 33, no. 1: 22–33.

———. 1978. *Stable Peace.* University of Texas Press.

———. 1988. "Moving from Unstable to Stable Peace." In *Breakthrough: Emerging New Thinking—Soviet and Western Scholars Issue a Challenge to Build a World Beyond War.* Edited by Anatoly Gromyko and Martin Hellman, 157–67. Walker & Company.

———. 1989. *Three Faces of Power.* Sage.

Hayek, Friedrich A. 1943. "The Facts of the Social Science." *Ethics* 54, no. 1: 1–13.

Heilbroner, Robert L. 1975. "Kenneth Boulding, *Collected Papers:* A Review Article." *Journal of Economic Issues* 9, no. 1: 73–79.

Kerman, Cynthia. 1974. *Creative Tension: The Life and Thought of Kenneth Boulding.* University of Michigan Press.

Kirzner, Israel. 1979. *Perception, Opportunity, and Profit: Studies in the Theory of Entrepreneurship.* University of Chicago Press.

Mott, Tracy. 2000. "Kenneth Boulding, 1910–1993." *Economic Journal* 110, no. 464: F430–44.

Nasar, Sylvia. 1993. "Kenneth Boulding, an Economist, Philosopher and Poet, Dies at 83." *New York Times.* March 20. At https://www.nytimes.com/1993/03/20/obituaries/kenneth-boulding-an-economist-philosopher-and-poet-dies-at-83.html.

Schelling, Thomas C. 1966. *Arms and Influence.* Yale University Press.

Scott, Robert. 2015. *Kenneth Boulding: A Voice Crying in the Wilderness.* Palgrave Macmillan.

Szenberg, Michael. 1993. "Kenneth E. Boulding: 1910–1993: In Memoriam." *American Economist* 37, no. 2: 3–4.

Chapter 12: Bruno Leoni by Michael C. Munger

Aranson, Peter H. 1988. "Bruno Leoni in Retrospect." *Harvard Journal of Law and Public Policy* 11, no. 3: 661–712.

Bassani, Luigi Marco, and Carlo Lottieri. 2021. "The Rise of the Sovereign State." Mises Wire. https://mises.org/mises-wire/rise-sovereign-state.

Boettke, Peter, and Rosolino Candela. 2014. "Hayek, Leoni, and Law as the Fifth Factor of Production." *Atlantic Economic Journal* 42, no. 2: 123–31

Buchanan, James, and Gordon Tullock. 1962. *The Calculus of Consent: Logical Foundations of Constitutional Democracy.* University of Michigan Press.

Empoli, D. da. 1993. "Public Choice in Italy." *Public Choice* 77, no. 1: 75–83.

Ferlito, Carmelo. 2013. "Bruno Leoni and the Socialist Economic Calculation Debate." In *Procesos de Mercado: Revista Europea de Economía Política* 10, no. 1: 37–64.

Hartwell, Max. 1995. *History of the Mont Pelerin Society*. Liberty Fund.

Hasnas, John. 2024. *Common Law Liberalism: A New Theory of the Libertarian Society*. Oxford University Press.

Hayek, F. A. 1960. *The Constitution of Liberty*. University of Chicago Press.

———. 1973. *Law, Legislation, and Liberty*. University of Chicago Press.

———. 2014. *The Market and Other Orders*. In *Collected Works of F. A. Hayek*. Edited by Bruce Caldwell, Vol. 15. University of Chicago Press.

In Mia Memoria. 1997. "Il Luogo dei Ricordi di Osvaldo Quero." https://web.archive.org/web/20161202170032/http://www.inmiamemoria.com/scatole_dei_ricordi/Quero/Osvaldo/Quero_Osvaldo___1110500.php.

La Stampa. 1967. "Professore dell'Università ucciso e sfigurato da un tipografo: il corpo nascosto in un garage." http://www.archiviolastampa.it/component/option,com_lastampa/task,search/mod,libera/Itemid,3/action,viewer/page,2/articleid,0117_01_1967_0277_0002_5047724.

———. 1970. "Condannate in appello a 24 anni Quero, l'uccisore del prof. Leoni." http://www.archiviolastampa.it/component/option,com_lastampa/task,search/mod,avanzata/action,viewer/Itemid,3/page,5/articleid,0131_01_1970_0120_0005_4813499.

Leoni, Bruno. 1961. *Freedom and the Law*. Van Nostrand/Princeton (commissioned by William Volker Fund). Reprinted in Expanded 3rd Edition (1991). Liberty Fund.

———. 1963. "Oggetto e limiti della scienza politica." *Il Politico* 28: 741–55.

Masala, Antonio. 2014. "Bruno Leoni and the Austrian Tradition." From the session on "Libertarianism: Intellectual History and Applications." Presented at the Austrian Economics Research Conference. Originally recorded March 23, 2013, at the Ludwig von Mises Institute in Auburn, Alabama. https://mises.org/podcasts/aerc-2013/bruno-leoni-and-austrian-tradition.

———. 2022. "Leoni, Hayek, and 'Il Politico.'" *Il Politico* 87, no. 2: 5–22.

Mingardi, Alberto. 2018a. "Bruno Leoni and the Search for Certainty in Law." Law and Liberty, November 7. https://lawliberty.org/classic/bruno-leoni-and-the-search-for-certainty-in-law.

———. 2018b. "Meet the Italian Scholar Who Influenced Hayek and Became a Founding Father of the Libertarian Movement." Foundation for Economic Education. https://fee.org/articles/meet-the-italian-scholar-who-influenced-hayek-and-became-a-founding-father-of-the-libertarian-movement.

Mises, Ludwig von. 1949. *Human Action: A Treatise on Economics*. Yale University Press.

North, Douglass C. 1990. *Institutions, Institutional Change, and Economic Development.* Cambridge University Press.

Posner, Richard A. 1980. "The Ethical and Political Basis of the Efficiency Norm in Common Law Adjudication." *Hofstra Law Review* 8: 487–507.

Priest, George L. 1977. "The Common Law Process and the Selection of Efficient Rules." *Journal of Legal Studies* 6, no. 1: 65–82.

Rothbard, Murray N. 1961. "Review of *Freedom and the Law.*" *New Individualist Review* 1, no. 1: 187–91.

Zywicki, Todd. 2003. "The Rise and Fall of Efficiency in the Common Law: A Supply-Side Analysis." *Northwestern Law Review* 97, no. 4: 1551–96.

———. 2015. "Bruno Leoni's Legacy and Continued Relevance," *Journal of Private Enterprise* 30, no. 1: 131–41.

Chapter 13: Edith Penrose by Richard N. Langlois

Alchian, Armen A. 1950. "Uncertainty, Evolution, and Economic Theory." *Journal of Political Economy* 58, no. 3: 211–21.

Bain, Joe S. 1959. *Industrial Organization.* John Wiley & Sons.

Barney, Jay. 1991. "Firm Resources and Sustained Competitive Advantage." *Journal of Management* 17, no. 1: 99–120.

Baumol, William J. 1962. "On the Theory of Expansion of the Firm." *American Economic Review* 52, no. 5: 1078–87.

Caves, Richard E. 1964. *American Industry: Structure, Conduct, Performance.* Prentice–Hall.

Chandler, Alfred D., Jr. 1959. "The Beginnings of 'Big Business' in American Industry." *Business History Review* 33, no. 1: 1–31.

———. 1962. *Strategy and Structure: Chapters in the History of the Industrial Enterprise.* MIT Press.

———. 1977. *The Visible Hand: The Managerial Revolution in American Business.* Belknap Press.

Coase, Ronald H. 1937. "The Nature of the Firm." *Economica*, 4, no. 16: 386–405.

———. 1972. "Industrial Organization: A Proposal for Research." In Victor R. Fuchs, ed., *Economic Research: Retrospect and Prospect, Volume 3, Policy Issues and Research Opportunities in Industrial Organization.* Columbia University Press for the National Bureau of Economic Research, 59–73.

Cyert, Richard M. and James G. March. 1963. *A Behavioral Theory of the Firm.* Prentice–Hall.

Foss, Nicolai J. 2002. "Edith Penrose: Economics and Stategic Management." In Christos Pitelis, ed., *The Growth of the Firm: The Legacy of Edith Penrose.* Oxford University Press, 147–64.

Friedman, Milton. 1953. "The Methodology of Positive Economics." In *Essays in Positive Economics.* University of Chicago Press, 3–43.

Kay, John. 2024. "The Story of Flight." *International Review of Applied Economics* 38, no. 1–2: 90–103.

Langlois, Richard N. 1986. "Rationality, Institutions, and Explanation." In Richard N. Langlois, ed., *Economics as a Process: Essays in the New Institutional Economics.* Cambridge University Press, 225–55.

———. 2023. *The Corporation and the Twentieth Century: The History of American Business Enterprise.* Princeton University Press.

Langlois, Richard N., and Roger G. Koppl. 1991. "Fritz Machlup and Marginalism: A Reevaluation." *Methodus* 3, no. 2 (December): 86–102.

Levallois, Clement. 2011. "Why Were Biological Analogies in Economics 'a Bad Thing'? Edith Penrose's Battles Against Social Darwinism and McCarthyism." *Science in Context* 24, no. 4: 465–85.

Levitt, Steven D., John A. List, and Chad Syverson. 2013. "Toward an Understanding of Learning by Doing: Evidence from an Automobile Assembly Plant." *Journal of Political Economy* 121, no. 4: 643–81.

Loasby, Brian J. 2002. "The Significance of Penrose's Theory for the Development of Economics." In Christos Pitelis, ed., *The Growth of the Firm: The Legacy of Edith Penrose.* Oxford University Press, 45–59.

Machlup, Fritz. 1963. *Essays on Economic Semantics.* Prentice–Hall.

———. 1967. "Theories of the Firm: Marginalist, Behavioral, Managerial." *American Economic Review* 57, no. 1: 1–33.

Mahoney, Joseph T., and Jackson Nickerson. 2022. "Oliver Williamson: A Hero's Journey on the Merits." *Journal of Institutional Economics* 18, no. 2: 195–207.

March, James G., and Herbert A. Simon. 1958. *Organizations.* John Wiley and Sons.

Marris, Robin. 1966. *The Economic Theory of "Managerial" Capitalism.* Macmillan.

McKenna, Christopher D. 2006. "Writing the Ghost-Writer Back In: Alfred Sloan, Alfred Chandler, John McDonald and the Intellectual Origins of Corporate Strategy." *Management & Organizational History* 1, no. 2 (May): 107–26.

Milgrom, Paul R., and John Roberts. 1992. *Economics, Organization and Management.* Prentice–Hall.

Mises, Margit von. 1976. *My Years with Ludwig von Mises.* Arlington House.

Nelson, Richard R., and Sidney G. Winter. 1982. *An Evolutionary Theory of Economic Change.* Harvard University Press.

———. 2002. "Evolutionary Theorizing in Economics." *Journal of Economic Perspectives* 16, no. 2: 23–46 (Spring).

Penrose, Angela. 2017. *No Ordinary Woman: The Life of Edith Penrose.* Oxford University Press.

Penrose, Edith T. 1951. *The Economics of the International Patent System.* Johns Hopkins University Press.

———. 1952. "Biological Analogies in the Theory of the Firm." *American Economic Review* 42, no. 5: 804–19.

———. 1959. *The Theory of the Growth of the Firm.* Basil Blackwell. First edition.

———. 1960. "The Growth of the Firm — a Case Study: The Hercules Powder Company." *Business History Review* 34, no. 1: 1–23.

———. 1995. *The Theory of the Growth of the Firm.* Oxford University Press. Third edition.

———. 2009. *The Theory of the Growth of the Firm.* Oxford University Press. Fourth edition.

Penrose, Perran, and Christos Pitelis. 2002. "Edith Elura Tilton Penrose: Life, Contributions and Influence." In Christos Pitelis, ed., *The Growth of the Firm: The Legacy of Edith Penrose.* Oxford University Press, 17–36.

Porter, Michael E. 1980. *Competitive Strategy.* The Free Press.

Richardson, G. B. 1960. *Information and Investment: A Study in the Working of the Competitive Economy.* Oxford University Press.

———. 1972. "The Organisation of Industry." *Economic Journal* 82, no. 327: 883–96.

———. 2002. "Mrs Penrose and Neoclassical Theory." In Christos Pitelis, ed. *The Growth of the Firm: The Legacy of Edith Penrose.* Oxford University Press, 37–44.

Rugman, Alan M., and Alain Verbeke. 2002. "Edith Penrose's Contribution to the Resource-Based View of Strategic Management." *Strategic Management Journal* 23(8): 769–80.

———. 2004. "A Final Word on Edith Penrose." *Journal of Management Studies* 41, no. 1: 205–17.

Simon, Herbert A. 1956. "Rational Choice and the Structure of the Environment." *Psychological Review* 63, no. 2: 129–38.

Sloan, Alfred P. 1964. *My Years with General Motors.* Doubleday.

Teece, David J. 1980. "Economies of Scope and the Scope of the Enterprise." *Journal of Economic Behavior & Organization* 1(3): 223–47 (September).

——— 1982. "Towards an Economic Theory of the Multiproduct Firm." *Journal of Economic Behavior & Organization* 3(1): 39–63 (March).

Teece, David J., Gary Pisano and Amy Shuen. 1997. "Dynamic Capabilities and Strategic Management." *Strategic Management Journal* 18(7): 509–33.

Tirole, Jean. 1988. *Theory of Industrial Organization.* MIT Press.

Uzawa, Hirofumi. 1968. "The Penrose Effect and Optimum Growth." *Economic Studies Quarterly* 19(1): 1–14.

Wernerfelt, Birger. 1984. "A Resource-Based View of the Firm." *Strategic Management Journal* 5(2): 171–80.

Williamson, Oliver E. 1964. *The Economics of Discretionary Behavior: Managerial Objectives in a Theory of the Firm*. Prentice Hall.

———. 1971. "The Vertical Integration of Production: Market Failure Considerations." *American Economic Review* 61(2): 112–23.

———. 1975. *Markets and Hierarchies: Analysis and Antitrust Implications*. The Free Press.

Winter, Sidney G. 1971. "Satisficing, Selection, and the Innovating Remnant." *Quarterly Journal of Economics* 85(2): 237–61.

Young, Allyn A. 1928. "Increasing Returns and Economic Progress." *Economic Journal* 38(152): 527–42 (December).

Chapter 15: Israel M. Kirzner by Rosolino Candela

Aeeni, Zeynab, Mahmoud Motavaseli, Kamal Sakhdari, and Ali Mobini Dehkordi. 2019. "Baumol's Theory of Entrepreneurial Allocation: A Systematic Review and Research Agenda." *European Research on Management and Business Economics* 25, no. 1: 30–37.

Arrow, Kenneth J. 1959. "Toward a Theory of Price Adjustment." In *The Allocation of Economic Resources: Essays in Honor of Bernard Francis Haley,* 41–51. Stanford University Press.

Arrow, Kenneth J., and Gerard Debreu. 1954. "Existence of an Equilibrium for a Competitive Economy." *Econometrica* 22, no. 3: 265–90.

Baumol, William J. 1990. "Entrepreneurship: Productive, Unproductive, and Destructive." *Journal of Political Economy* 98, no. 5: 893–921.

Boettke, Peter J., and Christopher J. Coyne. 2003. "Entrepreneurship and Development: Cause or Consequence?" *Advances in Austrian Economics* 6:67–88.

Candela, Rosolino A., Peter J. Jacobsen, and Kacey Reeves. 2022. "Malcom McLean, Containerization and Entrepreneurship." *Review of Austrian Economics* 35, no. 4: 445–65.

Demsetz, Harold. 1967. "Toward a Theory of Property Rights." *American Economic Review* 57, no. 2: 347–59.

———. 1983a. "The Neglect of the Entrepreneur." In *Entrepreneurship.* Edited by Joshua Ronen, 217–80. Lexington Books.

———. 1983b. "The Structure of Ownership and the Theory of the Firm." *Journal of Law & Economics* 26, no. 2: 375–90.

Douhan, Robin, Gunnar Eliasson, and Magnus Henrekson. 2007. "Israel M. Kirzner: An Outstanding Austrian Contributor to the Economics of Entrepreneurship." *Small Business Economics* 29, nos. 1–2: 213–23.

Hayek, F. A. [1956] 1967. "The Dilemma of Specialization." In *Studies in Philosophy, Politics and Economics,* 122–32. University of Chicago Press.

Henrekson, Magnus, and Tino Sanandaji, eds. 2012. *Institutional Entrepreneurship.* Edward Elgar.

Jones, Eric. [1981] 2003. *The European Miracle: Environments, Economies, and Geopolitics in the History of Europe and Asia.* 3rd ed. Cambridge University Press.

Kirzner, Israel M. 1963. *Market Theory and the Price System.* D. Van Nostrand.

———. 1966. *An Essay on Capital.* Augustus M. Kelley.

———. 1967a. "Divergent Approaches in Libertarian Economic Thought." *Intercollegiate Review* 3, no. 3: 101–8.

———. 1967b. "Methodological Individualism, Market Equilibrium, and Market Process." *Il Politico* 32, no. 4: 787–99.

———. 1971. "Entrepreneurship and the Market Approach to Development." In *Toward Liberty: Essays in Honor of Ludwig von Mises.* Vol. 2. Edited by F. A. Hayek, Henry Hazlitt, Leonard R. Read, Gustavo Velasco, and F. A. Harper, 194–208. Institute for Humane Studies.

———. 1972. "Advertising." *Freeman* 22, no. 9: 515–28.

———. 1973. *Competition and Entrepreneurship.* University of Chicago Press.

———. 1979. *Perception, Opportunity, and Profit: Studies in the Theory of Entrepreneurship.* University of Chicago Press.

———. [1978] 1985. "The Perils of Regulation: A Market Process Approach." In *Discovery and the Capitalist Process,* 119–49. University of Chicago Press.

———. 1988. "Some Ethical Implications for Capitalism of the Socialist Calculation Debate." *Social Philosophy and Policy* 6, no. 1: 165–82.

———. 1992. *The Meaning of Market Process: Essays in the Development of Modern Austrian Economics.* Routledge.

———. 1997. *How Markets Work: Disequilibrium, Entrepreneurship and Discovery.* IEA Hobart Paper no. 133. Institute of Economic Affairs.

———. 2009. "The Alert and Creative Entrepreneur: A Clarification." *Small Business Economics* 32, no. 2: 145–52.

———. [1960] 2009. *The Collected Works of Israel M. Kirzner: The Economic Point of View.* Liberty Fund.

———. [1989] 2016. *The Collected Works of Israel M. Kirzner: Discovery, Capitalism and Distributive Justice.* Liberty Fund.

———. 2019. "The Ethics of Pure Entrepreneurship: An Austrian Perspective." *Review of Austrian Economics* 32, no. 2: 89–99.

Lavoie, Don. 1991. "The Discovery and Interpretation of Profit Opportunities: Culture and the Kirznerian Entrepreneur." In *The Culture of Entrepreneurship*. Edited by Brigette Berger, 33–51. Institute for Contemporary Studies.

Li, David Daokui, Junxin Feng, and Hongping Jiang. 2006. "Institutional Entrepreneurs." *American Economic Review* 96, no. 2: 358–62.

Locke, John. [1690] 1980. *Second Treatise of Government*. Hackett.

Nozick, Robert. 1974. *Anarchy, State, and Utopia*. Basic Books.

Piketty, Thomas. 2014. *Capital in the Twenty-First Century*. Harvard University Press.

Rosenberg, Nathan, and L. E. Birdzell Jr. 1986. *How the West Grew Rich: The Economic Transformation of the Industrial World*. Basic Books.

Rothbard, Murray N. 1987. "Breaking Out of the Walrasian Box: The Cases of Schumpeter and Hansen." *Review of Austrian Economics* 1, no. 1: 97–108.

Schumpeter, Joseph A. [1911] 1934. *The Theory of Economic Development: An Inquiry into Profits, Capital, Credit, Interest, and the Business Cycle*. Harvard University Press.

———. [1942] 1947. *Capitalism, Socialism, and Democracy*. 2nd ed. Harper & Brothers.

Shughart, William F. II. 2014. "Airline Deregulation Act of 1978." *The Beacon*. October 24. At https://blog.independent.org/2014/10/24/airline-deregulation-act-of-1978.

Chapter 16: Thomas Sowell by Art Carden and Brian C. Albrecht

Alesina, Alberto, and Paola Giuliano. 2015. "Culture and Institutions." *Journal of Economic Literature* 53, no. 4: 898–944.

Brennan, Jason, and Christopher Freiman. 2022. "Why Paternalists Must Endorse Epistocracy." *Journal of Ethics and Social Philosophy* 21, no. 3: 329–53.

Carden, Art, Phillip W. Magness, John Meadowcroft, and Ilia Murtazashvili. 2022. "Slavery." Prepared for the *Edward Elgar Encyclopedia of Public Choice*.

Davis, William L., Bob Figgins, David Hedengren, and Daniel B. Klein. 2011. "Economics Professors' Favorite Economic Thinkers, Journals, and Blogs (Along with Party and Policy Views)." *Econ Journal Watch* 8, no. 2: 126.

Guiso, Luigi, Paola Sapienza, and Luigi Zingales. 2006. "Does Culture Affect Economic Outcomes?" *Journal of Economic Perspectives* 20, no. 2: 23–48.

Leonard, Thomas C. 2016. *Illiberal Reformers: Race Eugenics and American Economics*. Princeton University Press.

McCloskey, Deirdre Nansen, and Art Carden. 2020. *Leave Me Alone and I'll Make You Rich: How the Bourgeois Deal Enriched the World*. University of Chicago Press.

Rizzo, Mario, and Glen Whitman. 2019. *Escaping Paternalism*. Cambridge University Press.

Slobodian, Quinn. 2018. *Globalists: The End of Empire and the Birth of Neoliberalism.* Harvard University Press.

Smith, Adam. 1790. *The Theory of Moral Sentiments.* 6th ed. At https://www.adamsmithworks.org/documents/asw-edition. Last accessed May 3, 2023.

Sowell, Thomas. 1981. *Ethnic America: A History.* Basic Books.

———. 1993. *Is Reality Optional? And Other Essays.* Hoover Institution Press.

———. 1994. *Race and Culture: A World View.* Basic Books.

———. 1995. *The Vision of the Anointed: Self-Congratulation as a Basis for Social Policy.* Basic Books.

———. [1980] 1996. *Knowledge and Decisions.* Basic Books.

———. 1997. *Migrations and Cultures: A World View.* Basic Books.

———. 1999. *Conquests and Cultures: An International History.* Basic Books.

———. [1987] 2007. *A Conflict of Visions: Ideological Origins of Political Struggles.* Basic Books.

———. 2009. *Intellectuals and Society.* Basic Books.

———. 2015. *Wealth, Poverty, and Politics.* Basic Books.

Chapter 17: Julian Simon by Robert M. Whaples

Atkinson, Robert D. 2022. "The Abandonment of Growth and the Decline of the West." *The Independent Review* 27, no. 2: 201–26.

Blundell, John. 1998. "Remembering Julian." *Economist.* March 5. At https://www.economist.com/letters/1998/03/05/letters.

Covert, Thomas, Michael Greenstone, and Christopher R. Knittel. 2016. "Will We Ever Stop Using Fossil Fuels?" *Journal of Economic Perspectives* 30, no. 1: 117–38. Quotation from abstract. At https://www.aeaweb.org/articles?id=10.1257/jep.30.1.117.

Ehrlich, Paul. 1968. *The Population Bomb.* Ballantine Books.

Emmett, Ross B., and Jesse Grabowski. 2022. "Better Lucky Than Good: The Simon-Ehrlich Bet Through the Lens of Financial Economics." *Ecological Economics* 193:107322.

Geide-Stevenson, Doris, and Alvaro La Parra Perez. 2021. "Consensus Among Economists 2020: A Sharpening of the Picture." At https://www.researchgate.net/profile/Alvaro-La-Parra-Perez/publication/357526861_Consensus_among_economists_2020_A_sharpening_of_the_picture/links/62a23ce3416ec50bdb1995ea/Consensus-among-economists-2020-A-sharpening-of-the-picture.pdf.

Hammond, J. Daniel. 2020. "Malthus Was Not a Malthusian." *The Independent Review* 24, no. 4: 499–507.

Lindsay, Brink. 2022. "The Anti-Promethean Backlash." At https://brinklindsey.substack.com/p/the-anti-promethean-backlash.

Moore, Stephen, and Julian Simon. 2000. *It's Getting Better All the Time: 100 Greatest Trends of the Last 100 Years.* Cato Institute.

Our World in Data. 2022. "The Global Fertility Rate Has Continued to Decline to 2.3 Births per Woman." At https://ourworldindata.org/world-population-update-2022.

———. n.d. "World Population Living in Extreme Poverty, 1820 to 2015." At https://ourworldindata.org/grapher/world-population-in-extreme-poverty-absolute.

Perry, Mark J. 2010. "Julian Simon: More Right Than Lucky." *Carpe Diem* blog, February 20. At http://mjperry.blogspot.com/2010/02/julian-simon-more-right-than-lucky.html.

Sabin, Paul. 2013. *The Bet: Paul Ehrlich, Julian Simon, and Our Gamble over the Earth's Future.* Yale University Press.

Saint-Exupéry, Antoine de. [1943] 2000. *The Little Prince.* Harcourt.

Simon, Julian L. 1965a. "The Cause of the Newspaper Rate Differential: A Subjective-Demand-Curve Analysis." *Journal of Political Economy* 57, no. 5: 536–39.

———. 1965b. *How to Start and Operate a Mail-Order Business.* McGraw Hill.

———. 1968. "An Almost Practical Solution to Airline Overbooking." *Journal of Transport Economics and Policy* 2, no. 2: 201–2.

———. 1980. "The Pain of Failing a Ph.D. Oral Exam, and an Unfortunate Confusion in Economic Thought." *American Economist* 24, no. 2: 43–46.

———. 1981a. "Environmental Disruption or Environmental Improvement?" *Social Science Quarterly* 62, no. 1: 30–43.

———. 1981b. *The Ultimate Resource.* Princeton University Press.

———. 1989. "Lebensraum: Paradoxically, Population Growth May Eventually End Wars." *Journal of Conflict Resolution* 33, no. 1: 164–80.

———. 1996. *The Ultimate Resource 2.* Princeton University Press.

———. 2000. *The Great Breakthrough and Its Cause.* Edited by Timur Kuran. University of Michigan Press.

———. 2002. *A Life against the Grain: The Autobiography of an Unconventional Economist.* Transaction.

———, ed. 1995. *The State of Humanity.* Blackwell.

Thoreau, Henry David. [1854] 1951. *Walden.* Bramhall House.

Tupy, Marian L., and Gale L. Pooley. 2022. *Superabundance: The Story of Population Growth, Innovation, and Human Flourishing on an Infinitely Bountiful Planet.* Cato Institute.

Whaples, Robert. 2014. "Review of *The Bet: Paul Ehrlich, Julian Simon, and Our Gamble over Earth's Future.*" *The Independent Review* 19, no. 1: 137–40.

———. 2022. "Where Do the Poorest Americans Stand in the Income Distribution Among All People Ever Born?" *The Independent Review* 27, no. 1: 155–59.

Whaples, Robert, Christopher J. Coyne, and Michael C. Munger, eds. 2016. *Future: Economic Peril or Prosperity?* Independent Institute.

World Bank. 2022. *Poverty and Shared Prosperity 2022: Correcting Course.* World Bank.

Zitner, Aaron. 2023. "Poll Shows Shift in What Americans Value." *Wall Street Journal.* March 28, A4.

Chapter 18: Karl Mittermaier by Michael C. Munger

Boettke, Peter J. 1994. "Ludwig Lachmann and His Contributions to Economic Science." *Advances in Austrian Economics* 1:229–32.

Coase, Ronald H., and Richard Epstein. 2002. "The Intellectual Portrait Series: A Conversation with Ronald H. Coase." Liberty Fund. At https://oll.libertyfund.org/page/the-intellectual-portrait-series-a-conversation-with-ronald-h-coase.

Hume, David. 1739. "Of the Origin of Justice and Property." In *A Treatise of Human Nature.* At https://davidhume.org/texts/t/3/2/2.

Klein, Daniel B. 2020. "Karl Mittermaier and the Hands of Classical Liberalism." *Economic Affairs* 40, no. 2: 209–219.

Mises, Ludwig von. 1949. *Human Action: A Treatise on Economics.* Yale University Press.

Mittermaier, Karl H. M. 2018. "Menger's Aristotelianism." *Cambridge Journal of Economics* 42, no. 2: 577–94.

———. [1994] 2019. "The Invisible Hand and Some Thoughts on the Non-Existent in What We Study." Paper presented at the 2nd International Workshop on Methodology of Economics, Cambridge University. Reprinted in *Journal of Contextual Economics* 139, no. 1 (2019): 135–58.

———. 2020. *The Hand Behind the Invisible Hand: Dogmatic and Pragmatic Views on Free Markets and the State of Economic Theory.* Bristol University Press.

Munger, Michael C. 2010. "Endless Forms Most Beautiful and Most Wonderful: Elinor Ostrom and the Diversity of Institutions." *Public Choice* 143, no. 3: 263–68.

———. 2016. "Hayek's Political Insights: Emergent Orders and Laid-on Laws." In *Advances in Austrian Economics: Revisiting Hayek's Political Economy.* Edited by Peter Boettke and Virgil Storr, 145–61. Emerald.

North, Douglass C. 1990. *Institutions, Institutional Change, and Economic Development.* Cambridge University Press.

Rorty, Richard. 1982. *Consequences of Pragmatism.* University of Minnesota Press.

Rothbard, Murray. 1970. *Power and Market: Government and the Economy.* Institute for Humane Studies at George Mason University.

Rothschild, Emma. 1994. "Adam Smith and the Invisible Hand." *American Economic Review* 84, no. 2: 319–22.

Smith, Adam. [1776] 1994. *An Inquiry into the Nature and Causes of the Wealth of Nations*. Modern Library.

Stettler, Michael. 2019. "An Introduction to Karl Mittermaier and His Philosophy of Economics." *Journal of Contextual Economics* 139, no. 1: 123–34.

Truran, Peter. 2013. "Models: Useful but Not True." In *Practical Applications of the Philosophy of Science: Thinking About Research,* 61–67. Springer Briefs in Philosophy. Springer.

Chapter 19: Earl A. Thompson by Joshua R. Hendrickson

Barro, Robert J. 1974. "Are Government Bonds Net Wealth?" *Journal of Political Economy* 82, no. 6: 1095–1117.

Hendrickson, Joshua R. 2020. "The Riksbank, Emergency Finance, Policy Experimentation, and Sweden's Reversal of Fortune." *Journal of Economic Behavior and Organization* 171, 312–32.

Hickson, Charles R., and Earl A. Thompson. 1991. "A New Theory of Guilds and European Economic Development." *Explorations in Economic History* 28, 127–68.

Thompson, Earl A. 1967. "Debt Instruments in Both Macroeconomic Theory and Capital Theory." *American Economic Review* 57, no. 5: 1196–1210.

———. 1972. "The Taxation of Wealth and the Wealthy." *American Economic Review Papers and Proceedings* 62, no. 1–2: 329 –30.

———. 1974a. "Taxation and National Defense." *Journal of Political Economy* 82, no. 4: 755–82.

———. 1974b. "The Theory of Money and Income Consistent with Orthodox Value Theory," in G. Horwich and P. Samuelson, eds. *Trade, Stability, and Macroeconomics: Essays in Honor of Lloyd Metzler*. Academic Press, 427–53.

———. 1977. "A Reformulation of Macroeconomic Theory." UCLA Working Paper, No. 91.

———. 1979. "An Economic Basis for the 'National Defense' Argument for Aiding Certain Industries." *Journal of Political Economy* 87, no. 1: 1–36.

———. 1980. "On Labor's Right to Strike." *Economic Inquiry* 28, 640–53.

———. 1982. "Free Banking Under a Labor Standard." *The Role of Gold in Domestic and International Monetary Systems*, II, Annex B Report to Congress of the US Gold Commission, US G.P.O., March 1982, 502–4.

———. 1995. "The Gold Standard: Causes and Consequences," in David Glasner (ed.) *Encyclopedia of Business Cycles and Depressions*, Garland Publishing, 267–72.

———. 2001. "Alchian as a Teacher and an Economist." *International Society for New Institutional Economics* 3, no. 2: 11–13.

———. 2002. "What Globalization is Really All About." *Business and Economics Society International – Anthology*, 1–5.

———. 2006. "The Tulipmania: Fact or Artifact?" *Public Choice* 130, 99–114.

———. 2007. "From Social Security to Social Insecurity: The Genius of Democratic Politics." *Global Business and Economics Review* 9, no. 1: 1–7.

Thompson, Earl A., and Roger L. Faith. 1981. "A Pure Theory of Strategic Behavior and Social Institutions." *American Economic Review* 71, no. 3: 366–80.

Thompson, Earl A., and Charles R. Hickson. 2001. *Ideology and the Evolution of Vital Institutions: Guilds, the Gold Standard and International Cooperation.* Kluwer Academic Publishers.

———. 2006. "Predicting Bubbles." *Global Business and Economics Review* 8, nos. 3 and 4: 217–46.

Chapter 20: Robert D. Tollison by William F. Shughart II

Amacher, Ryan C., James C. Miller III, Mark Pauly, Robert D. Tollison, and Thomas D. Willet. 1973. *The Economics of the Military Draft.* General Learning Press.

Baumol, William J., and Janusz A. Ordover. 1985. "Use of Antitrust to Subvert Competition." *Journal of Law and Economics* 28, no. 2: 247–65.

Baxter, William F. 1980. "The Political Economy of Antitrust." In Tollison, Robert D. (ed.), *The Political Economy of Antitrust: Principal Paper by William Baxter*, 3–49. Lexington Books.

Bork, Robert H. 1978. *The Antitrust Paradox: A Policy at War with Itself.* Basic Books.

Bradbury, J. C. 2007. *The Baseball Economist: The Real Game Exposed.* Plume/Penguin.

Cowen, Tyler. 2024. *GOAT: Who Is the Greatest Economist of All Time and Why Does it Matter?* https://goatgreatesteconomistofalltime.ai/en.

Crain, Nicole V., and W. Mark Crain. 2010. "Determinants of Publication Productivity: An Empirical Analysis." *Public Choice* 142, nos. 3–4: 265–77.

Crain, W. Mark, and Nicole V. Crain. 2017. "Robert's Rules for a Knowledge-Creating Society." *Public Choice* 171, nos. 1–2: 29–32.

Ekelund, Robert B., Jr. 2013. "Public Choice and Religion." In Reksulak, Michael, Razzolini, Laura, and Shughart, William F. II (eds.), *The Elgar Companion to Public Choice, Second Edition*, 400–14. Edward Elgar.

———. 2017. "Memories of Bob Tollison: Memories of a Friendship." *Public Choice* 171, nos. 1–2: 39–43.

Ekelund, Robert B., Jr., Robert F. Hébert, and Robert D. Tollison. (2006). *The Marketplace of Christianity.* MIT Press.

Ekelund, Robert B., Jr., Robert F. Hébert, Robert D. Tollison, Gary M. Anderson, and Audrey B. Davidson. 1996. *Sacred Trust: The Medieval Church as an Economic Firm.* Oxford University Press.

Ekelund, Robert B., Jr., John D. Jackson, and Robert D. Tollison. 2017. *The Economics of American Art: Issues, Artists and Market Institutions.* Oxford University Press.

Ekelund, Robert B., Jr., and Robert D. Tollison. 1981. *Mercantilism as a Rent-Seeking Society: Economic Regulation in Historical Perspective.* Texas A&M University Press.

———. 1986. *Economics.* Little, Brown.

———. 1997. *Politicized Economies: Monarchs, Monopoly, and Mercantilism.* Texas A&M University Press.

———. 2011. *Economic Origins of Roman Christianity.* University of Chicago Press.

Ekelund, Robert B., Jr., Robert D. Tollison, and Rand Ressler. 2006. *Economics: Private Markets and Public Choice*, 7th ed. Addison–Wesley.

Emery, John. 2022. "Analyzing the 1969 Vietnam War Military Draft Lottery Using Tableau." *phData.* https://www.phdata.io/blog/analyzing-the-1969-vietnam-war-draft-lottery-using-tableau.

Faith, Roger L., Donald R. Leavens, and Robert D. Tollison. 1982. "Antitrust Pork Barrel." *Journal of Law and Economics* 15: 329–42.

Fleisher, Arthur A., III, Brian L. Goff, William F. Shughart II, and Robert D. Tollison. 1988. "Crime or Punishment? Enforcement of the NCAA Cartel." *Journal of Economic Behavior and Organization* 10, no. 4: 433–51.

Fleisher, Arthur A., III, Brian L. Goff, and Robert D. Tollison. 1992. *The National Collegiate Athletic Association: A Study in Cartel Behavior.* University of Chicago Press.

Goff, Brian L., William F. Shughart II, and Robert D. Tollison. 1997. "Batter Up! Moral Hazard and the Effects of the Designated Hitter Rule on Hit Batsmen." *Economic Inquiry* 35, no. 3: 555–61.

Goff, Brian L., and Robert D. Tollison (eds.). 1990. *Sportometrics.* Texas A&M University Press.

Kuhn, Thomas S. [1970] 2012. *The Structure of Scientific Revolutions*, 4th ed. University of Chicago Press.

Levitt, Steven D., and Stephen J. Dubner. [2005] 2020. *Freakonomics: A Rogue Economist Explores the Hidden Side of Everything.* Revised and expanded edition. William Morrow.

Levy, David M., and Sandra J. Peart. 2020. *Towards an Economics of Natural Equals: A Documentary History of the Early Virginia School.* Cambridge University Press.

Long, William F., Richard Schramm, and Robert D. Tollison. 1973. "The Determinants of Antitrust Activity." *Journal of Law and Economics* 16, no. 2: 351–64.

Mackay, Robert J., James C. Miller III, and Bruce Yandle (eds.). 1987. *Public Choice and Regulation: A View from Inside the Federal Trade Commission*. Hoover Institution Press.

McChesney, Fred S., and William F. Shughart II (eds.). 1995. *The Causes and Consequences of Antitrust: The Public-Choice Perspective.* University of Chicago Press.

———. 2010. "Public Choice Theory and Antitrust Policy." *Public Choice* 142, nos. 3–4: 385–406.

McCormick, Robert E., and Robert D. Tollison. 1981. *Politicians, Legislation, and the Economy: An Inquiry into the Interest-Group Theory of Government.* Martinus Nijhoff.

———. 1984. "Crime on the Court." *Journal of Political Economy* 92, no. 2: 223–35.

McKenzie, Richard B., and William F. Shughart II. 1998. "Is Microsoft a Monopolist?" *The Independent Review* 3, no. 2: 165–97.

Munger, Michael C. 2017. "Robert D. Tollison: A Remembrance." *Public Choice* 171, nos. 1–2: 63–65.

Olson, Mancur. 1965. *The Logic of Collective Action: Public Goods and the Theory of Groups.* Harvard University Press.

Sauer, Raymond D. 2017. "Robert D. Tollison: Father of Sportometrics, Friend and Colleague." *Public Choice* 171, nos. 1–2: 67–71.

Schumpeter, Joseph A. [1942] 2008. *Capitalism, Socialism, and Democracy*, 3rd ed. Harper & Row.

Seabright, Paul. 2024. *The Divine Economy: How Religions Compete for Wealth, Power, and People.* Princeton University Press.

Shughart, William F. II. 1990a. *Antitrust Policy and Interest-Group Politics.* Quorum Books.

———. 1990b. "Private Antitrust Enforcement: Competition, Deterrence, or Extortion?" *Regulation* 13, no. 2: 53–61.

——— (ed.). 2010. "Essays in Honor of Robert D. Tollison." *Public Choice* 142, nos. 3–4.

———. 2017a. "A Personal Remembrance." *Southern Economic Journal* 83, no. 3: 630–36.

———. 2017b. "Rest in Peace, Bob Tollison." *Public Choice* 171, nos. 1–2: 1–5.

———. 2017c. "Robert D. Tollison, In Memoriam." *The Independent Review* 22, no. 1: 153–57.

———. 2022a. "Antitrust Agonistes." *Journal of Law, Economics & Policy* 17, no. 3: 646–72.

———. 2022b. "On the Virginia School of Antitrust: Competition Policy, Law and Economics, and Public Choice." *Public Choice* 191, nos. 1–2: 1–19.

———. 2025. "In Memory of Robert B. Ekelund, Jr.: Career, Scholarship, and Retrospect." *Public Choice* 202, nos. 1–2: 287–91.

Shughart, William F. II, and Robert D. Tollison. 1985. "The Positive Economics of Antitrust Policy: A Survey Article." *International Review of Law and Economics* 5, no. 1: 39–57.

———. 1993. "Going for the Gold: Property Rights and Athletic Effort in Transitional Economies." *Kyklos* 46, no. 2: 263–72.

Stigler, George J. 1971. "The Economic Theory of Regulation." *Bell Journal of Economics and Management Science* 2, no. 1: 3–21.

Thornton, Mark. 2024. "Home Alone." *Public Choice* 202, nos. 1–2: 329–32.

Tollison, Robert D. 1970. "The Political Economy of the Military Draft." *Public Choice* 9: 67–78.

———. 1982. "Rent Seeking: A Survey." *Kyklos* 35, no. 4: 575–602.

———. 1983. "Antitrust in the Reagan Administration: A Report from the Belly of the Beast." *International Journal of Industrial Organization* 1, no. 1: 211–21.

———. 1985. "Public Choice and Antitrust." *Cato Journal* 4, no. 3: 905–16.

Tollison, Robert D., and Thomas D. Willett. 1979. "An Economic Theory of Mutually Advantageous Issue Linkages in International Negotiations." *International Organization* 33, no. 4: 425–49

Tullock, Gordon. 1967. "The Welfare Costs of Tariffs, Monopolies, and Theft." *Western Economic Journal* 5: 224–32.

Whaples, Robert M. 2024. "Review of *GOAT: Who is the Greatest Economist of All Time and Why Does it Matter?*" *The Independent Review* 28, no. 4. https://www.independent.org/publications/tir/article.asp?id=1964.

Chapter 21: Charlotte Twight by Mikayla Novak

Boettke, Peter J. 2012. *Living Economics: Yesterday, Today, and Tomorrow.* Independent Institute.

Cowen, Tyler. 2009. "Does Technology Drive the Growth of Government?" Paper presented to Mont Pelerin Society Stockholm General Meeting, June.

Crew, Michael A., and Charlotte Twight. 1990. "On the Efficiency of Law: A Public Choice Perspective." *Public Choice* 66, no. 11: 15–36.

Encyclopedia.com. n.d. "Twight, Charlotte Augusta 1944–." https://www.encyclopedia.com/arts/educational-magazines/twight-charlotte-augusta-1944.

Evancho, Bob. 1993. "The Politics of Economics." Boise State University Focus, Summer. https://scholarworks.boisestate.edu/cgi/viewcontent.cgi?article=1051&context=focus.

Higgs, Robert. 1987. *Crisis and Leviathan: Critical Episodes in the Growth of American Government.* Oxford University Press.

———. 2012. "Once More, with Feeling: Our System Is Not Socialism, but Participatory Fascism." Independent Institute blog, October 30. https://blog.independent.org/2012/10/30/once-more-with-feeling-our-system-is-not-socialism-but-participatory-fascism.

Higgs, Robert, and Charlotte Twight. 1987. "National Emergence and the Erosion of Private Property Rights." *Cato Journal* 6, no. 3: 747–72.

Holcombe, Randall G. 2018. *Political Capitalism: How Economic and Political Power Is Made and Maintained.* Cambridge University Press.

———. 2023. *Following Their Leaders: Political Preferences and Public Policy.* Cambridge University Press.

Kau, James B., and Paul H Rubin. 1981. "The Size of Government." *Public Choice* 37, no. 2: 261–74.

Kuran, Timur. 1995. *Private Truths, Public Lies: The Social Consequences of Preference Falsification.* Harvard University Press.

Meltzer, Allan H., and Scott F. Richard. 1981. "A Rational Theory of the Size of Government." *Journal of Political Economy* 89, no. 5: 914–27.

Olson, Mancur. 1982. *The Rise and Decline of Nations: Economic Growth, Stagflation, and Social Rigidities.* Yale University Press.

Rodrik, Dani. 1998. "Why Do More Open Economies Have Bigger Governments?" *Journal of Political Economy* 106, no. 5: 997–1032.

Rowley, Charles K., and Friedrich Schneider. 2004. *The Encyclopedia of Public Choice.* Kluwer Academic Publishers.

Tooze, Adam. 2022. "Welcome to the World of Polycrisis." *Financial Times,* October 29.

Twight, Charlotte. 1975. *America's Emerging Fascist Economy.* Arlington House Publishers.

———. 1988. "Government Manipulation of Constitutional-Level Transaction Costs: A General Theory of Transaction-Cost Augmentation and the Growth of Government." *Public Choice* 56, no. 2: 131–52.

———. 1992. "Constitutional Renegotiation: Impediments to Consensual Revision." *Constitutional Political Economy* 3, no. 1: 89–112.

———. 1993. "Channeling Ideological Change: The Political Economy of Dependence on Government." *Kyklos* 46, no. 4: 497–527.

———. 1994. "Political Transaction Cost Manipulation: An Integrating Theory." *Journal of Theoretical Politics* 6, no. 2: 189–216.

———. 1996. "Federal Control over Education: Crisis, Deception, and Institutional Change." *Journal of Economic Behavior & Organization* 31, no. 3: 299–333.

———. 2002a. *Dependent on D.C.: The Rise of Federal Control over the Lives of Ordinary Americans.* Palgrave.

———. 2002b. "Designing Dependence." *The Freeman: Ideas on Liberty* 52, no. 5: 10–12.

———. 2006. "Limited Government: *Ave Atque Vale*." *Independent Review* 10, no. 4: 487–512.

———. 2016. "Through the Mist: American Liberty and Political Economy, 2065." *Independent Review* 20, no. 3: 425–31.

Wagner, Adolph. [1883] 1958. "Three Extracts on Public Finance." In *Classics in the Theory of Public Finance*. Edited by Richard Musgrave and Alan T. Peacock, 1–16. Macmillan.

Wagner, Richard E. 1976. "Revenue Structure, Fiscal Illusion, and Budgetary Choice." *Public Choice* 25, no. 1: 45–61.

Chapter 22: Karen Vaughn by Jayme Lemke

Boettke, Peter J., Karen I. Vaughn, Bruce Caldwell, Jayme Lemke, and Viktor Vanberg. 2023. "*Essays on Austrian Economics and Political Economy* Book Panel." *Hayek Program Podcast.* February 22. At https://www.mercatus.org/hayekprogram/hayek-program-podcast/essays-austrian-economics-and-political-economy-book-panel.

Boulding, Kenneth E. 1971. "After Samuelson, Who Needs Adam Smith?" *History of Political Economy* 3, no. 2: 225–37.

Caldwell, Bruce. 2021. "JHET Interviews: Karen Vaughn." *Journal of the History of Economic Thought* 43, no. 3: 450–73.

Goldin, Claudia. 2021. *Career and Family: Women's Century-Long Journey Toward Equity.* Princeton University Press.

Lemke, Jayme, and Karen Vaughn. 2020. "Jayme Lemke and Karen Vaughn on Women in Economics." *Hayek Program Podcast.* March 26. At https://www.mercatus.org/hayekprogram/hayek-program-podcast/jayme-lemke-and-karen-vaughn-women-economics.

Moss, Laurence S., and Karen I. Vaughn. 1986. "Hayek's Ricardo Effect: A Second Look." *History of Political Economy* 18, no. 4: 545–65.

Storr, Virgil Henry, and Ginny Seung Choi. 2019. *Do Markets Corrupt Our Morals?* Palgrave Macmillan.

Vaughn, Karen I. 1980a. "Does It Matter That Costs Are Subjective?" *Southern Economic Journal* 46, no. 3: 702–15.

———. 1980b. "Economic Calculation Under Socialism: The Austrian Contribution." *Economic Inquiry* 18, no. 4: 535–54.

———. 1980c. *John Locke: Economist and Social Scientist.* University of Chicago Press.

———. 1988. "The Limits of Homo Economicus in Public Choice and in Political Philosophy." *Analyse & Kritik* 10, no. 2: 161–80.

———. 1990. "The Mengerian Roots of the Austrian Revival." *History of Political Economy* 22, no. S1: 379–407.

———. 1994. *Austrian Economics in America: The Migration of a Tradition.* Cambridge University Press.

———. 1996. "Economic Policy for an Imperfect World." *Southern Economic Journal* 62, no. 4: 833–44.

———. 1999. "Hayek's Implicit Economics: Rules and the Problem of Order." *Review of Austrian Economics* 11, no. 1: 129–44.

———. [1994] 2021a. "Can Democratic Society Reform Itself? The Limits of Constructive Change." In *Essays on Austrian Economics and Political Economy,* 191–206. Mercatus Center at George Mason University.

———. [1984] 2021b. "*The Constitution of Liberty* from an Evolutionary Perspective." In *Essays on Austrian Economics and Political Economy,* 207–21. Mercatus Center at George Mason University.

———. 2021c. *Essays on Austrian Economics and Political Economy.* Mercatus Center at George Mason University.

———. [2017] 2021d. "Friedrich Hayek's Defense of the Market Order." In *Essays on Austrian Economics and Political Economy,* 243–61. Mercatus Center at George Mason University.

———. [1999] 2021e. "Hayek's Theory of the Market Order as an Instance of the Theory of Complex, Adaptive Systems." In *Essays on Austrian Economics and Political Economy,* 173–89. Mercatus Center at George Mason University.

———. [1990] 2021f. "Profit, Alertness, and Imagination." In *Essays on Austrian Economics and Political Economy,* 73–80. Mercatus Center at George Mason University.

———. [1995] 2021g. "Should There Be an Austrian Welfare Economics?" In *Essays on Austrian Economics and Political Economy,* 137–52. Mercatus Center at George Mason University.

Chapter 23: Viviana Zelizer by Stefanie Haeffele and Jessica Carges

Belsie, Laurent. 2020. "Most Stimulus Payments Were Saved or Applied to Debt." *National Bureau of Economic Research: The Digest,* no. 10. At https://www.nber.org/digest/oct20/most-stimulus-payments-were-saved-or-applied-debt.

Boettke, Peter J., Christopher J. Coyne, and Peter T. Leeson. 2008. "Institutional Stickiness and the New Development Economics." *American Journal of Economics and Sociology* 67, no. 2: 331–58.

Boettke, Peter J., Stefanie Haeffele, and Virgil Henry Storr. 2016. *Mainline Economics: Six Nobel Lectures in the Tradition of Adam Smith.* Mercatus Center at George Mason University.

Buchanan, James M. 1964. "What Should Economists Do?" *Southern Economic Journal* 30, no. 3: 213–22.

Chamlee-Wright, Emily. 2010. *The Cultural and Political Economy of Recovery: Social Learning in a Post-Disaster Environment.* Routledge.

Frank, Robert H. 1987. "Book Review: *The Economic Mind: The Social Psychology of Economic Behavior* by Adrian Furnhamand and Alan Lewis." *Journal of Economic Literature* 25, no. 3: 1307–8.

Haeffele, Stefanie, and Virgil Henry Storr, eds. 2023. *Living Better Together: Social Relations and Economic Governance in the Work of Ostrom and Zelizer.* Palgrave Macmillan.

Halpern-Meekin, Sarah, Kathryn Edin, Laura Tach, and Jennifer Sykes. 2015. *It's Not Like I'm Poor: How Working Families Make Ends Meet in a Post-Welfare World.* University of California Press.

McCloskey, Deirdre. 2006. *The Bourgeois Virtues: Ethics for an Age of Commerce.* University of Chicago Press.

———. 2010. *Bourgeois Dignity: Why Economics Can't Explain the Modern World.* University of Chicago Press.

Mears, Ashley. 2011. *Pricing Beauty: The Making of a Fashion Model.* University of California Press.

Ostrom, Elinor. 1990. *Governing the Commons: The Evolution of Institutions for Collective Action.* Cambridge University Press.

Poteete, Amy R., Marco A. Janssen, and Elinor Ostrom. 2010. *Working Together: Collective Action, the Commons, and Multiple Methods in Practice.* Princeton University Press.

Smith, Adam. [1759] 1982. *The Theory of Moral Sentiments.* Liberty Fund.

Smith, Vernon L. 1998. "The Two Faces of Adam Smith." *Southern Economic Journal* 65, no. 1: 1–19.

Storr, Virgil Henry. 2012. *Understanding the Culture of Markets.* Routledge.

Storr, Virgil Henry, and Ginny Seung Choi. 2019. *Do Markets Corrupt Our Morals?* Palgrave Macmillan.

Velthuis, Olav. 2005. *Talking Prices: Symbolic Meanings of Prices on the Market for Contemporary Art.* Princeton University Press.

Weber, Max. [1904] 2002. *The Protestant Ethic and the Spirit of Capitalism: And Other Writings.* Penguin Classics.

Zelizer, Viviana A. 1979. *Morals and Markets: The Development of Life Insurance in the United States.* Columbia University Press.

———. 1985. *Pricing the Priceless Child: The Changing Social Value of Children.* Basic Books.

———. 2000. "How and Why Do We Care About Circuits?" *Accounts* (newsletter of the Economic Sociology section of the American Sociological Association), no. 1 (Fall): 3–5.

———. 2002. "La construction des circuits de commerce: Notes sur l'importance des circuits personnels et impersonnels." In *Exclusion et liens financiers: Rapport du Centre Walras.* Edited by Jean-Michel Servet and Isabelle Guérin, 425–29. Economica.

———. 2004a. "Circuits of Commerce." In *Self, Social Structure, and Beliefs: Explorations in Sociology.* Edited by Jeffrey C. Alexander, Gary T. Marx, and Christine L. Williams, 122–44. University of California Press.

———. 2004b. "Pricing the Priceless Child: The Changing Social Value of Children." In *The New Economic Sociology: A Reader.* Edited by Frank Dobbin, 135–61. Princeton University Press.

———. 2005. *The Purchase of Intimacy.* Princeton University Press.

———. 2011. *Economic Lives: How Culture Shapes the Economy.* Princeton University Press.

———. [1994] 2017. *The Social Meaning of Money.* Basic Books.

———. 2017. "A Dollar Is a Dollar Is Not a Dollar: Unmasking the Social and Moral Meanings of Monies." *Los Angeles Review of Books.* June 15. At https://lareviewofbooks.org/article/a-dollar-is-a-dollar-is-not-a-dollar-unmasking-the-social-and-moral-meanings-of-money.

———. 2022. "Pandemic Money Puzzles." In *The Euro at 20: The Future of Our Money.* Edited by Johannes Beermann, 466–84. Penguin Random House.

———. 2023. "How and Why Social Relations Matter for Economic Lives." In *Living Better Together: Social Relations and Economic Governance in the Work of Ostrom and Zelizer.* Edited by Stefanie Haeffele and Virgil Henry Storr, 11–28. Palgrave Macmillan.

Chapter 24: Don Lavoie by Peter J. Boettke

Boettke, Peter. 2002. "Remembering Don Lavoie (1951–2001): A Student's Perspective." *Review of Austrian Economics* 15, no. 1: 103–5.

———. 2021. *The Struggle for a Better World.* Mercatus Center at George Mason University.

Dreyfus, Hubert. 1972. *What Computers Can't Do.* Harper & Row.

Gadamer, Hans-Georg. 1960. *Truth and Method.* Continuum.

Lavoie, Don. 1985a. *National Economic Planning: What Is Left?* Ballinger.

———. 1985b. *Rivalry and Central Planning: The Socialist Calculation Debate Reconsidered.* Cambridge University Press.

———. 1986. "The Market as a Procedure for the Discovery and Conveyance of Inarticulate Knowledge." *Comparative Economic Studies* 28 (Spring): 1–19.

———. 1990. "Computation, Incentives and Discovery: The Cognitive Function of Markets in Market Socialism." *Annals of the American Academy of Political and Social Science* 507 (January): 72–79.

———, ed. 1991. *Economics and Hermeneutics.* Routledge.

McCloskey, Deirdre. 1985. *The Rhetoric of Economics.* University of Wisconsin Press.

Polanyi, Michael. 1951. *The Logic of Liberty.* University of Chicago Press.

———. 1958. *Personal Knowledge.* University of Chicago Press.

Credits

THE FOLLOWING CHAPTERS were originally articles published in *The Independent Review* 28, no. 2 (Fall 2023), copyright © 2023 by the Independent Institute:

"Alexander Hamilton as Economist: A Proper Verdict," by Richard M. Salsman originally published as "Alexander Hamilton as Economist: A Proper Verdict," *The Independent Review* 28, no. 2 (Fall 2023): 179–91; "Harriet Martineau: Economist as Storyteller and Traveler," by David M. Levy and Sandra J. Peart originally published as "Harriet Martineau: Economist as Storyteller and Traveler," *The Independent Review* 28, no. 2 (Fall 2023): 193–202; "Knut Wicksell: A Consistent Marginalist," by Diana W. Thomas originally published as "Knut Wicksell: A Consistent Marginalist," *The Independent Review* 28, no. 2 (Fall 2023): 203–211; "Ursula K. Hicks: Reviewer, Editor, and Gatekeeper," by Marianne Johnson originally published as "Ursula K. Hicks: Reviewer, Editor, and Gatekeeper," *The Independent Review* 28, no. 2 (Fall 2023): 213–24; "Friedrich A. Lutz: A Forgotten Monetary Economist and Social Philosopher," by Lachezar Grudev originally published as "Friedrich A. Lutz: A Forgotten Monetary Economist and Social Philosopher," *The Independent Review* 28, no. 2 (Fall 2023): 225–36; "Kenneth Boulding: Knowledge, Conflict, and Power," by Yahya Alshamy and Christopher J. Coyne originally published as "Kenneth Boulding: Knowledge, Conflict, and Power," *The Independent Review* 28, no. 2 (Fall 2023): 237–46; "Israel M. Kirzner and the Entrepreneurial Market Process: An Appreciation," by Rosolino Candela originally published as "Israel M. Kirzner and the Entrepreneurial Market Process: An Appreciation," *The Independent Review* 28, no.

2 (Fall 2023): 247–58; "Thomas Sowell: Uncommon Perspectives on Culture, Society, and Economics," by Art Carden and Brian C. Albrecht originally published as "Thomas Sowell: Uncommon Perspectives on Culture, Society, and Economics," *The Independent Review* 28, no. 2 (Fall 2023): 259–69; "Julian Simon: Irreplaceable Economist, Irreplaceable Man," by Robert M. Whaples originally published as "Julian Simon: Irreplaceable Economist, Irreplaceable Man," *The Independent Review* 28, no. 2 (Fall 2023): 271–80; "Karl Mittermaier: Economic Theory vs. Reality," by Michael C. Munger originally published as "Karl Mittermaier: Economic Theory vs. Reality," *The Independent Review* 28, no. 2 (Fall 2023): 281–89; "Karen Vaughn: Building an Austrian Approach to Public Choice," by Jayme Lemke originally published as "Karen Vaughn: Building an Austrian Approach to Public Choice," *The Independent Review* 28, no. 2 (Fall 2023): 291–300; "Don Lavoie: The Failures of Socialist Central Planning," by Peter J. Boettke originally published as "Don Lavoie: The Failures of Socialist Central Planning," *The Independent Review* 28, no. 2 (Fall 2023): 301–312; "Viviana Zelizer: Relational Exchange and Association," by Stefanie Haeffele and Jessica Carge originally published as "Viviana Zelizer: Relational Exchange and Association," *The Independent Review* 28, no. 2 (Fall 2023): 313–22.

Index

Note: Page numbers in bold refer to tables.

I

Q

R